SECOND EDITION

Listening to Music

Jay Zorn
University of Southern California

Prentice Hall, Englewood Cliffs, NJ 07632

Library of Congress Cataloging-in-Publication Data

Zorn, Jay D.
   Listening to Music / Jay Zorn. —2nd ed.
     p. cm.
   Includes bibliographical references and index.
   ISBN 0-13-035916-5
   1. Music appreciation.   I. Title.
MT6.Z77L6 1995
781.1'7—dc20   94-30741
                              CIP
                              MN

*I dedicate this book to my wife, June August.
Her continuous encouragement, editing expertise,
musical advice and many hours of work eased
the project from its inception to its completion.*

Publisher: *Bud Therien*
Interior and cover design: *Donna M. Wickes/Thomas Nery*
Production coordinator: *Bob Anderson*
Formatter: *Michael J. Bertrand*
Photo editor: *Lorinda Morris-Nantz*
Photo researcher: *Anita Dickhuth*
Editorial/production and supervision: *Jean Lapidus*
Marketing manager: *Alison Pendergast*
Editorial assistant: *Lee Mamunes*
Cover photo: *Joseph Sachs*

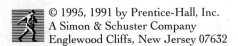
Printed in the United States of America
10 9 8 7 6 5 4 3

ISBN   0-13-035916-5
ISBN   0-13-147968-7 (with CDs)
ISBN   0-13-147950-4 (with cassettes)

Prentice-Hall International (UK) Limited, *London*
Prentice-Hall of Australia Pty. Limited, *Sydney*
Prentice-Hall Canada Inc.,*Toronto*
Prentice-Hall Hispanoamericana, S.A., *Mexico*
Prentice-Hall of India Private Limited, *New Delhi*
Prentice-Hall of Japan, Inc., *Tokyo*
Simon & Schuster Asia Pte. Ltd., *Singapore*
Editora Prentice-Hall do Brasil, Ltda., *Rio de Janeiro*

Contents

iii

PART FOUR: **ADJUNCT MUSIC**

24 North American Popular Music   355

25 Broadway Musical Theater   365

To the Student

Picture yourself a few years from now. You are entering a concert hall in your city to hear a performance by your local orchestra. Or perhaps on an out-of-town business or pleasure trip, you have chosen the concert as your evening's entertainment. Wherever you may be throughout the world, you feel at home entering that hall.

You feel comfortable there because you completed this music appreciation course and know that the great music of the world belongs to you. Reading the program, you understand the musical terms. You are familiar with the composers: their styles, significant passages in their lives, some of their music, how and where they earned their livelihoods. You are aware of the social, economic, and historical events that influenced them. Above all, you realize that they composed their music for your enjoyment.

As the concert starts, you are confident about concert procedure and etiquette and pleased that you can make sense out of the sounds you hear. You easily follow the composer's logic, the melodic themes, and the interplay of musical ideas heard throughout the orchestra. You recognize that this first piece is a concerto, a symphony, or an orchestral overture.

After the concert you'll be able to discuss the performance, feeling secure in your perceptions. In fact, your friends and business associates may acknowledge your expertise by asking questions or seeking your opinions.

Music belongs to everyone. Albert Einstein, an avid music lover, played the violin well into his old age. Commenting on his Theory of Relativity that led to space travel, Einstein said, "It occurred to me by intuition, and music was the driving force behind that intuition."

Listening to great music is an enchanting, exciting growth experience. You have a lifetime of listening ahead of you.

Organization

Listening to Music, Second Edition is arranged in four parts:

Part 1: The Musical Process The opening chapter focuses on ways of listening. Chapter Two explains how to take full advantage of concert attendance.

Part 2: The Musical Elements Detailed explanations and sound examples on the cassette tapes reinforce the book's presentation of the basic musical elements. Martin Bookspan, distinguished announcer for the Public Broadcasting System's classical music series, "Live at Lincoln Center," guides you through the "Musical Elements" demonstration. As your host on the recordings, he announces each music example on the tapes. Discussions in this section include the commonly used instruments and ensembles, and the classifications of the human voice.

Part 3: The Common Style Periods of Music Beginning with a basic survey of music before 1600, the text progresses chronologically from the Baroque style period through contemporary music of North America. Since most of the music chosen for discussion appears regularly on concert programs and includes works that audiences seem to favor, you are likely to encounter these pieces in your concertgoing.

Part 4: Adjunct Music Discussions of American popular music, Broadway musical theater, film music, and music of world cultures have been expanded in this new edition. Pops Orchestras now perform this music in their concerts.

Important Features

This new edition includes:

- 53 biographies of composers
- 14 Listening Insights Boxes
- 18 Historical Notes Boxes
- 38 detailed Listening Guides
- 8 pages of color art plates

Listening Insights: Fourteen *Listening Insights* give you practical suggestions for approaching and listening to various types of music, for example:

How to Listen to Classical Music
What to Listen for in Romantic Music
Enjoying Programmatic and Highly Descriptive Music
Listening to Nationalistic Music
Eclecticism in Music
Form in Early Broadway Musical Theater Songs

Historical Perspectives: Eighteen special information boxes highlight interesting facts about music. Here is a sampling:

What is the Secret of the Cremona Instruments?
Book and Music Printing
Use of Italian Terms in Music
Evolution of Public Concerts: The Baroque Period
Haydn's Labor Protest: The "Farewell Symphony"
Beethoven and the Changing Status of Composers
Opera in North America
Kern's Show Boat: The New Broadway Musical

The Listening Guides: Of the 38 detailed Listening Guides in the text, you will find 31 of the works on your cassette tapes. First, listen to each work until you are acquainted with it. Then, listen as often as you like while following the detailed listening guide.

The timing indications in the book will remind you at what point musical events occur on the recordings. For example, the second theme in the first movement of Beethoven's 5th Symphony enters 0:46 seconds after the piece begins. After several hearings, you will no longer need to watch the timings to follow the events. The more often you listen, the sooner you will be able to follow the events without the guides, just as you would at a live concert.

The goal of both the text and the course is your lifelong enjoyment of concert music. You have the vehicle to get there. Good luck on your journey.

⌁Acknowledgments

The production of such a complex project as *Listening to Music, Second Edition* requires the contribution of many talents. I would like to thank the following: special thanks to distinguished announcer Martin Bookspan whose musical expertise, dedication, and love of music permeates this project; James Wayne of Silverdisc Productions and his staff for their assistance in locating and producing the superior recordings; June August, President of Writing That Works, and her staff for editing and suggestions: Bud Therien, Prentice Hall publisher, whose vision guided this innovative project; Jean Lapidus, Prentice Hall production editor, who managed the final production; Donna Wickes, Prentice Hall, who designed my manuscript into a beautiful book; Leonard Stein, former Director of the Arnold Schoenberg Institute, for his judicious advice and editing of the chapter on Expressionism; Wayne Shoaf, Librarian/Archivist at the Arnold Schoenberg Institute, for his assistance in securing copies of photographs and artworks of expressionist composers; Frederick Lesemann of the University of Southern California, School of Music, for contributing his composition, *Metakinetic Invention, Version 2*, to the project and for his editing the chapter on Experimental and Technological Music; Bruce Broughton, award-winning film and television composer and lecturer at the University of Southern California, Music for Films Institute, for his contributions to the chapter on Music for films; William Doyle, El Camino College, for his reviews and creation of the *Student Workbook*.

I especially acknowledge my talented teaching assistants—more than 75 of them over the past twenty-two years. With their collaboration I have had the pleasure of presenting the material in this text. Observing them teach and receiving their feedback, I have learned from each of them. I am also indebted to the five thousand music appreciation students whose response and enjoyment of my materials have helped shape this text.

Finally, I thank the following colleagues for their suggestions and input for the project: Eleanor Hammer, Los Angeles Valley College; Giulio Ongaro, University of Southern California; Raymond A. Barr, University of Miami; Thomas L. Riis, University of Georgia; Dan Schultz, Walla Walla college; Elaine Morgan, City College of San Francisco; Edward Szabo, East Michigan University; Marc Peretz, Ball State University; Dan Dunavan, Southeast Missouri State University; James Klein, California State University, Stanislaus; Diane Touliatos, University of Missouri, St. Louis; Christine Smith, Middlebury College; K. Marie Stolba, Indiana University, Purdue Campus; Nelson Tandoc, De Anza College; Leo Kreter, California State University, Fullerton; Earl L. Clemens, Northern Illinois University.

Jay Zorn
University of Southern California
Los Angeles

✍ *The New York Times Supplements Program*

THE NEW YORK TIMES and PRENTICE HALL are cosponsoring a Themes of the Times: a program designed to enhance student access to current information of relevance in the classroom.

Through this program, the core subject matter provided in the text is supplemented by a collection of time-sensitive articles from one of the world's most distinguished newspapers, THE NEW YORK TIMES. These articles demonstrate the vital, ongoing connection between what is learned and what is happening in the world around us.

To enjoy the wealth of information of THE NEW YORK TIMES daily, a reduced subscription rate is available in deliverable areas. For information, call toll-free: 1-800-631-1222.

PRENTICE HALL and THE NEW YORK TIMES are proud to cosponsor Themes of the Times. We hope it will make the reading of both textbooks and newspapers a more dynamic, involving process.

Part 1: Prelude

✒ The Musical Process

The musical process begins with the composer's ideas and experiences, influenced by the era in which he or she lives. Manipulating into a coherent form the materials of music—*rhythm, melody, harmony, expression,* and *texture*—the composer constructs a framework to support those creative ideas.

Then, using *music notation,* composers put their ideas on paper. Notation is a system of visual symbols that represent sounds and sound qualities. Performers can then read and interpret these symbols and recreate the composer's ideas through the *performance medium*—the voices or instruments. Transformed into sound, music becomes accessible to you, the listener. You experience the music and respond.

CREATION
COMPOSER
(creator)

RECREATION
PERFORMER
(re-creator)

RESPONSE
PERCEIVER
(listener)

The Musical Process

musical ideas
↓
musical materials (elements)
(rhythm, melody, harmony, etc.)
↓
forms
(large: symphony, opera, etc.)
(detailed: rondo, sonata, etc.)
↓
↓
musical notation
↓
↓
↓
↓
↓
↓
medium
(instruments, voices)↓
↓
↓
↓
↓
↓
↓
↓
↓
listener-audience

CHAPTER 1

How to Listen to Music

Let's begin our musical journey with one of the most important links in the musical process—you. Composers create their music not for other musicians, music critics, or historians, but for you, the listener. Without the listener, music has no audience—the performers play to an empty house.

Looking at a panoramic landscape from a mountain, you have many possible vistas: close, distant, left, right. What you see results from the way you focus your attention. Similarly, the way you listen to music depends on how you focus. As you take in more and more of what you hear, that focus keeps changing.

If you are tired—perhaps after a busy day—you may have less energy with which to follow intricate music. But at those times when you feel relaxed or adventuresome, you may be more willing to accept a challenge.

Music, like all the arts, can accommodate all viewpoints. Each of us perceives differently. Your listening experience is your private world. There are no restrictions, no "correct" approaches to listening.

Following are some of the ways that many concertgoers listen to music.

⁊ *The Sensory Level*

Some listeners prefer letting the music wash over them without giving it much thought. This passive rather than active listening can be relaxing—like basking on a beach on a sunny day with the surf rushing back and forth over you. Because the *sensory level* is effortless and soothing, you can allow your brain to idle in neutral and your spine to tingle.

⁊ *The Emotional Level*

Music can speak directly to our emotions. If you've ever listened to music and found yourself daydreaming or reminiscing, you were listening at an *emotional level*. At this level, your emotions become part of the listening experience. There in your private world, that beautiful melody by Chopin stirs your deepest feelings—the ones that rarely rise to the surface, the feelings we seldom verbalize.

Metropolitan Opera star, Marilyn Horne, mezzo-soprano.

ஓ *The Contextual Level*

Some music supplies a background for a familiar event, activity, or environment. When we hear it, we immediately associate it with some context—a football game, a circus, a graduation. Even "patriotic" music falls into this category. In *contextual* listening, the association may become more important than the music itself.

ஓ *The Script Level*

Most music has no specific story for you to follow—although opera, ballet, and film music certainly do. But if you find yourself making up a story or unraveling a plot, you may be listening to music at the *script level*.

ஓ *The Musically Aware Level*

Great music has layers of subtleties that invite your involvement. Here, at the *musically aware level*, the excitement begins. You may still enjoy the sensory, emotional, and script levels, but as you grow more aware, the music engages your heightened understanding, and you are able to enjoy it for its own sake.

Reaching the Musically Aware Level

You don't have to be a trained musician to reach this level. Without any extra-musical guidance, pictures, or stories, you can develop the ability to focus on the music itself, understanding and experiencing the composer's creative choices.

When you achieve this awareness, you can follow the musical lines and patterns that the sounds create. You'll notice which instruments are performing, how the musical ideas are passed from instrument to instrument, the type of ornamentation in the melody, the texture or layers of parts, the quality of the harmony, and the forms the composer used to organize the music. The performer's tone quality, phrasing, consistency of style, and faithfulness to the composer's intentions will become clearer to you.

Chapters 3 and 4—"The Interaction of Basic Musical Elements" and "Performing Media: Instruments, Voices, and Ensembles," respectively— prepare you to reach the aware level. Then, each piece of music and its background information discussed in the remaining chapters will contribute to your experience and enjoyment.

CHAPTER 2

Becoming an Aware Concertgoer

✑ *What Types of Concerts Are There?*

Symphony Orchestra

Is there a difference between a "symphony" orchestra and a "philharmonic" orchestra? No. The designation means nothing. Both are symphony orchestras. New York City's main orchestra is the New York Philharmonic; Chicago's orchestra is the Chicago Symphony; Philadelphia's is the Philadelphia Orchestra. Typically, most symphony orchestra compositions call for orchestras consisting of 80 to 110 performers.

Chamber Orchestra

Popular during the seventeenth and eighteenth centuries, chamber orchestras were small groups that performed in the chambers of courts and palaces. Mozart and Haydn, for example, wrote for orchestras of twenty to forty performers because palace chambers accommodated only that many musicians—and usually a similar size audience. Today's chamber orchestras of thirty to sixty musicians perform music from all style periods, including contemporary.

Chamber Music Ensembles

Two to six musicians generally perform at chamber music concerts. Although any combination of two to twenty instrumental performers can be a chamber music ensemble, string quartets and trios, and brass and woodwind quintets predominate.

The term *chamber music* has the same roots as the term *chamber orchestra*: music performed in chambers or rooms of the courts and palaces of Europe. Chamber music ensembles have been popular at court since antiquity.

Vienna Chamber Orchestra.

Recitals

A recital features one or two musicians. Solo recitals are most commonly given by singers, pianists, or violinists.

Vocal Ensembles

LARGE CHOIRS Varying in size from 40 to 400 singers, large choirs and choruses perform both with and without instrumental accompaniment.

SMALL CHOIRS Often called an *a cappella choir* or *chamber choir*, a small choir consists of ten to thirty singers typically performing without piano or instrumental accompaniment. Taking its name from the small church choirs of the late Middle Ages and Renaissance periods (approximately A.D. 1000 to 1600), *a cappella* means "in the style of the church."

Especially popular around A.D. 1600 in Elizabethan England, informal *madrigal groups* provided court entertainment, usually accompanied by instruments. Today's madrigal singers still perform Elizabethan music, but they often expand their concerts to include music written for small vocal ensembles from any style period.

Samuel Ramey, Bass-Baritone.

CHURCH CHOIRS In churches as well as in concert halls, choirs perform many of the greatest masterpieces: *Messiah* oratorio by George Frideric Handel, *b minor Mass* by Johann Sebastian Bach, *Requiem* by Wolfgang Amadeus Mozart, *Requiem* by Giuseppe Verdi, and *Mass* by Leonard Bernstein.

Large Musical Productions

OPERA Opera is musical theater—orchestral and vocal music built around a libretto or story. Actually, opera is a combination of art forms: singing, instrumental performance, drama, poetry, scene design, costumes, and dance. The orchestra performs in a pit in front of the stage.

Vienna Boy's Choir.

BALLET Ballet also creates its effects by a wonderful blending of the arts: dance, drama, set design, costume design, and especially music. The music

Winnipeg Ballet.

John Williams.

provides the catalyst for the choreography—specifically designed dance steps and movement. Many great masters have composed specifically for ballet: Ludwig van Beethoven, Hector Berlioz, Peter Ilyich Tchaikovsky, Maurice Ravel, Igor Stravinsky, Sergei Prokofiev, Aaron Copland, and Leonard Bernstein.

Ballet orchestras usually perform in a pit in front of the stage. The number of players varies according to the music.

✌ How Can I Find Out About Concerts and Tickets?

Newspapers

Most concerts are advertised in the entertainment or arts sections of newspapers. Look for phone numbers, box-office location, dates and times, performers, and programs.

If you rely solely on newspaper advertisements for concert information, you may not get the best seats. By the time the advertisement appears, the house may have already been sold out and no seats are available.

Mailing Lists

For earliest notification, ask (by phone or short note) the concert hall or series management to put your name on the mailing list. For several years, you will receive advance brochures and order forms. You can buy tickets by mail before an event and get the price and seats you want.

Season Subscriptions

Once you are on mailing lists, you will receive invitations to become a season subscriber. Subscribers have the best seats. After you determine the series of programs and seats you prefer, you can reserve them for the entire season. As a season subscriber, you'll be notified of the coming concert season even earlier than those on the general mailing lists.

Box Office

If a performance isn't sold out, you can always purchase tickets at the box office. Arrive as early as possible. The first time you go to a concert or to a particular concert hall, ask box-office personnel to show you a detailed seating plan and advise you on the best seats.

Student-Rush Seats

Students may often have a considerable advantage over other concertgoers by being at the box office within an hour of the concert. Most orchestra concerts, operas, and ballets offer reduced price "student-rush" tickets. You must show current student identification, which usually entitles you to buy only one ticket.

Attending Open Rehearsals

Many opera companies and symphony orchestras have regularly scheduled rehearsals open to the public for a small fee. Ask at the box office about this. Seeing what goes on in preparation for a performance is fascinating. It is in rehearsal that conductors and performers do their main work—unifying the interpretation and polishing the performance.

☞ *How Can I Prepare for a Concert?*

Become Acquainted with the Music

Most concert music is available on recordings. Besides preparing for a concert, you can build your personal collection of classical-music recordings. Listen to the music you will be hearing at the concert whenever you can—on the car stereo, on a portable stereo, or at home.

To prepare for an opera, read a synopsis of the story in advance. You can usually find a printed version in the library or as an insert in a record album or compact disc recording. Several books, such as *Stories of the Operas* by Milton Cross, provide excellent synopses and brief discussions of most of the major operas.

☞ *The Conductor's Role*

WHAT DOES THE CONDUCTOR DO? As you watch a conductor during a performance, you might get the impression that setting the tempo and beating time are the conductor's main functions. They aren't. Almost any member of the orchestra can do those things. As important as beating time is, interpreting the music is more so.

Coordinating the ensemble's performance and *interpreting* the music are the conductor's most important responsibilities. The conductor's downbeat coordinates the start of the performance and sets the tempo, with the orchestra or chorus following and watching for changes.

To understand how conductors convey interpretation, you would have to attend a rehearsal or be on stage and watch how they use hands, face, and body to urge musicians to play louder or softer, more forcefully or heroically, more smoothly or tenderly. Public Television stations regularly broadcast symphony orchestra concerts. Camera closeups of the conductor's face help reveal the interpretative process. Look for these programs in your television listings.

Riccardo Muti.

Seiji Ozawa.

A soloist adds another dimension to a conductor's work because the orchestra accompaniment must be coordinated with the soloist's part. If, for instance, the soloist drags the tempo in a certain passage and speeds up in another, the conductor must inspire the entire orchestra to follow. Maintaining the balance between soloist and ensemble ensures that the soloist will be heard above the other instruments.

THE CONDUCTOR AS MUSIC SCHOLAR It takes a lifetime of study for a conductor to learn the great body of music for symphony orchestra, chorus, ballet, or opera. Guiding an ensemble is demanding: A conductor must research various resources and examine writings about the music. Even a composer's note to a colleague can be informative.

Why Do Some Conductors Use a Baton or Stick?

If you can think of the baton as an extension of the conductor's arm, you will understand why a conductor uses one. Players in all parts of the ensemble can see the conductor's beats more clearly. Using the baton to execute patterns maximizes visibility and reduces exertion.

Conductors of the past used other objects—rolled-up music, a violin bow, a cane—but none was as effective as the white baton. In the seventeenth century, the composer and conductor Jean-Baptiste Lully pounded beats on the floor with a wooden staff. During one performance, he smashed the staff into his foot, which became infected. Lully died of complications, a victim of his own enthusiasm.

How Do Conductors Communicate?

Most conductors use standard conducting patterns universally recognized by classically trained musicians and even by many folk and popular music performers. This communication is one example of how music performance can transcend geographic boundaries.

GETTING READY TO PLAY The conductor mounts the podium, waits until everyone in the orchestra is ready to perform, then raises his or her arms in the "ready position."

DOWNBEAT The downbeat is the first beat of any pattern. The conductor moves the baton down from the ready position to somewhere near the front of the waist. When the baton reaches bottom and begins to move upward, the downbeat is complete, and the performers begin to play.

Standard Conducting Patterns

The standard conducting patterns are illustrated to the right. The *meter*, or grouping of beats in the music, determines the pattern. Most music is grouped in recurring patterns—usually two, three, or four. Used less frequently are patterns of five and six beats.

Conducting Activity

Practice the standard conducting patterns for two, three, and four beats as shown. Then conduct the recorded music on the Student's Cassette Tape accompanying this text. Here are some suggestions:

The Two Pattern

Side B, Example 3   *Bach, Brandenburg Concerto No. 2, third movement: moderately fast tempo*

Side B, Example 7   *Mozart, Horn Concerto No. 2, third movement: fast tempo*

Side D, Example 10   *Copland, "Hoe Down" from Rodeo: very fast*

The Three Pattern

Side B, Example 1   *Bach, Cantata No. 140, opening chorus: moderate tempo*

Side B, Example 8   *Haydn, Symphony No. 94, third movement: moderate tempo*

The Four Pattern

Side A, Example 6   *Handel, "For unto Us a Child is Born" from Messiah: moderate tempo*

Side B, Example 2   *Vivaldi: The Four Seasons, op. 8, no. 1 "Spring" first movement*

ONE BEAT   TWO BEATS

THREE BEATS   FOUR BEATS

FIVE BEATS
(3 + 2)   (2 + 3)

SIX BEATS

Drawing of standard conducting patterns.

Conductor's Expression Indications

LEFT HAND The conductor's left hand indicates expression. For example, if the trumpets enter too loudly, the conductor, often looking like a police officer halting traffic, motions them to play more softly.

Urging the violins to play louder, the conductor might use another left-hand signal.

CUEING The left hand also signals a player or section to play. Imagine a cymbal player who has been following the music for fifteen minutes, waiting for his or her part. The conductor's cue increases the player's confidence that the crash of the cymbals will occur at the right moment—and avoid an embarrassing situation!

Left-hand expression: quiet—John Williams, conductor.

Left-hand cue — Neville Marriner.

Common Terms Used in Performance

On concert programs and throughout this text you will encounter many commonly used musical terms. Explanations for some of these terms appear in later chapters. Table 2-1 lists the most commonly used terms. (See Glossary for additional terms.)

✧ Table 2-1 Common Tempo Terms and Descriptions

from slow to fast

grave	extremely slowly and solemnly
largo	very slowly, broadly
lento	slow
adagio	slowly, leisurely
andante	slow to moderate walking pace
moderato	moderate
allegretto	moderately fast
allegro	fast, lively
vivace	very fast
presto	very fast
prestissimo	as fast as possible

Descriptions Often Used with Tempos

agitato	agitated
animato	animated
cantabile	singing style
con brio	with spirit
con fuoco	with fire
con moto	with movement
e or ed.	and
espressivo	expressively
grazioso	gracefully
ma	but
ma non troppo	but not too much
maestoso	majestically
meno	less
molto	very, much
piu	more

poco	little
poco a poco	little by little, gradually
sostenuto	sustained

Terms Indicating Tempo Changes

accelerando	quickening
ritardando	slowing
rallentando	gradual slowing
rubato	deliberate unsteady tempo

Terms for Loudness Levels from soft to loud

Abbreviation	Italian Term	English Meaning
pp or **ppp**	*pianissimo*	very soft
p	*piano*	soft
mp	*mezzopiano*	moderately soft
mf	*mezzoforte*	moderately loud
f	*forte*	loud
ff or **fff**	*fortissimo*	very loud

Terms and Symbols for Changes in Loudness

crescendo	becoming louder
decrescendo	becoming softer
or	
diminuendo	becoming softer

Other Performance Terms

a cappella	choir or voices without accompaniment
glissando	slide from pitch to pitch
legato	connected, smoothly
pizzicato	plucked strings, usually done with player's finger
staccato	detached, separated tones
tremolo	rapid repetitions of a tone or chord
vibrato	pulsating tones for expressiveness

LONDON SYMPHONY ORCHESTRA
MICHAEL TILSON THOMAS, Conductor

LUDWIG VAN BEETHOVEN

Symphony No. 5 in c minor, Op. 68 (1808)

     Allegro con brio
     Andante con moto
     Allegro, *leading into*
     Allegro

WOLFGANG AMADEUS MOZART

Concerto in A Major for Clarinet and Orchestra, K. 622 (1791)

     Allegro
     Adagio
     Rondo: Allegro

Franz Hoeprich, Clarinet Soloist

Intermission

PETER ILYICH TCHAIKOVSKY

Symphony No. 4 in f minor, Op. 36 (1877)

     Andante sostenuto; Moderato con anima
     Andantino in modo di canzona
     Scherzo: Pizzicato ostinato
     Allegro con fuoco

GEORGE GERSHWIN

Concerto in F Major for Piano and Orchestra (1925)

     Allegro
     Andante con moto
     Allegro con brio

Michael Tilson Thomas, Piano Soloist/Conductor

✧ Printed Concert Programs

Tempo indications in the printed program help you keep your place in the music because they show the speed of the movements. For instance, in the program on page 14, notice the indications for Gershwin's Concerto in F Major for Piano and Orchestra. *Allegro* means fast. *Andante con moto*—a moderate walking pace—is much slower. *Allegro con brio*, the third movement, means fast, with spirit. Using Table 2-1, try to figure out what each of the other tempo idications on the London Symphony program means.

✧ Catalog Systems for Composers' Works

The designation "Op. 68" after the title of Beethoven's symphony refers to the sequence among his compositions in which he wrote that work—*opus*, meaning "work" in Latin. In this case, Beethoven indicated that the Symphony No. 5 was approximately his sixty-eighth work. Most composers were not as consistent as Beethoven in cataloguing their music. Therefore, the opus numbers or other designations are rarely precise.

Instead of opus numbers, some composers' works bear other designations assigned much later by the person who catalogued the music. For instance, Ludwig von Köchel (1800–77) catalogued Mozart's numerous works. Instead of an opus number in the London Symphony Orchestra's program featuring the Mozart Clarinet Concerto, the designation is K. 622. Written only months before Mozart's untimely death in 1791, this concerto was one of Mozart's last works.

Table 2-2 provides a list of some of the most commonly used designations.

✧ Table 2-2 Common Music Catalog Designations

Composer	Designation	Cataloguer
Bach, J.S.	BWV (for "Bach-Werke Verzeichnis")	Wolfgang Schmieder: Thematisch-systematisches Verzeichnis der musikalischen Werke von Johann Sebastian Bach
Haydn	H. or Hob.	A. von Hoboken
Mozart	K.	Ludwig von Köchel
Schubert	D.	O. E. Deutsch
Vivaldi	R. or P.	Peter Ryom

CHAPTER 3

Part Two: The Musical Elements

The Interaction of Basic Musical Elements

✑Multimedia Presentation

Because music is a nonverbal art, it is best understood through its sounds. To assist in learning and reviewing the elements of music, this next section appears both in print and on the recordings provided with the book. Included also is a list of the music on the recordings.

Suggested Sequence

First, without looking at the book, listen to the "Elements of Music" recording (Side A, Example 1; CD 1, Track 1). Next, while listening, refer to the Summary of Basic Musical Elements at the end of Chapter 3 (page 26). Listen again to the recording, following along with the text's "Listening Activity" starting on page 26. If you need further clarification of your understanding of the elements, stop the recording and read the text before continuing with the recording.

LISTENING ACTIVITY ✦

MUSICAL ELEMENTS

Cassette Tape: Side A, Example 1
Compact Disc 1, Track 1
Running time: 30:06

Listen now to the Cassette Tape recording provided with this book.

Composers use an assortment of sound materials — *the elements of music* — to organize their ideas. Just as painters use colors, shapes, light, and textures to create their works, composers use *rhythms, scales, melodies, harmonies,* and *textures* to create theirs.

MUSIC
Leonard Bernstein, *Candide* Overture

✦ *Rhythm (Duration of Sound)*

Music is a temporal art, existing in time. Sounds occur and continue for a certain duration, flowing at specific rates of speed, or tempos. You may have referred to this as *rhythm*. While listening, we flow along in time with the music as if on a journey, for as long as it lasts.

Beat

PROMINENT BEAT When the beat is *prominent*, responding to it is easy. Even babies and animals react to a recurring, thumping beat. The beat motivates us to move — snap our fingers, tap our feet, sway, dance, march, exercise.

MUSIC
Recurring drum beat

MUSIC
Scott Joplin, "The Entertainer"

WEAK BEAT Some music has a *weak beat*, creating a feeling of floating, drifting, or gliding, as in this example by Claude Debussy.

MUSIC
Claude Debussy, *Afternoon of a Faun*

Tempo

The speed or *tempo* of the music also affects us. A slow tempo may evoke a mood of reflection or help us relax. A brisk tempo can lift our spirits. You won't find soldiers marching or aerobics classes exercising to music with a slow tempo. Both activities depend on the uplift a fast tempo creates.

We can measure the speed or tempo of the beat with a device called a *metronome*, invented in 1816 by Johann Maelzel (1772–1838).

Metronome

Metronome markings
MUSIC
Metronome ticking at 84
beats per minute

Measuring tempos
MUSIC
Edward Elgar, *Pomp and Circumstance*, March No. 1

MUSIC
Aaron Copland, "Hoe Down" from *Rodeo*

MUSIC
George Gershwin, Prelude II (tempo: 84 beats per minute)

MUSIC
George Gershwin, Prelude II, *Andante con moto e poco rubato* (walking tempo with movement and a little rubato)

Composers usually indicate the tempos for playing their works by notating the metronome setting at the beginning of the music. A tempo indication of 84 in the music means that the basic beats should proceed at eighty-four beats per minute.

That's a good tempo for a graduation march—for example, Edward Elgar's march *Pomp and Circumstance*.

Without a metronome, you can measure tempo the same way you measure your pulse. First, find your pulse on the inside of your wrist below your thumb. Turn off the recording and count the number of pulse beats in 20 seconds, using a second hand or timer. Then turn the tape on again. Do that now.

In 20 seconds, you probably counted 22 to 30 beats. Multiply the *number* you counted by three, and you'll have your pulse rate.

Now try to measure the tempo of "Hoe Down" from Aaron Copland's ballet *Rodeo*. Using a second hand or a stopwatch, count the number of beats you hear in 20 seconds.

PERCEPTION OF TEMPO Our perception of whether a tempo is fast or slow tends to correspond to our individual pulse rate. We perceive a tempo as moderate (*moderato* in Italian) when it is close to our own pulse—usually between 65 and 90 beats per minute.

Listen to George Gershwin's "Prelude II," which runs about 84 beats per minute.

How did you react to a tempo close to your own pulse?

STEADY TEMPO The tempo in most music usually remains steady—especially if dancers or marchers are trying to move with the music.

FLEXIBLE TEMPO (RUBATO) Did you notice that the tempo in the Gershwin piece was not entirely steady? In highly personal and emotional music, the performer often uses a flexible approach to the beat. The musical term for this is *rubato*, meaning "robbed" in Italian. To execute rubato, performers vary the pace of the music slightly by increasing the speed for some beats and slowing it down for others.

Listen again to Gershwin's "Prelude" and notice how the performer conveys the emotional quality of the music through *rubato*.

Meter (Groupings of Beats)

Rhythmic groupings in most concert music are predictable. Created by stressed and unstressed beats, the recurring group is called a *meter*. Two, three, and four beats are the most common meters.

TRIPLE METER Waltzes, for instance, use recurring rhythmic patterns of three beats, usually with the first beat of the pattern accented. A three-beat pattern is called a *triple meter.*

/		/		/		/		/		/
ONE	-	two	-	three	-	ONE	-	two	-	three
STRONG	-	weak	-	weak	-	STRONG	-	weak	-	weak
BEAT	-	beat	-	beat	-	BEAT	-	beat	-	beat

Listen to the triple meter in Johann Strauss' *Blue Danube Waltz.*

DUPLE METER Because marches are intended for marchers with *two* feet, recurring groups of two or *duple meter* are standard:

	/		/	/		/
	ONE	-	two	ONE	-	two
	STRONG	-	weak	STRONG	-	weak
	BEAT	-	beat	BEAT	-	beat
marchers:	LEFT	-	right	LEFT	-	right

DETERMINING THE METER Here's how to determine the meter of the music. Listen for the recurring pattern of strong, accented beats and weak, unaccented beats. Mark the beats on a piece of paper. Indicate an accented beat with a long line and an unaccented beat with a shorter one.

Examples:

Duple　　　/　　/　　/　　/　　/　　/

　　　　　　　2　　　　　2　　　　　2

MUSIC
Johann Strauss (the Younger), *Blue Danube Waltz*

MUSIC
John Philip Sousa, "The Stars and Stripes Forever," trio section

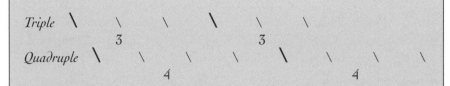

MUSIC
Richard Wagner, Overture to *Die Meistersinger von Nürnberg*, opening section

Minuet
MUSIC
Joseph Haydn, Symphony No. 94, third movement

MUSIC
Paul Desmond, "Take Five"

Ahmad Jamal Trio.

Jazz rhythms

You will now hear the opening section of the overture to the opera *Die Meistersinger*, by Richard Wagner. Determine the meter by marking on your paper the accented and unaccented beats.

Did you hear the four pattern, or *quadruple meter*?

Listen to this next example and figure out the meter by marking the beats.

The music is a *minuet* by Joseph Haydn. The minuet was a popular *triple-meter* dance in the eighteenth century.

LESS COMMON METERS If you can't fit two, three, or four beats in a pattern, chances are you are listening to music with a less common meter, such as five, seven, or eleven.

Listen to "Take Five" by jazz composer Paul Desmond of the Dave Brubeck Quartet. Can you hear the five-beat meter?

MULTIPLES OF TWO (DUPLE METER) You may perceive meters such as four and eight as *duple meter*. Meters that are multiples of two tend to sound like a duple meter. Without looking at the printed notation, you will often not recognize the difference.

MULTIPLES OF THREE (TRIPLE METER) The same holds for some multiples of three, such as 6, 9, and 12. A listener may hear them as *triple meter*.

SIX BEATS Six is a multiple both of two and of three. Depending on the tempo, you may hear six beats as either duple or triple meter.

SYNCOPATION Some music, especially jazz, uses rhythm patterns with unexpected accents. Or, there may be silence where you would anticipate an accent. This type of rhythm is called *syncopation*.

Listen again to Scott Joplin's ragtime piece "The Entertainer." Joplin used syncopated rhythms throughout.

MUSIC
Scott Joplin, "The Entertainer"

RHYTHMIC OSTINATO Twentieth-century composers are especially fond of using a repetitive pattern called *rhythmic ostinato*. Jazz, rock, and dance music often depend on ostinato for the driving rhythm that motivates movement.

Listen for the ostinato in the text piece by Igor Stravinsky.

MUSIC
Igor Stravinsky, *The Rite of Spring*, "Sacrificial Dance"

SILENCE Silence is also an important part of music. Listen to the opening of this piano sonata by Ludwig van Beethoven. Notice how the moments of silence create a dramatic effect.

MUSIC
Ludwig van Beethoven, Piano Sonata No. 8, Op. 13, first movement

Printed notes

∿Pitch (Melody and Harmony)

Pitches or tones are the materials of *melodies* and *harmonies*. Pitches appear on paper as *notes*. Performers read the notes and play or sing the corresponding pitches.

Melody

A melody is a succession of individual pitches that makes sense when you perceive them as a group. This is similar to perceiving a sentence from a group of individual words. Listen to this section from Felix Mendelssohn's Violin Concerto. Notice how the succession of pitches creates a coherent melody.

MUSIC
Felix Mendelssohn, Violin Concerto, first movement

Describing Melodies

As listeners, we can describe melodies and pitches in a number of ways.

PROMINENT OR NOT PROMINENT Is the melody *prominent* or *not prominent*? A prominent melody forms a coherent whole. You can often hum or remember a prominent melody after you've heard it a few times. Even the first time you hear it you can follow it. A melody is *not prominent* if you have trouble following it. When a succession of pitches sounds fragmented or aimless, you can describe the melody as *not prominent*.

MUSIC
Arnold Schoenberg, *Suite for Piano*, "Praeludium"

Listen to this twentieth-century piece by Arnold Schoenberg. Because the melody sounds fragmented, you may find it a challenge to remember or to hum it. For this reason you would probably describe it as *not prominent*.

LENGTH OF PHRASE   Another aspect of a melody is its length of *phrase* or melodic idea. Is the melodic idea *short* or *long*?

Short melodic idea. What we notice immediately about Beethoven's Symphony No. 5 is the unusual shortness of the opening phrase. Beethoven uses this short statement as a structural element throughout the first movement. When a melodic idea is used in this manner, that statement is called a *melodic motive*.

MUSIC
Ludwig van Beethoven, Symphony No. 5, first movement

Listen again as the orchestra plays this section of Beethoven's Symphony No. 5. Notice how the rhythmic idea (short, short, short, long) persists even when the melody changes. Therefore, the opening motive is also a *rhythmic motive*.

Long melodic idea. Contrast Beethoven's short idea with the longer idea in Wagner's Overture to *Die Meistersinger*.

MUSIC
Richard Wagner, Overture to *Die Meistersinger von Nürnberg*, opening section

Cadences. Notice how the melody keeps moving forward until it seems to arrive at a resting place. In music, we call these arrivals *cadences*.

ORNAMENTED MELODIES   Some melodies are plain—the opening of Beethoven's Symphony No. 5, for example. Others are ornamented with trills and embellishments. The type of *ornamentation* used is often a matter of the prevailing taste and fashion of the composer's time.

Listen to this section of Wolfgang Amadeus Mozart's variations of the French folk song "Ah, vous dirai-je maman." We know it as "Twinkle, Twinkle, Little Star." First, the plain, unornamented melody.

MUSIC
Wolfgang Amadeus Mozart, main theme. Variations "Ah, vous dirai-je maman," K. 265

Trills. Now listen to the variations. Mozart ornaments the melody with *trills* —a rapid alternation of two pitches.

Repetition, Imitation, and Sequence

Composers want you to become familiar with their melodic ideas. To help you, they may use musical devices such as *repetition*, *imitation*, and *sequence*.

REPETITION Hearing a phrase or melody again enables you to recognize it quickly. Repetition is like bringing a character from a play back on stage.

Listen to this catchy "Turkish March" by Mozart. You may almost memorize it the first time you hear it, but Mozart eases the job by repeating it for you.

IMITATION Imitation is a form of repetition. We hear a motive or a melody. Shortly thereafter, we hear it played again either by another voice or instrument, or by the same voice or instrument in a higher or lower range. That restatement is called *imitation.*

Listen to this section from Johann Sebastian Bach's *Brandenburg Concerto No. 2*. Notice how the melody, stated first by the trumpet, is imitated by the oboe, then by the violin, and finally by the flute.

Canons and rounds. A *canon* is an imitation that continues throughout an entire work. Examples are "Row, Row, Row Your Boat" and "Frère Jacques." We sometimes refer to these songs as *rounds* or *circle canons* if different voices keep coming around to the same melody.

SEQUENCE Sequences are another form of repetition: The same instrument repeats the melodic idea, using slightly different pitches.

Listen again to the opening of the Beethoven piano sonata. Beethoven takes the opening motive through a series of sequences.

Listen for *repetition*, *imitation*, and *sequences* in the opening section of the first movement of Beethoven's Symphony No. 5. Notice how Beethoven manipulates the melodic motive using different pitches. This is called a *sequence*. Then the motive is passed around the orchestra. This is called *imitation*.

Notice which instruments imitate the motive until that section comes to a cadence. First, you will hear the violins in a low range. Then, the violas imitate the melody. Next, the violins continue the imitation in a higher range. Then the full orchestra repeats the opening statement, followed by *imitation* and *sequences* until the next cadence.

MUSIC
Wolfgang Amadeus Mozart, K. 265, Variation No. 12

MUSIC
Wolfgang Amadeus Mozart, "Turkish March" from Sonata in A Major, K. 331

MUSIC
Johann Sebastian Bach, *Brandenburg Concerto No. 2*, third movement

MUSIC
Ludwig van Beethoven, Piano Sonata No. 8, Op. 13, opening

MUSIC
Ludwig van Beethoven, Symphony No. 5, first movement

MUSIC
C major scale and chord

MUSIC
c minor scale and chord

James Galway: flutist.

MUSIC
Pitches C, E, and G individually, then together

Scales

Scales consist of ascending or descending pitches arranged in specified patterns. Most melodies in Western concert music are based on one of two common scales: *major* and *minor*.

MAJOR SCALE   In general, the major scale has a bright, happy quality.

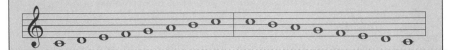

MINOR SCALE   The minor scale has a more plaintive quality.

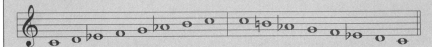

While you listen to concert music, try to discern the major or minor quality of the music you hear. The way you feel when you hear the music can sometimes be a clue.

OTHER SCALES   To add freshness to their music, many twentieth-century composers have organized pitches in other than major and minor scale patterns. These innovations will be discussed in later chapters.

Harmony

Combinations of pitches sounded simultaneously create harmony. You will now hear three pitches. First, they are sounded individually, as they would be in a melody. Then, they are sounded together to form harmony.

CHORD   When those three pitches were sounded simultaneously, they became a *chord*—a major chord.

CONSONANT CHORDS The chord you just heard evokes a feeling of stability and *balance*. This type of chord is *consonant*. Listen to it again.

DISSONANT CHORDS In some chords, the pitches within the chord seem to clash with one another. They may even sound unpleasant or disagreeable to you. These types of chords are *dissonant*.

Listen to these three chords. You'll have no trouble picking out the one dissonant chord from the two consonant chords.

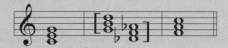

Did you recognize the second chord as the dissonant chord? If not, listen again.

MAJOR AND MINOR CHORDS We also describe chords by their quality, referring to them as *major chords* or *minor chords*.

Listen now to five chords. They alternate between major and minor chords, starting and ending with major.

Textures

With these musical threads—*rhythms, scales, melodies,* and *harmonies*—composers weave their ideas into *textures*. Using layers of sounds, they create a musical fabric. Most concert music employs three types of texture: *monophonic, homophonic,* and *polyphonic*.

MONOPHONIC TEXTURE A *monophonic texture* is a melody alone—without harmony, other melodic lines, or accompaniment.

HOMOPHONIC TEXTURE Seldom does music use monophonic texture. The most common texture is a melody with a harmonic accompaniment of some sort. This combination of melody and chordal accompaniment is called *homophonic texture*. An example of this texture would be produced by a singer with guitar accompaniment.

Here is the same Beethoven melody supported by a harmonic accompaniment. Notice the *homophonic texture*.

POLYPHONIC TEXTURE *Polyphonic texture* is more complicated. In polyphonic texture you hear several independent, overlapping melodic lines.

MUSIC
C major chord

MUSIC
consonant and dissonant chords

MUSIC
C major, f minor, E-flat major, a minor, and D-flat major

MUSIC
Ludwig van Beethoven, Piano Sonata No. 8, Op. 13, second movement (melody only)

MUSIC
Ludwig van Beethoven, Piano Sonata No. 8, Op. 13, second movement (original form)

MUSIC
George Frideric Handel,
Messiah, Chorus: "For
unto Us a Child Is Born"

Listen to this opening section of "For unto Us a Child Is Born" from George Frideric Handel's *Messiah*. The constant overlapping of melodic lines is an example of *polyphonic texture*.

You have just heard some of the basic materials used in music — *rhythms, scales, melodies, harmonies,* and *textures*. As you listen to the remaining recorded music with this book, you will become more familiar with them.

Itzhak Perlman.

❧ *Table 3-1* Summary of Basic Musical Elements

Rhythm (Duration of Sound)

beat prominence: strong, weak	rubato
tempo: slow, medium, fast	ostinato
meter: duple, triple, quadruple, other	rhythmic motive
	silence
	syncopation

Melody

prominent	imitation
not prominent	sequences
short phrase	repetition
long phrase	scales: major, minor
cadence	other scales: chromatic,
ornamented	pentatonic, whole-tone,
plain	gapped, tone-row

Harmony

mostly consonant	major and minor chords
mostly dissonant	

Texture

monophonic
polyphonic
homophonic

CHAPTER 4

Performing Media: Instruments, Voices, and Ensembles

Performers bring music to life. By singing or playing instruments, performers achieve the second step in the musical process—delivering composers' ideas to you, the listener.

Dedicated to giving the best possible performances, musicians not only spend a lifetime perfecting their skills but also constantly search for better and more interesting instruments. To meet these demands, manufacturers continually improve their traditional instruments and occasionally introduce new ones, most recently electronic and computer-generated instruments.

✍ Acoustics of Vocal and Instrumental Sound

All voices and musical instruments need three basic components to function: an *energy source*, a *vibrating element*, and a *resonating chamber*. An energy source (air, bow, mallets) sets a vibrating element (strings, lips, vocal cords) into motion. For the sound to be audible, a resonating chamber (tube, drum, wooden box) must amplify it. Air waves then carry the sound to the listener.

Try it yourself. Put your fingers on your larynx. Take a breath and exhale, saying "ah." Your exhaled breath is the energy source that makes your vocal cords vibrate. Your mouth and head cavities serve as resonating chambers that shape and amplify the sound.

Notice the difference between the sounds you produce when your mouth is closed and when it is open. Also notice that the more energy you exert, the louder the sound you produce.

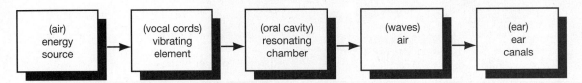

Instrumental Performing Media

Instruments fall into at least one of six categories:

- string
- woodwind
- brass
- percussion
- keyboard
- electronic

How Instruments Produce Sound

Timbre
(*tam*-ber)

Many variables contribute to an instrument's tone and sound production. Differences in size, shape, and construction materials alter *timbre* — the quality of the tone. Table 4-1 presents an overview of the acoustical components of the most common musical instruments.

⏳*Performing Media and Performances: Solo Instruments and Ensembles*

Solo Recitals

A recital can feature almost any instrument. Except for keyboard performances, recitals most typically present a soloist with an accompanist. For example, a violinist or cellist usually has a piano accompanist.

Ensembles

Although any combination of instrumentalists can play together in an *ensemble*, here are the most common:

❧ Table 4-1 *Acoustics of Commonly Used Instruments*

	Instrument	Energy	Vibrator	Resonator
WOODWIND	flute/piccolo	air	air over mouth hole	metal tube
	oboe	air	double reed	wood tube
	English horn	air	double reed	wood tube
	clarinet	air	single reed	wood tube
	bassoon	air	double reed	wood tube
	saxophone	air	single reed	metal tube
BRASS	trumpet	air	player's lips	brass tube
	French horn	air	player's lips	brass tube
	trombone	air	player's lips	brass tube
	baritone horn	air	player's lips	brass tube
	tuba	air	player's lips	brass tube
STRING	violin	bow	string	wood box
	viola	bow	string	wood box
	cello	bow	string	wood box
	string bass	bow	string	wood box
	harp	finger	string	wood box
	guitar	finger or pick	string	wood box
	mandolin	finger or pick	string	wood box
	banjo	finger or pick	string	wood box
PERCUSSION	cymbals	hands/arms	cymbals	metal disks
	snare drum	hands/arms w/stick	drum head (plastic or skin)	metal or wood cylinder
	bass drum	w/mallet	drum head	wood cylinder
	timpani	w/mallets	timpani heads	metal bowls
KEYBOARD	piano	fingers/hammers	strings	wood box
	harpsichord	fingers/plectrum	strings	wood box
	organ	fingers/air	air columns	metal and wood pipes
	celesta	fingers/hammers	steel bars	wood box
ELECTRONIC	synthesizer	fingers/electricity	transistors	loudspeaker

Chamber ensembles

New York Woodwind Quintet

Canadian Brass Quintet

SMALL ENSEMBLES   Combinations of only a few instruments are called *chamber ensembles*.

String trio: one violin, one viola, one cello
String quartet: two violins, one viola, one cello
Woodwind quintet: one flute, one oboe, one clarinet, one French horn, and one bassoon
Brass quintet: two trumpets, one French horn, one trombone, and one tuba

LARGE ENSEMBLES   The *symphony orchestra* and the *wind ensemble* are the most common large instrumental ensembles. Both ensembles may vary in size and instrumentation, according to the demands of the music. For special works, unusual instruments may be brought in. Our discussion of these ensembles begins with the symphony orchestra.

✣ The Orchestra and Its Instruments

Classical-music concerts by symphony orchestras are by far the most popular and well attended. Concertgoers love the rich variety of tone colors emanating from the individual instruments as well as from the ensemble as a whole. Artistic directors of orchestras have an extensive body of works to choose from. Many of the large orchestral works have maintained a broad appeal from one generation to the next.

The Juilliard String Quartet

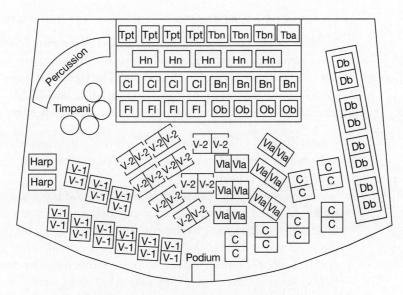

Typical Large Symphony Orchestra Seating Arrangement

❧ **Table 4-2   Numbers of Performers in Typical Orchestra**

Section	Instrument	Abbreviation	Number in Orch.
String	first violins	V-1	18
	second violins	V-2	16
	violas	Vla	12
	cellos	C	12
	double basses	Db	8
Woodwind	flutes (including piccolo)	Fl	4
	oboes (including English horn)	Ob	4
	clarinets	Cl	2–4
	bassoons (including contrabassoon)	Bn	2–4
Brass	trumpets	Tpt	4
	French horns	Hn	4–6
	trombones (including bass trombone)	Tbn	3–4
	tuba	Tba	1
Percussion	cymbals		1
	snare drum		1
	bass drum		1
	timpani		(2–6) 1
	chimes, marimba, bells, xylophone, triangle, miscellaneous		1
	harp		1–2

Sections of the Orchestra

Modern orchestras use similar seating arrangements for the four main sections: *string, woodwind, brass,* and *percussion.* A conductor may vary the seating somewhat at his or her discretion. The figure on page 31 shows the approximate placement of the instruments, and Table 4-2, the typical numbers of instruments used in today's major orchestras.

STRING SECTION   With more than half the musicians playing *violins, violas, cellos* (short for *violoncellos*), and *string basses,* the string section is the foundation of the orchestra.

The violins, the smallest of the string family, have the highest pitch range. Divided into two subsections—first and second violins—all the violinists sit together next to the conductor (see figure on page 31). Much of the time, you will hear the first violins carry the melody or theme in an orchestral piece. Sometimes the second violins play the same melody as the first violins; at other times they play a harmony part.

Similar in appearance to a violin, the viola is slightly larger and plays in a lower range. Violas are usually placed next to the violins, as shown in the chart.

Although similar in shape to both the violin and the viola, the cello (or violoncello) is much larger. Cellists, who place their heavy instruments between their legs, often use a special forward-tilting chair for balance. A long pin supports the bottom of the instrument on the floor. Because of its larger size and longer strings, the cello produces pitches in a range lower than those of either the violin or the viola. You will most often find the cellos to the extreme right of the conductor.

The bass, the largest string instrument, is also known by several other names: double bass, contrabass, bass viol, standing bass, string bass. Usually behind the cellos on the outer edge of the orchestra, a bass player may perform standing up or partially sitting or leaning on a tall stool.

String players produce sounds by drawing a *bow* across the strings. For a special effect, strings may be plucked (*pizzicato* in Italian). To soften and change the timbre, string players can use a device called a *mute* on their instruments.

WOODWIND SECTION   Usually seated directly in front of the conductor behind the strings, the woodwinds make up the second most important section of the orchestra. The full section consists of *piccolo, flutes, oboes, English horn, clarinets, bassoons,* and *contrabassoon. Saxophones* may occasionally join the woodwind section for modern or jazz-influenced music.

Originally, all woodwind instruments were made of wood. Now, flutes and piccolos are nearly always metal. Whether wood or metal, all modern woodwinds have elaborate keying mechanisms that facilitate rapid playing.

Violin
(vy-uh-*lin*)

Viola
(vee-*oh*-luh)

Cello
(*chel*-oh)

Violoncello
(*vee*-uh-lun-*chel*-oh)

String bass
(bayse)

Bow
(bo)

Pizzicato
(pits-ih-*kah*-toh)

Mute

Flute

Piccolo
(*pik*-uh-loh)

Playing in the highest range of the flute section and the orchestra, the piccolo is the smallest woodwind. The flute is next in range and size. A flutist or piccolo player produces tones by blowing across a hole at the head of the instrument.

Placed next to each other, the oboe and English horn both have a set of double reeds. The oboe has a highly audible, "reedy" sound. Its pitches are consistent and easily heard. For this reason, the first oboist usually sounds the "A" for the orchestra to tune by.

Slightly larger than the oboe, the English horn is distinguished by the curved pipe between its reeds and the body of the instrument. Neither English nor a horn, the instrument probably received its name because someone noticed that it resembled an angled hunting horn. In the early nineteenth century, when the instrument was introduced, "cor anglé" ("angled horn" in French) sounded similar to "cor anglais" ("English horn"). The name stuck.

Clarinets use a single reed. Capable of a wide range of pitches and timbres, clarinets vary in size from smaller, high-pitched soprano clarinets to large, deep-pitched bass clarinets. The clarinet's upper register, higher than an oboe's, can be heard above the orchestra. The middle register can sound mellow, and the lower register, rich and "woody."

Saxophones also use a single reed. Although they have always been made of brass, saxophones are included in the woodwind category. The instruments range in size from the high soprano saxophones to the low baritones and basses.

With its double reeds, the bassoon is closely related to the oboe. Notice the photos of a bassoon and its larger version, the contrabassoon, so you will recognize them. Both are made of large wooden tubes, with long pipes connecting their reeds to the body of the instrument.

BRASS SECTION   The brass section, named for the construction material of its instruments, includes *trumpets*, *French horns*, *trombones*, and *tubas*. All brass players produce sounds by forcing air through their lips. This creates a buzzing or vibration that is funneled into the instrument through a mouthpiece. Then, the unique construction of the individual instrument shapes and resonates these initial sounds differently.

Because the brass instruments are powerful enough to produce the loudest sounds in the orchestra, they are usually placed behind the woodwinds, or in the outer ring of the orchestra.

Smallest of the section, the trumpets produce the highest tones. Depending on the requirements of a particular piece, players use trumpets of different sizes and pitches.

Distinguished from the other brasses by its mellower tones, the French horn can produce a wide range of pitches. This versatile instru-

Orchestra violin section

English horn

Oboe

Clarinet

Saxophone

Bassoon

Members of an orchestra's woodwind section (left to right: flute, oboe, bassoon, clarinet).

Trumpet

French horn

ment can easily blend with either the woodwinds or the brass. Though not visible in the photo, the horn players' right hands are partially inside the bell.

Trombone

Playing in the middle and lower ranges of the brass section, the trombone is the only brass instrument without valves. Instead, the instrument has a telescoping slide that changes the length of its tubing, and therefore its pitch.

Bass trombone

Music often calls for the addition of a bass trombone. Its larger tubing and slightly larger bell make it capable of playing low and loudly.

Tuba

The tuba, easily recognized by its size, is the largest brass and is capable of playing the lowest tones in the section. To prevent the tuba from overpowering other instruments in the orchestra, its bell is pointed toward the ceiling.

The sousaphone, a popular marching band instrument (not an orchestra brass), is similar to a tuba. Named for "the March King," John Philip Sousa, the sousaphone is shaped so that a player can carry it while marching.

Brass mutes

Placing various mutes into the bell of a brass instrument will change its sound. The cone-shaped "straight" mute makes any of the brasses sound more like a woodwind instrument. The "cup" mute mellows sounds, and the "wa-wa" mute is often used in jazz pieces.

PERCUSSION SECTION   Percussionists are usually placed at the outer perimeter of the ensemble. Members of this section strike, rub, shake, jiggle, pound, beat, or crash their instruments to produce a host of specialized sounds.

Members of an orchestra's brass section (front, left to right: French horn, trumpet; rear: trombones.

Orchestra percussion section: (left to right) bass drum, tom tom, timbale, marimba, snare drums, conga drum, timpani, bass drum. Photo: Robert Millard ©

Drums

Some percussion instruments play defined pitches—for example, chimes, glockenspiel, celesta, bells, xylophone, and marimba. Others do not, including drums of various sizes and shapes. Some drums, such as snare and field drums, are played with sticks. Others, such as the bass drum, are played with padded mallets. Still others, such as the bongos and conga drums, are played with the hands.

Timpani

The timpani, or kettledrums, deserve special mention for two reasons. First of all, they were the first percussion instruments to join the symphony orchestra. They made their debut in an opera orchestra around 1670. Later, Johann Sebastian Bach used them in some of his larger works. Two timpani were standard in Mozart's and Haydn's orchestras. In the nineteenth century, a third, fourth, and even more timpani joined the symphony orchestra as needed for particular works.

Second, they are the only drums tuned to specific pitches. Consisting of large, shiny copper bowls, timpani are impressive. Each bowl is topped with a stretched skin or plastic head. The player uses an assortment of padded mallets to produce the desired effects. A pedal mechanism on today's timpani facilitates changing pitches and retuning during performances.

Exotic

Various cultures have contributed to the percussion section:

Africa: drums, wood blocks, gourds, xylophone
Islamic North Africa and Turkey: various cymbals, triangle, bass drum
Asia: Korean temple blocks, Chinese gongs, Indonesian finger cymbals

South and Central America: maracas, timbales, bongos, conga drum, claves, cow bell

Europe: castanets, tambourine

(For a more detailed discussion of the contributions of world cultures to Western concert music, see Chapter 27.)

The Turkish cymbals in the orchestra are either hit with a stick or mallet or crashed together. Because the player may wait through pages of music for the brief cymbal part, he or she often plays other instruments in the section.

Sound effects

Including almost any sounds in the percussion section is possible: whips, thunder, bird calls, breaking glass, crashing cars, blasting cannons, firing rifles, roaring aircraft, and an infinite variety of electronically produced effects. George Gershwin called for taxi horns to add realistic street sounds in his orchestral piece *An American in Paris*. Ottorino Respighi enhanced the atmosphere of *The Pines of Rome* by adding recordings of genuine bird calls.

Note: All the recordings in this chapter will be discussed in more detail later in the text. In most cases, the text also contains a detailed listening guide of each work.

Becoming Familiar with the Instruments

Associating the sounds you hear with the instruments you see at concerts or on television is the best way to become familiar with them. Use this next listening activity to become acquainted with the instruments.

Zubin Mehta conducting the New York Philharmonic.

LISTENING ACTIVITY ∽

BRITTEN, *THE YOUNG PERSON'S GUIDE TO THE ORCHESTRA*.

▌ *Compact Disc 4, Track 21*

While you listen to *The Young Person's Guide to the Orchestra* by Benjamin Britten (1913–76), follow along with the listening guide. As each instrument is introduced, notice its sounds when it performs with its section and then later, as a solo instrument. Listen again, this time associating sounds with the pictures of the string, woodwind, brass, and percussion sections of the orchestra.

Written to introduce concertgoers to orchestral instruments, *The Young Person's Guide to the Orchestra* is a set of variations and fugue based on a theme by the seventeenth-century English composer Henry Purcell (*per*-sul, 1659–95).

Purcell's theme

The work is in three sections:

Part one is a statement of Purcell's *theme*. First, the entire orchestra plays the theme. Next, each section plays it in turn—starting with the woodwinds, then the brass, the strings, and finally the percussion.

Variations

Part two of the piece is a set of thirteen variations on Purcell's theme. Britten uses this to introduce individual instruments (see Listening Guide).

Fugue

Part three is a fugue—a compositional device in which other voices or, as in this case, instruments imitate with polyphonic texture a central subject.

LISTENING GUIDE

BRITTEN, *THE YOUNG PERSON'S GUIDE TO THE ORCHESTRA*, OP. 34,
"VARIATIONS AND FUGUE ON A THEME BY PURCELL"

▌ *Compact Disc 4, Track 21*
▌ *Running time: 18:07*

Please turn to page 38 for the Guide.

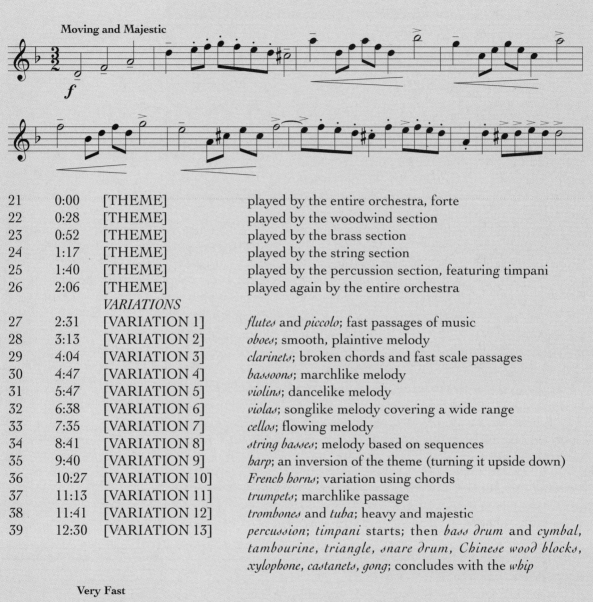

21	0:00	[THEME]	played by the entire orchestra, forte
22	0:28	[THEME]	played by the woodwind section
23	0:52	[THEME]	played by the brass section
24	1:17	[THEME]	played by the string section
25	1:40	[THEME]	played by the percussion section, featuring timpani
26	2:06	[THEME]	played again by the entire orchestra
		VARIATIONS	
27	2:31	[VARIATION 1]	*flutes* and *piccolo*; fast passages of music
28	3:13	[VARIATION 2]	*oboes*; smooth, plaintive melody
29	4:04	[VARIATION 3]	*clarinets*; broken chords and fast scale passages
30	4:47	[VARIATION 4]	*bassoons*; marchlike melody
31	5:47	[VARIATION 5]	*violins*; dancelike melody
32	6:38	[VARIATION 6]	*violas*; songlike melody covering a wide range
33	7:35	[VARIATION 7]	*cellos*; flowing melody
34	8:41	[VARIATION 8]	*string basses*; melody based on sequences
35	9:40	[VARIATION 9]	*harp*; an inversion of the theme (turning it upside down)
36	10:27	[VARIATION 10]	*French horns*; variation using chords
37	11:13	[VARIATION 11]	*trumpets*; marchlike passage
38	11:41	[VARIATION 12]	*trombones* and *tuba*; heavy and majestic
39	12:30	[VARIATION 13]	*percussion*; *timpani* starts; then *bass drum* and *cymbal*, *tambourine*, *triangle*, *snare drum*, *Chinese wood blocks*, *xylophone*, *castanets*, *gong*; concludes with the *whip*

		FUGUE	
40	14:43	[SUBJECT]	based on the theme, played by *piccolo*
	15:04	[SUBJECT]	played by *flutes*
	15:20	[SUBJECT]	played by *oboes*
	15:26	[SUBJECT]	played by *clarinets*
	15:37	[SUBJECT]	played by *bassoons*
	15:49	[SUBJECT]	played by *first violins*
	15:51	[SUBJECT]	played by *second violins*
	15:59	[SUBJECT]	played by *violas*
	16:05	[SUBJECT]	played by *cellos*
	16:13	[SUBJECT]	played by *string basses*
	16:25	[SUBJECT]	played by *harp*
	16:39	[SUBJECT]	played by *French horns*
	16:45	[SUBJECT]	played by *trumpets*
	16:55	[SUBJECT]	played by *trombones* and *tuba*
	17:01	[SUBJECT]	played by *upper strings* and *woodwinds*; [THEME] played in long tones by *brasses*

[CODA]
17:47 Percussion enters forte
18:00 Ending chord by the entire orchestra

✺ How the Orchestra Developed

Toward the end of the eighteenth century, Joseph Haydn's 30-piece court orchestra consisted of part-time musicians who had to double as servants, cooks, and stable hands to make a living. A generation later, Ludwig van Beethoven was limited to 40 or 50 poorly trained instrumentalists, many of whom had difficulty reading his demanding music.

Today's symphony orchestra, with highly skilled, professional performers playing the assortment of instruments we have come to know, developed during the latter part of the nineteenth century. Among the factors influencing this development were the emergence of both new and improved instruments, the growing popularity of public concerts in larger halls, and the establishment of funding sources to support expanded orchestras.

Before the Seventeenth Century

CHAMBER ENSEMBLES Chamber ensembles were the main instrumental groups before the seventeenth century. Two to eight musicians performed on an as-needed basis to entertain in the chambers or rooms of a palace or manor house. Composers did not specify the instruments because they didn't know which ones would be available. So it was possible to hear a piece played on a different combination of instruments from one performance to the next.

The Roman Catholic Church, the leading employer of musicians before that time, was more interested in vocal music. Although an ensemble of instruments was occasionally featured in the church service, the instrumentalist's primary role was to accompany the singers.

The Beginnings of Instrumentation

Gabrieli
(gah-bree-*ay*-lee)

In Venice around 1600, Giovanni Gabrieli (c.1555–1612) surveyed the possibilities offered by the huge interior of St. Mark's Basilica, where he was first organist and composer. He realized that instruments playing in different locations of the church could produce very rich sound effects. So he experimented with different combinations of instruments until he was satisfied with the results.

To ensure the balance and quality of that sound, Gabrieli did specify which instruments should play. Thus, we had the beginning of standardized *instrumentation*, which made it possible for a complex instrumental composition to be performed with the same instrumentation at each performance.

Monteverdi
(mohn-teh-*vehr*-dee)

Another great Italian composer, Claudio Monteverdi, built on Gabrieli's ideas to set up the first orchestra with stable instrumentation. In 1607, he hired 40 musicians to accompany his opera *Orfeo* (*or*-fay-oh).

2	flutes (one high and one low)
2	oboes
1	very high trumpet (clarino)
3	high trumpets
4	medium trumpets
2	cornets (looking and sounding different from the modern cornet, and made either of wood or of ivory)
2	small violins
2	violins (regular size)
10	viole da braccia (similar to the modern violin)
3	viole da gamba (similar to the modern cello)
2	double-bass viols (string bass)
2	deep-tone lutes (a cross between a guitar and a mandolin)
5	assorted keyboard instruments, including harpsichords

The String Instruments Achieve Perfection

Between 1650 and 1700, there was a breakthrough in the construction of string instruments. This breakthrough was the next important step in the

LISTENING ACTIVITY ॐ

GABRIELI, MOTET, *IN ECCLESIIS*

Cassette Tape: Side A, Example 5
Compact Disc 1, Track 5
Running time: 9:00

Listen to Gabrieli's interesting motet, *In ecclesiis*, performed by singers, instruments, and organ. Gabrieli composed this work for the Basilica di San Marco (St. Mark's) in Venice, which was a hub of world trade around 1600. Gabrieli's musical services attracted visitors from around the globe. To maintain their interest, he kept the pace of his music lively and interesting. As you listen to the following plan for the various sections of *In ecclesiis*, note how Gabrieli keeps changing his performing media:

- organ
- organ and soprano
- contrasting choirs and organ
- tenor with organ accompaniment
- contrasting choirs and organ
- brasses and other instruments
- altos and tenors with instrumental accompaniment
- contrasting choirs with instruments and organ
- contrasting choirs and organ
- contrasting choirs with instruments
- contrasting choirs with instruments and organ

development of the orchestra. In the northern Italian town of Cremona, a few generations of craftsmen achieved near-perfection in creating their string instruments. Niccolo Amati (1596–1684), Antonio Stradivari (1644–1737), and Giuseppe Bartolomeo Guarneri (1698–1744) crafted priceless instruments cherished and played today by such soloists as Itzhak Perlman, Midori, Nigel Kennedy, Nadja Salerno-Sonnenberg, Yo-Yo Ma, and Lynn Harrell.

Amati
(ah-*mah*-tee)

Stradivari
(strah-deh-*vah*-ree)

Guarneri
(gwahr-*nay*-ree)

HISTORICAL PERSPECTIVE

What Is the Secret of the Cremona Instruments?

With all our modern technology, why haven't we been yet able to replicate the quality of string instruments created by the Cremona craftsmen? What makes those instruments so great? Not only are their tones beautiful, but their sounds resonate over the symphony orchestra.

Theories abound about the secrets of these instruments, but all theories remain unproved: the secrets died with the craftsmen.

Some have conjectured that there were special qualities in the varnish and glue. Perhaps. Another suggests that the instruments were crafted from wood soaked in the polluted waters of Venice. What "magical" powers this particular water may have transferred, no one knows. But recent analyses indicate that the soaking seems to have created a specially porous wood, which, may indeed, amplify sound.

LISTENING ACTIVITY ∾

VIVALDI, *THE FOUR SEASONS*, SPRING,
FIRST MOVEMENT: ALLEGRO

Cassette Tape: Side B, Example 2
Compact Disc 1, Track 30
Running time: 3:10

Listen to the first movement of the "Spring" Concerto of Vivaldi's *The Four Seasons*, which features a violin soloist with a string chamber orchestra.

SOLO PERFORMERS   Around 1700, several composers, Antonio Vivaldi in particular, were inspired by the improved string instruments. A violinist himself, Vivaldi grew up in Venice about 100 miles east of Cremona, and later taught at a girl's orphanage in Venice. Of his 500 concertos (music for one or several soloists with orchestra) featuring various instruments, he composed almost half for the violin.

VIRTUOSO PERFORMERS   Vivaldi's violin concertos were more technically demanding than earlier string music. With the availability of superior instruments, musicians aspired to become *virtuosos*—solo performers with exceptional technical ability.*

Virtuosos
(vur-choo-*oh*-sohs)

Highly proficient soloists could now earn more money—a fact that motivated other instrumentalists to attain virtuosity. After 1700, trumpeters, hornists, flutists, oboists, and bassoonists joined the ranks of virtuosos. A harpsichord or a chamber orchestra usually accompanied soloists.

Concertos
(con-*chayr*-tos)

Chamber Orchestra

Because most of the performances took place in the court chambers, the larger Baroque instrumental ensemble is called a *chamber orchestra*. Not yet containing the variety of instruments associated with the modern symphony orchestra, the chamber orchestra consisted mainly of string instruments, a few winds, and harpsichord, often with the composer playing and conducting from the harpsichord. This is illustrated in the figure below.

Concerto Grosso

With more instrumentalists becoming virtuosos, composers of the early eighteenth century began to write concertos featuring several soloists in the same piece of music. To distinguish this work from a concerto for one or two instruments, composers called it *concerto grosso*, or "large concerto."

The Baroque Chamber
Orchestra (10 to 20 players)
———

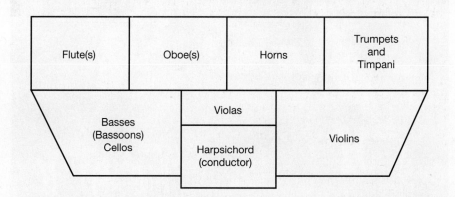

*In music, we use either the Italian plural ending of words (concerti, virtuosi) or the English ending (concertos, virtuosos).

LISTENING ACTIVITY ⚮

BACH, *BRANDENBURG CONCERTO NO. 2* IN F,
THIRD MOVEMENT

Cassette Tape: Side B, Example 3
Compact Disc 1, Track 34
Running time: 3:01

Bach's six *Brandenburg Concertos* are among the most exciting examples of the concerto grosso. Concerto No. 2 features four virtuoso performers—*trumpet, flute, oboe,* and *violin*—with a small string chamber orchestra and harpsichord. Listen to the third movement. Notice how each of the four soloists contributes to the entire work. In Chapter 8, we will return to this work and discuss it in detail.

Haydn directing a court chamber orchestra from the harpsichord.

The Court Orchestra Evolves

By the latter part of the eighteenth century, almost every European court of the ruling nobility had its small resident orchestra. The 15 to 30 part-time players were on call to provide familiar entertainment for their employers and guests.

The words "familiar entertainment" are significant; aristocrats didn't like surprises. Catering to this desire for predictability, court composers wrote music with standardized instrumentation for these small resident orchestras. Thus, members of the aristocratic leisure class could be assured of comparable entertainment, no matter where they traveled.

Haydn's Contributions

Over a 30-year span of composing more than 100 symphonies for the classical orchestra, Joseph Haydn contributed significantly to the development of the orchestra. Adding a pair of timpani (kettledrums) to the standard orchestra and gradually phasing out the harpsichord, Haydn influenced Wolfgang Amadeus Mozart and other contemporaries to follow his lead. These refinements paved the way for the birth of the "modern" orchestra.

Beethoven's Expanded Orchestra

Beethoven, who often expressed his reluctance to appear in palaces, took his music to larger halls where the middle class could gather. Consequently, a larger orchestra evolved to produce enough sound to fill the available space and be heard by larger audiences. As orchestras moved into larger halls, composers further explored the expressive potential of the orchestral sound.

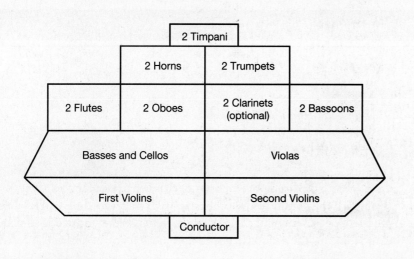

Table 4-4 The Classical Orchestra (18–30 players)

LISTENING ACTIVITY ა

HAYDN, *SYMPHONY NO. 94* IN G,
THIRD MOVEMENT

Cassette Tape: Side B, Example 8
Compact Disc 2, Track 1
Running time: 5:32

Listen to the third movement of Haydn's *Symphony No. 94*. It is derived from an eighteenth-century dance (the minuet) in triple meter. Note that the sound of this small symphony orchestra is similar to orchestras you have heard before.

For his *Symphony No. 1*, Beethoven used an orchestra similar in size to the ones Haydn and Mozart used (see Table 4-3). A few years later, for his *Symphony No. 5*, Beethoven added a piccolo, contrabassoon, and three trombones, thus increasing the size and power of the orchestra.

By 1824, for his last symphony, the *Ninth*, Beethoven's orchestra had nearly doubled in size. Now it included such new percussion instruments as the triangle, bass drum, and cymbals (see Table 4-3). In the last movement of the *Ninth Symphony*, Beethoven calls for four soloist singers and a large chorus to perform with the orchestra.

LISTENING ACTIVITY ა

BEETHOVEN, *SYMPHONY NO. 5*, FIRST MOVEMENT

Cassette Tape: Side C, Example 1
Compact Disc 2, Track 17
Running time: 7:18

Listen to the first movement of Beethoven's popular *Symphony No. 5*. Compare the sound of the orchestra with the recording of Haydn's *Symphony No. 94*. You will notice that though instrumentation is similar, Beethoven calls for a slightly larger and more forceful orchestra.

↝ *Table 4-3* Beethoven's Early, Middle, and Late Orchestras

Symphony No. 1 (1800)	Symphony No. 5 (1808)	Symphony No. 9 (1824)
2 Flutes	1 Piccolo	1 Piccolo
2 Oboes	2 Flutes	2 Flutes
2 Clarinets	2 Oboes	2 Oboes
2 Bassoons	2 Clarinets	2 Clarinets
2 Horns	2 Bassoons	2 Bassoons
2 Trumpets	1 Contrabassoon	1 Contrabassoon
Timpani	2 Horns	4 Horns
First Violins	2 Trumpets	2 Trumpets
Second Violins	3 Trombones	3 Trombones
Violas	Timpani	Timpani
Cellos	First Violins	Triangle
Basses	Second Violins	Cymbals
	Violas	Bass Drum
	Cellos	First Violins
	Basses	Second Violins
		Violas
		Cellos
		Basses
		4 Vocal soloists
		Large chorus

Nineteenth-century Expansion of the Orchestra

Inspired by Beethoven, other nineteenth-century composers continued to enlarge the orchestra. Berlioz added players in the wind and percussion sections. He also incorporated improved versions of existing instruments as well as newly invented instruments such as the tuba, English horn, saxophone, and contrabassoon. Berlioz was even adventuresome enough to try several experimental instruments not usually found in orchestras (ophicleide, basset horn, Sax horn, for example). This last group of instruments had technical and tonal problems and was discontinued.

BRASS VALVES AND WOODWIND KEYS   By the 1830s, many brass instruments had valves, enabling them to play in all keys. Formerly, brass instruments were largely limited to playing fanfares and bugle calls. Only a few early brass players could manage the instrument's extreme high register, where a few more pitches were available. Bach had a specific, talented trumpet player in mind when he wrote that demanding trumpet part in his *Branden-burg Concerto No. 2* (Cassette Tape, Side B, Example 3).

The trombone, which uses a telescoping slide to produce pitches other than bugle calls, retains its basic mechanism to this day.

A new system of keying, invented in 1832 by the flutist Theobald Boehm, eventually allowed flutes, clarinets, oboes, and bassoons to be played faster and with greater ease. The woodwind keys, much like typewriter keys, allowed the players to open holes in the body of the instrument formerly out of reach of the player's fingers.

With the capabilities of both woodwind and brass instruments, composers began creating more important musical roles for them in the orchestra as well as for concerto performance. Though not employed as frequently as the string section in the orchestra during the nineteenth century, the woodwind and brass sections were significantly elevated in importance.

Rising Standards of Performance

Gewandhaus
(guh-*vahnd*-howse)

When the composer Felix Mendelssohn accepted appointment in 1835 as conductor of the Gewandhaus Orchestra in Leipzig, Germany, he began transforming the orchestra. He energetically recruited the best players in Europe. Thus Mendelssohn established the Gewandhaus Orchestra as the finest of its day. Living composers clamored to have the Gewandhaus Orchestra play their works, and audiences were able to hear superb performances of great masterpieces.

LISTENING ACTIVITY ॐ

Symphonie
(sam-foh-*nee*)
fantastique
(fahn-tahs-*teek*)

BERLIOZ, *SYMPHONIE FANTASTIQUE*, FIFTH
MOVEMENT, "DREAM OF A WITCHES' SABBATH"

| *Cassette Tape: Side C, Example 2*
| *Compact Disc 2, Track 26*
| *Running time: 10:20*

Listen to the fifth movement of Hector Berlioz's *Symphonie Fantastique* and focus on the variety of instrumental timbres in the orchestra. In addition to the woodwinds and brass just mentioned, you'll hear chimes and a high-pitched clarinet. To create the scary atmosphere of a graveyard, complete with sounds of rattling bones, Berlioz requests all string players to turn their bows around and strike the strings with the wood side. This special effect is called *col legno* (Italian for "with wood").

col legno
(cohl-*lehn*-yo)

The Virtuoso Orchestra Emerges

To meet the performance demands of late-nineteenth-century composers—particularly Richard Wagner, Richard Strauss, Nikolai Rimsky-Korsakov, and Gustav-Mahler—orchestras hired virtuoso performers for every section, giving us the orchestra we know today.

Then in 1913, Igor Stravinsky, for his ballet *The Rite of Spring (Le Sacre du printemps)*, gave new prominence to the percussion section. Stravinsky calls for between 110 and 115 players for *The Rite of Spring*:

Strings (66 players)
>   18 first violins
>   16 second violins
>   12 violas
>   12 cellos
>   8 string basses

Woodwinds (23 players)
>   2 piccolos
>   3 flutes (3rd doubling as 2nd piccolo)
>   1 alto flute in G
>   4 oboes (4th doubling as 2nd English horn)
>   2 English horns
>   1 clarinet in D
>   3 clarinets in A and B-flat
>   2 bass clarinets
>   3 bassoons
>   2 contrabassoons

Brass (19 players)
>   1 trumpet in D
>   4 trumpets in C (4th doubling as bass trumpet)
>   1 bass trumpet in E-flat
>   8 horns
>   3 trombones
>   2 tubas

Percussion (4-7 players—some percussionists play more than one instrument)
>   5 timpani (played by 2 players)
>   1 bass drum
>   1 pair of cymbals
>   1 set of tam tam (Chinese gong)
>   1 set of antique cymbals (tiny, 2 1/2 to 3 inches)
>   1 triangle
>   1 guiro (a serrated African gourd scraped with a stick)

Wagner
(*vahg*-ner)
Strauss
(shtrowss)
Rimsky-Korsakov
(*rim*-skee *kohr*-suh-koff)
Mahler
(*mah*-ler)
Sacre du printemps
(*sac*-ruh doo pran-*ton*)

LISTENING ACTIVITY ∽

STRAVINSKY, *THE RITE OF SPRING*, "SACRIFICIAL DANCE"

Cassette Tape: Side D, Example 2
Compact Disc 3, Track 1
Running time: 4:33

Listen to the "Sacrificial Dance" from *The Rite of Spring* ballet by Igor Stravinsky. Notice how he maintains a strong percussive drive throughout the entire piece.

The Wind Ensemble

Especially during the twentieth century, wind ensembles have become popular concert attractions. These groups include concert bands, symphonic bands, wind orchestras, or wind bands. Consisting primarily of wind instruments and an occasional string bass, wind ensembles may vary in size and instrumentation.

Since Biblical times, outdoor music without string instruments has been associated with invading armies, powerful rulers, and successful conquests. Now wind ensembles are associated with popular concerts, summer outdoor concerts in park bandstands, and holiday celebrations. These ensembles bring music to masses of people who otherwise might never have the opportunity to enjoy a traditional symphony orchestra concert.

Around the turn of the twentieth century, the fine professional bands of John Philip Sousa, Arthur Pryor, and Patrick Conway spread the popularity of these ensembles throughout North America. During the World Wars, bands marched in parades, provided inspiration at patriotic rallies and War Bond drives, and performed concerts throughout the world.

Today, with the abundance of fine performing ensembles in high schools, colleges, and the military, contemporary composers have found a new, profitable outlet writing music for wind bands. Wind ensembles now have a wide variety of music from which to choose their concert programs.

∽ *Keyboard Instruments*

Keyboards of various sizes, sounds, and shapes have been popular since the Greeks invented a version of the organ, the water-powered *hydraulis,* sometime between 250 and 120 B.C. The *organ*, *harpsichord*, *piano*, and *electronic music synthesizer* now predominate at concert music performances.

Organ

Often called "the king of instruments," the organ is the largest and most powerful in the keyboard category. The sound from its hundreds of individual pipes fills such churches as St. Peter's in Rome, St. Mark's in Venice, St. Paul's in London, and the Washington Cathedral in Washington, D.C.

Early giant organs made great physical demands on the operators. For example, the organ installed in England's Winchester Cathedral in the tenth century required 70 energetic men to pump and jump and huff and puff to work the 26 bellows that provided air to its more than 400 pipes. The aerobics of these operators made it possible for the organist to produce music.

Today, most organs use electric energy to move the air through the pipes. Some pipes sound like woodwind instruments, others like brasses; still others produce sounds unique to the organ. The organist can select and combine any of the various pipes to create interesting timbres, similar to combining instruments in orchestration.

Most organs have at least two keyboards, and many have three or four, making it easier for the player to shift between the various combinations of pipes and timbres. Organists can produce additional tones on a pedalboard, playing with their toes and heels of both feet.

Harpsichord

Until the advent of the pianoforte in the eighteenth century, European music patrons favored the harpsichord for both solo and chamber ensemble performance. Though similar in shape to a modern grand piano, the harpsichord produces its tone and sound quite differently.

When a harpsichordist strikes a key, a mechanism activates a plectrum, a picklike device made of bird quill or leather. This device plucks a string, resulting in a brittle twang. Hitting a piano key, by contrast, activates a felt-covered hammer that strikes the strings, producing full, more mellow tones.

A drawback to the harpsichord is that all tones have equal volume, no matter how hard the player hits the keys. To achieve a modest contrast in the volume, some harpsichords have an additional keyboard that strikes louder-sounding strings. On the other hand, an advantage of the harpsichord is that its lighter tone is useful for accompanying singers.

LISTENING ACTIVITY ᴔ

BACH, *FUGUE IN G MINOR* (THE LITTLE)

Cassette Tape: Side B, Example 4
Compact Disc 1, Track 39
Running time: 3:44

Listen to the recording of the *Fugue in g minor* (The Little) by Johann Sebastian Bach, composed in the early eighteenth century. Note the power and variety of sounds the organ produces. Try to imagine the famous organist Bach performing this work in one of the world's greatest cathedrals.

Fortepiano
(*for*-tay-pee-*an*-oh)

Piano

Johann Sebastian Bach was not impressed by the piano collection of King Frederick the Great of Prussia. Although the monarch had specially invited Bach in 1747 to try out his array of newly invented instruments, the great master found them all in a rudimentary state of development.

Starting in 1770, however, 20 years after Bach's death, piano makers began significantly improving their instruments. In a 1777 letter to his father, Wolfgang Amadeus Mozart expressed his enthusiasm about the new instruments. Having them available, Mozart later added to the growing repertoire for the piano by composing 27 concertos and 20 sonatas.

By 1800, piano makers had produced an instrument very similar to the modern piano—short for *fortepiano* (meaning "loud-soft" in Italian). For the first time, a keyboard instrument had been named for its capabilities. Keyboard artists could control dynamic shadings—very soft to very loud—with the touch of their hands.

Championed by such composer-performers as Ludwig van Beethoven, Franz Schubert, Robert Schumann, Felix Mendelssohn, Frederic Chopin, Johannes Brahms, and Franz Liszt, the piano enjoyed its golden era. With its greater expressive capabilities, the piano emerged as the preferred keyboard instrument of the nineteenth century, figuring prominently as a sign of status in every prosperous and educated home.

LISTENING ACTIVITY ☙

MOZART, VARIATIONS ON "AH, VOUS DIRAIS-JE, MAMAN," K. 265

Cassette Tape: Side B, Example 5
Compact Disc 1, Track 45
Running time: 2:49

Listen to the sound quality of the harpsichord in this excerpt from Mozart's variations on the French folk song "Ah, vous dirais-je, maman."

Mozart at the harpsichord

Electronic synthesizer keyboard

Electronic Instruments

ELECTRONIC KEYBOARDS AND SYNTHESIZERS   Recently, electronic keyboards and electronic music synthesizers have paralleled the piano's popularity. Actually, the term "synthesizer" does not adequately describe these instruments. Early synthesizers were designed to imitate the timbre of harpsichords, organs, violins, flutes, and other instruments. They still are able to produce these sounds, but they are also capable of much more. When combined with computers, synthesizers can create virtually unlimited varieties of sounds.

LISTENING ACTIVITY ☙

LESEMANN, *METAKINETIC INVENTION*, VERSION 2

Cassette Tape: Side D, Example 5
Compact Disc 3, Track 13
Running time: 2:00

While listening to Frederick Lesemann's *Metakinetic Invention*, Version 2, note the wide variety of sounds the synthesizer produces.

LISTENING ACTIVITY ॐ

CHOPIN, *FANTASIE-IMPROMPTU*, OP. 66

Cassette Tape: Side C, Example 5
Compact Disc 2, Track 35
Running time: 4:42

Listen to the *Fantasie-Impromptu* by Frederic Chopin. Chopin's music allows pianists to display their technical brilliance and the instrument's expressiveness.

ॐ Human Voice

Many people consider the human voice, with its tremendous range of sound and emotion, to be the most expressive musical instrument. Think of the differences between the jazz "scat" singer, the crooner, the rapper, the Gospel singer, the pop vocalist, and the opera singer.

For classical music there are several general voice classifications, as shown in Table 4-4.

LISTENING ACTIVITY ॐ

MOZART, *DON GIOVANNI*, "MADAMINA"

Cassette Tape: Side B, Example 10
Compact Disc 2, Track 13
Running time: 5:53

Listen to the famous "Catalog" aria "Madamina," featuring a *basso buffo* ("comic bass" in Italian) singing the role of Leporello from Mozart's opera *Don Giovanni*. Pay special attention to the quality of the singer's voice.

✏ Table 4-4 General Voice Classifications

FEMALE VOICES	soprano	the highest voice
	mezzo-soprano (*met*-soh)	the next highest, usually with a slightly darker timbre (*mezzo* = "middle" in Italian)
	contralto (alto)	lowest female voice, heavier and darker timbre than soprano
MALE VOICES	tenor	the highest male voice
	baritone	lower, with darker timbre than tenor
	bass (*basso*, It.)	the lowest and darkest timbre

Samuel Ramey, bass-baritone

✏ Table 4-5 Operatic Voice Classifications

SOPRANOS	coloratura	usually high range with great vocal agility (Olympia in Offenbach's *Tales of Hoffmann*)
	dramatic	powerful, dramatic roles (Aida in Verdi's *Aïda*)
	lyric	lighter timbre, sweeter roles, ingenue—young leading lady (Mimi in Puccini's *La Bohème*)
TENORS	robusto	full, powerful voice roles (the Duke in Verdi's *Rigoletto*)
	lyric	lighter timbre; smooth, lyrical singing roles (Rodolfo in Puccini's *La Bohème*)
	heldentenor (heroic tenor)	powerful, expressive, agile (Walther in Wagner's *Die Meistersinger*)
BARITONE-BASSES	profondo	deep range; powerful, solemn roles (Commendatore in Mozart's *Don Giovanni*)
	cantante	smooth, lyrical singing roles (Don Giovanni in Mozart's *Don Giovanni*)
	buffo	agile, comic roles (Leporello in Mozart's *Don Giovanni*)

LISTENING ACTIVITY ✒

PUCCINI, *TURANDOT*, ACT III, ARIA

Cassette Tape: Side C, Example 6
Compact Disc 2, Track 38
Running time: 3:00

Act III of Giacomo Puccini's opera *Turnadot* opens with a chorus, followed by an aria by a *lyric tenor*. Chapter 14 discusses this opera in greater detail.

Opera Singers

For opera, additional subclassifications are used to describe the character, timbre, and type of roles, as shown in Table 4-5.

Summary of Terms

Boehm key system
bow
brass mutes
brass quintet
col legno
concerto
concerto grosso
contrabassoon
electronic keyboards
energy source
English horn
ensembles; chamber
  ensembles
instrumentation
keyboard instruments:
  electronic keyboards
  harpsichord
  organ
  pianoforte
  synthesizer

mute
orchestration
pizzicato
resonating chamber
saxophones
string quartet
string trio
symphony orchestra
synthesizer
timbre
vibrating element
virtuoso
virtuoso orchestra
Voices:
  female voices:
    coloratura
    contralto (alto)
    dramatic soprano
    lyric soprano

female voices:
  (continued)
  mezzo-soprano
  soprano
male voices:
  baritone
  bass
  basso buffo
  basso cantante
  basso profondo
  heldentenor
  lyric tenor
  robusto tenor
  tenor
wind ensemble
woodwind quintet

CHAPTER 5

Part Three:
The Common Style Periods of Music
An Introduction to Musical Styles

❧ Why Study Musical Styles?

Musical styles reflect the tastes and cultural attitudes of the age in which they are created. People want their arts to have certain characteristics, and artists usually give the people what they want—although this is less true in the twentieth century.

Artists also influence one another and tend to use similar vocabulary in creating their artworks. In music, composers of the same style period tend to reflect that style. We cannot study all the works of any style period, but we can come to know representative works. With that foundation, we can understand music we haven't heard before.

For example, the music of Haydn and that of Mozart sound similar. The more familiar you become with the compositions of these two masters, the more you'll recognize their similarities in *style*.

Rather than present all style periods since the beginning of time, we have focused our listening upon the musical styles you are most likely to hear at concerts—mainly music composed after A.D. 1600—although we will take a brief look at the music that preceded it.

HISTORICAL PERSPECTIVE

Styles in Music

Stylistic similarities extend beyond music. Parallel trends have always existed among other arts, philosophy, and even fashion. Artists and musicians seem to have an uncanny knack of anticipating these trends—often more accurately than business and governments do. Art, therefore, not only reflects society and imitates life but also influences society and changes life.

STYLISTIC EXCEPTIONS   Not all composers of a particular age compose with a similar style. Some resist falling into the general style of their contemporaries. Others may adhere to an earlier style instead. Composers may express their creativity through innovation: They strive to produce new forms of expression. For instance, the Finnish composer Jan Sibelius (1865–1957), though creating most of his works in the twentieth century, chose a musical style more characteristic of the preceding century. Listening to his music, you will place it in an earlier style period.

"Summertime" from Act I of Gershwin's opera *Porgy and Bess.* Although they have changed dramatically through the centuries, musical styles continue to influence and reflect cultural trends.

STYLISTIC GENERALIZATIONS Effectively describing the vast variety of composers and their music requires some generalization. As we encounter exceptions, we will point out how their music deviates from others of their time.

Style periods of Western art music are usually divided into eras, as follows:

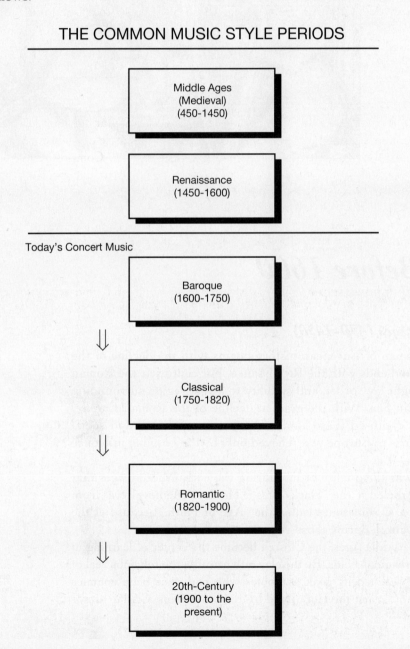

THE COMMON MUSIC STYLE PERIODS

Middle Ages
(Medieval)
(450-1450)

Renaissance
(1450-1600)

Today's Concert Music

Baroque
(1600-1750)

⇓

Classical
(1750-1820)

⇓

Romantic
(1820-1900)

⇓

20th-Century
(1900 to the present)

CHAPTER 6

Music Before 1600

✎ *The Middle Ages (450–1450)*

This 1,000-year span of European history begins with the decline of the Roman Empire and ends with the Renaissance. For centuries, the Roman legions had brought law, order, and stability to a vast region surrounding the Mediterranean Sea. With the gradual decline of the Roman Empire, German nations captured these lands. The ensuing political and social chaos in many parts of Europe was relieved only by the growing influence of Christianity.

So dismal was the quality of life during the early Middle Ages that historians once labeled it the "Dark Ages." The late Medieval era, from A.D. 1000 onward, is sometimes called the "Age of Faith" because of the strength of the Church during those years.

During the Middle Ages, the Church became the center of learning in both secular and religious fields. By the eleventh century, the religious zeal of the Middle Ages reached its peak as nobles who had once been enemies formed alliances to reclaim the Holy Land from the Moslems. Clad in armor

Thirteenth-century Gothic cathedral in Burgos, Spain.

and carrying colorful flags, they led vast armies to Turkey, the Arabian Peninsula, and North Africa—on foot—in a series of bloody and costly Crusades.

As a "holy war," the Crusades failed. They were successful, however, in changing the socioeconomic structure of Europe by weakening feudalism and expanding the cultural perspective of the people.

Construction of the Gothic Cathedrals

An important development occurred in the twelfth and thirteenth centuries: construction began on many of the great Gothic cathedrals of Europe. Among the most notable are:

> France   *Notre Dame (Paris), 1163; Bourges, 1195; Chartres, 1194*
> Spain   *Burgos, 1221; Toledo, 1227*
> England   *Salisbury, 1220; Gloucester, 1332*

HIERARCHY OF COMMON PEOPLE, CHURCH, AND STATE
Reaching toward God and the heavens, the Gothic arches and spires of the great cathedrals, together with the castles of the nobility, symbolized the medieval view of society.

Notre Dame
(*noh*-truh *dahm*)

Bourges
(*boorj*)

Chartres
(*shart*)

Burgos
(*boor*-gos)

Toledo
(toh-*lay*-do)

Salisbury
(*sahlz*-burry)

Gloucester
(*glos*-tur)

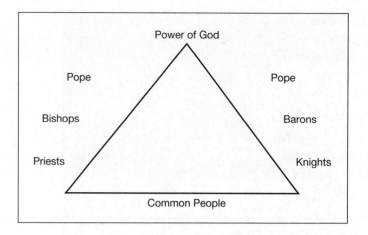

ঌ Music in the Middle Ages

Gregorian Chants

The largest body of music that has survived from before the year 1000 is *Gregorian chant*. This is also known as *Catholic liturgical chant, plainsong, plainchant*, or simply *chant*. Its identifiable characteristic is its *monophonic texture*—a melody without harmony or accompaniment. All singers perform the same melody in unison. The texts of Gregorian chants are in Latin.

Since the chants used in the Catholic service chants were passed on mainly through oral tradition, many were getting lost in the process. Gregory I (The Great), Pope from A.D. 590 to 604, charged his monks with the task of organizing the remaining monophonic chants that incorporated Hebrew and Roman melodies so that they would be better preserved.

Some two centuries later, a notation was devised to further assist in their preservation. Since his reforms saved that literature, we tend to call medieval monophonic chants "Gregorian chants," even though most of the chants used in Catholic Church services today were composed after Pope Gregory's time.

Music in the Church Service

Developing from Judaic roots, early Christian church liturgy borrowed much of its material from the Hebrew services: hymns praising God and asking for forgiveness and psalms sung responsively between a soloist and the congregation.

THE MASS   Late in the sixth century, Pope Gregory standardized the rituals of the church service as part of his efforts to organize the liturgy. The most important of these liturgical celebrations is the *Mass*. The Mass consists of two different kinds of texts. The *Ordinary* portions of the Mass are repeated in nearly every Mass, hence the name "ordinary." The *Proper* portions are specific to particular celebrations in the Church calendar; therefore, those sections change according to the day of the year. Here are the portions of the Mass most often set to music:

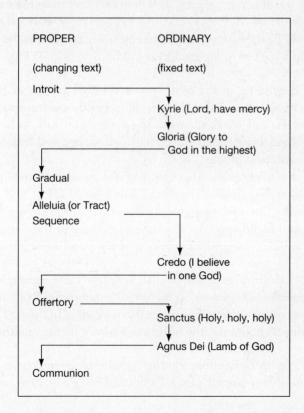

PROPER

(changing text)

Introit

Gradual

Alleluia (or Tract)

Sequence

Offertory

Communion

ORDINARY

(fixed text)

Kyrie (Lord, have mercy)

Gloria (Glory to God in the highest)

Credo (I believe in one God)

Sanctus (Holy, holy, holy)

Agnus Dei (Lamb of God)

LISTENING ACTIVITY ❧

GREGORIAN CHANT: *ALLELUIA PASCHA NOSTRUM*

Cassette Tape: Side A, Example 2
Compact Disc 1, Track 2
Running time: 0:42

Listen to the Gregorian chant *Alleluia Pascha Nostrum* from an early Catholic Mass. Notice that all the men sing the melody in unison with no harmony.

The Lute Player and the Harpist, engraved by Israhel van Meckenem.

Secular Music of the Middle Ages

Examining the body of extant music before the eleventh century, you might suppose that church music was almost the only type of music that existed. We'll never know. Unfortunately, most of the nonreligious or *secular* music for dancing, singing, and general entertainment has been lost to us. The performers did not know how to preserve it through music notation. We know from paintings and illuminated manuscripts, however, that music formed a part of many medieval events.

MINSTRELS   Beginning in the tenth century, small groups of professional poet-musicians wandered the French countryside performing in castles, palaces, taverns, and town squares. These common folk, called *minstrels*, were the newscasters of their day. Their songs reported folk legends, recent events, and local gossip.

These minstrels were also the original vaudevillians—performing magic tricks, telling jokes, juggling, doing acrobatics, and exhibiting trained animals. But society treated these itinerant strangers as outcasts. Perhaps minstrels did not take the time to document their songs because they were too busy struggling to make a living—and fleeing from officials.

TROUBADOURS   Beginning in the twelfth century, some secular songs composed by *troubadours* began to be recorded in notation. Troubadours were knights in the courts of Provence in southern France. In this age of chivalry, they rhapsodized about love, the beauty of women, honor, and the Crusades.

TROUVÈRES   Not to be outdone by their southern counterparts, noblemen in the courts of northern France composed songs in their own dialect.

Known as *trouvères*, these musical poets of the twelfth and thirteenth cen-   (tru-*vair*)
turies lyricized about the familiar topics of love and chivalry.

GERMAN MINNESINGERS   Modeled after the troubadours, German knights-
of-the-court developed their own music. Love (*Minne* in Old German) was
also the main subject for their songs. Among these are watcher's songs,
warning lovers of the approach of dawn. Many others celebrated the beauty of women and of nature.

GERMAN MEISTERSINGERS   Throughout the fourteenth, fifteenth, and sixteenth centuries, middle-class *Meistersingers* (mastersingers) built upon the
Minnesingers' tradition. Forming guilds, these Meistersingers established
rigid rules for songwriting just as the trade guilds had done. They even
made aspiring songwriters take tests to demonstrate their adherence to
"the rules."

MONOPHONIC NOTATION   Although surviving medieval songs were notated in
monophonic texture—melody only—literary descriptions and paintings
suggest that the songs were accompanied by an instrument, usually a harp
or a lute (a guitar-like instrument). Some harmony may have been used,
but this is only conjecture.

Instrumental Music in the Middle Ages

Pictures show medieval dancers accompanied by flutes, recorders, oboe-
like instruments (shawms), and early violins of various sizes. Some pictures show trumpets and drums—although royalty usually reserved these
instruments for ceremonial purposes.

Dances in the Middle Ages.

BEGINNINGS OF POLYPHONY   An important musical development occurred
during the ninth century: A second musical line began to be performed
with the monophonic chant. This created a texture called *polyphony*, meaning "many sounds."

One theory about the advent of polyphony is interesting, but unproved.
The theory contends that men and boys were singing the Gregorian chants
together—the boys singing the same melody in a high range as the mature
men sang in a low range. When the soprano voices of some of the adolescent boys suddenly "cracked," this created an inner voice and a different
pitch between the high part and the lower part. Church musicians called
this early harmony *organum*.

Evidently, the monks liked the sound of organum. In addition to   organum
improvising this new line of music during performance, they began indi-   (*or*-guh-num)
cating it in the music written after about A.D. 1000.

Sit glo- ri - a Do- mi- ni in Sae- cu- la   lae- ta- bi- tur Do- mi- nus in o - pe - ri- bus su- is

Notre Dame, Paris,
side view.

Leonin
(lay-oh-*nan*)
Perotin
(pay-roh-*tan*)

Music in the Cathedral of Notre Dame

With the building of the great Gothic cathedrals in the Middle Ages came the need for larger choirs. This, in turn, created employment for resident cleric-composers whose duties included composing and arranging music for church services.

THE SCHOOL OF NOTRE DAME   Until the construction of Notre Dame in Paris, composers had been mostly anonymous. Then, for the first time, two important music director-clerics of this new cathedral rose to prominence in the musical world—Leonin (1163-90) and Perotin (fl. 1200). Their works so influenced other church composers that they were referred to as the "School of Notre Dame."

LISTENING ACTIVITY ❧

LEONIN, "ALLELUIA, DIES SANCTIFICATUS"

Cassette Tape: Side A, Example 3
Compact Disc 1, Track 3
Running time: 0:53

Both Leonin and Perotin used polyphonic texture, assigning the original chant to the lower voice. Listen to this excerpt from Leonin's "Alleluia, Dies Sanctificatus" from the Proper portion of the Mass.

Notice his use of organum. The lower voice holds unusually long tones. The upper voice moves faster and more freely, creating two independent musical lines, or polyphony.

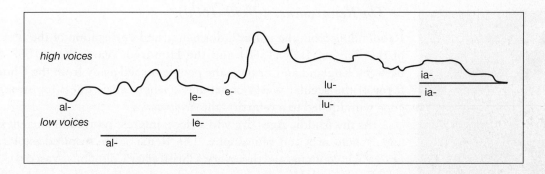

⌒ *Important Composers of the Middle Ages*

TROUBADOUR SECULAR SONGS
Marcabru   (fl. 1128–50)

Bernart de Ventadorn   (died c. 1195)

Adam de la Halle   (c. 1250–c. 1290)

CHURCH MUSIC OF NOTRE DAME
Leonin   (c. 1163–90)

Perotin   (fl. 1200)

CHURCH AND SECULAR MUSIC
Philippe de Vitry   (1291–1361)
 French prelate, composer, and theorist, known for his treatise *Ars nova* (new art), which explained early-fourteenth-century theory.

Guillaume de Machaut   (c. 1300–77)
 French court composer, cleric, and poet. Considered one of the greatest composers of the Middle Ages.

Francesco Landini   (c. 1325–97)
 One of the greatest Italian composers of the Middle Ages. Most of his compositions are *ballate*, a type of polyphonic song.

Johannes Ciconia   (c. 1373–1412)
 Born in France, Ciconia wrote church music and also secular madrigals, motets, and polyphonic vocal works.

John Dunstable   (c. 1390–1443)
 English composer who wrote mostly polyphonic music for the Mass and several secular songs.

Interior Notre Dame, Paris.

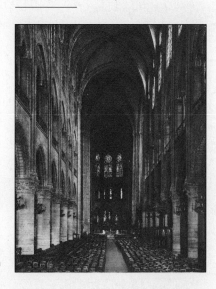

Statue of David by
Michelangelo at the Galleria
dell-Accademia, Florence, Italy.

Machiavelli
(mah-kyah-*vel*-le)
Leonardo da Vinci
(dah--*veen*-chee)

Michelangelo
(mee-kul-*ahn*-jah-loh)

⤳ The Renaissance (1450–1600)

Rebounding from the cultural dormancy and devastation of the first wave of the Plague (Italy, 1348) and the Hundred Years' War (1337–1453) between England and France, the people turned away from the Church in favor of the secular world of art and science. Their quest for strength to cope with life led to a rebirth—the *Renaissance*.

As the Middle Ages drew to a close, interest revived in ancient Greek and Roman arts and philosophy. The Renaissance inspired exploration, practical inventions, and discovery. Christopher Columbus, Vasco da Gama, and Ferdinand Magellan discovered and explored new lands, Nicolai Copernicus and Galileo Galilei expanded our knowledge of the universe through astronomy.

Humanism

In contrast to the focus on the sacred in Medieval thought, the Renaissance was an age of *humanism*. Individual achievement took on a new importance. Artists proudly signed their works. The humanistic spirit awakened an optimism that all things were possible and knowable.

RENAISSANCE "MAN"   Artists, philosophers, inventors, and scientists enthusiastically crossed disciplines. Niccolò Machiavelli (1469–1527), for instance, was not only a political official but also a political philosopher, historian, essayist, and author of the famous treatise, *The Prince*.

Perhaps Leonardo da Vinci (1452–1519) epitomizes the Renaissance man. He is best remembered for his fresco of *The Last Supper* and the painting *Mona Lisa*. His genius also provided the world with a legacy of inventions and knowledge in anatomy, architecture, hydraulics, hydrology, geology, meteorology, mechanics, machinery and gears, military weaponry and fortifications, human and avian flight, optics, mathematics, botany, and more.

Leonardo's breadth of accomplishments is rivaled by that of Michelangelo Buonarroti (1475-1564), Italian sculptor, painter, architect, and poet. His sculptures *David*, *Moses*, and the *Pietà*, and his paintings on the ceiling of the Sistine Chapel at the Vatican in Rome are among the greatest accomplishments in the history of Western art.

⤳ Music in the Renaissance

In contrast to the other arts, music of the Renaissance had fewer significant innovations. As opportunities for performance increased, so did the number of composers, each contributing technical refinements to the new style.

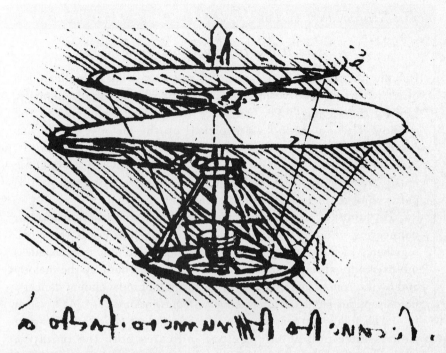

Sketch of helicopter by Leonardo da Vinci.

Close-up of Michelangelo's painting of Jeremiah the prophet at the Sistine Chapel in Rome, commissioned by the Vatican as part of the counter-Reformation.

Although religious music was still predominant, the demand for secular music increased. Court musicians were hired to entertain in the homes of the wealthy. Small instrumental groups performed in courtyards, on balconies, and in various rooms—thus the term *chamber music*.

RESIDENT COURT COMPOSER   With their own chapels and resident clergy, the courts of the aristocracy were self-contained. The resident court composer was responsible for supplying all music—religious music for chapel, chamber music for instrumentalists, dance music and songs for solo entertainers, and choral music for the court choir.

THE MADRIGAL   Madrigals, still performed today, were composed for small groups of singers expressly for court entertainment. Originating in the Italian courts, the first madrigals were sung in Italian. Important Italian madrigal composers were Carlo Gesualdo (1560–1613), Luca Marenzio (1553–99), and Claudio Monteverdi (1567–1643).

As madrigals spread to other countries, they were written in the language of the court. English madrigals became extremely popular during Shakespeare's time and appear today on concerts of choral groups. Some

LISTENING INSIGHTS

Listening to Polyphonic Music

Polyphonic texture is sophisticated and somewhat complicated—often with four or five melodies sung or played simultaneously. During the Renaissance, one voice (or part) usually started the melody. Then, a second voice picked up the melody, which was continually passed around through the several parts.

As listeners, we tend to focus on the melody. In polyphonic music, that melody or fragments of it constantly shifts from part to part, requiring us to shift our attention with the music.

In addition to the recognizable melody, composers use other connecting and supporting music—the glue that holds the work together. Much of the beauty of Renaissance polyphony is its seamless interweaving of parts and the harmonies created both by the melody and by the connecting material—like a group of independent dancers, doing separate steps yet interacting with one another.

The following graphic representation of a section of four-part Renaissance polyphonic texture indicates both the imitative entrances of the melody and the connecting material (counterpoint).

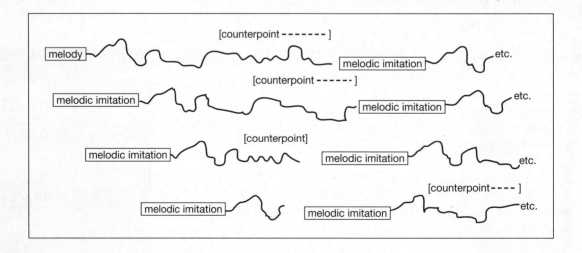

of the leading English madrigal composers were Thomas Morley (1557-1602), Thomas Weelkes (1575-1623), and John Wilbye (1574-1638).

Romantic love, sometimes erotic love, was high on the list of favorite madrigal subjects. But many madrigals reflected on nature, and some were settings of sonnets or pious devotions.

POLYPHONY CONTINUES   Characterized by many independent musical lines, polyphony continued throughout the Renaissance to dominate the musical texture of secular as well as sacred music. Creating as many as five and six parts, composers usually separated or staggered entrances of voices. In contrast to Middle Ages polyphony, Renaissance polyphony is mostly *imitative*; that is, the voices all sing the same or similar melody, starting at different times. This note-against-note or melody-against-melody technique is also referred to as *counterpoint*.

Palestrina

Of the many Renaissance composers, Giovanni Palestrina stands out as one of the most respected by listeners and musicians. His seamless counterpoint is a model of both the creativity and craftsmanship of the period.

Palestrina
(pah-luh-*stree*-nuh)

GIOVANNI PIERLUIGI DA PALESTRINA (C. 1525–94)

Palestrina's early biographical data is sketchy, but we do know that Palestrina was born in a small town near Rome—probably the town of Palestrina. (The translation of *da Palestrina* is "from Palestrina.")

At about the age of 12, he was a choirboy in the church of Santa Maria Maggiore in Rome. At 19, Palestrina became the organist for the cathedral at Sant Agapito in Palestrina. His employer there, the Bishop of Palestrina, who later became Pope Julius III, asked Palestrina to accompany him in 1550 to the Vatican as his resident composer and music director.

After Pope Julius' death in 1555, Palestrina found it difficult to stay at the Sistine Chapel of St. Peter's. Although Palestrina was not a priest, the politically scheming Vatican officials objected to his marriage and lack of celibacy. His original appointment irked them as he had been appointed against regulations because he supported Pope Julius III.

Leaving the Vatican, Palestrina became employed by a wealthy cardinal. In 1571, he returned to the Sistine Chapel where he spent the last 23 years of his life serving a succession of Popes until his death at age 69.

PRINCIPAL WORKS

Sacred Vocal Music: Over 100 Masses including *Missa Papae Marcelli* and *Missa brevis;* 375 motets; 35 Magnificat settings; 68 offertories; lamentations, litanies, sacred madrigals, hymns.
Secular Vocal Music: Over 140 madrigals.

LISTENING ACTIVITY ॐ

PALESTRINA: MASS: *DE BEATA VIRGINE* KYRIE
LARGE FORM: MASS

Cassette Tape: Side A, Example 4
Compact Disc 1: Track 4
Running time: 3:37

Listen to the recording of Giovanni Palestrina's late-sixteenth-century polyphonic treatment of the "Kyrie" section from the ordinary of the Mass *De Beata Virgine* (*To The Blessed Virgin*). Four separate voice parts weave in counterpoint. The melody (*cantus* in Latin) of this Kyrie is an old Gregorian chant, around which Palestrina added other voice parts.

Notice that the sopranos begin and the altos enter with counterpoint, after which the tenors and basses imitate the sopranos and altos. What you hear in this style is almost constant imitation, prompting you to shift your focus to whichever voice enters with the melody.

ॐ Important Composers of the Renaissance

Franco-Flemish Composers

Jacob Arcadelt (c. 1505–c. 1567)
    Wrote mainly *chansons* (songs) and madrigals.
Gilles Binchois (c. 1400–60)
    Composed *chansons* for the court of Philip the Good of Burgundy.
Jacobus Clemens (c. 1510–c. 1567)
    Composed mostly music for the church.
Guillaume Dufay (c. 1400–74)
    The leading composer of his day in Burgundy, Dufay wrote Masses and motets for church services and *chansons* for the courts.
Heinrich Isaac (c. 1450–1517)
    Composed both church and secular music.
Clement Jannequin (c. 1475–1560)
    Wrote mainly *chansons* for the French courts.

Josquin des Pres (c. 1440–1521)
  One of the greatest composers of the Renaissance, Josquin was born
  in France but spent most of his productive life in Italy. He wrote both
  Masses and secular *chansons*.

Claude Le Jeune (1528–1600)
  Composed motets and *chansons*.

Orlando di Lasso (1532–94)
  Lasso, or Lassus as he was known in Italy, was born in the
  Franco–Flemish north. One of the greatest composers of the period,
  Lasso worked in Milan, Naples, Rome, and Munich. He composed
  both sacred and secular vocal music.

Jacob Obrecht (c. 1452–1505)
  Composed church music and *chansons*.

Johannes Ockeghem (c. 1430–97)
  Known for his canons and intricate counterpoint, Ockeghem wrote
  both church and secular music.

Claudin de Sermisy (c. 1490–1562)
  Known mainly as a composer of *chansons*.

Jan Sweelinck (1562–1621)
  Mainly known for his keyboard music, Sweelinck also wrote *chansons*.

Adrian Willaert (c. 1480–1562)
  Born in the Franco-Flemish north, Willaert made his way to St. Mark's
  in Venice, where he was renowned as a church composer and teacher.
  He also composed *chansons*.

Italian Composers

Costanzo Festa (c. 1490–1545)
  Composed church music at the Papal Chapel in Rome, though he is
  best known for his Italian madrigals.

Andrea Gabrieli (c. 1533–85)
  Andrea Gabrieli preceded his nephew Giovanni Gabrieli as first
  organist at St. Mark's in Venice. He composed both church music and
  madrigals.

Giovanni Gabrieli (c. 1555–1612)
  Composed church music, concerti, instrumental music, and madrigals.
  (More on Gabrieli in Chapter 8.)

Carlo Gesualdo (c. 1560–1613)
  Mainly known for his innovative chromatic madrigals.

Luca Marenzio (c. 1553–99)
  Though known mainly for his madrigals, Marenzio also composed
  many sacred motets.

Claudio Monteverdi (1567–1643)
  Known for his late opera works in the Baroque period, he wrote many madrigals as a young composer. (More on Monteverdi in Chapter 8.)
Giovanni da Palestrina (c. 1525–94)
  Considered one of the greatest Renaissance church composers (see biography).

Spanish Composers

Antonio de Cabezon (c. 1510–66)
  Mainly keyboard compositions.
Cristobal de Morales (c. 1500–53)
  An important church composer.
Tomàs Luis de Victoria (c. 1549–1611)
  The most important Spanish church composer of the period.

German Composers

Hans Leo Hassler (1564–1612)
  Hassler wrote German polyphonic *lieder* (songs) and also church music.

English Composers

William Byrd (1543–1623)
  One of the best English composers prior to the Baroque. He composed church music, keyboard music, and songs.
John Dowland (1562–1626)
  A prolific composer, Dowland wrote songs for several voices and also music for the lute.
Thomas Morley (c. 1557–1602)
  Morley is known mainly for his popular English madrigals.
Thomas Tallis (c. 1505–85)
  Tallis wrote his most important works for the church.
John Taverner (c. 1490–1545)
  One of England's finest church-music composers.
Thomas Weelkes (c. 1557–1623)
  Weelkes wrote some of the most popular English madrigals.

Summary of Terms

Age of Faith

cantus

chamber music

Chartres

counterpoint

Dark Ages

Gloucester

Gothic Cathedrals

Humanism

lute

madrigal

Mass

Meistersingers

Minnesingers

minstrels

Notre Dame

Old Roman chants

ordinary Mass portion

organum

plainchant

plainsong

proper Mass portion

Salisbury Cathedral

troubadours

trouvères

Summary of Non-musicians

Gregory I (Pope, called The Great) c. 540–604

Leonardo da Vinci (1452–1519)

Machiavelli (1469–1527)

Michelangelo (1475–1564)

CHAPTER 7

The Baroque Style Period

ᕱ Protestant Reformation

When Martin Luther nailed a list of grievances on the door of Palast Church in Wittenburg, Germany, his protests included the widespread practice among Catholic clergy of selling indulgences to forgive sins and the lack of relevancy of the traditional church service. Thus in 1517 during the Renaissance Period, the Protestant Reformation gradually challenged the omnipotence of the Church of Rome. By 1532, the Reformation had spread to Sweden, Scotland, and France, and soon after, across most of Europe.

CHANGING CHURCH SERVICE Luther, a priest himself, doubted that his parishioners could derive full value as passive observers of the traditional Latin service that the Roman Catholic Church offered. In his own services, Luther made two important changes to make the liturgy more accessible to his congregation:

- *Language change* Luther translated his services from Latin into German, the language of his congregants.
- *Congregational singing* In his desire to involve the entire congregation, Luther wrote easily learned, easily sung hymns with a German text. Even those who could not read could learn to sing them. (Today, most denominations throughout the world use books of hymns, or hymnals, for congregational singing.)

∽ Counter-Reformation

Between 1545 and 1564, Roman Catholic church leaders met intermittently at the Council of Trent to devise strategies to deal with the Reformation. Result: the *Counter-Reformation,* which included a mandate for making the church more attractive—if not in substance, at least in image.

Portrait of Martin Luther painted by Lukas Cranach.

St. Peter's Basilica, Rome
Bernini
(bayr-*nee*-nee)
Bramante
(brah-*mahn*-tay)
The Cupola of St. Peter's in Rome

BAROQUE FACADES How did church leaders decide to accomplish this new image?

Eye appeal: Highly ornate Baroque facades gave an architectural facelift to drab exteriors of older churches. Architects designed and built new, elaborate, Baroque-style churches.

One of the first projects became the showcase of the Vatican in Rome—St. Peter's Basilica (1546–1664). The exterior was completed in the early seventeenth century with its rows of columns later designed by Gianlorenzo Bernini (1598–1680). Michelangelo, who simplified an earlier plan by Donato Bramante (1444–1514), is largely responsible for the dome and present appearance of the church. *Gold leaf* and colorful brocaded *tapestries* adorn the altar. Bernini and other sculptors created statues of the Trinity, Holy Family, and important saints for the interior and exterior.

STAINED GLASS An important art form since the building of the great Gothic cathedrals in the Middle Ages, stained glass enjoyed a revival during this period. Baroque-style churches continued using stained-glass windows depicting scenes from the Bible. The colorful, cartoon-like scenes were useful instructional tools to help the mostly illiterate congregation understand church history and beliefs. (See Color Plate 4.)

Counter-Reformation Succeeds

The mission of the Counter-Reformation was accomplished by 1600, and the initial impact of Protestantism had waned. Having experienced self-renewal, the Catholic Church was to play a new role in the arts from 1600 to 1750.

HISTORICAL PERSPECTIVE

Book and Music Printing

Books   Until 1453, very few people had access to books or could even read. That year, Johannes Gutenberg [*goot*-en-berg] (c. 1390–1468) of Mainz, Germany, printed the first book using moveable type—a Bible. Printing remained a slowly developing art and books an expensive commodity for another 200 years. It is understandable that most people outside the clergy or royalty had little access to the printed word.

Music   The first music was printed in 1501 by Ottaviano Petrucci (peh-*troo*-chee) of Venice. Petrucci used Gutenberg's process of moveable type.

Sixteenth-century facade of the Gothic Duomo in Mantua, Italy.

ॐ Overview of the Baroque Period (1600–1750)

IMPORTANT COMPOSERS	Giovanni Gabrieli, Claudio Monteverdi, Heinrich Schütz, Jean-Baptiste Lully, Archangelo Corelli, Henry Purcell, Alessandro Scarlatti, Domenico Scarlatti, Jean-Philippe Rameau, Antonio Vivaldi, Johann Sebastian Bach, George Frideric Handel
ARTISTS	Gianlorenzo Bernini, Caravaggio, El Greco, Frans Hals, Rembrandt van Rijn, Peter Paul Rubens, Anthony Van Dyke
WRITERS	John Donne, John Milton, Alexander Pope, William Shakespeare, Jonathan Swift, Jean-Baptiste Molière
PHILOSPHERS	Francis Bacon, René Descartes, Thomas Hobbes, John Locke, Bernard Spinoza
SOCIAL, POLITICAL, AND CULTURAL EVENTS	First opera (c. 1600), Shakespeare's *Hamlet* (1600), King James version of the Bible (1611), Pilgrims land in America (1620), first opera house (1637), reign of Louis XIV (1643–1715), Newton's physical laws, beginning of Age of Enlightenment, expansion of Colonialism

Characteristics of Baroque Music

GENERAL	Music often sounds heavy, grand, and expansive; often includes both singers and instruments
PERFORMING MEDIA	Chamber orchestra, chorus and chamber orchestra, soloist(s) and chamber orchestra, chamber ensembles, organ, harpsichord
RHYTHM	Steady beats, running bass, complicated driving rhythms; meters: 2, 3, 4, 6; usually slowing of tempo at the end of the piece
MELODY	Major and minor melodies; sequence, imitation, and elaborate ornamentation
HARMONY	Strong harmonic movement; harmonic sequences and recurring cadences; major and minor tonalities
EXPRESSION	Contrasting layers of dynamics, echo imitation used; loud and soft juxtaposed—no crescendo or diminuendo

TEXTURE

Mainly polyphonic, thick texture; one or more melodies in high parts with countermelodies; harmonic filler parts and continuous bass line; occasional homophony (sounding together)

FORMS

Concerto, concerto grosso, suite, oratorio, cantata, opera; trio sonata and other sonatas for instruments, keyboard prelude, fugue, toccata

CHAPTER 8

Baroque Music (1600–1750)

Despite the early Counter-Reformation's cosmetic innovations that radically changed the outward appearance of the church, its music was hardly affected. Even with the craftsmanship of Giovanni Palestrina, its greatest master, Renaissance church music, though beautiful, was still mostly austere, reserved, somewhat colorless, and usually performed *a cappella*—without instruments.

✑ *Baroque Vocal Music*

The New Baroque Music

Venice of 1600 was the commercial maritime center of the world, hosting visitors and merchants from many countries. It was also here that musical innovations in church services first appeared.

As you have already read in Chapter 4, Giovanni Gabrieli, music director of Basilica of St. Mark, took seriously the order of the Council of Trent to make church services more interesting. Experimenting by placing

a cappella
(a kah-*pel*-lah)

Antiphonal

Concertato

Concert

Concerto

In ecclesiis
(in eh-*clay*-cease)

Exterior of the Basilica of St. Mark in Venice.

groups of singers in one alcove (balcony) of the nave, brass players in other alcoves, a boy's choir in another, and other choirs and instrumentalists in still other areas, Gabrieli developed a highly appealing music. Adding another dimension, Gabrieli included the great organ of St. Mark.

CONCERTED MUSIC   Gabrieli's experiments produced stereophonic or multiphonic music—music coming from several directions—also called *antiphonal* style. Perhaps more important is the term *concertato*, from which we derive *concert* and *concerto*. Both terms mean "bringing contrasting performing groups together." Gabrieli's concerted music contrasted different choirs of voices with the organ and with other instruments. As Gabrieli alternated choirs and instruments—left and right, front and rear—the sounds enveloped listeners as never before.

Below is a simplified floor plan for typical performances in the Basilica of St. Mark of Gabrieli's concerted compositions such as *In ecclesiis*.

Where Did the Name "Baroque" Come From?

Although we now refer to the style period between 1600 and 1750 as Baroque, the actual term *Baroque* appeared in the late eighteenth century. Classical artists, looking back on the work of their predecessors, derived the term from a Portuguese word describing irregular pearls. These artists felt that the highly ornate Baroque architecture, statues, and music were not as orderly as their more controlled art.

Interior of the Basilica of St. Mark in Venice.

Simplified drawing of floor plan at the Basilica of St. Mark for the performance of *In ecclesiis*.

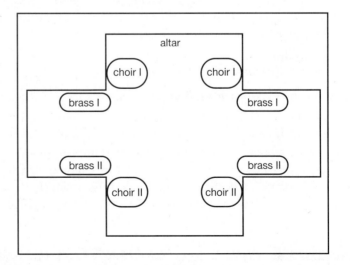

LISTENING ACTIVITY ॐ

GABRIELI: IN ECCLESIIS
FORM: MOTET

Cassette Tape: Side A, Example 5
Compact Disc 1: Track 5

Listen to Gabrieli's motet *In ecclesiis* and follow along with the listening guide. From locations shown in the figure on page 82, voices and instruments perform the five verses and five *alleluias*. A *motet* is a type of polyphonic sacred composition for voices, popular with composers during the Renaissance and Baroque style periods.

Gabrieli uses the text as inspiration for his new concerted music. For example, Verse 2, "In omni loco..." (In every place of worship, praise Him), "every place" suggested for Gabrieli that the motet literally should be performed in every place in St. Mark's Basilica. And so performers were assigned various locations in the great basilica.

Notice the many short, contrasting sections often using dance-like rhythms. Then notice the rousing finale. Gabrieli's intent was to keep listeners interested.

GABRIELI'S OTHER INNOVATIONS   To achieve the right balance in this complicated mix of instruments, Gabrieli introduced two lasting innovations in music:

Specific Instrumentation: He designated instruments to play on specific parts, beginning the practice of instrumentation or orchestration.

Expression: He placed expression indications of soft (*piano*) and loud (*forte*) in the printed music.

Motet
(moh-*tet*)

LISTENING GUIDE

GABRIELI: *IN ECCLESIIS* FORM: MOTET

Cassette Tape 1: Side A, Example 5
Compact Disc 1: Track 5
Running time: 8:59

5	0:00	[Organ introduction]	triple meter, major tonality, ending in a clear cadence	
6	0:29	Verse 1	"In ecclesiis benedicite Domino" (Praise the Lord in the congregation), moderate tempo, duple meter	sopranos (Chorus I) organ
7	:45	Alleluia	"Alleluia," triple meter, smoothly, faster (*f*), cadence	sopranos (Chorus I), Chorus II, organ
8	1:02	Verse 2	"In omni loco…" (In every place of worship praise him"), duple meter, moderate tempo cadence	tenors (Chorus I), organ
	1:38	Alleluia	"Alleluia," triple meter, faster cadence	tenors (Chorus I), Chorus II, organ
9	1:52	(Sinfonia)	(instrumental interlude), duple meter, cadence	brass, organ
10	2:35	Verse 3	"In Deo, salutari meo…" (In God, who is my salvation and glory…);dance-like character; alternating altos, tenors, and brass; cadence	altos (Chorus I), tenors (Chorus I), brass, organ
	4:34	Alleluia	"Alleluia," triple meter, loud alternating choirs and brass, cadence	altos (Chorus I), tenors (Chorus I), Chorus II, brass
11	4:50	Verse 4	"Deus meus, te vocamus…" (My God, we invoke thee…); duple meter; soft; alternating sopranos, tenors and organ; cadence	sopranos (Chorus I), tenors (Chorus I), organ
	6:26	Alleluia	"Alleluia," triple meter, alternating choirs	Chorus I, Chorus II, organ
12	6:43	Verse 5	"Deus, adjutor noster aeternam" (God, our eternal judge), duple meter, alternating soft and loud, choirs and brass, cadence	Chorus I, Chorus II, brass, organ
13	8:34	Alleluia	"Alleluia," triple meter, alternating choirs and brass	Chorus I, Chorus II, brass, organ
	8:38	Cadence	Final cadence, long full chord, ***forte***	tutti (everyone)

The Sensory Appeal of the Catholic Church Service

Church service

Baroque music had finally become as sensorily appealing as the visual arts. The rites of the Catholic Church now involved all five senses:

sound bells during the service; rich blends of voices, keyboards, mixed instruments

sight beautiful statues; stained-glass windows; ornate, gold leaf altar; ceiling and wall frescos; brocaded, jeweled vestments; huge candles; choreographed movement of priests, altar boys, and congregants

taste the flavor of the wine and wafer of Holy Communion

touch the handling of rosary beads; the feel of the floor, benches, and goblets; genuflection and contact with the holy water

smell the aroma of burning incense and candles

∿ *Baroque-style Vocal Music*

Concertato Style

Music combining vocal and instrumental ensembles remained popular throughout the period in *opera, oratorio, cantata,* and the *Mass.* In addition to Gabrieli, several other great Baroque composers championed the concertato style: Claudio Monteverdi, Heinrich Schütz, Georg Philipp Telemann, George Frideric Handel, and Johann Sebastian Bach.

HISTORICAL PERSPECTIVE

Use of Italian Terms in Music

You may wonder why music uses so many Italian terms, especially for expression and tempo indications. Some examples are *piano, allegro,* and *rallantando* (see Glossary). After Gabrieli introduced these terms in his new concerted music, European composers who had come to Venice to study with him brought the new terms back to their native countries. Italian soon became the international language of music.

Since Gabrieli's time, the vocabulary has greatly expanded. In addition to Italian, composers occasionally use their native languages. This, of course, makes the description less universal than Italian and may pose interpretation problems to performers not conversant in a particular language.

Baroque Opera

One of the most important innovations of the early Baroque era was opera. The first full-length operas were staged around 1600 in northern Italy. Although drama with music existed in the Middle Ages and Renaissance in the form of mystery plays and other liturgical dramas, nothing prepared audiences for the operas of the early 1600s. With their spectacular combinations of dramatic solo singing, emotional choruses, orchestral music, scenery, and dance, attending the opera soon became one of the most fashionable pastimes in Italy.

Venice and Florence hosted some of the earliest opera performances. Claudio Monteverdi, after his *Orfeo* (1607), moved opera from elite court performances to increasingly larger and larger public audiences. Open to the general public as well as the aristocracy, the first opera house was built in Venice in 1637.

Late-Baroque (1740) opera performance in the opera house in Turin, Italy. Notice the narrow stage and small orchestra typical of the time (painting by Pietro Domenico Olivero).

CLAUDIO MONTEVERDI (1567–1643)

The birthplace of Monteverdi (mohn-teh-*vehr*-dee) was Cremona, Italy, the famous violin-making center. He began his music career as a string player, later becoming *maestro di cappella* (music director) at the court of Mantua. *Orfeo* (1607), Monteverdi's earliest opera, premiered in Mantua, then played in Venice.

After Giovanni Gabrieli's death in 1612, Monteverdi soon replaced him at St. Mark's in Venice, the most prestigious appointment in Italy at that time. There, Monteverdi quickly established a reputation for his operas as well as for his religious music. Unfortunately, many of his operas have been lost.

During 1630 and 1631, Venice suffered heavy losses from the Plague. To give thanks for its passing, Monteverdi wrote a stirring *Gloria* in concertato style. Soon after, he took holy orders in the Church and spent approximately 10 years concentrating primarily on sacred music.

In his later years, Monteverdi returned to opera. His last, *L'incoronazione di Poppea* (The Coronation of Poppea), which premiered in Venice in 1642, is still in the repertoire of today's opera companies.

PRINCIPAL WORKS

Operas: *Orfeo* (1607), *Arianna* (1608), *Il ritorno d'Ulisse in patria* (The Return of Ulysses to His Country, 1640), *L'incoronazione di Poppea* (The Coronation of Poppea, 1642)

Secular Vocal Music: Nine books of madrigals for five to eight voices and instruments, 25 Scherzi Musicali for voices and instruments, canzonettas

Sacred Vocal Music: *Vespers* (1610), *Gloria* (1631) for voices and instruments, Masses, psalms

Characteristics of Early Opera

Perhaps Monteverdi's operas have timeless appeal because they contain most of the same characteristics found in more contemporary operas.

LIBRETTO   The *libretto* ("little book" in Italian) is the story or play upon which the opera is based. Some of the earliest opera stories were adaptations of classic Greek dramas, such as *Orfeo* (Orpheus) and *The Return of*   Libretto

Ulysses to His Country. Since then, composers have used stories from later times, including their own.

Although opera quickly spread to England and France, the Italian language remained the favorite until the eighteenth century. Not only had the opera tradition developed in Italy, but for many years Italian was considered the most suitable language for singing. Today, an opera can be in any language. In fact, as a result of the unusual popularity of opera, some are translated from the original into the language of the country where the performance takes place.

SOLOISTS   Rarely are lines spoken in opera; therefore, principal characters must be trained singers. The variety of voices—sopranos, altos, tenors, and basses—adds interest to the production.

Early opera, however, occasionally used male voices in female roles. Only in the more enlightened and in the principal operatic centers, such as Venice, were women allowed on stage. (This was also the custom in England for plays by Monteverdi's contemporary, William Shakespeare [1564–1616]).

Several of the male protagonists' roles—heroes, generals, etc.—called for an extremely high range. Often, these were sung by a *castrato*. To ensure a supply of virtuoso singers, opera producers in the 17th and 18th centuries arranged for the castration of some of the boys before their voices changed. Apparently, a boy who was a candidate for *castrato* had to have an unusual timbre: the upper range of a woman and the voice and power of a boy.

You may wonder why anyone would subject himself to castration, or how a boy's parents could consent to such an operation. To understand this practice, keep in mind that opera singers were major celebrities, with all the advantages that come with stardom. Therefore, many families, foreseeing a financially secure future for their children, agreed to the uncomfortable operation.

By the late eighteenth century, when women were permitted on stage to sing the female roles, the castrato gradually became a rarity. (Moreschi, the last of the castrati, died in 1922.)

BEL CANTO   Operatic *Bel canto* ("beautiful singing" in Italian) represents the lilting flow of the melody, often containing elaborate embellishments improvised at the time of performance. To perform *bel canto*, a singer must be capable of a highly expressive delivery. This requires extensive training. Thus, when *bel canto* emerged in seventeenth-century Venice, so did employment opportunities for teachers of vocal technique. Venice became the European center for the training of singers.

Castrato

Bel Canto

RECITATIVO To advance the story of the opera more quickly, opera composers used the technique of *recitativo* (recitative)—a speechlike style of singing. Because singing takes more time than dialogue, the recitative offers an effective compromise between talking and singing. The accompanying orchestra or keyboard instruments are usually lighter than for arias because the text or story is most important in the recitative.

Recitativo
(reh-chee-tah-*tee*-voh)

ARIA The solo song or *aria* began to dominate opera soon after its inception. In the aria, the vocal power, virtuosity, and expressiveness of the singer can be given free reign. Even today, the prospect of hearing a great performer deliver a magnificent solo draws enthusiastic audiences to opera productions. In some cases, a few good arias have made the difference in creating a successful opera.

Aria

ARIA FORM By the early thirteenth century, operas often contained a series of arias, connected by recitative. These arias usually have a three-part form:

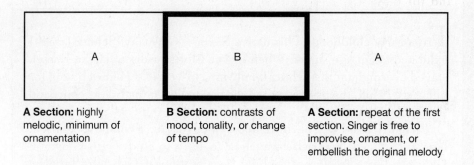

A Section: highly melodic, minimum of ornamentation

B Section: contrasts of mood, tonality, or change of tempo

A Section: repeat of the first section. Singer is free to improvise, ornament, or embellish the original melody

ENSEMBLES (DUETS, TRIOS, QUARTETS) *Duets, trios*, and *quartets* are songs for two, three, and four singers. Often using the same three-part form (A-B-A) as arias, these multivoice songs add dramatic interest and musical variety to the opera.

CHORUSES From the earliest Greek plays, *choruses* of singers or choral speakers added depth to the drama by providing commentary on the action. Opera choruses, present since Monteverdi's operas, add realism and drama to the plot. Chorus members played the parts of soldiers, peasants, or other onlookers. The music for chorus provides a balance and contrast to the solo singing.

ORCHESTRA Monteverdi pioneered the use of the orchestra to provide an overture or introduction to the opera and to play musical interludes during the performance. To establish a mood, he introduced evocative sounds in the orchestra such as *tremolo* and *pizzicato* (see Glossary).

Overture
Tremolo
(*treh*-mo-loh)

To accompany recitatives and arias, Monteverdi and his contemporaries preferred only a few instruments, or even just a lute or a harpsichord. Because the earliest operas were performed in court, in rooms without an orchestra pit, a full ensemble probably would have overpowered the singers, and the audience would have had difficulty understanding the text. By Handel's time, singers performed on elevated stages, making it possible for an orchestra and a harpsichord to accompany recitatives, arias, and choruses.

Baroque Oratorio

Another popular vocal form, the *oratorio*, developed during the late Renaissance. The name derives from the small prayer chapel, or oratorio, within the church where these works were first performed.

HEINRICH SCHÜTZ (1585–1672)

From early childhood in his native Saxony, Germany, Schütz (*shoots*) exhibited talent as a singer. When Prince Moritz, ruler of Hesse-Kassel, stayed overnight at the Schütz family inn, 13-year old Heinrich sang for him. As a result, the prince invited the boy to live at the Kassel court and sing in the choir.

Heinrich did well at court, and Prince Moritz, a composer himself, later subsidized Heinrich's traveling to Italy to study with Giovanni Gabrieli. Once in Venice, Schütz became one of Gabrieli's favorite pupils. After Gabrieli's death in 1612, Schütz returned to Germany to become *Kapellmeister*, music director, at the Lutheran court of Dresden. There, Schütz carried on the polychoral work of his Venetian master, working Gabrieli's style into the Lutheran service.

Unfortunately for Schütz, the Dresden court was constantly overburdened with debts. He was poorly paid and miserable because he was never allowed to change positions. Finally, at the age of 70, after 55 years of servitude, Schütz was released from his Dresden position. He continued composing until his death two years later.

PRINCIPAL WORKS

Oratorios: Christmas Oratorio (1664), *The Seven Last Words of Christ on the Cross* (1657)

Passions: St. Matthew (1666), *St. Luke* (1666), *St. John* (1666)

Secular Vocal Music: Italian madrigals (1611)

Two outstanding composers of oratorios were Heinrich Schütz and George Frideric Handel. In response to the Protestant movement's goal to reach parishioners about their religion, these composers set Bible stories to music.

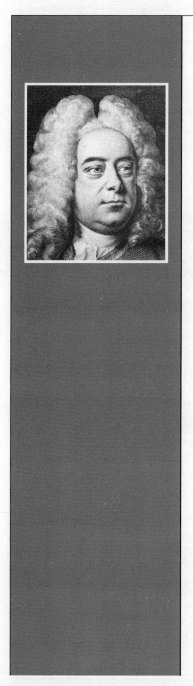

GEORGE FRIDERIC HANDEL (1685–1759)

Handel was born in Halle, Germany, near Berlin, into a family of clergy and doctors who concentrated their efforts on financial security rather than on the arts. His father, who died a week before George's twelfth birthday, had encouraged his son to study law. But an event two years earlier had influenced Handel profoundly.

Hearing that his father planned a short trip to visit his older son Karl, valet to Duke Johann Adolf, ten-year-old George wanted to go along. When his father left without him, a disappointed but determined young Handel followed after his father's carriage on foot until he caught up with him. During the visit, George stayed in the palace chapel. Although he had studied music for only two years, Handel sat down at the organ and began to play. The duke heard his playing and was sufficiently impressed to present the boy with a gift of money. The elder Handel allowed his son to use the gift for music lessons.

At 18, Handel entered the University of Halle and within a few weeks accepted a one-year contract to be church organist of the Domkirche—a position that provided a salary, lodging, and prestige. Money was not an issue for Handel: He had an income from his father's estate. So when his contract was up, he left Halle for Hamburg, a lively, sophisticated, wealthy commercial center. In addition to church-supported music, Hamburg had a magnificent opera house with 1,675 seats. Handel worked as a violinist in the opera orchestra.

Handel's first opera, *Almira*, was a success when it premiered at the Hamburg Opera in January 1705. In 1706, after his fourth opera, Handel left Hamburg to study composition with Italian opera composers. He arrived in Florence, but because it was not a center of music, Handel went on to Rome. There he met the violinist and conductor Arcangelo Corelli, whose techniques for bowing and for managing an orchestra impressed Handel. Corelli insisted on the highest professional standards: An orchestra must behave and perform as an ensemble, with accuracy and consistency.

Venice, the opera center of the world, won Handel completely. He remained there until early 1708, when he returned to Palazzo Bonelli in Rome, the home of Handel's patron Marchese Ruspoli, who commissioned him to compose an oratorio for Easter, six weeks away. The two performances of *The Resurrection* were well received.

Handel returned to Germany with a pocketful of letters of recommendation. In June 1710, George the Elector of Hannover appointed him *Kapellmeister* (music director). But Handel needed more activity than Hannover could offer, so he went to London, where his music had its first local performance in early December at the famous Haymarket Theatre. And in February 1711, his opera *Rinaldo* had its successful premiere at the Queen's Theatre.

After a year, he reluctantly returned to Hannover, using his time there to learn English. In the autumn of 1712, the Elector again granted Handel permission to return to London on the condition that he return promptly. Once back in London, Handel ignored his promise, remaining there for two years. Then, coincidence caused an embarrassing predicament between 32-year-old Handel and his employer. Following the death of Queen Anne in 1714, King George I ascended to the throne—the same George who had been Elector of Hannover. Rather than create an unpleasant confrontation, George accepted Handel's apology and, to show there were no hard feelings, doubled his salary.

In 1720, Handel became the director of the newly opened Royal Academy of Music. In addition to his composing, his responsibilities took him all over Europe to audition opera singers. His operas, including *Giulio Cesare* (1724) and *Rodelinda* (1725), premiered at the Academy.

After a long career in which he achieved fame and fortune mainly as an opera and oratorio composer, Handel's health declined. Although losing his eyesight, he continued conducting and performing at the keyboard but composed very few works during his last years. Handel remained in London until his death at the age of 74.

PRINCIPAL WORKS

Operas: Over 40 operas in Italian. *Rinaldo* (1711), *Giulio Cesare* (1724), *Rodelinda* (1725), *Alcina* (1735), *Serse* (1738)

Oratorios: Over 30 oratorios. *Athalia* (1733), *Alexander's Feast* (1736), *Saul* (1739), *Israel in Egypt* (1739), *Messiah* (1742), *Samson* (1743), *Judas Maccabaeus* (1747), and *Solomon* (1749)

Secular Vocal Music: Over 100 Italian cantatas; trios, duets, songs

Instrumental Music: Water Music (1717) and *Music for Royal Fireworks* (1749), 6 concerti grossos, Op. 3 (1734), 12 grand concertos, Op. 6 (1740), organ concertos

Chamber Music: Trio sonatas for recorder, flute, oboe, violin

Keyboard Music: Harpsichord suites, chaconnes, airs, preludes, fugues

HANDEL'S ORATORIOS   Despite his success as a German composer of Italian-style operas for English audiences, Handel owed his later career to the oratorio. In 1728, after London audiences had heard John Gay's *Beggar's Opera* in English, they began to lose interest in Italian-language opera. Wisely switching to composing oratorios with English texts, Handel quickly regained his stature as the most popular composer in London.

A financial consideration also motivated the switch: The Church of England, like most other churches at the time, banned all stage productions during the pre-Easter season of Lent. Oratorios, however, had religious subject matter. Besides, they contained no acting, costumes, or staging and were usually performed in churches. Fitting into a loophole, oratorios were permitted.

Immediately acclaimed, Handel's oratorios played throughout Lent, indulging London audiences in their desire to be entertained. Handel's appeal also extended to London's large Jewish population, which enjoyed his Old Testament oratorio subjects: *Solomon, Judas Macabbaeus*, and *Israel in Egypt*, for example.

English Baroque Soloists and Monteverdi Choir, John Eliot Gardiner, Conductor.

LISTENING ACTIVITY ॐ

HANDEL, *"For Unto Us a Child Is Born"*
CHORUS FROM *MESSIAH*
LARGE FORM: ORATORIO

Cassette Tape: Side A, Example 6
Compact Disc 1, Track 14

Listen to the chorus "For Unto Us a Child Is Born" from Handel's *Messiah*. Written more than 250 years ago, this work gives us a glimpse of Handel's genius for writing exhilarating choral music.

Notice the extensive use of imitation and sequences in the voice parts. Notice also how Handel's music reflects the text. For the opening text, "For unto us a Child is born…" Handel has the orchestra play softly with delicate music. Later, for "And the government shall be upon His shoulder…" the music is more aggressive.

The climax of the chorus comes with a musical fanfare together with the text, "And His Name shall be called Wonderful, Counsellor, the mighty God, the everlasting Father, the Prince of Peace."

LISTENING GUIDE

HANDEL, *"For Unto Us a Child Is Born"* CHORUS FROM *MESSIAH*
LARGE FORM: ORATORIO

Cassette Tape: Side A, Example 6
Compact Disc 1: Track 14
Running time: 4:16

Introduction
14   0:00   Main Melody   violin section of the orchestra, moderate tempo, *f*, moderate tempo, 4 meter, major tonality, basso continuo

15   0:14   Main Melody   sopranos enter, **p**, accompanied by orchestra, moves with sequences, "For unto us…"

SOPRANOS

For un - to us a Child is born,   un - to   us   a Son is giv - en,

     0:28   Main Melody   imitated by tenors, **p**, "For unto us…"

TENORS

For un - to   us a Child is born,

     0:31   Main Melody   imitated by sopranos, then running sixteenth-note counterpoint, "For unto us a Child is Born…"

     0:44   Main Melody   imitation by altos, **p**, imitated by basses, running sixteenth-note counterpoint in basses, "For unto us…"

16   1:04   Second Melody   stated by tenors, **mf**, imitated by sopranos, then altos and basses together

TENORS

and   the gov - ern - ment shall   be   up-on His shoul   -   der

17   1:21   Fanfare Theme   chorus and orchestra together, homophonic texture, **ff**, violins with steady sixteenth notes.

     1:34   Main Melody   stated by altos, **p**, imitated by altos and tenors, **f**, then running sixteenth-note counterpoint in tenors, "For unto us…"

     1:48   Second Melody   stated by altos, **mf**, imitated by basses, "And the government…"

     2:03   Fanfare Theme   all voices and orchestra homophonically, **ff**, violins steady sixteenth notes, "Wonderful, Counsellor…"

2:15	Main Melody	sung by tenors, ***p***; similar to beginning with imitations by the soprano, alto, and basses; "For unto us…"
2:33	Second Melody	started by tenors; ***mf***; imitated by sopranos, then altos and basses together; "And the government…"
2:51	Fanfare Theme	All voices and orchestra, homophonically, ***ff***, violins steady sixteenth notes, "Wonderful, Counsellor…"
3:04	Main Melody	sung by basses; ***f***; imitated by sopranos, altos, and tenors together; followed by altos and tenors singing running sixteenth-note counterpoint together with strings; "For unto us…"
3:20	Second Melody	stated by sopranos, quickly imitated by altos, imitated by tenors and basses together, then all voices together homophonically, "And the government…"

	3:34	Fanfare Theme	all voices and orchestra together homophonically, *ff*, "Wonderful, Counsellor…"
	3:50	Chorus section ends with a cadence.	

Coda

18	3:54	Main Melody	orchestra restatement, *ff,* cadence with ritardando (slowing down)
	4:11	Final chord held.	

HISTORICAL PERSPECTIVE

Handel's *Messiah*

Handel composed *Messiah* in only 24 days—an amazing feat for a three-hour work containing some of the grandest music ever written. Waving off food and often sleep, Handel worked feverishly to complete the monumental work.

In April 1742, the public first heard the work in Dublin, Ireland's Music Hall. Handel had staged a special preview during an open rehearsal to build the public's anticipation for a formal premiere a few days later. His strategy worked. So great was the clamor for tickets after the preview that hundreds of people had to be turned away.

Dublin's Music Hall had no seats. Those attending *Messiah* had to stand for hours. In the interest of space, comfort, and additional sales, ticket holders were alerted in advance: Women were not to wear their customary hoops; men had to forgo their swords. Despite these minor inconveniences, *Messiah* was a huge success. In fact, a special charity performance of the oratorio at the Dublin Cathedral raised enough money to free 142 people from debtors' prison.

Today, at concert performances of *Messiah*, audiences often stand up during the "Hallelujah" chorus. This practice goes back to Handel's day when King George II, inspired by that section, rose to his feet. His subjects dutifully followed, thus inaugurating the tradition.

Messiah was first performed in New York in 1770. Since then, cities in North America have joined those throughout the world in presenting *Messiah* during the holiday season. Fans of *Messiah* can participate in singalong performances assisted by professional choruses and orchestra. Watch your local newspapers for the opportunity.

The Baroque Cantata

Cantata
(can-*tah*-tuh)

The cantata, another vocal form popular in the Baroque, features soloists, chorus, and orchestra.

The form of the cantata is similar both in style and in general format to the oratorio (see characteristics summarized in Table 8-1). The cantata, however, is much shorter than the oratorio.

Lutheran Cantata
Secular Cantata

Cantatas performed as part of the Lutheran Church service usually glorified New Testament subjects. Secular cantatas, however, used popular themes. Bach's charming "Coffee Cantata" is an example of a secular cantata. He wrote this work for a Collegium Musicum student choir that assembled regularly at Zimmermann's Coffee House in Leipzig. The text, a comedy by the poet Picander, expresses women's desire to partake in the pleasure of drinking coffee and their objections to being excluded from the cafés.

❧ Table 8-1 Baroque Opera, Oratorio, and Cantata Compared

	Opera	Oratorios	Cantata
text or plot	usually secular	religious, Old and New Testament	religious and secular
language	Italian	local language	local language
staging	yes	no	no
scenery	yes	no	no
costumes	yes	no	no
characters	yes	yes	yes
acting	yes	no	no
soloists	yes	yes	yes
overture	yes	yes	yes
recitatives	yes	yes	yes
arias	yes	yes	yes
duets, trios	yes	yes	yes
chorus	yes	yes	yes
orchestra	yes	yes	yes
keyboard	harpsichord	organ/ harpsichord	organ/ harpsichord

JOHANN SEBASTIAN BACH (1685–1750)

Born in Eisenach, Germany, into a distinguished family of professional musicians, Bach (*bahk*) lived and worked throughout his life within a 100-mile radius of his birthplace. The family Bach took great pride in having been elevated to the middle class, a status that included the opportunity to attend university. They also took seriously the responsibility of preparing each new generation of the family for a career in music. Bach received most of his musical training from his oldest brother, Johann Christoph, an organist, with whom Bach lived after he was orphaned at the age of 10.

At 18, Bach secured his first appointment—violinist in the small, private orchestra of Duke Johann Ernst of Saxe-Weimar. But the assignment also relegated him to a variety of menial, subservient tasks unrelated to music. Realizing that quitting the post could damage his reputation, Bach instead resisted those tasks until, less than a year later, the court dismissed him. However, he was to return to Weimar five years later.

During the interval, Bach served four years as church organist in Arnstadt and one year at St. Blasius in Muhlhausen. It was in Arnstadt that Bach and a cousin from his father's side, Maria Barbara, caused a stir. Maria Barbara, a singer, appeared as soloist for vocal pieces Bach had composed for the church service. Church officials objected: There had been no precedent in Arnstadt for a woman to be a soloist. Bach was able to withstand the criticism, and later, he and Maria Barbara were married.

Under the Duke Wilhelm Ernst, the arts thrived in Weimar. The new duke appreciated and encouraged his organist, and Bach composed hundreds of organ works to play for him. The duke also acquired Italian musical works for his court orchestra, including compositions by Antonio Vivaldi, whose concerto structure greatly impressed Bach.

In 1717, when Bach did not receive a promotion to *Kapellmeister*, the top post for a musician at court, he indignantly requested his release. Angered by the request, the duke sent Bach to prison, where he remained for four weeks until the duke dismissed him.

Soon afterward, Prince Leopold of Cöthen hired Bach as his court *Kapellmeister*. Bach was very productive, composing *The Well-Tempered Clavier* for harpsichord, secular cantatas, orchestral music for chamber ensembles, concertos, and duo and trio sonatas. On a trip to Berlin to find a new harpsichord, Bach gave a command performance at the palace of Christian Ludwig of Brandenburg. Two years later (1721), Bach sent to Ludwig six concertos for the court orchestra—the famous *Brandenburg* Concertos.

After the death of Maria Barbara, Bach remarried in 1721. He dedicated a book of clavier works to his new wife, Anna Magdalena. From these two marriages, Bach fathered many children, several of whom pursued a career in music.

In May 1723, Bach and his family arrived in Leipzig where he assumed the prestigious post of Kantor of St. Thomas School, which also included music directorship for the city of Leipzig and its four principal churches. Bach also was director of the Collegium Musicum, which gave weekly performances throughout the year.

It was in Leipzig that Bach composed some of his greatest works, including *St. Matthew Passion* (1727). He began his *Mass in b minor* and, in 1733, submitted the "Kyrie" and "Gloria" as part of his application for the post of court composer for the King of Poland. Bach did receive that appointment, which he maintained in addition to his post in Leipzig. Under the patronage of Poland's Roman Catholic king, Bach was able to complete the *Mass* in 1749.

Bach remained in Leipzig until his death at age 65. Although blind (like Handel) in his last years, Bach remained an active composer and performer.

PRINCIPAL WORKS

Sacred Choral Music: St. John Passion (1724), St. Matthew Passion (1727), Christmas Oratorio (1734), Mass in b minor (1749), Magnificat in D (1723), nearly 300 church cantatas: No. 4 "Christ lag in Totesbanden" (Christ lay in the bonds of death, 1724), No. 80 "Ein feste Burg" (A mighty fortress, 1730), No. 140 "Wachet auf" (Sleepers, wake!, 1731), motets, chorales, sacred songs, arias

Secular Vocal Music: Over 30 cantatas: No. 211 "Coffee Cantata" (1732), No. 212 "Peasant Cantata" (1742)

Orchestral Music: Brandenburg Concertos 1-6 (1721), 4 orchestral suites (1725, 1731), harpsichord concertos, sinfonias

Chamber Music: 6 sonatas and partitas for solo violin (1720), 6 sonatas for violin and harpsichord (1723), 6 suites for solo cello (1720), *Musikalisches Opfer (Musical Offering,* 1747), flute sonatas, trio sonatas

Keyboard Music: Chromatic fantasia and fugue (1720), "The Well-Tempered Clavier" (1722, 1742), "Goldberg Variations" (1741), 6 English Suites (1724), 6 French Suites (1724), 6 partitas (1731), Italian Concerto (1735), French Overture (1735), *The Art of Fugue* (1745), 600 chorale preludes, hundreds of preludes and fugues, inventions, suites, concertos, dances, toccatas, fantasias, and sonatas

LISTENING ACTIVITY ↝

BACH, CANTATA NO. 140, (BWV 140)
OPENING CHORUS
LARGE FORM: CANTATA

Cassette Tape: Side B, Example 1
Compact Disc 1: Track 19

Listen to the opening chorus from Bach's Cantata No. 140 "Wachet auf" ("Wake Up!"). In an elaborate, lively setting, Bach employs the *chorale melody* written by Philip Nicolai (1556–1608).

Notice the use of the animated polyphonic texture combined with instrumental accompaniment. After an instrumental introduction, the sopranos sing Nicolai's chorale melody. Then, different sections of the choir imitate the chorale melody.

Notice how Bach's music emphasizes the action words employed in the text: *wake up! where? where? cheer up!; stand up! prepare yourself!; go forth!* Here is the text:

Wachet auf, ruft uns die stimme	Wake up, call to us the voices
Der Wächter sehr hoch auf der Zinne,	Of watchmen high on the tower,
Wach' auf, du Stadt Jerusalem!	Wake up, thou town of Jerusalem!
Mitternacht heißt diese Stunde;	It is now the hour of midnight;
Sie rufen uns mit hellem Munde:	They call us with shining faces:
Wo seid ihr klugen Jungfrauen?	Where are you now, clever maidens?
Wohl auf, der Bräut'gam kommt,	Cheer up, the Bridegroom (Jesus) comes
Steht auf, die Lampen nehmt! Alleluia!	Stand up, and take your lamps! Halleluja!
Macht euch bereit zu der Hochzeit,	Prepare yourselves, the wedding nears,
Ihr müsset ihm entsprungen gehn.	You must go forth to welcome Him.

LISTENING GUIDE

BACH, CANTATA NO. 140, (BWV 140) OPENING CHORUS
LARGE FORM: CANTATA

Cassette Tape: Side B, Example 1
Compact Disc 1: Track 19
Running time: 6:06

Introduction (A)

19	0:00	Introduction Theme	played by the orchestra, *mf*, triple meter, dotted rhythm ("long, short"), major tonality, alternating imitation between violin and oboe

20	0:07	Instrumental Countermelody	alternating imitations between violin and oboe

Chorus B)

21	0:28	Chorale Melody	sung by sopranos; "Wachet auf" (Wake up!); polyphonic texture; counterpoint imitations by altos, then tenors, then basses

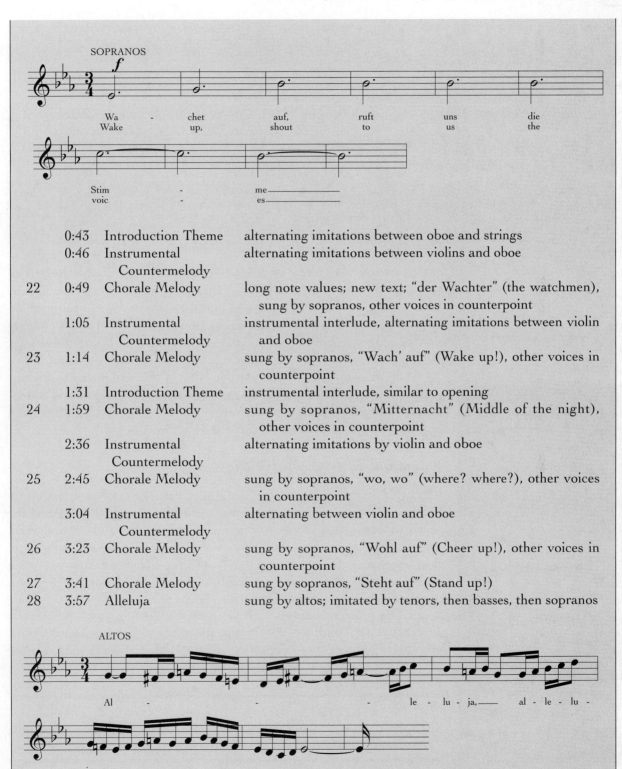

SOPRANOS

Wa - chet auf, ruft uns die
Wake up, shout to us the

Stim - me
voic - es

	0:43	Introduction Theme	alternating imitations between oboe and strings
	0:46	Instrumental Countermelody	alternating imitations between violins and oboe
22	0:49	Chorale Melody	long note values; new text; "der Wachter" (the watchmen), sung by sopranos, other voices in counterpoint
	1:05	Instrumental Countermelody	instrumental interlude, alternating imitations between violin and oboe
23	1:14	Chorale Melody	sung by sopranos, "Wach' auf" (Wake up!), other voices in counterpoint
	1:31	Introduction Theme	instrumental interlude, similar to opening
24	1:59	Chorale Melody	sung by sopranos, "Mitternacht" (Middle of the night), other voices in counterpoint
	2:36	Instrumental Countermelody	alternating imitations by violin and oboe
25	2:45	Chorale Melody	sung by sopranos, "wo, wo" (where? where?), other voices in counterpoint
	3:04	Instrumental Countermelody	alternating between violin and oboe
26	3:23	Chorale Melody	sung by sopranos, "Wohl auf" (Cheer up!), other voices in counterpoint
27	3:41	Chorale Melody	sung by sopranos, "Steht auf" (Stand up!)
28	3:57	Alleluja	sung by altos; imitated by tenors, then basses, then sopranos

ALTOS

Al - - - le - lu - ja,— al - le - lu -

ja,—

		Coda (A)	
29	4:33	Introduction Theme and orchestral interlude	
		Instrumental Countermelody	
	4:41	Chorale Melody	sung by sopranos, "Macht euch" (Prepare yourselves!), other voices in counterpoint, chorus section, ends with cadence
	5:33	Introduction Theme with	exactly like opening, slowing tempo for the final cadence
		Instrumental Countermelody	
	6:02	Final Chord	f, major tonality

Performance of a Lutheran cantata.

USE OF CHORALES IN THE BAROQUE LUTHERAN CANTATA   Simple hymns or chorales, an important part of the Lutheran Church service during the Baroque, were usually incorporated into the cantata. Martin Luther himself had been a lover of music, a singer, and a composer. He felt strongly that the congregation should take part in the musical portion of the service. To that end, Luther composed many chorales for his own services.

Luther's original chorales included only a text and melody—no harmony—and were intended for the congregation to sing in unison. Subsequent Lutheran Church composers harmonized the original chorales. Of all these, Bach's harmonizations are the most famous.

↝ Baroque Instrumental Music

The Baroque Concerto

Developed during the Baroque period, the concerto quickly became the principal instrumental form. At that time a harpsichord and a chamber orchestra of mostly string instruments accompanied the soloist. As a form, the concerto continued its popularity into the nineteenth and twentieth centuries, and today's audiences can hear renowned soloists perform concertos with symphony orchestras.

CONCERTO FORM   With few exceptions, the concerto has retained the same overall three-movement form that had developed during the Baroque period:

The Concerto Plan

FIRST MOVEMENT	*Fast* (Allegro)
SECOND MOVEMENT	*Slow* (Adagio, Andante, or similar tempo)
THIRD MOVEMENT	*Fast* (Allegro)

LISTENING INSIGHTS

Evolution of Public Concerts: The Baroque Period

Today, we use the term *concert* for all kinds of public music performances: anyone can buy a ticket and attend. However, before the Baroque period, attendance of concerts—presented in academic settings or in private residences—was restricted to a privileged few. Public concert halls were virtually unheard of. Only in church could common people hear performances of fine music.

Venice: The First Opera House Opera made the first important breakthrough in offering music performances to the general public. The milestone: the opening in 1637 of Teatro San Cassiano in Venice. As a major commercial trading center, Venice attracted merchants from all over the world. Its lively economy helped to create a thriving middle-class population, eager and able to pay for entertainment and exposure to the arts. By 1700, with its 17 opera houses, Venice had become the opera capital of the world.

London Starting in 1672 and continuing for six years, the public could attend the first non-opera performances in London's Whitefriars. Building on the popularity of those afternoon concerts, a London coal merchant named Thomas Britton began in 1678 to sponsor weekly performances in his storehouse loft. These "Coal-House Concerts" continued for 36 years.

Other Early Opera Houses

1652	Vienna
1671	Paris (Academie de Royale Musique)
1656	London
1678	Hamburg Staatsoper
1705	Haymarket Theatre, London
1725	Prague
1731	Covent Garden, London

Dates of Interest

1725	first public concert in Paris
1731	first public concerts in Boston, Massachusetts, and Charleston, South Carolina
1735	first performance of ballad opera (*Flora*), Charleston

ANTONIO VIVALDI (1678–1741)

A Venetian by birth, Vivaldi (vee-*vahl*-dee) was the son of a leading violinist at the Basilica of St. Mark. At an early age, he began studying music with his father.

Still in his youth, Vivaldi was ordained a priest. Because of his bright red hair, he was known as *il prete rosso* (the red-headed priest). More interested in music than the priesthood, Vivaldi pursued his first love. As a violinist in Venice, he often performed in the orchestra at St. Mark's.

At 25, Vivaldi was appointed teacher of violin and orchestra director at the Ospedale della Pietà (Hospital of Piety), a girls' orphanage specializing in music. The school had an exceptional orchestra and many outstanding instrumental soloists. For his students, Vivaldi wrote many of his concertos, including works for violin, cello, oboe, piccolo, flute, bassoon, trumpet, guitar, and mandolin—whatever instrument the girls played.

His most famous work in the concerto genre is the programmatic *Four Seasons,* a group of four concertos featuring a solo violin. Each concerto depicts a different season of the year.

At 49, Vivaldi accepted the invitation of Emperor Charles VI of Vienna to become court composer. He remained there until his death at the age of 63.

PRINCIPAL WORKS

Many of Vivaldi's nearly 800 works have been lost.

Concertos: About 500—including 344 solo concertos (about 230 violin concertos, 81 concertos for two or more soloists), *The Four Seasons*

Chamber Music: Over 90 sonatas and trios for instruments

Operas: Over 45 operas: *Giustino* (1724), *Griselda* (1735)

Sacred Choral Music: Three oratorios, psalm settings, motets

Secular Cantatas: About 40 cantatas

VIVALDI'S CONCERTOS   Because of the concerto's immense popularity at court and at public concerts, just about every eighteenth-century composer wrote concertos. The most prolific was Antonio Vivaldi (1678–1741), who composed more than 500 concertos.

CONCERTO GROSSO Composers realized that they could add even more interest to the already popular concerto by featuring more than one or two soloists. They called this "large concerto" a *concerto grosso*.

While Bach was employed as music director at the court of Cöthen, one of his duties was to supply music for court entertainment. It was here that he composed his famous six *Brandenburg* Concertos. Numbers one, two, four, and five are concerto grossos.

LISTENING ACTIVITY ॐ

VIVALDI, *THE FOUR SEASONS*
CONCERTO FOR VIOLIN AND STRINGS IN E MAJOR,
OP. 8, NO. 1 "SPRING," FIRST MOVEMENT: ALLEGRO
LARGE FORM: CONCERTO

Cassette Tape: Side B, Example 2
Compact Disc 1: Track 30

You may recognize Vivaldi's popular *Four Seasons* as background music in film and television productions. The entire work consists of four violin concertos, each based on a descriptive sonnet and focused on a different season of the year. Many scholars believe that Vivaldi wrote the sonnets.

Previously, we discussed how other Baroque composers, specifically Handel and Bach, derived musical inspiration from the texts they used. Vivaldi chose to describe the seasons instrumentally. To assist with interpretation, Vivaldi had the sonnets printed in each player's musical score. The following is a translation of the sonnet for the first movement of the "Spring" concerto:

Spring has arrived, and festively
The birds greet it with cheerful song
And the brooks, caressed by soft breezes
Murmur sweetly as they flow.

The sky is covered with a black mantel
Lightning and thunder announce a storm
When the storm dies away to silence, the birds
Return with their melodious songs.

LISTENING GUIDE

VIVALDI, THE FOUR SEASONS
CONCERTO FOR VIOLIN AND STRINGS IN E MAJOR,
OP. 8, NO. 1 "SPRING," FIRST MOVEMENT: ALLEGRO
LARGE FORM: CONCERTO

Cassette Tape: Side B, Example 2
Compact Disc 1: Track 30
Running time: 3:10

30	0:00	Introduction Theme	*"Spring has arrived…"* violin soloist accompanied by a string orchestra; allegro; *f;* quadruple meter; E major; theme repeats *p*
31	0:13	Ritornello Theme	violin solo and orchestra; *f;* syncopated melody, theme repeats *p*
32	0:28	Bird Calls	*"and festively, the birds greet it with cheerful song"* soloist and other violins answer each other with trills and scale runs
	1:00	Ritornello Theme	returns in violins, accompanied by other strings and continuo; *f*
	1:07	Murmuring Brook	*"And the brooks…"* smoothly, alternating pitches; *p*
	1:29	Ritornello Theme	returns in violins, accompanied by other strings and continuo
33	1:36	Storm Section	*"The sky is covered with a black mantel…"* quick scale runs (lightning); arpeggios (fury of the storm)
	2:02	Ritornello Theme	solo violin; all strings and continuo; *f*
	2:09	Bird Calls	*"…the birds return…"* violin trills and scales
	2:26	Introduction Theme	like introduction: violin soloist and full group
	2:51	Ritornello Theme	*f;* repeated *p;* cadence

Buxtehude
(*books*-tih-*hoo*-duh)

Couperin
(koo-*pran*)

Rameau
(rah-*moh*)

Scarlatti
(skahr-*lah*-tee)

Telemann
(*tay*-lih-mahn)

~ Baroque Keyboard Music

The two most famous Baroque composers, Bach and Handel, were also virtuoso keyboard artists. Both played organ and harpsichord, the popular keyboards of the day. Other composers who wrote extensively for the keyboard are Dietrich Buxtehude (c. 1637–1707), François Couperin (1668–1733), Jean-Philippe Rameau (1683–1764), Alessandro Scarlatti (1660–1725), Domenico Scarlatti (Alessandro's son, 1685–1757), and Georg Philipp Telemann (1681–1767).

LISTENING ACTIVITY ❧

BACH, *Brandenburg* Concerto No. 2,
Third Movement
Large Form: Concerto Grosso

Cassette Tape: Side B, Example 3
Compact Disc 1, Track 34

Listen to the third movement, Allegro assai (quite fast), of Bach's *Brandenburg* Concerto No. 2. This concerto grosso features four soloists—on trumpet, flute, oboe, and violin.

LISTENING GUIDE

BACH, *Brandenburg* Concerto No. 2,
Third Movement
Large Form: Concerto Grosso

Cassette Tape: Side B, Example 3
Compact Disc 1: Track 34
Running time: 3:01

34 0:00 Main Melody stated by the solo *trumpet*, *f*, with cello and harpsichord (basso continuo) accompaniment, allegro, duple meter (2), F major tonality

35	0:08	Main Melody	imitated by the *oboe, trumpet* in counterpoint
36	0:25	Main Melody	imitated by the *violin, trumpet,* and *oboe* in counterpoint
37	0:33	Main Melody	imitated by the *flute, oboe,* and *violin* in counterpoint
	0:59		Orchestra strings enter with short accompaniment and counterpoint melodies in solo parts
	1:11	Main Melody	stated by *violin, flute* in counterpoint, with cello and harpsichord continuo
	1:23	Main Melody	imitated by *oboe, flute,* and violin in counterpoint
	1:30	Main Melody	imitated by both cello and harpsichord in orchestra, other instruments in counterpoint
38	1:40	Melodic Fragment	imitated by *trumpet* and *flute*
	1:47	Melodic Fragment	stated by *oboe,* imitated by *violin,* later by *flute, violin,* then *trumpet,* back to *oboe,* then *flute* play running sixteenth notes
	2:16	Main Melody	stated in *oboe,* imitations by *flute,* cello, and harpsichord in orchestra, *trumpet* then *flute* running sixteenth notes
	2:52	Main Melody	final statement by *trumpet* accompanied by all soloists and orchestra, sudden slowing of tempo on last few beats
	2:57	Final Chord	F major tonality

Bach at keyboard with his family in a nineteenth-century etching.

❧ Plate 1

Le Concert champêtre: la musique (*The Musicians of a Country Concert*) *A chamber music ensemble including (left to right) a harpsichord, lute, recorder and a bass viol. (See Chapters 4 and 6)*

Source: Giraudon/Art Resource

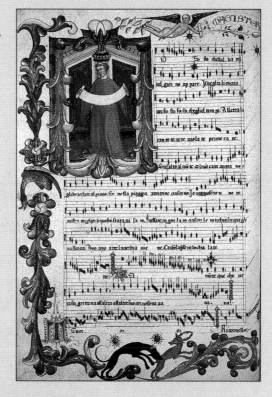

❧ Plate 4
The stained glass rose window of Chartres Cathedral in France. The great Gothic cathedral contains some of the best original stained glass windows that date back to the thirteenth century. (See Chapters 6 and 7)

Source: © Tetrel/Explorer/Photo Researchers

↬ Plate 5
Frederick the Great (1712-86), King of Prussia, performing by candlelight as concerto soloist with his court chamber orchestra. (See Chapter 8)

↬ Plate 6 (left)
Seven-year-old Wolfgang Amadeus Mozart at the piano, with his sister Nannerl singing, and his father, Leopold playing the violin. Note the many pillows the tiny Wolfgang had to use to reach the keyboard. (See Chapter 10)

↬ Plate 7 (below)
The Circle of the Lustful *is an early Romantic engraving by artist-poet William Blake.*

The Fugue

Bach is known for his *fugues*, devilishly difficult to perform, especially on an organ. The fugue uses three or four highly independent parts (polyphony) and is written in either three or four voices. The term *voice* refers to the number of independent parts in the fugue.

Fugue
(*fyoog*)

The fugue's main ingredient is *imitative counterpoint*. In a four-voice fugue, a melody, called a *subject*, is stated in one voice, imitated by a second voice, imitated again by a third, and then a fourth. In a constant overlapping of parts, the first voice continues playing in *counterpoint*, using music other than the main subject. The second voice takes over the subject; then the third voice plays the subject while the second voice moves into the role of counterpoint, played together with the first voice. Here is a graph of the exposition section of a fugue:

Imitative counterpoint
Subject

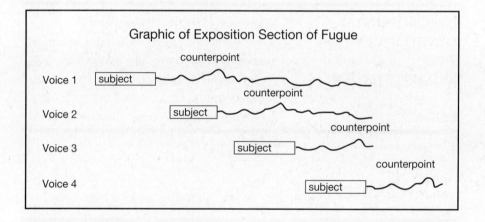

EXPOSITION   Because it exposes the main theme or subject, the opening section of the fugue is called the *exposition*. Most commonly, a fugue has only one subject or melody. Once all voices have exposed the subject and counterpoint, the exposition concludes.

DEVELOPMENT (EPISODES)   This second section develops the melodic ideas presented during the exposition. The developmental section events are also referred to as *episodes* when the subject of the fugue is broken into fragments. Composers usually handle the subject in a development section by moving it around in sequences, changes of keys, and fragmented imitations.

Episodes

RECAPITULATION   When the *recapitulation* begins, the development ends. Now we hear a restatement of the subject in its original key, similar though not identical to the exposition.

Stretto

CODA   A short *coda* usually ends the fugue. *Coda*, the Italian word for "tail," means an ending section. The fugal coda occasionally contains a short section called a *stretto*. Here the subject is imitated by the voices in close succession.

PERFORMING FUGUES   The challenge in performing a fugue on an organ is to keep each voice a distinctly independent melodic line. To sound all the parts, an organist must play more than one melody with each hand and must use both feet on the pedal board.

ॐ **Table 8-2**   Overall Form of the Fugue

EXPOSITION (A)	exposing of subject by all parts
DEVELOPMENT (B)	free, fantasy section, containing imitation, sequences, and modulations of key
RECAPITULATION (A)	restatement of subject, similar to exposition
CODA	concluding section (may include a stretto)

LISTENING ACTIVITY ॐ

BACH, FUGUE IN G MINOR (LITTLE) (BWV 578)
FORM: 4-VOICE FUGUE

| *Cassette Tape: Side B, Example 4*
| *Compact Disc 1, Track 39*

Listen to Bach's Fugue in g minor. It is known as the "Little" fugue to distinguish it from other fugues Bach wrote in the g minor key. Because the main subject (main melody) of the fugue is stated at the beginning, try to remember it and follow it as it is imitated by other parts and as it goes through transformations.

LISTENING GUIDE

BACH, FUGUE IN G MINOR (LITTLE) (BWV 578)
FORM: 4-VOICE FUGUE

Cassette Tape: Side B, Example 4
Compact Disc 1: Track 39
Running time: 3:32

Exposition (A)

39   0:00   SUBJECT—VOICE 1   played in middle register, moderate tempo, duple meter (4), g minor tonality

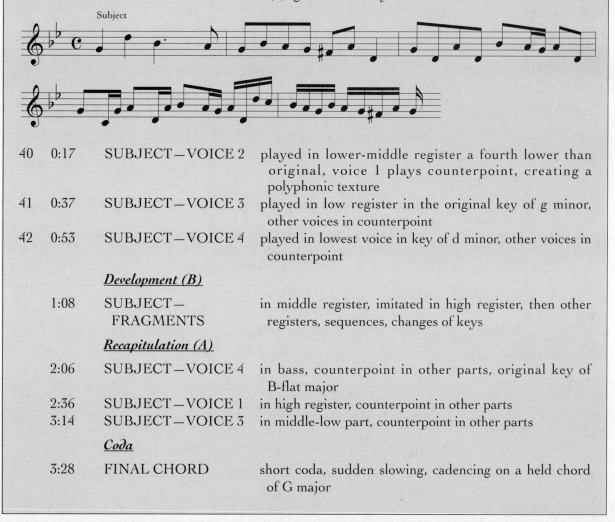

40   0:17   SUBJECT—VOICE 2   played in lower-middle register a fourth lower than original, voice 1 plays counterpoint, creating a polyphonic texture

41   0:37   SUBJECT—VOICE 3   played in low register in the original key of g minor, other voices in counterpoint

42   0:53   SUBJECT—VOICE 4   played in lowest voice in key of d minor, other voices in counterpoint

Development (B)

1:08   SUBJECT— FRAGMENTS   in middle register, imitated in high register, then other registers, sequences, changes of keys

Recapitulation (A)

2:06   SUBJECT—VOICE 4   in bass, counterpoint in other parts, original key of B-flat major

2:36   SUBJECT—VOICE 1   in high register, counterpoint in other parts

3:14   SUBJECT—VOICE 3   in middle-low part, counterpoint in other parts

Coda

3:28   FINAL CHORD   short coda, sudden slowing, cadencing on a held chord of G major

Summary of Terms

antiphonal	development	multiple soloists
aria	duet	opera
aria form	embouchure	oratorio
Baroque	exposition	overture
Beggar's Opera	expression indications	pizzicato
bel canto	fugue	recapitulation
cantata	imitative counterpoint	recitativo
castrato	instrumentation	secular cantata
chorales	Kapellmeister	stretto
choruses	libretto	subject
coda	Lutheran cantata	tremolo
concertato	maestro di cappella	trio
concerto grosso	Mass	
counterpoint	motet	

The Classical Period (1750–1820)

⁓ Political and Social Background

Two contrasting moods characterized the Classical Period. Inside the castles and palaces, the complacent aristocracy settled into a predictable life of manners, morals, and music. Outside the walls, the frenzied people began rising in revolt. The result was a tug-of-war between guardians of the status quo and insurgents who wanted control of their own destinies.

- 1776 — the United States sheds its domination by the British Monarchy.
- 1789 — Parisian citizens storm the Bastille.
- 1790 — Hapsburg troops suppress a revolution for independence in Brussels, Belgium.
- 1792 — angry French mobs take over the Tuileries Palace.
- 1793 — Louis XVI, Marie Antoinette, their children, and scores of aristocrats are guillotined.
- 1795 — angry French citizens stage the Bread Riots and White Terror against the aristocracy.

Dancing the popular minuet at court.

As the eighteenth century drew to a close, Europe was a crazy quilt of wars. Spain declared war on a Britain weakened from its loss to the United States. Napoleon's armies invaded Germany, Italy, and Austria and defeated the Turks in Cairo, Egypt.

To drown out the cries of the mobs, the aristocracy demanded more music. Avoiding the reality of change, royalty retreated into greater self-indulgence, dependent for their comfort on the toil of the lower classes. Legions of servants served dinner on gold plates. Other hirelings, including musicians such as Haydn and Mozart, were meagerly paid to entertain their employers and their guests.

COURT FUNCTIONS   Once a court function was scheduled, servants delivered ornate invitations and returned with acceptances. On the appointed day, guests arrived in the afternoon for drinks, snacks, and chit-chat. Later, they retired to the guest rooms to nap before changing clothes for dinner.

COURT CONCERTS AND BALLS   After overindulging in the food and drink, the entourage strolled into the music room. During the short concert, several guests would talk incessantly, others would doze noisily, and the rest would listen intermittently. Concert over, the guests would again nap and change dress for the ball, where they would dance into the morning hours.

THE MUSICIAN'S LIFE   Most French, German, and Austro-Hungarian courts maintained a staff of resident musicians to become a small orchestra on call for concerts, operas, and dances. Considered servants, the musicians often had to put down a serving tray to pick up a violin bow.

The discovery of Pompeii's ruins in 1748 renewed interest in Greek and Roman art.

❧ *Classical Origins*

Buried since A.D. 79 in the volcanic ash from Mt. Vesuvius lay the cities of Pompeii and Herculaneum. Archeologists excavated these ruins in 1748, uncovering Greek and Roman art, architecture, and artifacts. Their discoveries helped to promote a renewed interest in classical art. Symmetry and simple symmetrical classical proportions became fashionable in the arts throughout the eighteenth century.

As applied to music of this era, the concept of *classical* is appropriate because of its emphasis on clarity of sound and on symmetry of form. This application certainly describes the music of the great classical composers—Haydn, Mozart, and early Beethoven.

FOCUS ON FORM AND SYMMETRY In court manners and daily life as well as in the arts, form and symmetry were in high regard. Notice in the photograph of the eighteenth-century mansion how the architectural design of the building consists of three parts:

As we discuss the music of the Classical Period in the next chapter, you will discover how often the A B A form is used. Its balance and symmetry pervade classical forms.

A	B	A
First Section	Contrasting Section	Repetition of First Section

An eighteenth-century aristocratic mansion in Munich, Germany.

๛ *Overview of the Classical Period (1750–1820)*

Important Composers	Joseph Haydn, Wolfgang Amadeus Mozart, early and middle Ludwig van Beethoven works
Writers	Robert Burns, Johann Wolfgang Goethe, Thomas Jefferson, Samuel Johnson, Alexander Pope, Johann Schiller
Artists	Jacques-Louis David, Jean-August Ingres
Philosophers	Denis Diderot, David Hume, Immanuel Kant, Jean-Jacques Rousseau, Voltaire (Francois-Marie Arouet)
Social. Political, and Cultural Events	Factory system begins in England; James Watt's steam engine; American and French Revolutions; Napoleon in power; Catherine the Great of Russia; Hapsburgs rule Austria, Hungary, Italy, Spain, and The Netherlands; the American Constitution; The Age of Reason

CHARACTERISTICS OF CLASSICAL MUSIC

General	Elegant, restrained, stable, balanced, mostly predictable, with clear musical ideas: you seem to know the music even on first hearing
Performing Medium	Symphony orchestra, chamber orchestra, soloists and orchestra, piano, chamber ensembles, opera companies
Rhythm	Simple, regular rhythms with steady beat; steady tempos with little change; meters mostly 2, 3, 4, 6
Melody	Lightly ornamented melodies; running scale patterns and broken chords; imitation and sequences, symmetrical phrases
Harmony	Chords by thirds, mostly built on scale tones; strong tonal center (key); major and minor tonalities
Expression	Moderate use of crescendo, diminuendo; neither very soft nor very loud (mostly *p, mf, f*)
Texture	Basically homophonic—melody (usually on top) with chordal accompaniment; some polyphony, mainly in development sections; polyphony is less formal than Baroque era
Forms	Clear-cut, easy to follow, sections set off by obvious cadences and stops; exact repetition of sections; detailed forms: two-part and three-part forms; sonata, rondo, minuet and trio, theme and variations; large forms; symphony, concerto, sonata, string trio and quartet; opera; some oratorios and masses

CHAPTER 10

Music of the Classical Period

✧ *Mozart*

Why would some biographers characterize Wolfgang Amadeus Mozart as an intractable genius, quarrelsome with and rebellious toward his patrons? What experiences had molded the young, undisciplined Wolfgang?

Raised in the luxury of the Hapsburg palaces, the infant prodigy was caressed and spoiled by Empress Maria Theresa. How surprising—even demeaning—it must have been to the adolescent Mozart when he realized that a composer was little more than a hired hand! No special station accompanied his employment in the court of the Prince-Bishop of Salzburg. His employer praised him extravagantly but paid him relatively poorly.

✧ *Haydn*

Financially, as his spacious homes seem to attest, Joseph Haydn fared well. Employed by the Esterházy family for more than thirty years, Haydn led a considerably more stable life than Mozart.

The young prodigy Mozart being introduced to Maria Theresa at the Schönbrunn Palace, seat of the Hapsburg empire.

Haydn also grumbled about his employer's treating him as a servant. Having to live in a tiny apartment over the kitchen at the Esterházy palace was offensive to him. But Haydn was not as openly rebellious as Mozart, preferring instead to take little jabs at the aristocrats through his music.

⁊ *Young Beethoven*

About the same time Mozart was in Vienna writing some of his greatest works, Ludwig van Beethoven (*bay*-toh-ven, 1770–1827) was growing up in Bonn, Germany. Beethoven had always idolized Mozart, yearning for the day he could study with him (see the box in Chapter 11: "Beethoven Meets Mozart"). But when Beethoven finally settled in Vienna in 1792, Mozart was dead, and Beethoven studied with Haydn and other composers.

In 1778, Ludwig's father heard about the success Leopold Mozart had had with young Wolfgang. So he dressed his eight-year-old son in short pants and tried to foist him off as an infant piano prodigy. There is more on Beethoven, including his biography, in the next chapter.

WOLFGANG AMADEUS MOZART (1756–1791)

One of music's greatest child prodigies, Mozart displayed his extraordinary musical ability at the age of four by performing in public on both violin and piano. At five, Mozart started composing music, and by the age of eight, he had composed his first symphony. Mozart completed his first oratorio at eleven and his first opera at twelve.

When he was six, Wolfgang toured the great courts of Europe with his sister, Maria Anna (Nannerl), playing the violin and the piano to the amazement of his aristocratic audiences. Their tours were supervised by their nurturing father, Leopold (1719–87). To promote his talented children, he had curtailed his own musical career as a violinist and court composer in Salzburg, Austria.

For all his prodigious beginnings and genius, Mozart never had the benefit of a stable patron, though recent evidence finds that his financial situation was considerably better than previously thought (see "Mozart Myths Revealed" box). In 1781, after resigning from his position as concertmaster (principal violinist) in the court orchestra of the Archbishop of Salzburg, Mozart went to Vienna to make his way as a freelance musician.

Soon after his arrival in Vienna he met and married Constanze Weber, with whom he had six children, of whom only two survived into adulthood—the same as the average survival rate in the eighteenth century.

It was in Vienna with opera that Mozart and his public realized his greatest talents. His German singspiels (comic opera with spoken dialogue) *Die Entführung aus dem Serail* (The Abduction from the Harem, 1782) and *Die Zauberflöte* (The Magic Flute, 1791) were successes and major departures from traditional Italian-language opera that had dominated opera since its inception.

Mozart's taste for expensive clothes, entertainment, and travel led him to outspend his income and prompted him to borrow heavily from his father and friends. After he died, some of his creditors went after his estate.

At 35, Mozart died prematurely (see "Mozart Myths Revealed" box), leaving a legacy of more than 600 compositions in almost every form.

PRINCIPAL WORKS

Symphonies: 50 symphonies: No. 35 (*Haffner*, 1782); No. 36 (*Linz*, 1783); No. 38 (*Prague*, 1786); No. 39 (1788); No. 40 (g minor, 1788); No. 41 (*Jupiter*, 1788).

Concertos: 23 piano concertos: No. 15, *K. 450 (1784); No. 17 K. 453 (1784); No. 18, K. 456 (1784); No. 19, K. 459 (1784); No. 20, K. 466 (1785); No. 21, K. 467 (1785); No. 23, K. 488 (1786); No. 25, K. 503 (1786). 5 violin concertos; concertos for flute, flute and harp, oboe, clarinet, bassoon, horn; Sinfonia Concertante for oboe, clarinet, bassoon, and horn, K. 279b.

Other Orchestral Music: serenades: Serenata notturna, K. 239 (1776); *Eine kleine Nachtmusik*, K. 535 (1787); divertimentos; cassations; dances

Chamber Music: 26 string quartets; 6 string quintets; clarinet quintet; flute quartets; piano quartets; piano trios; 1 string trio; violin sonatas (with piano)

Piano Music: 17 sonatas; rondos; variations; fantasias; piano duets

Operas: 20 operas: *Idomeneo* (1781); *Die Entführung aus dem Serail* (The Abduction from the Harem, original in German, *1782); Le nozze di Figaro* (The Marriage of Figaro, 1786); *Don Giovanni* (1787); *Così fan tutte* (Women Are Like That, 1789); *Die Zauberflöte* (The Magic Flute, original in German, 1791)

Choral Music: 18 masses: No. 16 (Coronation, 1779); Requiem (1791, unfinished); Exultate jubilate (1773); oratorios; sacred music

*K. refers to Ludwig Köchel (*ker*-shul, 1800–77) an attorney and amateur musician who catalogued most of Mozart's works according to their composition dates. Because of Mozart's pressing need to make money with his compositions, he rarely had time to catalogue his extensive output.

Esterházy Palace, called the "Hungarian Versailles."

HISTORICAL PERSPECTIVE

Haydn's Labor Protest: The "Farewell" Symphony

Haydn's Symphony No. 45 ("Farewell") is an example of his efforts on behalf of musicians. He composed it to protest the fact that members of his orchestra were not permitted to bring their wives and families to the Esterházys' palace in Eisenstadt, about 30 miles south of Vienna. Being away from their families for long periods and having to live in crowded and uncomfortable servant's quarters made life difficult for the musicians.

Haydn composed this clever symphony for one evening's court concert. The first three movements of the symphony were uneventful. In the middle of the fourth movement, according to Haydn's instructions, the second horn player and the first oboist packed up their instruments, blew out their reading candles, and walked out of the hall. Soon, others followed—the bassoonist, the second oboist, cellists and bassists, then the violas and violins. All departing players blew out their candles and made a quiet exit. Finally, with only one candle burning, two violinists finished the symphony.

Haydn's labor protest produced the desired result: Prince Esterházy took the hint and declared an extended leave for the performers to visit their families.

JOSEPH HAYDN (1732–1809)

Born in Rohrau, a little town in eastern Austria near the Hungarian border, Haydn began music studies at an early age. At eight, he received a scholarship to study in Vienna, where he became a member of the Vienna Boy's Choir. Later, he held several court posts as a violinist, composer, and music director.

In 1761, Haydn was engaged as court composer and music director in the courts of the Esterházy family. Powerful and wealthy, this Hungarian family had palaces both in Hungary and in Austria. During his 30-year tenure there, Haydn provided weekly operatic performances and orchestral concerts.

After the death of Haydn's Esterházy patron, the concert impresario Johann Peter Salomon made a special trip from London to offer Haydn a commission. Now in his sixties, Haydn found this period of his career to be fruitful. He wrote his 12 famous "London" symphonies—Nos. 93-104—for the concerts in that city.

Having become a famous and wealthy artist, Haydn spent his remaining years comfortably in Vienna. There he composed his last works, which included the two great oratorios inspired by his London visits—*The Creation* and *The Seasons*.

Among his great contributions, Haydn helped establish the symphony and the string quartet as major instrumental forms. He was a mentor and friend of Mozart and a teacher of young Beethoven.

PRINCIPAL WORKS

Symphonies: 106 symphonies: No. 45 (*Farewell*, 1772); Nos. 82-87, Paris Symphonies; No. 92 (*Oxford*, 1789); No. 94 (*Surprise*, 1791); No. 100 (*Military*, 1794); No. 101 (*Clock*, 1794); No. 103 (*Drum Roll*, 1795); No. 104 (*London*, 1795)

Concertos: numerous concertos for piano, harpsichord, organ, violin, cello, horn, oboe, trumpet

Chamber Music: More than 70 string quartets; 32 piano trios; string trios

Piano Music: 54 piano sonatas

Operas: Six German operas for marionettes, at least 15 operas in Italian (many were lost)

Choral Music: 14 masses; oratorios: *The Seven Last Words of Christ* (1796); *The Creation* (1798); *The Seasons* (1801)

Young Beethoven. Engraving by Johann Neidl after a drawing by Stainhauser.

ᐧᔕ *Concerts in the Classical Period*

Court and Subscription Concerts

Orchestra and chamber music concerts took place mostly at court and at the stately homes of the aristocracy.

With growing frequency, subscription performances were offered in town to the general public. Because few public concert halls existed, many of the early sites were meeting halls.

With their guarantee of prepaid ticket sales, composers began regarding subscription concerts as an important source of income. Mozart wrote many of his orchestral works for public subscription concerts in Vienna. In his later years, Haydn traveled throughout Europe to perform his music at subscription concerts.

CONCERT PROGRAMS   Different from today's programs, eighteenth-century concerts consisted mainly of new music or music by living composers. The composer was usually present, participating either as conductor or soloist. Motivated by the need to create their personal performing repertories, composers had little interest in performing music by other composers.

Because music publishing was not yet very efficient, composers such as Mozart and Haydn had to carry their original, handwritten copies to concerts. Printed music by other composers were hard to come by. Dead composers, no longer around to promote their works, were gradually forgotten. By 1800, therefore, works by Bach, Handel, and others were seldom performed.

Classical Music Forms

Catering to their patrons' wishes for predictability, composers wrote their works in recognizable forms. So fond were audiences of these familiar forms that composers used them repeatedly. Using a similar symphonic plan, Haydn composed 106 symphonies and Mozart, 50. The challenge for the composer was to create fresh, interesting works while using similar forms.

MULTIMOVEMENT PLANS (LARGE FORM)   In addition to the symphony, most multimovement works, such as *string quartets, sonatas,* and *concertos,* used the same forms. That is why, if you've heard one symphony by Haydn, another of his symphonies may sound familiar to you the first time you hear it, and also why music by Haydn may sound similar to music by Mozart.

Typical Multimovement Instrumental Forms

- Concerto (three movements)
- Symphony (four movements)
- String trio and quartet (three or four movements)
- Sonata for solo instrument and piano (three or four movements)

First performance of Haydn's *Creation.*

THE CONCERTO (THREE MOVEMENTS)   Since its development in the Baroque period, the concerto form continued to be an audience favorite in the Classical
period. Featuring a soloist and an orchestra, the concerto allowed great pianists such as Mozart and Beethoven to display their virtuosity. The first and
last movements typically included a *cadenza*, a highly virtuosic solo passage.

The Concerto Plan

FIRST MOVEMENT	***Fast*** (allegro). Usually the most involved and serious movement. Often *sonata form* used as detailed form with the orchestra playing the exposition and the soloist entering on the repeat of the exposition. One or two cadenzas for the soloist in the movement.
SECOND MOVEMENT	***Slow*** (adagio, andante, or similar tempo). Usually a songlike movement, with prominent melody. Many detailed forms used such as sonata, rondo, and theme and variations.
THIRD MOVEMENT	***Fast*** (allegro). Usually having the fastest tempo, with a light and witty style. Often rondo detailed form is used with another cadenza for the soloist.

cadenza

THE CLASSICAL-PERIOD SYMPHONY (FOUR MOVEMENTS)   The overall form of the
four-movement symphony is similar to the concerto with the addition of a
dance movement as the third movement. Most Classical-period symphonies contain *four* movements, or large uninterrupted sections.

Occasionally, composers omitted the dance movement, producing a three-movement symphony with an overall form back in line with the concerto—*fast-slow-fast.*

Typically, the tempo and mood of each movement of the four-movement symphony follows this plan:

The Symphony Plan

FIRST MOVEMENT	*Fast* (allegro). Usually the most involved and serious movement. Occasionally, a slow introduction opens the work. Most often the sonata form is used.
SECOND MOVEMENT	*Slow* (adagio, andante, or similar tempo). Usually a songlike movement, with prominent melody. Many forms used: sonata, theme and variations, rondo.
THIRD MOVEMENT	*Moderately fast* (allegretto or menuetto). The popular dance of the period, the minuet, was used most often for this movement. The form is minuet and trio (song form and trio).
FOURTH MOVEMENT	*Fast* (allegro). Usually having the fastest tempo, this movement ends the symphony with a light and happy mood. Sonata or rondo forms are the most common forms.

Detailed Forms

The four movements of the symphony or the three movements of the concerto are the overall plan or form. Movements are the outer structure, much like the structure of a building. Within each movement, composers organize their music in more specific forms. These forms, then, would be like the detailed infrastructure of a building.

Musical forms are guidelines; a composer may modify them to suit the needs of a particular work. Therefore, from work to work there can be slight differences within the same form. Here are the most commonly used classical forms used for movements in instrumental music:

- Theme and variations
- Rondo
- Minuet and trio (song form and trio)
- Sonata

THEME AND VARIATIONS FORM   A *theme and variations* uses one main theme throughout the movement, usually stated at the beginning of the piece. Then, each succeeding section presents a variation or modification. Because the theme is usually recognizable throughout its transformations, this form is easy to follow.

LISTENING INSIGHTS

How to Listen to Classical Music

The key to enjoying Classical-period music is recognizing and following its *forms*. In no other style period is the understanding of form so important.

Mozart's and Haydn's audiences knew these forms well. Most of them played instruments and had studied music as part of their court education. Knowing the rules of the game, they followed the form with its themes (melody or melodic fragment). They enjoyed noticing the subtle deviations composers used with a particular form.

You can easily follow the overall form (symphony, concerto, sonata) because there are usually pauses between movements. Once you understand the typical plan for these works, you know which movement you are hearing.

Within each movement, the detailed forms are usually built around one or two clearly stated themes or melodies that are repeated several times. As you listen to them, try to remember the themes so that you will recognize them when they return or are modified later in the work.

LISTENING ACTIVITY ~

MOZART, VARIATIONS, "AH, VOUS DIRAI-JE, MAMAN"
(TWINKLE, TWINKLE, LITTLE STAR), K. 265
FORM: THEME AND VARIATIONS

Cassette Tape: Side B, Example 5
Compact Disc 1, Track 43

Listen to this abridged version of Mozart's variations on a popular French children's tune of his day, "Ah, vous dirai-je, maman" (Oh, what do you want me to tell you, mama?) — you may know it as "Twinkle, Twinkle, Little Star." In 1778, while performing in Paris, Mozart heard the tune and wrote twelve variations to it.

Since you probably know the theme, you will be able to recognize it throughout its variations. Mozart clearly states it at the beginning and then repeats it. Notice the differences between the variations.

LISTENING GUIDE

MOZART, VARIATIONS, "AH, VOUS DIRAI-JE, MAMAN"
(TWINKLE, TWINKLE, LITTLE STAR), K. 265
FORM: THEME AND VARIATIONS

Cassette Tape: Side B, Example 5
Compact Disc 1, Track 43
Running time: 2:49

43   0:00   MAIN THEME   moderately fast tempo, duple meter; C major tonality [MAIN THEME] and sections repeated exactly.

44   0:56   VARIATION 1   same tempo, running sixteenth notes (four to a beat) in the upper register incorporate pitches of the main theme; all sections repeated; clear cadence

45   1:53   VARIATION 2   same tempo and key; modified main theme in the upper register while bass plays running sixteenth notes

THEME AND VARIATIONS FORM

A main theme	A¹ variation 1	A² variation 2	A³ variation 3	A⁴ variation 4

RONDO FORM *Rondo* was one of the favorite forms for last movements of concertos and sonatas. Catchy, identifiable rondo themes were also used occasionally in symphonies and string quartets. Listening to a rondo in a fast movement, you will immediately notice its light, humorous style. Though there are many plans for a rondo, its principal ingredients are a recurring main theme contrasted with several shorter, less important themes. The following are the most typical plans:

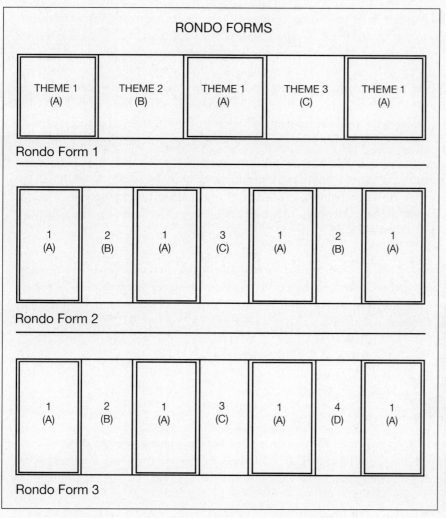

RONDO FORMS

| THEME 1 (A) | THEME 2 (B) | THEME 1 (A) | THEME 3 (C) | THEME 1 (A) |

Rondo Form 1

| 1 (A) | 2 (B) | 1 (A) | 3 (C) | 1 (A) | 2 (B) | 1 (A) |

Rondo Form 2

| 1 (A) | 2 (B) | 1 (A) | 3 (C) | 1 (A) | 4 (D) | 1 (A) |

Rondo Form 3

Mozart, aged 21, four years before departure to Vienna.

HISTORICAL PERSPECTIVE

Mozart Myths Revealed

Over the past two hundred years since Mozart's death at the age of 35, many myths have developed about his life. Recent investigations by physicians, economists, and historians seem to dispel some of these myths.

Lived in Poverty?   That Mozart earned very little money, eked out a meager living, and died impoverished is not true. Mozart was too busy composing to keep accurate records of his finances, and his own accounting omitted major opera and other commissions, as well as many performances. A reasonable estimate of Mozart's earnings would certainly place him in an upper-middle-class category. How much did he earn? Responsible economists have given up their efforts to convert the value of florins in the 1780s to that of today's dollars. The bottom line is that Mozart was no pauper, but rather a moderately affluent composer who chose to live beyond his means. As a young composer who was in demand, he apparently did not anticipate such an early death.

Murdered by a Rival?   Because Mozart's death was premature, its cause was surrounded by mystery. Rumors persisted that Antonio Salieri (1750–1825) of *Amadeus* fame poisoned Mozart out of jealousy. However, newer theories strongly suggest that kidney disease, not poisoning, was the cause.

Dumped into Communal Grave?   It is true that after his death, Mozart was unceremoniously dumped into a common grave at the Central Cemetery of Vienna. However, according to historian Volkmar Braunbehrens (*Mozart in Vienna: 1781–1791*), Emperor Joseph II decreed in 1784 that all bodies were to be buried as follows:

- put in a communal grave far removed from the city
- covered in a linen sack without a coffin
- sprinkled with lime
- left unmarked with no headstones at the grave site.

Sanitary and practical reasons governed the emperor's decree: He wanted to avoid the spread of disease and drinking-water contamination, and to help the bereaved conserve their financial resources. Mozart was treated the same as all other citizens of Vienna during this period.

LISTENING ACTIVITY ❧

BEETHOVEN, SONATA NO. 8 IN C MINOR,
OPUS 13 (*PATHÉTIQUE*)
LARGE FORM: PIANO SONATA
DETAILED FORM: RONDO

Cassette Tape: Side B, Example 6
Compact Disc 1, Track 46

The rondo from Beethoven's Sonata No. 8 (opus 18) has the second of the three forms shown on page 129. Listen especially to the opening main theme, as it will return throughout the work. After several hearings, you should be able to become familiar with the other themes as well. Then, you will really grasp the entire form.

Mozart's apartment in fashionable section of Vienna.

LISTENING GUIDE

BEETHOVEN, SONATA NO. 8 IN C MINOR,
OPUS 13 (*PATHÉTIQUE*)
LARGE FORM: PIANO SONATA; DETAILED FORM: RONDO

Cassette Tape: Side B, Example 6
Compact Disc 1, Track 46
Running time: 4:16

46	0:00	THEME 1	main rondo theme, *p*; fast duple meter; c minor tonality
	0:19	THEME 1	extension after cadence chords and silence
	0:37	[TRANSITION MUSIC]	fast triplet patterns

47	0:48	THEME 2	**p** crescendo to **f**, cadence

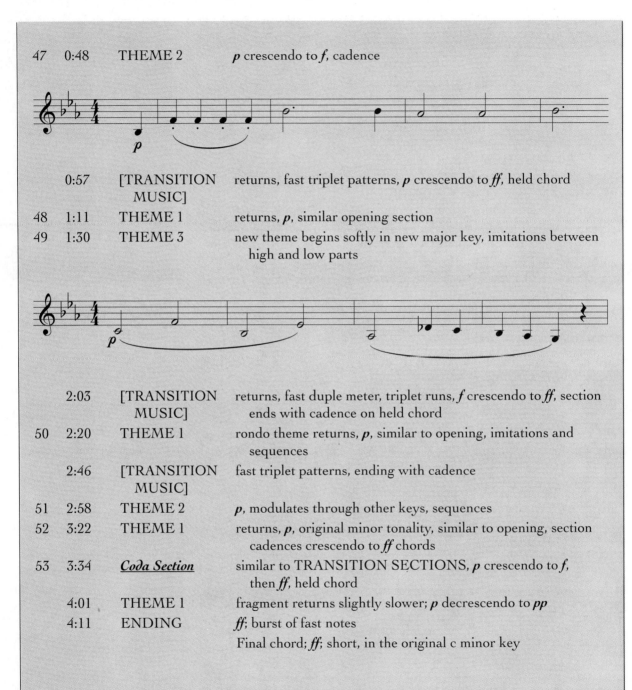

	0:57	[TRANSITION MUSIC]	returns, fast triplet patterns, **p** crescendo to **ff**, held chord
48	1:11	THEME 1	returns, **p**, similar opening section
49	1:30	THEME 3	new theme begins softly in new major key, imitations between high and low parts

	2:03	[TRANSITION MUSIC]	returns, fast duple meter, triplet runs, **f** crescendo to **ff**, section ends with cadence on held chord
50	2:20	THEME 1	rondo theme returns, **p**, similar to opening, imitations and sequences
	2:46	[TRANSITION MUSIC]	fast triplet patterns, ending with cadence
51	2:58	THEME 2	**p**, modulates through other keys, sequences
52	3:22	THEME 1	returns, **p**, original minor tonality, similar to opening, section cadences crescendo to **ff** chords
53	3:34	_**Coda Section**_	similar to TRANSITION SECTIONS, **p** crescendo to **f**, then **ff**, held chord
	4:01	THEME 1	fragment returns slightly slower; **p** decrescendo to **pp**
	4:11	ENDING	**ff**; burst of fast notes
			Final chord; **ff**; short, in the original c minor key

LISTENING ACTIVITY ∽

MOZART: HORN CONCERTO NO. 2 IN E-FLAT
MAJOR, K. 417
THIRD MOVEMENT: ALLEGRO
LARGE FORM: CONCERTO; DETAILED FORM:
RONDO

Cassette Tape: Side B, Example 7
Compact Disc 1, Track 54

The playful rondo movement you are about to listen to is from one of Mozart's four horn concertos, written in his later years in Vienna. Mozart composed these concertos for his friend, hornist Joseph Leutgeb, with whom he had performed in the Salzburg court orchestra.

Knowing that the rondo or Theme 1 is presented at the beginning, be prepared to become familiar with it so that you can recognize it when it returns.

The form of this rondo may be charted as follows:

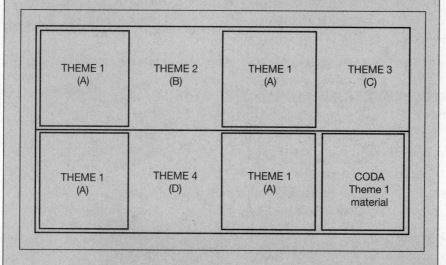

| THEME 1 (A) | THEME 2 (B) | THEME 1 (A) | THEME 3 (C) |
| THEME 1 (A) | THEME 4 (D) | THEME 1 (A) | CODA Theme 1 material |

LISTENING GUIDE

MOZART: HORN CONCERTO NO. 2 IN E-FLAT MAJOR, K. 417
THIRD MOVEMENT: ALLEGRO
LARGE FORM: CONCERTO; DETAILED FORM: RONDO

Cassette Tape: Side B, Example 5
Compact Disc 1, Track 54
Running time: 3:24

54	0:00	THEME 1(A)	horn solo with orchestra accompaniment, rondo theme, homophonic texture, fast, duple-compound meter, E-flat major key
		THEME 1(A)	orchestra without soloist repeats rondo theme, *f*
55	0:18	THEME 2(B)	lighter, same key, horn questions, strings answer
		TRANSITION	fanfarelike transition to cadence, B-flat major
		CADENZA	solo horn featuring trills, transitions back to main theme
56	1:00	THEME 1(A)	exact repeat of opening main rondo theme, horn then orchestra, E-flat major
		TRANSITION	fanfarelike transition
57	1:26	THEME 3(C)	legato (smooth) melody, c minor key, horn solos, strings answer with playful ornaments
		TRANSITION	fanfarelike transition, horn, imitated by strings
58	1:56	THEME 1(A)	similar to opening section, horn solo then orchestra imitation, *f*, E-flat major
59	2:13	THEME 4(D)	legato melody first in solo horn, then imitated by orchestra, *p*
		TRANSITION	similar fanfarelike transition, trills in horn
		THEME 1(A)	fragments of main theme
60	3:04	THEME 1(A)	horn with main theme, orchestra with fanfarelike fragments from transition, faster tempo, solo horn imitates transition fanfare, orchestra imitates, *f*, final cadence in original key of E-flat major

MINUET AND TRIO Mozart and Haydn realized the advantages of keeping the interest and attention of the audiences. Wisely catering to their fondness for dancing, especially the *minuet*, the composers included a minuet as the third movement of many of their symphonies, chamber music pieces, and even in some of their piano music. With its moderately fast tempo in triple meter, the minuet provides an effective contrast to the other movements in multimovement plans.

Minuet

The basic minuet and trio form has three parts:

Trio

MINUET AND TRIO FORM

Minuet Section (A)–strongly rhythmic, triple meter, dance-style

Theme 1	Theme 1–modified

both sections repeat

Theme 2	Theme 2–modified

both sections repeat

Trio Section (A)–lighter, smoother style

Theme 3	Theme 3–modified

both sections repeat

Theme 4	Theme 4–modified

both sections repeat

Minuet Section (A)–same as beginning

Theme 1	Theme 1–modified

usually no repeats

Theme 2	Theme 2–modified

usually no repeats

Schönbrunn Palace in Vienna, the seat of the Hapsburg Empire and the center of court life in eighteenth-century Austria.

HISTORICAL PERSPECTIVE

What Was Haydn's Surprise?

Haydn did not name his Symphony No. 94 "Surprise"—audiences did, because of one loud, unexpected chord (*ff*) in the second movement, following a simple, quiet *andante* theme. In 1791, during the symphony's first performance in London at one of the famous "Salomon" concerts, this surprising chord startled the audience. Haydn later denied having planned the effect "to make the ladies scream."

Sonata-allegro

SONATA FORM   Movements of symphonies, concertos, sonatas, string quartets, and many other works of the classical period often use sonata form. In a fast movement, this is called *sonata-allegro*. Typically, you will hear this form in at least the first movement of a multimovement work.

Haydn and Mozart often used a sonata form for two or three of the four movements in their symphonies. Mozart's Symphony No. 40, for instance, employs sonata form in movements one, two, and four, with minuet and trio form in the third movement.

LISTENING ACTIVITY ❧

HAYDN, SYMPHONY NO. 94 (*SURPRISE*)
THIRD MOVEMENT: ALLEGRO MOLTO
LARGE FORM: SYMPHONY; DETAILED FORM:
MINUET AND TRIO
(SONG FORM AND TRIO)

Cassette Tape: Side B, Example 8
Compact Disc 2, Track 1

Listen to the third movement from Haydn's Symphony No. 94 (*Surprise*). The movement is a typical classical-period minuet and trio.

Follow along with both the Listening Guide and the minuet and trio form chart.

In the minuet section, the strong three-beat meter is obvious. Repeated sections of [THEME 1] and [THEME 2] are typical.

The trio section offers a lighter, more lyrical contrast to the heavier and louder minuet section.

LISTENING GUIDE

HAYDN, SYMPHONY NO. 94 (*SURPRISE*)
THIRD MOVEMENT: ALLEGRO MOLTO
LARGE FORM: SYMPHONY; DETAILED FORM: MINUET AND TRIO
(SONG FORM AND TRIO)

Cassette Tape: Side B, Example 8
Compact Disc 2, Track 1
Running time: 5:32

MINUET (A)

1   0:00   THEME 1   played by violins and bassoons, full orchestra, *f*, then contrasting quieter sections, fast, triple meter, strongly rhythmic dance-style, major key (G major), homophonic texture, sequences

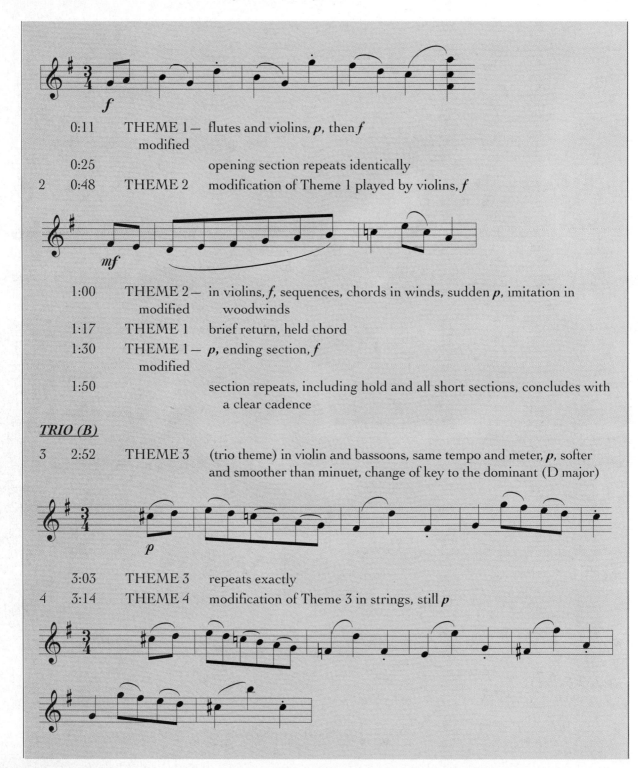

	0:11	THEME 1— modified	flutes and violins, *p*, then *f*
	0:25		opening section repeats identically
2	0:48	THEME 2	modification of Theme 1 played by violins, *f*

	1:00	THEME 2— modified	in violins, *f*, sequences, chords in winds, sudden *p*, imitation in woodwinds
	1:17	THEME 1	brief return, held chord
	1:30	THEME 1— modified	*p,* ending section, *f*
	1:50		section repeats, including hold and all short sections, concludes with a clear cadence

TRIO (B)

| 3 | 2:52 | THEME 3 | (trio theme) in violin and bassoons, same tempo and meter, *p*, softer and smoother than minuet, change of key to the dominant (D major) |

| | 3:03 | THEME 3 | repeats exactly |
| 4 | 3:14 | THEME 4 | modification of Theme 3 in strings, still *p* |

3:40	THEME 4	repeats exactly

MINUET (A)

5	4:04	THEMES 1 & 2	loud, *f*, the minuet section with both themes returns, but without repeating shorter sections, *f*
	5:30		full orchestra, *f*, final chord in G major.

Sonata Form

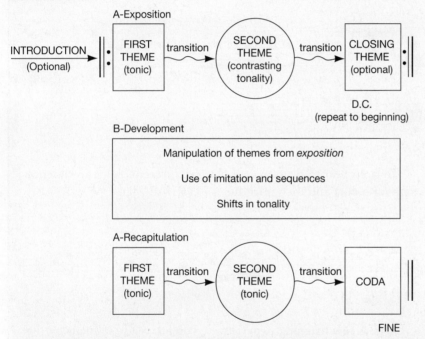

LISTENING ACTIVITY ❧

MOZART, SYMPHONY NO. 40 (G MINOR), K. 550
FIRST MOVEMENT: MOLTO ALLEGRO
LARGE FORM: SYMPHONY; DETAILED FORM: SONATA

Cassette Tape: Side B, Example 9
Compact Disc 2, Track 6

Listen a few times to the first movement—Molto Allegro—of Mozart's Symphony No. 40 in g minor. Use the first hearing just to get acquainted with the overall progress of the work. Subsequent hearings will increase your familiarity with the themes or melodies Mozart has used to take us on a symphonic journey through the form.

The entire movement is constructed from two main themes:

[THEME 1] is a rapid theme which uses sequences and running notes.

To help you find your way, Mozart presents a clear cadence (stopping point) and then introduces [THEME 2].

After a few listening experiences, you are ready to focus on the detailed form of the movement. Because it is in traditional sonata form, you should be able to follow its progress using both the Listening Guide and the Sonata Form Chart.

LISTENING GUIDE

MOZART, SYMPHONY NO. 40 (G MINOR), K. 550
FIRST MOVEMENT: MOLTO ALLEGRO
LARGE FORM: SYMPHONY; DETAILED FORM: SONATA

Cassette Tape: Side B, Example 9
Compact Disc 2, Track 6
Running time: 8:02

Exposition (A)

6	0:00 2:01)	THEME 1	played by violins, full orchestra, *p*, duple meter (4), g minor key, homophonic texture.

7	0:32 (2:33)	TRANSITION THEME	in violins, *f*, complete cadence and pause

8	0:51 (2:52)	THEME 2	played by violin, then clarinet, *p*, major key

	1:27 (3:27)	THEME 1 — fragments	alternating soft and loud
	1:41 (2:01)	THEME 1 — fragments	used for cadence, violins, *f*, cadence, then pause exposition (complete) repeats

		Development (B)	
9	4:00	THEME 1— fragments	played by violins, *p*, fragments in sequence modulates through several keys
	4:05	THEME 1— fragments	*f*, alternating imitations of low strings and woodwinds and sequences
	4:47	THEME 1— fragments	in violins, *p*, imitations between strings and woodwinds, sequences
	5:03	THEME 1— fragments	in violins, *f*, imitated by low strings
	5:12	THEME 1— fragments	in flutes, imitations by clarinets, *p*, sequences, transition to recapitulation

		Recapitulation (A)	
10	5:18	THEME 1	returns in violins, *p*, g minor tonality, similar to opening section
	5:49	TRANSITION THEME	returns in violins, *f*, imitated by low strings and woodwinds, *f*, sequences modulates through several keys
	6:12	TRANSITION THEME	in violins; *f*; scale runs in strings to a cadence; pause
11	6:31	THEME 2	returns in strings alternating with woodwinds, p, crescendo to *f*.
	7:12	THEME 1— fragments	alternating imitations by woodwinds, *p*,
	7:16	THEME 1— fragments	alternating between violins (*f*) and woodwinds (*p*)

		Coda	
12	7:42	THEME 1— modified	in violins, *p*, imitated by viola and woodwinds, *p*
	7:57		cadence of three strong g minor chords in full orchestra, *f*

✠ Classical-period Opera

Opera—the musical theater of the classical period—was the favorite entertainment of both the middle class and the aristocracy. From its debut in Italy around 1600, opera grew in popularity throughout Europe.

Although most concertgoers of today know Haydn and Mozart chiefly through their symphonic, piano, and chamber music, both depended heavily on their operas for a living and a reputation. Haydn composed more than 25, some of which were lost. Of those that remain, six are in German, written for marionette theater, and 19 are in Italian. Of Mozart's 12 major operas, nine are in Italian, and three in German.

Today Haydn's operas are seldom produced, but several of Mozart's are part of the standard repertory for most professional companies: *Don Giovanni, Così fan tutte, The Magic Flute,* and *The Marriage of Figaro.*

Opera Language

Why were most of Haydn's and Mozart's operas in Italian, even though they were written for German-speaking audiences? Because opera first appeared in Italy, the Italian language was considered traditional. Even the German-born Handel, composing operas for his English audiences, preferred an Italian libretto.

Mozart was the first important composer to break this tradition with *The Abduction from the Harem* and *The Magic Flute.* Written in German, both operas were first performed in the *singspiel* or folk theater, rather than in the traditional opera house. The predominantly middle-class audiences spoke only German, and had no interest in Italian opera. To them, opera was a show, and they wanted the show in their native language.

Singspiel
(*Zing*-shpeel)

Many come to know Mozart best through his operas. They demonstrate his genius, his wit, and his uncanny sense of drama. No other composer of his day so keenly understood the qualities of good theater.

Soprano Sheri Greenawald, as Donna Elvira, and baritone Timothy Noble, as Leporello, performing "Madamina" from Mozart's *Don Giovanni.*

Mozart raised opera to new standards. Many of the plots for his operas were daring attacks on the decadence of the aristocracy. *The Marriage of Figaro*, for instance, exposes the aristocracy's frivolous court antics. His *Abduction from the Harem*, with its dancing, choruses of sailors, and light-hearted entertainment, directly influenced nineteenth-century operetta composers, including Gilbert and Sullivan, and modern Broadway musical theater.

LISTENING ACTIVITY ∾

MOZART, *DON GIOVANNI*, "MADAMINA"
LARGE FORM: OPERA, DETAILED FORM, ARIA

❚ *Cassette Tape: Side B, Example 10*
❚ *Compact Disc 2, Track 13*

Before you listen to the aria "Madamina," also known as the "Catalog" aria, from *Don Giovanni*, here is some information on the background and plot of the opera to help place this charming aria in context.

BACKGROUND   Don Giovanni is the Italian name of Don Juan, the legendary Spanish philanderer. Completely disregarding the feelings and ethics of his victims, he seduced his way through Europe with ladies of every class, compulsively gratifying his own pleasures.

Convention-driven audiences of the late 1700s may not have sympathized with this unscrupulous cad, but they were fascinated by his ability to overthrow restrictions in order to follow his heart — or at least his hormones.

Mozart wrote this opera in 1787, eleven years after the American Revolution and two years before the French Revolution. Daringly, Mozart and his librettist, Lorenzo da Ponte (1749-1838), reworked the Don Juan legend to fit contemporary Seville — though any European court would have served as well — and poked fun at the excesses of court life.

PLOT   As the curtain rises, Don Giovanni's servant Leporello is nervously guarding the courtyard, grumbling about having to work so late at night. His unappreciative master has sneaked into young Donna Anna's room to seduce her. With Donna Anna struggling to fight off her attacker, she and Don Giovanni noisily stumble down the palace stairs. Her father, the commandant, comes to her rescue with drawn sword, challenging Don Giovanni to a duel. In the skirmish, Don Giovanni kills the commandant and then flees.

In the second scene, Leporello mockingly consoles Donna Elvira after she complains that his master had seduced and deserted her. In one of the opera's comic moments, Leporello sings the "Madamina" aria. He pulls out a huge scroll, rolls it open across the stage, and summarizes Don Giovanni's numerous affairs with women: 640 in Italy, 231 in Germany, 100 in France, 91 in Turkey, and 1,003 in Spain.

LISTENING GUIDE

MOZART, *DON GIOVANNI*, "MADAMINA"
LARGE FORM: OPERA, DETAILED FORM, BARITONE ARIA

Cassette Tape: Side B, Example 10
Compact Disc 2, Track 13
Running time: 5:53

13   0:00   [orchestral introduction, Allegro, duple meter (4), *p*, major key (D Major)]
　　0:02   [Leporello enters singing softly]

Madamina, il catalogo è questo	My dear lady, this is a list
Delle belle, che amo il padron mio,	Of the beauties my master has loved,
Un catalogo egli è, che ho fatt'io.	A list which I have compiled.
Osservate, leggete con me.	Observe, read along with me.

　　0:23   [orchestral interlude, *f*, continuous downward scales, staccato, like laughter]
　　0:27   [Leporello sings softly]

In Italia seicento e quaranta,	In Italy, six hundred and forty,
In Alamagna dueccento e trentuna	In Germany, two hundred and thirty-one
Cento in Francia, in Turchia, novatuna,	One hundred in France, in Turkey, ninety-one.

　　0:42   [tempo slows and style becomes more lyrical]

	Ma in Ispagna son già mille e tre!	But in Spain, already one thousand and three!
1:02	[gradual crescendo to *f*]	

	V'han fra queste contadine,	Among these are peasant girls,
	Cameriere, cittadine,	Servant girls, city girls,
	V'han contesse, baronesse,	Countesses, baronesses,
	Marchesane, principesse,	Marchionesses, princesses,
	E v'han donne d'ogni	And women of every rank,
	grado, d'ogni forma, d'ogni età!	every shape, every age!
1:22	[repetition of previous melodies, *p*]	

	In Italia seicento e quaranta,	In Italy, six hundred and forty
	In Alamagna duecento e trentuna,	In Germany, two hundred and thirty-one,
	Cento in Francia, in Turchia, novatuna.	One hundred in France, in Turkey, ninety-one.
	Ma in Ispagna son gia mille e tre!	But in Spain, already one thousand and three!
	V'han fra queste contadine,	Among these are peasant girls,
	Camerierei, Cittadine,	Servant girls, city girls.
	V'han contesse, baronesse,	Countesses, baronesses,
	Marchesine, principesse,	Marchionesses, princesses,
	E v'han donne d'ogni	And women of every rank,
	grado, d'ogni forma, d'ogni età!	every shape, every age!
	[The entire opening section comes to a clear cadence.]	

14 2:23	[slower tempo in triple meter, in minuet style, *p*]	

Nel - la   bion - da   e - gli ha l'u - san - za

	Nella bionda egli ha l'usanza	With a blonde it is his habit
	Di lodar la gentilezza;	to praise her kindness;
	Nella bruna, la costanza;	In a brunette, her faithfulness;
2:51	[music oozes sweetness]	
	Nella bianca la dolcezza.	In the light blond, her sweetness.
	Vuol d'inverno la grassotta,	In winter he likes fat ones
	Vuol d'estate la magrotta.	In summer he likes thin ones.
3:12	[crescendo, tempo slows to a held tone]	
	E la grande maestosa,	He calls the tall ones majestic.
3:35	[staccato tones, poking fun]	
	La piccina è ognor vezzosa;	The little ones are always charming.

		Delle vecchie fa conquista	He seduces the old ones
		Pel piacer di porle in lista.	For the pleasure of adding to the list.
15	3:57	[softly, almost spoken]	

Sua passion predominante — His main passion
È la giovin principiante. — Is the young beginner.
Non si picca se sia ricca, — It doesn't matter if she's rich,
Se sia brutta, se sia bella, — Ugly or beautiful
Se sia ricca, brutta, se sia bella — If she is rich, ugly or beautiful.
Purchè porti la gonnella, — As long as she wears a skirt,

Coda

16 4:50 [slower and slower]

Voi sapete quel che fa — You know what happens.
Purchè porti la gonnella, ecc. — As long as she wears a skirt, etc.

fa,_____ quel che fa,_____

5:23 [vocalizing on *fa* and humming]

quel che fa! — You know what happens!
quel che fa! — You know what happens!

5:38 [cadences and running tones in the orchestra]
5:46 [final tones]

Summary of Terms

cadence	recapitulation	song form and trio
concerto	rondo form	string quartet
development	singspiel	subscription performances
exposition	sonata form	symphony
minuet and trio form	sonata-allegro	theme and variation form
opera		

CHAPTER 11

Beethoven: Bridge to Romanticism

*The first association that springs to anyone's mind when serious music is
mentioned is "Beethoven." . . . What is the meat-and-potatoes of every
piano recital? A Beethoven sonata. . . . What did we play in our symphony
concerts when we wanted to honor the fallen in war? The Eroica. . . .
What is every United Nations concert? The Ninth.*

—*Leonard Bernstein**

One of the most troubled yet greatest geniuses in music, Beethoven
changed the course of music and influenced all composers who succeeded
him. Not only did his music become the exemplar for the nineteenth century, but his independence became an inspiration for all musicians.

Beethoven led the way for freelance composers to shed their depen-
dence on noble patrons and achieve financial security as freelance professionals.

*Leonard Bernstein, *The Joy of Music.* New York: Simon & Schuster, 1967.

LUDWIG VAN BEETHOVEN (1770–1827)

From his early years in his native Bonn, Germany, Beethoven (*bay*-toh-ven) showed extraordinary talent at the piano, performing his first public concert at the age of eight. His father, a musician at the court in Bonn, had Ludwig study composition, organ, and violin as well as piano.

At 13, Beethoven was hired as assistant organist at the court in Bonn. In 1790 and again in 1792, Haydn made special trips to see Beethoven on his way from Vienna to London. Haydn encouraged Beethoven's patrons to send young Ludwig to Vienna for more intensive studies. They were convinced, and later in 1792, the 21-year-old Beethoven was off to Vienna, the center of musical life. His music was well received there.

Despite his success, Beethoven was moody and withdrawn. At 26, he began to lose his hearing and in 1802 considered suicide, as documented in his *Heiligenstadt Testament* (see box).

Transcending his increasing deafness, Beethoven actively composed during his entire life. Within his lifetime, his music was performed extensively throughout continental Europe and the United Kingdom—although in his later years he couldn't hear it played. Beethoven was recognized by his contemporaries as the greatest living composer. He died a relatively wealthy man at the age of 56.

PRINCIPAL WORKS

Symphonies: 9 symphonies: No. 3 in E-flat Major (*Eroica*, 1803); No. 5 in c minor (1808); No. 6 in F Major (*Pastoral*, 1808); No. 7 in A Major (1812); No. 9 in d minor (*Choral*, 1824)

Concertos: 5 piano concertos: No. 5 (*Emperor*, 1809); Violin Concerto (1806); Triple Concerto for Piano, Violin and Cello (1804)

Overtures and incidental music: Leonore Overtures nos. 1, 2, and 3 (1805–6); *Coriolan* Overture (1807); *Egmont* Overture (1810)

Chamber Music: 17 string quartets; 5 string trios; piano quintet; sonatas for piano and violin; octet for wind instruments (1793)

Piano Music: 32 sonatas: No. 8 (*Pathétique*), Op. 13; No. 14 (*Moonlight*); Op. 27; No. 2; No. 21 (*Waldstein*), Op. 53; No. 23 (*Appassionata*), Op. 57

Opera: Fidelio (1805)

Choral Music: Mass in D (*Missa solemnis*, 1819–23)

Songs: An die ferne Geliebte (*To the Distant Beloved*), song cycle for tenor and piano (1816)

HISTORICAL PERSPECTIVE

Beethoven's Deafness

Increasing deafness began plaguing Beethoven shortly after his arrival in Vienna in 1792. At the age of 30, he wrote to a boyhood friend, "…my ears continue to hum and buzz day and night. For almost two years I have stopped attending social functions, because I find it impossible to tell people: I am deaf!"

To find a cure, he went from one physician to another, each of whom subjected him to painful but useless treatments. One of his doctors suggested that he take thermal bath treatments in the little town of Heiligenstadt outside Vienna. So during the summer of 1802, a desperate Beethoven rented rooms there and bathed at the local thermal baths.

When by the end of the summer he was no better, a deep depression overcame him. On October 6, contemplating suicide, Beethoven wrote a letter containing his will and testament to his brothers Carl and Johann. Written as a letter addressed to the world and to be opened only after his death, the Heiligenstadt Testament expresses his ambivalence about living or dying.

Composing was a struggle for Beethoven, in contrast to Mozart's fluency. Yet his output was considerable, and his influence on future composers was enormous.

Beethoven was only 18 on July 14, 1789, when Parisians stormed the Bastille and Napoleon Bonaparte was just beginning his military career. Having grown up in a highly formalistic society dominated by the aristocracy, Beethoven witnessed the social changes that ultimately resulted in new forms of government. Through his music, he articulated the transition from Classicism to the freer forms of the Romantic Period.

HISTORICAL PERSPECTIVE

Beethoven's Heiligenstadt Testament

For my bothers Carl and Johann Beethoven

Oh my fellow men, who consider me or describe me as hostile, obstinate, or misanthropic, how greatly you do me wrong. You do not know the secret reason why I appear this way.

Since childhood I have been filled with love of humanity, and a desire to do good things. But for the last six years, I have been afflicted with an incurable complaint, made worse by incompetent doctors. From year to year my hopes for a cure have been gradually shattered. Finally, I must accept the prospect of *permanent deafness* (which may take years to cure, if at all possible).

Though born with a passionate and sociable temperament, I was soon obliged to seclude myself and live in solitude. When I tried to ignore my infirmity, it became worse. Yet I could not bring myself to say to people: Speak up, shout, for I am deaf! Alas! how could I possibly refer to the impairing of *a sense* which should be more perfectly developed in me than in others—a sense which once was perfect.

...Oh, I cannot do it: so forgive me, if I withdraw from you. My pain is double because it makes people misjudge me. But I cannot relax with others, nor even enjoy conversations or mutual confidences. I must live alone, coming out only when necessity demands. When I'm with others, I am filled with burning anxiety that they will notice my condition.

...How humiliating when someone standing beside me has heard a flute playing and *I heard nothing*.

...I have been considering suicide, but my *art* has held me back. For indeed how could I die before I have composed all the music I feel inside.

...Now I realize I must be patient.

...Oh my fellow men, when some day you read this, remember that you have done me wrong. Let me take comfort from the thought that there may be some other unfortunate person who has also risen above the obstacles imposed by nature, to be in the ranks of noble artists and human beings.

You, my brothers Carl and Johann, after my death, ask Professor Schmidt, if he is still living, to describe my disease and to attach this document to his record, so that the world and I may be reconciled as much as possible. I appoint you both heirs to my small property (if I may so describe it). Divide it honestly, live in harmony, and help one another. You know that you have long ago been forgiven for the harm you did me.

I again thank you, my brother Carl, in particular, for the affection you have shown me recently. I hope your life is better and more carefree than mine. Urge your children to be *virtuous*, for only virtue can make a person happy. Money can't. I speak from experience. Only my virtue and my art have kept me from killing myself until now.

Farewell and love one another. I thank all my friends, and especially *Prince Lichnowsky* and *Professor Schmidt*. I would like one of you to take care of Prince [Lichnowsky]'s instruments, provided you do not quarrel over them. If you ever need money, sell them. I shall be glad, in my grave, if I can still do something for you both.

Well, that is all. Joyfully I go to meet Death. If it comes before I have developed all my artistic gifts, then in spite of my hard fate, I would like to postpone it. Even if I do die, I'll be content, for death will free me from this continual suffering. Come, whenever you like, with courage I will go to meet you.

Farewell. When I am dead, I deserve to be remembered by you, because I have often thought of you and tried to make you happy. Be happy.

Ludwig van Beethoven

Heiligenstadt
October 6th
1802

RENEWED CREATIVE MOOD   Emerging from this depression with new determination, Beethoven completed his Symphony No. 2. He went on to compose for another 25 years, producing his greatest music during the last years of his life.

Beethoven's Keyboard Music

BEETHOVEN'S SEARCH FOR A MORE SUITABLE INSTRUMENT   As Beethoven's deafness intensified, so did his demand for more sound from his piano. The keyboards used by his contemporaries, Mozart and Haydn, did not satisfy him—they were not strongly built or versatile enough. Nor were they loud enough for the larger public concert halls that increasingly became the center of concert activity in the nineteenth century. So, in the early 1800s, Beethoven turned to John Broadwood, an Englishman who built both ships and pianos, and to Viennese piano builder Johann Streicher, commissioning them to build larger, sturdier instruments similar to today's concert grands.

The new Broadwood and Streicher pianos were louder and more suitable for the large public concert halls than for the chambers at court or

---

HISTORICAL PERSPECTIVE

Beethoven Meets Mozart

When Beethoven was a young child, his father pressured him to emulate Mozart, first as a keyboard *wunderkind*, and then as a composer. Beethoven might have grown up resenting Mozart, yet he idolized him. It was Beethoven's dream to study composition with the great master, only fourteen years his senior.

In 1787, at the age of 17, Beethoven journeyed from his native Bonn to the great cultural center of Vienna. Historical documentation is missing for much of this short trip; however, several accounts indicate that Beethoven actually met with Mozart briefly and performed for him at his studio.

According to these accounts, Beethoven's first selection was a piano piece he had been practicing. Apparently, Mozart was only mildly impressed with young Beethoven's keyboard ability—Vienna had many gifted young pianists. Sensing this, Beethoven asked Mozart to supply him with a melody upon which he could improvise. Mozart did so, and Beethoven proceeded to dazzle Mozart and his friends with a stirring improvisation. Turning to his friends. Mozart declared, "Keep an eye on this man. Someday he will give the world something to talk about."

After only two weeks in Vienna, Beethoven had to rush to the bedside of his gravely ill mother in Bonn. She died a few days later. Not until 1792 did Beethoven return to Vienna. Mozart had died only months before his arrival.

the rooms in Beethoven's own lodgings. His loud music disturbed the neighbors, and his energetic piano playing in the middle of the night compounded the situation. As a result, Beethoven was evicted from some 80 apartments in and around Vienna. Buildings throughout that city have plaques stating "Beethoven Lived Here."

Beethoven's Orchestral Music

Public concert halls require more sound to fill them than the smaller chambers at court. Because of this, and also because of new avenues of emotional expression that Beethoven was exploring in his music, he began writing for more instruments and increasing the size of the orchestra. He also composed longer and structurally more complex symphonies than Haydn's and Mozart's 20-minute works. Beethoven's Ninth Symphony, for example, takes about one hour and ten minutes to perform.

Beethoven used traditional Classical-period forms, expanding them to fit his Romantic viewpoint. Here are noticeable characteristics of Beethoven's symphonic works:

- The loudness of the orchestra increased along with the number of instruments.
- Developmental sections (free sections or side journeys) occur within almost all sections of the form (exposition, coda, etc.).
- Traditional forms became freer. He treated these forms with great originality in his later works.

Beethoven's Schwarzpanierhaus studio, one of Beethoven's many studios in and around Vienna. The piano in this sketch is a Broadwood.

Concert Hall in the Streicher piano factory in Vienna. Beethoven performed on Streicher pianos in concerts in Vienna.

LISTENING ACTIVITY ✺

BEETHOVEN, SONATA NO. 8 IN C MINOR,
OPUS 13 (*PATHÉTIQUE*)
LARGE FORM: PIANO SONATA; DETAILED FORM: RONDO

Cassette Tape: Side B, Example 6
Compact Disc 1, Track 48
Running time: 4:16

Listen again to the Rondo from Beethoven's Sonata No. 8 in c minor. In Chapter 10, you followed the same work using the Listening Guide. For this hearing, try to follow the form and the musical events without the Listening Guide, as you normally would at a concert.

Beethoven composed this sonata in 1799 during his early years in Vienna. We are not sure why he titled the work *Pathétique*. We do know that he composed it at the onset of his hearing problems, only three years before writing his Heilingenstadt Testament.

The Rondo in *Pathétique* shows a tinge of sadness. Classical rondos are usually extremely jolly, so this minor-keyed rondo tends toward the more melancholy moods of Romanticism. Following a basic rondo form, its main theme keeps returning, alternating with contrasting themes.

Again, the form for this Beethoven rondo is:

Theme 1 (A)	Theme 2 (B)	Theme 1 (A)	Theme 3 (C)	Theme 1 (A)	Theme 2 (B)	Theme 1 (A)

- Music occasionally moves from one movement to the next without the usual breaks.
- Themes from one movement are occasionally restated in another.
- Changes in tempo within a movement are more frequent than in previous Classical-period works.
- Coda or finale sections are usually longer, more elaborate, and triumphant than those of Haydn and Mozart. They usually conclude with repeated, powerful chords.

LISTENING ACTIVITY ❧

BEETHOVEN, SYMPHONY NO. 5,
FIRST MOVEMENT, ALLEGRO CON BRIO
LARGE FORM: SYMPHONY;
DETAILED FORM: SONATA-ALLEGRO

Cassette Tape: Side C, Example 1
Compact Disc 2, Track 17

Following along with the Listening Guide, listen to the first movement of Beethoven's Symphony No. 5 in c minor. Notice how Beethoven builds a monumental structure from a simple idea. The approach is similar to that of an architect who uses a geometric shape such as a rectangle or triangle as the fundamental building shape throughout a structure. Buckminster Fuller's geodesic domes of interlocking polygons are architectural examples.

Beethoven's building idea is the famous theme that he later uses both as a melodic motive and as a rhythmic motive.

The overall form of the first movement is traditional classical sonata form. Notice, however, that Beethoven extends the coda to last as long as each of the other sections.

EXPOSITION (124 measures)
[THEME 1]   [THEME 2]
              holds   horn strings   full orch. exposition
‖: —————————————— . . . . ——————————————:‖ repeats
   ff p–   <f ff p   <f ff   p   < ff   ff
DEVELOPMENT (123 measures)
[THEME 1] fragments
hns. hold   brass
—————————————————————————————————————
ff p–   *crescendo*   ff ff ff diminuendo *pp ff pp ff*
RECAPITULATION(128 measures)
[THEME 1]   [THEME 2]
              oboe solo   bassoons   full orch   codetta
                                  . . . strings   //////
——————————————————————————————————————
ff p   <ff   p < ff   ff   p   *crescendo* ff   ff
CODA (127 measures)
[THEME 1]   [THEME 2]   [THEME 1]
full orch.   alternating
                   strings & woodwinds   :‖
——————————————————————————————————————
ff   f   ff   ff ff pp   ff

LISTENING GUIDE

BEETHOVEN, SYMPHONY NO. 5,
FIRST MOVEMENT, ALLEGRO CON BRIO
LARGE FORM: SYMPHONY;
DETAILED FORM: SONATA-ALLEGRO

Cassette Tape: Side C, Example 1
Compact Disc 2, Track 17
Running time: 7:18

Exposition

| 17 | 0:00 | THEME 1 | played by unison strings and clarinet; *ff*; duple meter, fourth tone |
| | (1:25) | | held, same idea repeated as a sequence in the key of c minor |

	0:06	THEME 1	played softly by second violin, imitated by other strings; c minor;
	(1:31)		crescendo to *f* chords by full orchestra
	0:13	THEME 1	played by full orchestra; *ff*; fourth tone held
	(1:39)		
	0:21	THEME 1	transition section started by violins; *p*; imitations throughout the
	(1:47)		orchestra; crescendos to loud chords, then silence
18	0:48	THEME 1—	French horn introduces next theme; *ff*; major key
	(2:09)	modified	

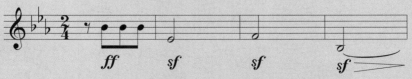

| | 0:46 | THEME 2 | played softly by violins, imitated by clarinets, then flutes; motive of |
| | (2:14) | | Theme 1 played softly by cellos and basses every fourth measure |

Violins

p

19	1:06	THEME 1—	(closing section) played by violins, other instruments added,
	(2:32)	modified	building to loud chords
20	(1:26)	**_Exposition_** repeats	
		Development	
21	2:51	THEME 1	played by French horns; *f*; then strings, with fourth tone held
	2:57	THEME 1	started in violins, then alternating imitations between woodwinds and strings; gradual crescendo
	3:21	THEME 1— modified	full chords in winds, repeated tones of first theme, followed by silence
	3:40	THEME 1— fragments	two-tone motive (part of Theme 1); imitations throughout sections of the orchestra; reducing to one-tone imitations followed by alternating one-tone imitations
	3:51	THEME 1—fragments	
	4:09	THEME 1—fragments	stated suddenly and loudly
		Recapitulation	
22	4:14	THEME 1	played by full orchestra; *ff*; fourth tone held
23	4:32		short oboe cadenza, ending on held tone
	4:44	THEME 1— modified	acts as transition section, starting softly; then getting louder as it is imitated by different instruments
	5:04	THEME 1— modified	played by bassoons
24	5:08	THEME 2	started by violins; *p*; then alternating imitations; gradual crescendo; C major
		Coda	
25	5:43	THEME 1	rhythmic pattern; alternating imitations between winds and strings containing many repeated tones
	5:52	THEME 1— modified	imitations, then two-tone motive developed
	6:05	THEME 2— modified	four-tone pattern; ascending sequences played by strings, then alternating imitations between woodwinds and strings, reducing to two-tone patterns

6:55	THEME 1	full orchestra; *ff*; played twice with fourth tone held
7:04	THEME 1	softly in strings, then suddenly loud by entire orchestra;
7:10		series of loud chords
7:17	[FINAL CHORD]	in c minor

SYMPHONY NO. 6 (PASTORAL)   After the mighty Fifth Symphony, Beethoven began searching for new inspiration and direction for his music. Although not as schooled in the traditional forms as court audiences, his new audiences at public concerts enjoyed the power and emotionalism in his music.

Music notebooks in hand, Beethoven roamed both the Vienna Woods and the Grinzing Woods near Heilingenstadt seeking inspiration. Caught up in the beauty of the countryside, he worked quickly on his new work. Beethoven was touched by the romantic feelings of the woods; the delicate settings; the rustic life of the peasants; the wonders of nature.

Beethoven's Symphony No. 6 depicts the feelings that nature inspired in him. Titling his composition "The Pastoral Symphony, more the expression of feeling than painting" was evidence of that inspiration.

Beethoven goes on to affix highly descriptive phrases to each of the five movements. The goal is to transport the audience out of the concert hall and into nature:

Beethoven's Symphony No. 6 (Pastoral), Opus 68

Movement	Tempo indication	Beethoven's movement titles
First Movement:	Allegro ma non troppo	"The awakening of joyful feelings upon arriving in the country"
Second Movement:	Andante molto mosso	"Scene by the brook"
Third Movement: *(into next movement without a break)*	Allegro	"Merry gathering of country folk"
Fourth Movement: *(into next movement without a break)*	Allegro	"Thunderstorm"
Fifth Movement:	Allegretto	"Happy, thankful feelings after the storm: shepherd's song"

HISTORICAL PERSPECTIVE

Beethoven and the Changing Status of Composers

Before Beethoven, composers were almost totally dependent on either the church or the courts for employment. Mozart, for example, who lost his post with the Archbishop of Salzburg, struggled as a freelance musician. He was just beginning to achieve financial independence when his career ended with his untimely death.

Beethoven succeeded as a freelance musician. When he first arrived in the great musical city of Vienna, he accepted employment by the aristocracy. He tried to fit in, outfitting himself in the newest fashions and even taking dancing lessons. But the clothes made him uncomfortable, and he claimed he had difficulty moving in time with the music.

Beethoven felt out of place among some of his frivolous and snobbish patrons. First of all, he resented having to occasionally use the servants' entrance when he arrived to perform. Furthermore, when members of his audience talked during his playing, he became angry and often walked out in the middle of a piece.

So Beethoven searched for a new audience. Influenced by the social and political change around him, he took control of his life by organizing and performing in concerts for the middle class at the public concert hall or public buildings. What is more, he usually turned a profit.

Toward the end of the eighteenth century, public concerts had grown rapidly in importance. The famous Salomon Concerts from 1791 to 1795 in London enabled the aging Haydn to amass more money than he ever could have from his wages at the Esterházy court. Beethoven studied briefly with Haydn during some of those years. He must have been encouraged by Haydn's financial successes with the London audiences, because Beethoven began developing new public concerts in Vienna.

Music Publishing: A New Source of Income

Mozart had earned negligible royalties from his few published works—some of which were distributed without his knowledge. But Beethoven was a shrewder businessman and knew how to negotiate a profitable deal, often with a sizable advance. Stories are told about his negotiating with two or more publishers at a time, playing them against each other until he won his price. Eventually royalties were his main source of income. Beethoven's success in negotiating encouraged future composers to follow his example.

THE GREAT NINTH SYMPHONY (CHORAL)   Beethoven composed his first eight symphonies over a 12-year span, between 1800 and 1812. Yet it would be another 12 years before he would release his tradition-shattering Ninth Symphony for its first performance. With the Ninth Symphony, Beethoven completely crossed the bridge into Romanticism.

Schiller
(*shill*-er, 1759–1805)

Beethoven attended the premiere performance of this work in Vienna on May 7, 1824, on a program featuring only his music. Word had spread of this premiere, and a large and distinguished audience streamed into the concert hall for the performance. Throughout the concert, they saw the composer himself standing at the podium, next to the conductor.

After the finale, the audience spontaneously rose for a standing ovation—cheering, applauding, waving handkerchiefs. Beethoven heard none of this adulation. Finally, one of the soloists tugged on his sleeve so he would turn around to acknowledge the applause.

For the first time in a symphony, a chorus and vocal soloists performed with the orchestra. Beethoven set to music a poem that seems to have meant a great deal to him throughout his life: Friedrich Schiller's "Ode to Joy." Its main idea embraced the spirit of emerging Romanticism—the joy of the universal brotherhood: "Alle Menchen werden Brüder" (All men become brothers).

Inspired by the grandeur of the Ninth Symphony, Romantic-period composers began writing larger, more emotional works, many containing choruses and soloists delivering texts and stories.

Summary of Terms

Appassionata Sonata	Heiligenstadt Testament	*Pastoral* Symphony
Choral Symphony	*Moonlight* Sonata	*Pathétique* Sonata
Emperor Concerto	Ninth Symphony	rondo form
Eroica Symphony	"Ode to Joy"	sonata form

CHAPTER 1

The Romantic Period (1820–1900)

"The road of excess leads to the palace of wisdom."

–William Blake, Proverbs of Hell

After 1820 and throughout the nineteenth century, Romanticism became the predominant style, not only in music, but in all the arts—a style and outlook that reflected a new concern with emotional expression.

Beholden to the Church and the aristocracy for financial support, artists had worked under tight constraints. Now, with other sources of income open to them, composers no longer had to defer to patrons. Thus liberated, artists could create art by their own standards and for art's sake. Throwing themselves into their work, many were victims of burnout, dying young. Excess, exuberance, and optimism often followed by pessimism and depression characterized this creative mode.

Self-sustaining and self-reliant, arts and artists gave impetus to the lively, great cultural centers—Paris, Vienna, Prague, Budapest, Leipzig, Dresden, Amsterdam, and London. Public concert associations, philharmonic orchestral societies, and opera and ballet companies were established throughout Europe and the United States.

161

Delacroix's "Liberty Leading
the People" (1830).

At last, artists were celebrities—respected members of society. Suddenly they were invited to the homes of the wealthy, not just as entertainers but as honored guests.

Romantic Subjects

In art, literature, and music, the Romantic movement was characterized by intense introspection and a fascination with the supernatural and exotic. Some favorite subjects included:

- nature
- beauty
- love
- death
- the supernatural
- the mystical, magical, and mysterious
- travel, distant lands, and exotic cultures
- adventure
- drug-induced states
- the brotherhood of man
- the individual and the common man
- the superman and hero

Romanticism in Music

EVOCATIVE TITLES FOR MUSICAL WORKS   Romantic subjects inspired evocative titles: Beethoven's *Pastoral* Symphony, Mendelssohn's *Scottish* Symphony, Schumann's *Spring* Symphony, Brahm's *Tragic Overture*, Dukas' *Sorceror's Apprentice*. When listening to these works, we can visualize the stories or images that the titles suggest.

PROGRAM MUSIC   Public support was at a new peak, challenging composers to find ways of communicating with audiences unfamiliar with the classical forms. Composers offered new ideas in the titles and stories, and this influenced audiences to become involved with the passion of the music.

To carry these ideas further, some composers provided a detailed scenario or *program* to follow along with the music. Examples are Berlioz's *Symphonie fantastique*. Liszt's *Faust* and *Dante* symphonies, and Strauss's tone poems, *Don Juan*, *Death and Transfiguration*, and *A Hero's Life*.

EMOTIONAL MUSIC   Romantic composers became fascinated with the possibilities of deep emotional expression offered by expanded use of the musical elements and instrumental tone colors. Audiences were enthralled by these exotic and emotional works.

What about today's audiences? If you examine programs from any major orchestra or opera company, you will find that at least half the music is from the Romantic period. We still favor Romantic music. It gives us an opportunity to experience our feelings.

Overview of the Romantic Period (1820–1900)

Important Composers	Ludwig van Beethoven, Hector Berlioz, Georges Bizet, Alexander Borodin, Johannes Brahms, Anton Bruckner, Frédéric Chopin, Claude Debussy, Henri Duparc, Anton Dvořák, Edward Elgar, Gabriel Fauré, César Franck, Mikhail Glinka, Charles Gounod, Edvard Grieg, Franz Liszt, Gustav Mahler, Felix Mendelssohn, Modest Mussorgsky, Jacques Offenbach, Giacomo Puccini, Nicolai Rimsky-Korsakov, Camille Saint-Saëns, Franz Schubert, Robert Schumann, Jan Sibelius, Bedřich Smetana, Johann Strauss, Jr. and Sr., Richard Strauss, Peter Tchaikovsky, Giuseppe Verdi, Carl Maria von Weber, Richard Wagner
Visual Artists	William Blake, Paul Cézanne, Honoré Daumier, Edgar Degas, Eugene Delacroix, Paul Gauguin, Francisco Goya, Claude Monet, Pierre-Auguste Renoir, Auguste Rodin, Georges Seurat, Joseph Turner, Vincent van Gogh
Writers	Louisa May Alcott, Honoré de Balzac, Anne, Charlotte, and Emily Brontë, Elizabeth Browning, Robert Browning, George Gordon Lord Byron, Anton Chekhov, Samuel Coleridge, Charles Dickens, Emily Dickinson, Fyodor Dostoevski, Nathaniel Hawthorne, Heinrich Heine, Victor Hugo, Henrik Ibsen, Henry James, John Keats, Henry Wadsworth Longfellow, Edgar Allan Poe, Aleksandr Pushkin, George Sand, Percy Bysshe Shelley, Marie-Henri Stendhal, Robert Louis Stevenson, Harriet Beecher Stowe, Alfred Lord Tennyson, William Thackeray, Leo Tolstoy, Mark Twain, Walt Whitman, Oscar Wilde, William Wordsworth
Philosophers	Auguste Comte, Ralph Waldo Emerson, Friedrich Engels, Ernst Haeckel, Georg Hegel, Thomas Henry Huxley, Søren Kierkegaard, Karl Marx, John Stuart Mill, Friedrich Nietzche, Arthur Schopenhauer, Herbert Spencer, Henry David Thoreau

Social, Political, and Cultural Events	Industrial revolution, steamboat, railroads, photography, telegraph, telephone, phonograph, Monroe Doctrine, California Gold Rush, unification of Germany and Italy, reign of Victoria, "Gay '90s," Darwin's *The Descent of Man*, American War Between the States

CHARACTERISTICS OF ROMANTIC MUSIC

General	Music has an emotional, subjective quality with frequent mood changes; expansive sound with large ensembles; intimate music with small ensembles; literature or extra-musical ideas often serve as basis for the music.
Performing Media	Large symphony orchestras, piano, chamber music ensembles, opera and ballet companies
Rhythm	Rubato used often; changing tempos within sections and movements; more complex rhythms than in previous periods
Melody	Long, flowing, emotion-laden melodies; also short themes representing ideas or people; major and minor melodies with chromatic alterations; instrumental melodies with wide leaps and range
Harmony	Tonal (key-centered), but with increasing use of modulations and chromatic tones; rich, complex harmonies
Expression	Full range of dynamics (extremely soft to extremely loud); extensive use of crescendo and diminuendo
Texture	Mainly homophonic (melody with accompaniment); occasional use of polyphony
Forms	Some continued use of Classical period forms; symphony, often with titles; concerto; new, small piano forms (nocturne, ballade, étude, waltz, mazurka); opera, ballet, symphonic tone poem, concert overture; programmatic and descriptive works

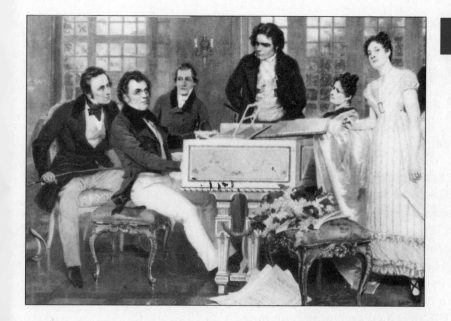

CHAPTER 13

Early Romantic Music

∾ Orchestral Music

Berlioz
(*behr*-ly-ohz)

Hector Berlioz's life typifies the spirit of the Romantic period. Although he placated his father, a respected physician, by attending one semester of medical school in Paris, Berlioz had other plans. And after his first experience with a cadaver, his medical career ended. His own account states:

> At the sight of that terrible charnel-house—the fragments of limbs, the grinning heads and gaping skulls, the bloody quagmire underfoot and the atrocious smell it gave off, the swarms of sparrows wrangling over scraps of lung, the rats in their corner gnawing the bleeding vertebrae—such a feeling of revulsion possessed me that I leapt through the window of the dissecting-room and fled for home...*

*Hector Berlioz, *Memoirs*. New York: Alfred A. Knopf (Publisher of First American Edition). 1969.

Now he could pursue his real interest, music. Though Berlioz had learned to read music, composed a few little works while a youngster, and could perform a few pieces on flute and guitar, he was far from an accomplished musician. His father, fearing that his son's strong interest in music would interfere with his becoming a doctor, blocked his boyhood music studies. Specifically, his father prevented Hector from studying piano, the traditional instrument of composers. Yet at 19, Berlioz pursued his new career with enthusiasm. True to the Romantic spirit that *anything is possible if you really want to accomplish it*, Berlioz studied music in Paris, then in Italy, and eventually became one of the world's greatest composers.

Berlioz's Orchestration

Most composers write at a keyboard because it enables them to work on a number of parts at once. Therefore, their notation of orchestral music usually resembles keyboard music, with occasional suggestions about which instruments might play which ideas. Later, they orchestrate the music — renotate it for full orchestra. The process is similar to that of many painters who first sketch their ideas on a piece of paper. Then, they transfer the idea to a large canvas and develop the painting in a full range of colors.

Because Berlioz could neither compose nor play his works at the piano, he started immediately to notate an entire orchestral score. What started as a handicap — his inability to play the piano — intensified Berlioz's determination. Driven by his vision, he learned about each of the orchestral instruments until he was able not only to compose but to orchestrate brilliantly, setting a standard for those who followed.

HISTORICAL PERSPECTIVE

Berlioz's Innovative Orchestration

Berlioz, the creative orchestrator, treats the listener to many interesting and unusual sounds, featuring unusual instruments and instrumental effects. In the "Witches' Sabbath" from the *Symphonie fantastique*, you will hear a high clarinet (E-flat clarinet) playing sounds that resemble squeaking laughter. Also featured are tubas and chimes, rare in orchestras at that time.

Occasionally, Berlioz calls for the string performers to play with mutes attached to the bridges of their instruments — *con sordini* (con sor-*dee*-nee). Also, he calls for the players to run their bows very close to the bridges, producing eerie, glassy sounds — *sul ponticello* (sool pon-tee-*cell*-o). To simulate dancing skeletons — perhaps an image that remained from his disgust in the dissecting-room — Berlioz requires the string players to turn their bows around and strike the strings with the wood portion to produce a sound like clattering bones — *col legno battuta* (cohl-*len*-yoh bah-*too*-tah).

HECTOR BERLIOZ (1803-1869)

Born in a little town near Lyon, France, Berlioz (*behr*-ly-ohz) began studying music seriously at 19, taking lessons in composition and orchestral instruments in Paris. Because of his late start, he was not accepted as a music student at the Paris Conservatory. Ironically, later in his career he was hired to teach orchestration and composition at the Conservatory.

Objecting to his choice of music for a career, his parents cut off his allowance. To support his studies, Berlioz gave music lessons and held odd jobs in the theater. He struggled until 1830, when he won the prestigious Prix de Rome.

Now with funds, he continued his studies in Rome. When he returned to Paris, he threw himself into composition and was accepted into the Parisian artistic community, which included the musicians Frédéric Chopin and Franz Liszt, the artist Eugene Delacroix, and the writers Victor Hugo and George Sand.

Berlioz, fascinated with instrumental effects and new instruments, employed his latest discoveries in his orchestral works. As a professor at the Paris Conservatory, Berlioz wrote the first important orchestration textbook, *Treatise on Instrumentation*. Because Berlioz was interested in the dramatic quality of music, his works often contain detailed stories.

PRINCIPAL WORKS

Orchestral: Symphonie fantastique (1830); *Harold in Italy* (viola concerto, 1834); *Roméo et Juliette* (Romeo and Juliet, 1839); *Le Carnaval romain* (The Roman Carnival, 1844)

Wind Band: Grande Symphonie funèbre et triomphale (Grand Funeral and Triumphant Symphony, 1840)

Operas: Benvenuto Cellini (1838); *Les Troyens* (The Trojans, 1858); *Béatrice et Bénédict* (1862)

Choral: Requiem (1837); *Te Deum* (1849); *L'enfance du Christ* (The Childhood of Christ, 1854)

(sam-fo-*nee* fahn-tah-*steek*)

SYMPHONIE FANTASTIQUE   The events surrounding the creation of *Symphonie fantastique* exemplify Berlioz's Romantic spirit. In Paris, he attended an English-language performance of Shakespeare's *Hamlet* by a London company. Though he did not understand one word of English, Berlioz became instantly infatuated with the actress who played Ophelia, Harriet Constance Smithson (1800–54).

Vowing to marry her, he began writing letters to her. To further demonstrate his love, Berlioz dedicated his *Symphonie fantastique* to her. He even made Harriet the central character in the symphony by weaving a melody that represented her throughout the fabric of this five-movement, programmatic orchestral work. Berlioz called this type of central theme an *idée fixe*.

Idée fixe
(ee-*day feex*)

HECTOR BERLIOZ AND HARRIET SMITHSON   Dedicating his *Symphonie fantastique* to Harriet Smithson was part of Berlioz's strategy. He invited her to a performance of the work, explaining that she had been the inspiration and was the central character. So impressed was Harriet that she consented to his courtship. Berlioz learned some English. Harriet learned some French. A few years later, they married.

In spite of its romantic beginnings, the marriage came to a stormy ending. With Harriet out of his life, Berlioz was forced to seek other inspirations for his passionate creative genius.

Hector Berlioz at age 29. Oil portrait by Signol (1832).

Harriet Smithson at age 28, after a portrait by Dubufe (1828).

LISTENING ACTIVITY ✣

BERLIOZ, *SYMPHONIE FANTASTIQUE*,
FIFTH MOVEMENT: *"DREAM OF A WITCHES' SABBATH"*
LARGE FORM: SYMPHONY; DETAILED FORM:
SECTIONAL FORM

Cassette Tape: Side C, Example 2
Compact Disc 2, Track 26

Before you listen to the music, read the program that Berlioz wrote for the fifth and last movement of his *Symphonie fantastique*. Because he wanted his audience to know the story Harriet had inspired, Berlioz wrote it out in detail. The entire story is usually printed in the concert program or on the record jacket.

INTRODUCTION

*A young musician of morbid sensitivity and ardent imagination poisons himself with opium in a moment of amorous despair. The narcotic dose, while too weak to kill him, plunges him into deep hallucinations. His strange visions, sensations, feelings, and memories are translated in his brain into musical ideas and images. Even his beloved becomes a melody for him and his fixation with her (*idée fixe*) haunts him.*

FIFTH PART *"Dream of a Witches' Sabbath"*

He sees himself at a Witches' Sabbath. Shadowy figures, sorcerers, and monsters of every kind have gathered for his burial. Strange noises, groans, bursts of laughter, and faraway cries seem to be answered by other cries. He hears the melody of his beloved again, but now lacking its noble and gentle quality, it is nothing more than a dance tune, mocking, trivial, and grotesque.

She (the beloved) arrives at the Sabbath, greeted by shouts of joy. She joins the diabolical orgy...The funeral bell tolls, a burlesque parody of the Dies irae, dies illa *("Day of wrath, O judgment day"). While the day of wrath melody continues, the witches dance.*

The plan Berlioz uses for the last movement of his *Symphonie fantastique* is a *sectional form*:

Introduction
Theme 1—*idée fixe*: "Beloved Theme Modified"
Theme 2—*Dies irae, dies illa:* from the Gregorian chant "Day of wrath, O judgment day"
Theme 3—"Witches' Round Dance." A loosely constructed fugue.
Coda

Here is the original *idée fixe*, the "beloved" melody, introduced in the first movement:

When this melody (*idée fixe*) reappears in the fifth movement, it is transformed into:

LISTENING GUIDE

Berlioz, *Symphonie fantastique*,
Fifth Movement: "Dream of a Witches' Sabbath"
Large Form: Symphony; Detailed Form: Sectional Form

Cassette Tape: Side C, Example 2
Compact Disc 2, Track 26
Running time: 10:20

Introduction

26	0:00		violins and violas tremolo; *pp*; cellos and basses upward swoop; *p* < *mf*, three times capped off with soft thud on bass drum; duple meter (4), moderately slow

	0:11		woodwind-held chords, over rapidly repeated figures in upper strings into pizzicato strings, answered by winds
	0:32	FANFARE MOTIVE	playing staccato (short tones); *f* in piccolo, flutes, and "squeaky" E-flat clarinet ending with downward glissando (smear), imitated by muted horn over bass drum roll; *ppp*
	0:55		similar to opening with upward swoops
	1:20	FANFARE MOTIVE	returns in the same instruments, but louder; *pppp*; muted horn imitates still softer; *mf*; over quiet bass drum roll

Idée Fixe — "Beloved Melody"

27	1:37	THEME 1—fragment "Beloved Melody"	clarinet plays mocking dance style; *ppp*; over percussion; duple meter (2) compound, Allegro

	1:45	[TRANSITION SECTION]	transition section, sudden full orchestra; *ff*; faster, triplet patterns; section ends with clear cadence chord
	1:57	THEME 1 — "Beloved Melody"	played by E-flat clarinet; *f*; accompanied by woodwinds, later flute added to the melody with rapid arpeggio figures in bassoon and cellos; other instruments join in crescendo to *ff*
	2:27	[TRANSITION SECTION]	transition section full orchestra chord; *ff*; then descending and ascending chromatic scale triplet figures into string descending syncopated pattern, changing into descending long tones in bass instruments, quieter to held bass tone
28	3:10	TOLLING BELLS	ominous sounding bells/chimes, *ff*, three sets of three notes C-C-G; each set interrupted by [WITCHES' ROUND DANCE fragment]

Dies Irae

29	3:39	THEME 2 — *Dies irae* part 1	played by tubas, *f*, slow 2 meter, [TOLLING BELLS] continue

Tubas and Bassoons
Allegro

	4:01	THEME 2 — *Dies irae* part 1	imitated by *f* brass section, twice as fast; then imitated by *f* woodwinds and pizzicato strings, twice as fast as brass section; ending with upward swoop similar to the beginning
30	4:17	THEME 2 — *Dies irae* part 2	tubas; *ff*; imitated by pizzicato basses and cellos; then imitated by brass section twice as fast; then woodwinds and pizzicato strings twice as fast as brass section; ending with upward swoop

| 4:43 | THEME 2—*Dies irae* part 1 | returns in tubas and bassoons; *f*; syncopated low strings; brass section imitates twice as fast; then woodwinds and pizzicato strings twice as fast as brass section, ending with upward swoop, [TOLLING BELLS] continue |
| 5:20 | THEME 3—fragment Witches' Round Dance | transition section in strings, *mf*, several times, *crescendo* to cadence chord, *ff* |

violins and violas

Witches' Round Dance (loosely constructed fugue)

| 31 | 5:38 | THEME 3—Witches' Round Dance | duple meter compound, slower tempo; fugue started in low strings, imitated in upper strings; then woodwinds, punctuated by loud, syncopated brass figures; later section quiets down |

7:28	THEMES 2 AND 3— fragments	horns; *f*; [DIES IRAE], strings; *p*; [WITCHES' ROUND DANCE]; long transition over bass drum roll, gradual *crescendo* to loud syncopated figures; section ends with a cadence
7:35	THEME 3—Witches' Round Dance	returns, *ff*, in strings, original tempo, continues through brass entrances
8:33	THEME 2—*Dies irae*	returns in winds, *ff*, continues together with [THEME 3] in strings, *ff*

	9:03	THEME 3—fragments	transition section ("spooky" resembling dancing ghosts and skeletons), trill ornaments in upper strings, *f*, rattling wood part of their bows (*col legno battuta*) over the strings, staccato woodwinds (laughingly), then brass chords, full orchestra-held chord
		CODA	
32	9:41	THEME 2—*Dies irae*	returns in tubas, *f*, twice as fast, then woodwinds twice as fast
	9:42	[CODA MATERIAL]	full orchestra, *ff*, triplet figures dominate, then loud chords, descending chromatic scale in trombones
	10:25	[FINAL CHORD]	held, *ff*

✑ *The Romantic Art Song*

Lied (pl., Lieder)
(leed, leed-er)

The small, intimate *art song* (*Lied* in German) epitomizes Romantic music. A composer of Romantic art songs chose an existing poem—a work that stood on its own—and set it to music to heighten the drama of the text. Subjects included nature, beauty, love, death, and heroism.

Song Cycle

When a group of songs were designed to be performed together, often around a common subject or musical idea, composers placed them in a *song cycle*.

L I S T E N I N G   I N S I G H T S

What to Listen for in Romantic Music

To enjoy Romantic music more fully, look for extra-musical clues that have possibly contributed to the composer's inspiration for the music. The most obvious clues come from the title of the work— *Spring* Symphony, *Faust* Symphony, *Italian* Symphony, *1812 Overture*. Before you listen to the music, anticipate how the composer might convey the title's meaning through the music. While you listen, decide whether the music confirms your images.

Read the printed concert program or notes accompanying the recording for the title and other clues. You may also find background information about the music and the composer in the library.

FRANZ SCHUBERT (1797–1828)

Showing early musical talent, Schubert (*Shoo*-bert) studied violin with his father and piano with his brother. He became a choirboy in the Imperial Chapel of his native Vienna (Vienna Boy's Choir) and, as one of the benefits, he was able to study music and other subjects at Vienna City School. At the age of 13, Schubert studied composition with Salieri.

Schubert did well in school, and at the age of 18 he became a schoolmaster, like his father. But he was unhappy teaching young students and resented the rigidity of the teaching profession. Schubert's real interest was composing, which he was able to do full time when he left his teaching post at age 21.

Schubert's meager income provided him a near-pauper's existence, occasionally alleviated by the help of his more fortunate friends.

His last five years were fraught with illness, but he kept composing until his death at the age of 31. Like Mozart, he died young in Vienna, yet he left the world a bounty of beautiful music.

PRINCIPAL WORKS:

Orchestral: 9 symphonies: No. 5 in B-flat Major (1816); No. 8 (*Unfinished*, 1822), No. 9 (*Great*, 1825); Concert overtures; Incidental music: *Rosamunde* (1823)

Chamber Music: 15 string quartets: *Death and the Maiden* (1824), String Quartet in C (1828); piano quintet: *The Trout* (1828)

Piano Music: 21 sonatas, 6 *Moments musicaux* (1828), impromptus, dances, fantasias, variations, marches

Songs: about 600: "An die Musik" (To Music), "Ave Maria," "Erlkönig" (The Erlking), "Der Wanderer" (The Wanderer), "Die Forelle" (The Trout); Song Cycles: *Die schöne Müllerin* (The Beautiful Maid of the Mill, 1823), *Winterreise* (Winter's Journey, 1827)

Operas: Alfonso und Estrella (1822), *Fierabras* (1823)

Choral Music: 30 choral works, including seven masses

A musical evening with Schubert at the piano and the singer Vogl at his right.

Art Song Performances

Performances of art songs became a favorite entertainment during the Romantic period. Originally held in the homes of the wealthy, these performances were part of an evening that typically included poetry readings and philosophical discussions. Guests included an assortment of poets, novelists, painters, musicians, philosophers, and patrons of the arts. As the popularity of the art song spread, performances often moved to small concert halls and were open to the general public.

PIANIST'S ROLE IN ART SONGS In performing art songs, the singer and the pianist have an equal role. Accompanist and vocalist share the melodic ideas, providing a context for the poetry. The musical dialogue and constant interaction between soloist and accompanist elevate both the poetry and the music to a high artistic plane.

German Art Song Composers

The most notable composers of German art songs (*Lieder*) were Franz Schubert, Robert Schumann, Felix Mendelssohn, Johannes Brahms, Franz Liszt, Hugo Wolf (1860–1903), Richard Strauss, and Gustav Mahler.

French Art Song Composers

Gabriel Fauré (1845–1924) and Henri Duparc (1848–1933) used poems in their native French, as did the twentieth-century composers Claude Debussy, Maurice Ravel, Francis Poulenc, and many others.

Scandinavian Art Song Composers

Of the Scandinavian composers, Edvard Grieg (1865–1931) wrote many of the most beautiful songs in the genre.

LISTENING ACTIVITY ❧

SCHUBERT, *ERLKÖNIG* (*ERLKING*)
LARGE FORM: ART SONG; DETAILED FORM:
THROUGH COMPOSED

**| *Cassette Tape: Side C, Example 3*
| *Compact Disc 2, Track 33***

Before following the Listening Guide and recording of Schubert's *Erlkönig* (Erlking), read the text. In this art song, Schubert chose a poem by one of the great German poets, Johann Wolfgang Goethe (1749–1832). Germanic legend describes the Erlking as a messenger of death who kills everyone he touches. The subjects, death and the supernatural, are typically Romantic.

Notice that there are four character roles in the poem, challenging the singer to distinguish among the characters by using distinctly different voice qualities for each portrayal:

- a narrator
- an ill child
- the child's father on horseback
- the beckoning Erlking

The form for the song is ***through-composed***—the melodies keep changing with little or no return.

through-composed

Notice how the piano, playing its repeated triplet patterns, adds to the agitated mood, and how the accompaniment enhances the ideas in the text.

Schnell (fast)

LISTENING GUIDE

SCHUBERT, *ERLKÖNIG* (*ERLKING*)
LARGE FORM: ART SONG; DETAILED FORM: THROUGH COMPOSED

Cassette Tape: Side C, Example 3
Compact Disc 2, Track 33
Running time: 4:14

33   0:00   triplet patterns in piano continue throughout, f, key of g minor, ominous sounding
triplet runs in bass

0:23   *Narrator*

Wer reitet so spät durch Nacht und Wind?	Who rides so late through the night and wind?
Es ist der Vater mit seinem Kind;	It is a father with his child.
Er hat den Knaben wohl in dem Arm,	He holds the young boy within his arm,
Er faßt ihn sicher, er hält ihn warm.	He clasps him tightly, he keeps him warm.

0:56   *The Father*

"Mein Sohn, was birgst du so bang dein Gesicht?"	"My son, why do you hide your face in fear?"

1:05   *The Child* (with fear)

"Siehst, Vater, du den Erlkönig nicht	"See, father, isn't that the Erlking?
Den Erlkönig mit Kron' und Schweif?"	The Erlking with crown and cape?"

1:22   *The Father* (calming his child)

"Mein Sohn, es ist ein Nebelstreif."	"My son, it's only a misty cloud."

1:32   *The Erlking* (sweetly)

"Du liebes Kind, komm, geh' mit mir!	"You lovely child, come, go with me!
Gar schöne Spiele spiel' ich mit dir;	Such pleasant games I'll play with thee!
Manch' bunte Blumen sind an dem Strand,	The fields have bright flowers to behold,
Meine Mutter hat manch' gülden Gewand."	My mother has many robes of gold."

1:54   *The Child*

"Mein Vater, mein Vater, und hörest du nicht,	"My father, my father, now don't you hear
Was Erlkönig mir leise verspricht?"	What the Erlking whispers in my ear?"

2:07	*The Father*	
	"Sei ruhig, bleibe ruhig, mein Kind;	"Be calm, stay calm, my child;
	In dürren Blättern säuselt der Wind."	The dry leaves rustle when the wind blows wild."
2:18	*The Erlking* (beckoning)	
	"Willst, feiner Knabe, du mit mir geh'n?	"My fine boy, won't you go with me?
	Meine Töchter sollen dich warten schon;	My daughters shall wait on thee,
	Meine Töchter führen den nächtlichen Reih'n	My daughters nightly revels keep,
	Und wiegen und tanzen und singen dich ein.	They'll sing and dance and rock you to sleep.
	Sie wiegen und tanzen und singen dich ein."	And sing and dance and rock you to sleep"
2:36	*The Child*	
	"Mein Vater, mein Vater, und siehst du nicht dort	"My father, my father, can't you see him there
	Erlkönigs Töchter am düstern Ort?"	The Erlking's daughters in that dark place?"
2:49	*The Father*	
	"Mein Sohn, mein Sohn, ich seh' es genau,	"My son, my son, all I can see
	Es scheinen die alten Weiden so grau."	Is just the old gray willow trees."
3:00	triplet patterns in the piano	
3:07	*The Erlking*	
	"Ich liebe dich, mich reizt deine schöne Gestalt,	"I love you, your form enflames my sense;
	Und bist du nicht willig, so brauch' ich Gewalt."	Since you are not willing, I'll take you by force."
3:19	*The Child*	
	"Mein Vater, mein Vater, jetzt faβt er mich an!	"My father, my father, he's now grabbing my arm,
	Erlkönig hat mir ein Leid's getan!"	The Erlking wants to do me harm!"
3:34	*The Narrator*	
	Dem Vater grauset's, er reitet geschwind,	The father shudders, he speeds through the wind,
	Er hält in Armen das ächzende Kind,	He holds the moaning child in his arms,

4:00	*The Narrator* (music slows)	
	Erreicht den Hof mit Müh und Not;	He reaches home with pain and dread:
	In seinen Armen das Kind war tot!	In his arms, the child lay dead!
4:13	final chord in g minor	

ROBERT SCHUMANN (1810–1856)

Schumann (*shoo*-mahn) was born in Zwickau, Germany, near Leipzig. His father, a writer and publisher, sent Robert to Leipzig University to study law. But Robert's strong interests in music and literature distracted him, and he never attended classes.

At 19, he studied piano with Friedrich Wieck (*veek*). It was then that Robert met his teacher's nine-year-old daughter Clara, a piano prodigy. Robert moved into Wieck's home as a lodger the following year. In 1840, he married Clara Wieck, then 21. Clara became one of the nineteenth century's leading concert pianists and greatest exponent of her husband's music. Their famous love affair was the subject of several Hollywood films.

Probably as a result of unsuccessful medical treatments for a sore due to syphilis, Schumann began to have major difficulties with the flexibility of his fingers. It was devastating to his planned career as a piano performer.

Unable to perform in public, he followed his abiding interest in literature and journalism, founding the *Neue Zeitschrift für Musik* (The New Journal for Music), which is still in existence. As its editor and leading writer, Robert became one of the first and finest music critics, calling attention to such creative geniuses as Schubert, Berlioz, Mendelssohn, Chopin, and Brahms.

Toward the end of his life, he was plagued by depression, hallucinations, and erratic behavior. He even attempted suicide by throwing himself into the icy winter waters of the Rhine River. After being rescued from his suicide attempt, Schumann was taken to an asylum, where he died later that year at the age of 46.

PRINCIPAL WORKS

Orchestral Music: 4 symphonies: No. 1 (*Spring*, 1841), No. 3 (*Rhenish*, 1850); Piano Concerto in a minor (1845)

Chamber Music: 23 works for various chamber music groups

Piano Music: "Abegg" Variations, Op. 1 (1830); *Papillons* (Butterflies), Op. 2 (1831); *Carnaval*, Op. 9 (1835); and *Kinderszenen* (Scenes from Childhood)

Songs: Over 275 songs, including several song cycles: *Frauenliebe und Leben* (A Woman's Love and Life, 1840) and *Dichterliebe* (A Poet's Love, 1840)

CLARA [WIECK] SCHUMANN (1819–96)

As early as the age of 21, Clara had written in her diary, "I once thought that I possessed creative talent, but I have given up this idea; a woman must not desire to compose—not one has been able to do it, and why should I expect to?"

At the age of five, Clara began piano lessons with her father, Friedrich Wieck, a noted piano teacher in Leipzig, Germany. She progressed so rapidly that by the age of nine, she performed a full piano recital in the famous Gewandhaus concert hall in Leipzig. The following year her father organized a concert tour, and Clara performed throughout central Europe, traveling as far as Paris. Her fame quickly spread, and by the age of 16 she was recognized as a highly talented child prodigy. Among her admirers were Felix Mendelssohn, Frédéric Chopin, and of course, Robert Schumann, her future husband. After hearing Clara perform, the great virtuoso-pianist Franz Liszt declared that she had "complete technical mastery, depth, and sincerity of feeling."

While still in her teens, Clara had several of her piano compositions published. Because of her widespread fame, she had an easier time at this age getting her works published than most of her women contemporaries. This would change later in her life.

Clara continued concertizing through her teen years with great acclaim. Her successes on the stage were dampened by conflicts in her personal life. Clara and Robert Schumann had fallen in love, much to the chagrin of her father, who felt that marriage to Robert would threaten her brilliant career. Robert had moved in to the Wiecks' house as a 20-year-old piano student and lodger when Clara was only 11. When Clara was 18, Robert asked Professor Wieck to give his permission for Clara to marry him. Friedrich refused, and a bitter legal as well as personal battle began that ended with the law courts ruling that the two lovers could marry. By then, the two lovers were the talk of Europe's musical world.

Clara and Robert married in 1840. Much of Friedrich's concerns became a reality. Clara's performing and composing career waned for several years while she bore eight children, seven of whom lived beyond childhood. Clara tended to a very busy household, which later included a boarder and music student by the name of Johannes Brahms.

After Robert's illnesses, attempted suicide, and eventual death in an asylum, Clara continued both her composing and performing, though in a more limited way. She was no longer the child prodigy, and her composing was thwarted by nineteenth-century prejudice against women's asserting themselves in the arts and commerce.

Clara became a celebrated pianist specializing in the music of both Schumann and Brahms. Clara and Johannes Brahms maintained a caring though mostly long-distance relationship that was rumored to have been quite serious. Mysteriously they destroyed each other's correspondence. In addition to performing as she grew older, Clara became an influential teacher, working for some years at the Leipzig Conservatory of Music and later at the Hoch Conservatory in Frankfurt. She died at the age of 76.

PRINCIPAL WORKS

Orchestral and Chamber Music: Concerto in a minor (1837); Three Romances for Violin and Piano (1853); Trio in g minor for Violin, Cello, Piano (1846)

Piano Music: Romance-Variations on a Theme of Robert Schumann (1853); Soirée musicales (1836); numerous works in many forms, such as variations, caprices, nocturnes, mazurkas, waltzes, and scherzos

Choral Music: Choral Songs for a cappella mixed choir (1848)

Songs: numerous songs (lieder)

Early daguerreotype photograph of Robert and Clara Schumann.

LISTENING ACTIVITY ❧

SCHUMANN, *"WIDMUNG"* (*DEDICATION*)
LARGE FORM: ART SONG; DETAILED FORM:
THREE-PART SONG FORM (A B A)

Cassette Tape: Side C, Example 4
Compact Disc 2, Track 34

Robert composed the song "Widmung" (Dedication) for Clara and had it performed at their wedding. The text is by the German poet Friedrich Rückert (1788–1866).

Notice how the mood of the music and of the poetry fit. For instance, when the text states "Du bist die Ruh', du bist der Frieden"

("You are rest, you are peace"), the music changes from the excited opening to a more peaceful mood. After the singer finishes, the piano continues playing a little postlude with a musical quote from Schubert's "Ave Maria" (Hail Mary) — to show Schumann's heightened devotion to Clara:

Original key

LISTENING GUIDE

SCHUMANN, *"WIDMUNG"* (*DEDICATION*)
LARGE FORM: ART SONG; DETAILED FORM:
THREE-PART SONG FORM (A B A)

Cassette Tape, Side C, Example 4
Compact Disc 2, Track 34
Running time: 2:06

34   0:00   *piano introduction, fast, triple meter, rubato, key of A-flat major,* **mf**

Du meine Seele,	You are my soul,
du mein Herz,	you are my heart
Du meine Wonn',	You are my joy,
o du mein Schmerz,	you are my grief,
Du meine Welt,	You are my world
in der ich lebe,	in which I dwell,
Mein Himmel du,	My heaven,
darein ich schwebe,	wherein I roam.
O du mein Grab,	Oh you my grave
in das hinab	into which
Ich ewig meinen Kummer gab.	I forever cast my grief.

*music calms down, becomes softer, **p**, smoother, key change to C♯ major, later back to F major*

0:33   Du bist die Ruh',   You are rest,
            du bist der Frieden,   you are peace,
         Du bist vom Himmel   You are from heaven
            mir beschieden.   my answer,
         Daβ du mich liebst,   That you love me,
            macht mich mir wert,   bestows on me my worth.
         Dein Blick hat mich   Your glance gives
            vor mir verklärt,   my eyes their light,
         Du hebst mich liebend   Your love transfigures me,
            über mich
         Mein guter Geist,   My good spirit,
            mein besseres Ich!   my better self!

1:00   *music returns to the beginning sections, **f***
         Du meine Seele,   You are my soul,
            du mein Herz,   you are my heart,
         Du meine Wonn',   You are my joy,
            o du mein Schmerz,   you are my grief
         Du meine Welt,   You are my world
            in der ich lebe,   in which I dwell,
         Mein Himmel du,   My heaven,
            darein ich schwebe,   wherein I roam.
         Mein guter Geist,   My good spirit,
            mein besseres Ich!   my better self!

1:46   *musical quote from Schubert's "Ave Maria," rubato and ritardando*

〜 Romantic Piano Music

Nineteenth-century Piano

The piano of the nineteenth century was greatly superior to the earliest versions in Frederick the Great's collection that Bach had found wanting. Enlarged, with an improved mechanism and more keys, the piano was now capable of producing a full range of expression and levels of dynamics. It became the perfect medium with which to display the virtuosity of the Romantic keyboard performer in public concert halls.

Salon Concerts

Salon concerts in the homes of wealthy music enthusiasts became the vogue for piano music as well as for art song performances. The hosts invited a select group of sophisticated guests to hear a piano recital by Chopin, Schubert, Mendelssohn, Clara Schumann (1819–96), Liszt, and the influential piano teacher-composer Anton Rubinstein (1829–1894). To accommodate the general public, these piano recitals were occasionally held in small concert halls.

Anton Rubinstein

FRÉDÉRIC CHOPIN (1810–1849)

Born near Warsaw, Poland, Chopin (sho-*pan*) gave his first piano recital there at the age of eight. Concentrating mainly on piano performance, he studied at the Warsaw Conservatory until he was 19.

Frédéric's father, a Frenchman, had left France to avoid serving in Napoleon's army. In Poland the elder Chopin was a political activist who vehemently opposed the czarist Russian occupation. Because the family lived in fear of reprisal, they thought Frédéric would be safer elsewhere so he could advance his career.

After Frédéric left Poland, he concertized first in Vienna, then throughout Germany. He finally settled in Paris, where the artistic community quickly accepted him. Among his friends were the painter Delacroix, musicians Liszt and Berlioz, and the writers Victor Hugo, Honoré de Balzac, Alexandre Dumas (père), Heinrich Heine, and George Sand.

Sand was actually a woman, Aurore Dudevant. To become published, she was forced to use a man's name and circumvent the prejudice against women writers. She and Chopin lived together for years, and she nursed him through his bouts with tuberculosis. He finally died from the disease at 39. True to the romantic and nationalistic spirit, his body was buried in Paris, but his heart was returned to Poland for burial.

Chopin's legacy of piano compositions are among the greatest ever written.

PRINCIPAL WORKS

Orchestral Music: 2 concertos for piano and orchestra, No. 1 in e minor (1830); No. 2 in f minor (1830)

Piano Music: hundreds of pieces in a variety of short forms: ballades, preludes, fantasies, impromptus, nocturnes, polonaises, scherzos, études (studies), variations, and waltzes

Published Piano Music

The popularity of both the public performances and the salon perform-ances encouraged composers to create and publish an unsurpassed variety of piano music. Learning to play the piano was considered an essential ele-ment of a nineteenth-century education, particularly among middle-class and wealthy families. The demand for published music increased, and com-posers now had a lucrative outlet for their works.

Intimate Piano Music

To take full advantage of the instrument's expressive potential and to hold the interest of their audiences, Chopin, Liszt, Mendelssohn, Brahms, and

---

LISTENING ACTIVITY ~

CHOPIN, *FANTAISIE-IMPROMPTU*, OP. 66
LARGE FORM: SMALL ROMANTIC PIANO FORM;
DETAILED FORM: THREE-PART SONG FORM (A B A)

Cassette Tape: Side C, Example 5
Compact Disc 2, Track 35

Listen to the *Fantaisie-Impromptu* by Chopin. Lasting under five minutes, the piece covers a wide range of expression and allows the performer to dazzle the audience. Notice the slight deviations from steady tempo—*rubato*—which enhance the emotional mood of the piece.

The title, *Fantaisie-Impromptu*, gives two clues to the nature of the music. *Fantaisie*, or "fantasy," denotes whimsy, a fanciful vision, a pleasant daydream. *Impromptu* suggests extemporaneous or impro-vised music. Though Chopin notated the music on paper, he wanted the music to suggest a feeling of spontaneity.

Chopin's melody in the middle section (B) is so appealing that during the 1940s it was turned into a popular song called "I'm Always Chasing Rainbows."

The detailed form, A-B-A, that Chopin uses here is one of the most popular in music. Often called three-part song form because of its extensive use in songs, the first and last sections (A) are similar and bracket a contrasting middle section (B).

LISTENING GUIDE

CHOPIN, *FANTAISIE-IMPROMPTU*, OP. 66
LARGE FORM: SMALL ROMANTIC PIANO FORM;
DETAILED FORM: THREE-PART SONG FORM (A B A)

Cassette Tape: Side C, Example 5
Compact Disc 2, Track 35
Running time: 4:42

Section A

35	0:00	THEME 1	Allegro, duple meter, rubato throughout, sixteen-note patterns in upper voice and triplet patterns in the bass, c-sharp minor tonality, *f* diminuendo to *p*, then brief swells crescendo and diminuendo
	0:48		chromatic runs from high to low, slowing and modulating to D-flat major tonality

Section B

36	1:03	THEME 2	moderate tempo, softer, homophonic texture—melody with ornaments in high voice, rolling triplet arpeggios in bass accompaniment

Section A

37	3:03	THEME 1	presto (very fast) like the beginning, c-sharp minor tonality, crescendos and diminuendos
			chromatic runs from high to low, still c-sharp minor tonality

Coda

	3:57	THEME 2	*ff* gradual diminuendo and slowing of tempo, brief restatement of melody from section B in bass, ending with two rolling chords, very soft

other composers generally wrote fewer of the longer, more formal piano pieces, such as the sonata. Instead, they developed a variety of simple, intimate forms, generally lasting two to five minutes.

- ballades
- capriccios
- consolations
- études (studies)
- fantasies
- impromptus
- mazurkas

- nocturnes
- polonaises
- preludes
- rhapsodies
- scherzos
- songs without words
- waltzes

MENDELSSOHN'S CONCERTS   As the newly appointed conductor of the Leipzig Gewandhaus Orchestra, 26-year-old Felix Mendelssohn addressed his musicians, imploring them to make their orchestra the best in Europe. He was able to motivate them, and they worked harder than ever before. Finally, the orchestra did earn that distinction under Mendelssohn's direction.

To compensate them for their extra work, Felix used his own money to double the salaries of his players. He also established the first pension plan for orchestral musicians. Treated like professionals, they had greater feelings of self-esteem.

Mendelssohn created a new type of concert offering. Until his time, orchestras primarily played works by living composers, with rare performances of music by dead composers. Aware that a wealth of great orchestral music was being neglected simply because the composer was no longer around to promote it, Mendelssohn assembled programs similar to what we find today—works by several composers, from several style periods. He staged concerts featuring Handel's oratorios, Bach's works for chorus and orchestra, and Mozart's and Beethoven's symphonies.

Mendelssohn showcased his contemporaries, too. Struggling composers could come to him for his generous financial help. By featuring their music in his Gewandhaus concerts, Mendelssohn enabled both audiences and publishers to become familiar with the works of Franz Schubert, Robert Schumann, Hector Berlioz, Luigi Cherubini, Franz Liszt, Giacomo Meyerbeer, Johannes Brahms, and Frédéric Chopin.

Hundreds of musicians and composers were indebted to Mendelssohn for his nurturing. During his short life, he served as a catalyst for promoting music as a desirable profession.

FRANZ LISZT (1811–86)

Liszt (*list*) was born near Sopron in the Austro-Hungarian empire. Because Sopron was once predominantly Austrian, Liszt's native language was German. The town is 40 miles south of Vienna and only 12 miles from the Esterházys' Austrian palace in Eisenstadt where Haydn worked. During Haydn's time, Liszt's father was one of the managers of the Esterházys' summer palace in Hungary, which Haydn frequently visited.

Liszt exhibited enormous talent as a pianist and was sent to Vienna to study with Antonio Salieri and Karl Czerny (*chair*-nee) (1791–1857). Following his piano debut in London at 11, Liszt began touring the musical capitals of Europe and was soon considered the greatest piano virtuoso of the nineteenth century.

Settling in Paris at 16, Liszt was quickly welcomed into the inner circles of great artists: Berlioz, Heine, Hugo, Sand, and later Chopin. With Paris as his home base, Liszt toured extensively throughout central Europe, Russia, Turkey, the British Isles, Spain, and Portugal.

At 38, he accepted the position of musical director to the Grand Duke of Weimar (*vy*-mar), near Leipzig. There, Liszt devoted himself mainly to composing and conducting. He also introduced several works of his friend Richard Wagner. That friendship became family when Liszt's daughter, Cosima, married Wagner.

At 50, Liszt moved to Rome and went through a religious stage there, taking minor orders in the Catholic church. Later, he continued traveling and performing until his death at age 74 in Bayreuth (*by*-royt), Germany. Liszt's music is known for its extra-musical associations, either through their titles, or from specific programs.

PRINCIPAL WORKS

Orchestral Music: Faust Symphony (1854); *Dante Symphony* (1856); Symphonic Poems: *Tasso* (1849); *Les Préludes* (1854); Piano Concertos No. 1 in E-flat (1849); No. 2 in A (1849); *Totentanz* for Piano and Orchestra (1849).

Piano Music: Transcendental Studies (1851); *Traveler's Album* (1836); *Six Consolations* (1850); Sonata in b minor (1853); Hungarian Rhapsodies, ballades, études (studies).

FELIX MENDELSSOHN (1809–47)

Felix was born in Hamburg, Germany, into one of Europe's wealthiest and most interesting families. His grandfather, the noted writer and philosopher Moses Mendelssohn (*men*-dl-sun), was a political and financial advisor to King Friedrich the Great of Prussia. (Moses was largely responsible for the assimilation of Jews into German society.) Felix's father, Abraham, started the banking business that influenced European affairs until the Nazi era.

When Felix was an infant, his family moved to Berlin. He began receiving a thorough education through tutors when he was very young. Many people—including Felix's teachers and Goethe, a frequent visitor at the Mendelssohn home—described the boy as "an exceptionally attractive, agreeable, and talented child."

His musical talents were often compared to Mozart's. Performing brilliantly on the piano at an early age, Felix displayed his genius by writing six symphonies by the age of 12, seven more by 14, and *A Midsummer Night's Dream* Overture at 17.

The Mendelssohns' Berlin home was a meeting place for some of the most influential artists and thinkers of the world. Felix's father added the name Bartholdy to the family name because of the pressures of anti-Semitism. Although he tried to pass the name on to his children, they both vehemently rejected its use—Felix often signing letters to his sister, Fanny, "Felix 'not-Bartholdy' Mendelssohn."

Traveling extensively throughout Germany, England, Scotland, and Italy, Felix incorporated his impressions into musical compositions. At 26, he became conductor and musical director of the Gewandhaus (guh-*vahnd*-house, "Cloth Hall") Orchestra in Leipzig, a post he held for the rest of his life.

Also in Leipzig, he founded one of Europe's great schools of music, the Leipzig Conservatory. After the death of his beloved sister Fanny, his health began to fail. Mendelssohn died several months later at 37.

PRINCIPAL WORKS

Orchestral Music: 12 string symphonies; 5 full orchestra symphonies: No. 3 (*Scottish*, 1842), No. 4 (*Italian*, 1833), No. 5 (*Reformation*, 1832); Overtures: *A Midsummer Night's Dream* Overture (1826), *Calm Sea and Prosperous Voyage* (1828), *The Hebrides (Fingal's Cave) Overture* (1830), *Ruy Blas Overture* (1839), Piano Concertos: No. 1 in g minor (1831), No. 2 in d minor (1837); Violin Concerto in e minor (1844)

Chamber Music: 6 string quartets, 2 string quintets

Piano Music: 48 Lieder ohne Worte (Songs Without Words)

Choral Music: oratorios in the Handel tradition: *St. Paul* (1836), *Elijah* (1846).

FANNY MENDELSSOHN (1805–47)

Four years older than her brother Felix, Fanny was described as equally talented. As with Felix, Fanny began piano lessons with her mother. She made such excellent progress in her piano studies that by the age of 13, she could play from memory Bach's entire *Well-Tempered Clavier.* Forgoing a performing career for a husband and a family, Fanny married the painter Wilhelm Hensel. However, she and her family did travel extensively throughout Europe, with extended stays in Milan, Venice, Naples, and Genoa.

Fanny remained an excellent pianist as well as a composer, though most of her compositions were unpublished during her life. Because of the discrimination against women composers, she had to publish six of her songs, which were well received, under Felix's name.

Fanny and brother Felix remained close throughout their short lives, consulting each other on personal as well as on musical matters.

Like her brother, Fanny nurtured new composers at the Elternhaus in Berlin, where she, like Felix, produced performances of their works. Fanny's death at the age of 41 was a dramatic, tragic event. It happened on stage during a rehearsal of Felix's *Walpurgisnacht* cantata at the Elternhaus. Felix was devastated by Fanny's untimely death and went into a deep depression, took ill, and he too died a few months later.

PRINCIPAL WORKS (OVER 200, SOME PUBLISHED WORKS FOLLOW)

Chamber Music: Trio in d minor for Violin, Cello, and Piano (Op. 11)

Piano Music: Romances Without Words (7) (Op. 2, 6, 8); *Der Jahr* (The Year) a suite of 13 pieces, various sonatas

Songs: Six Lieder (Op. 1), Six Lieder (Op. 7); Six Lieder (Op. 9); Five Lieder (Op. 10)

Choral Music: Gartenlieder (17 songs for unaccompanied mixed choir); *Gartenlieder* (6 songs for unaccompanied mixed choir) (Op. 3, 1846); *Nachtreigen* for unaccompanied mixed choir (1829); Oratorio (on Biblical themes), for vocal soloists, chorus, and orchestra (1831)

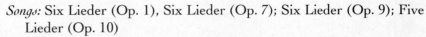

LISTENING ACTIVITY ❧

MENDELSSOHN, CONCERTO FOR VIOLIN AND ORCHESTRA
IN E MINOR, OP. 64 (1844)
FIRST MOVEMENT: ALLEGRO MOLTO APPASSIONATO
(VERY LIVELY AND PASSIONATELY)
LARGE FORM: CONCERTO;
DETAILED FORM: SONATA-ALLEGRO

▌*Compact Disk3, Track 35*

Mendelssohn's Violin Concerto appears only on the compact disc recording and not on the Cassette Tapes. If you have that recording, you can follow along with the Listening Guide. If you are building your personal recording collection, be sure to acquire this popular concerto.

Mendelssohn's Violin Concerto in e minor is one of the most frequently played violin concertos today. He composed the work in 1844 for his friend Ferdinand David, a famous violinist. The concerto is in the typical concerto form of three movements: fast-slow-fast.

Traditionally, audiences would applaud the soloist after the first movement of a concerto, interrupting the mood of music. Inspired by Beethoven's Piano Concerto No. 5 (*Emperor*), Mendelssohn indicates no stops between movements for the audience to applaud. Both composers wanted audiences to concentrate on the music rather than on the soloist.

Mendelssohn, like Beethoven, also wrote out the soloist's cadenzas, insisting that they be played as written. Thus,

Mendelssohn did not allow soloists to improvise or insert their own cadenzas in his violin concerto.

The first movement is in classical sonata form. After only a three-beat quiet orchestral introduction, the violin soloist enters with the main theme. This is a minor departure: In most Classical-period concertos there are two expositions, one by the orchestra and one by the soloist.

One of the outstanding features of this movement is its lyricism. All three melodies—Theme 1, Transition Theme, and Theme 2—are warmly melodic, allowing the soloist to display his or her rich violin tone quality and expressiveness.

LISTENING GUIDE

MENDELSSOHN, CONCERTO FOR VIOLIN AND
ORCHESTRA IN E MINOR, OP. 64 (1844)
FIRST MOVEMENT: ALLEGRO MOLTO APPASSIONATO
(VERY LIVELY AND PASSIONATELY)
LARGE FORM: CONCERTO;
DETAILED FORM: SONATA-ALLEGRO

Compact Disk 3, Track 35
Running time: 11:42

EXPOSITION

35   0:00   THEME 1   in solo violin, *p*, after a three-beat orchestral introduction,
                                  song-like duple meter, e minor tonality

	0:29		solo violin passage, *f*, after short orchestra chords, *f*, repeated in sequence, violin continues with sequences accompanied by orchestra.
	0:57	THEME 1	full orchestra without soloist, *ff*, original tempo and key, section moves into new theme
36	1:29	TRANSITION THEME	introduced by the orchestra, *p*, then played by solo violin, same key (e minor)

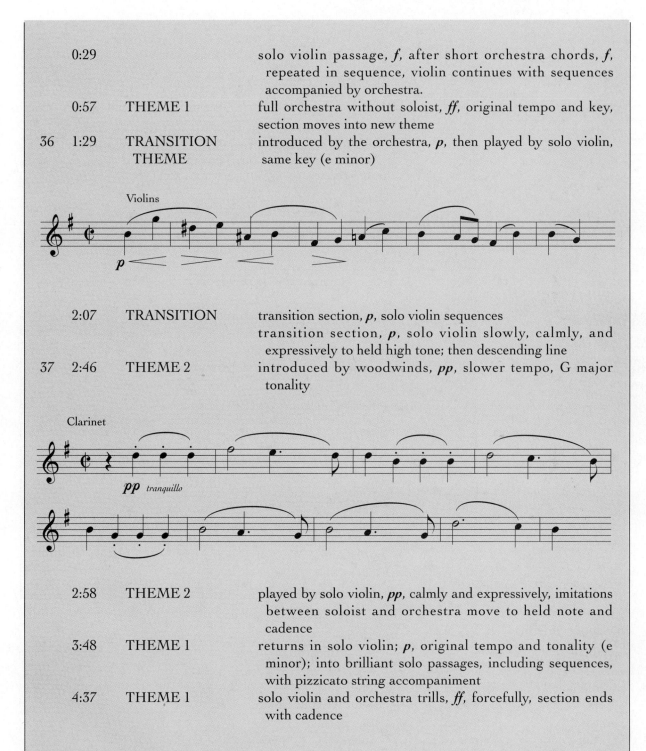

	2:07	TRANSITION	transition section, *p*, solo violin sequences
			transition section, *p*, solo violin slowly, calmly, and expressively to held high tone; then descending line
37	2:46	THEME 2	introduced by woodwinds, *pp*, slower tempo, G major tonality

	2:58	THEME 2	played by solo violin, *pp*, calmly and expressively, imitations between soloist and orchestra move to held note and cadence
	3:48	THEME 1	returns in solo violin; *p*, original tempo and tonality (e minor); into brilliant solo passages, including sequences, with pizzicato string accompaniment
	4:37	THEME 1	solo violin and orchestra trills, *ff*, forcefully, section ends with cadence

DEVELOPMENT

38	4:58	TRANSITION THEME fragments THEME 1—fragments	both used, rubato
	5:57	THEME 1— fragments	in solo violin, **_pp_**, descending sequences, orchestra crescendos to held loud dominant chord
39	6:22	CADENZA	unaccompanied solo violin; arpeggios, trills, fragments of [THEME 1], rapid arpeggios, diminuendo; transition back to orchestra

RECAPITULATION

40	7:51	THEME 1	played softly by the orchestra, original tempo and key
	8:07	TRANSITION THEME— fragments	played first by orchestra, **_ff_**, then sequences, played by solo violin; becomes softer, slows down, modulates to new key
	8:37	THEME 2	returns _first in_ woodwinds, then solo violin, E major tonality; section ends with held high note, and cadence
	9:48	THEME 1— fragments	played softly by orchestra, followed by solo violin passages accompanied by pizzicato strings; orchestra crescendo
	10:28	TRANSITION	loud orchestra chords separate unaccompanied solo violin passage, similar to cadenza
	10:31	THEME 1— fragments	solo violin, **_ff_**, separated by orchestra trills, **_ff_**, then diminuendo

CODA

41	10:54	TRANSITION THEME— fragments	played softly by the solo violin; faster tempo, increasingly faster and louder until the end
	11:38		**_ff_**, e minor, orchestra stops, except solo bassoonist who holds one tone, softly as a transition to the second movement

Summary of Terms

art song	lieder	salon concerts
ballades	mazurkas	scherzos
consolations	nocturnes	song cycle
études	orchestration	songs without words
fantasies	polonaises	tone poems
idée fixe	preludes	waltzes
impromptus	rhapsodies	

CHAPTER 14

Romantic Opera

Opera is dramatized music. With its sung dialogue, elaborate costumes and scenery, cast of characters, and dancing—all accompanied by an orchestra—opera naturally lends itself to Romanticism.

Audiences have always been drawn to opera as a contrast to everyday realism. Though some operas are based on realistic plots, most operas transport you to another time and place, to idealized love, to magic and mystery. Operatic superheros and superbeings can do what no mortal can. By its very nature, then, opera became a very popular medium for nineteenth-century Romantic composers and audiences.

Adding Dimension to Instrumental Music

With singers performing a text in his Ninth Symphony, Beethoven strove to say more than instrumental music alone could convey. With grand opera, all the subjects, spirit, and extra-musical ideas associated with Romanticism materialized in the grandest manner—many within the same opera. Here are a few examples:

- *Fidelio* (1805) by Ludwig van Beethoven
  heroism, love, death
- *Der Freischütz* (1821) by Carl Maria von Weber
  magic, mystery, the supernatural
- *La Traviata* (1853) by Giuseppe Verdi
  love, death, beauty
- *Die Walküre* (1870) by Richard Wagner
  hero, supernatural, love
- *Carmen* (1875) by Georges Bizet
  the common man, love, death, exotic cultures
- *Madama Butterfly* (1904) by Giacomo Puccini
  distant lands, travel, exotic cultures, love, death
- *Turandot* (posthumous, 1926) by Giacomo Puccini
  distant lands, travel, exotic cultures, love, death

Earlier Opera

Until the early nineteenth century, operas were primarily a series of songs (arias and duets). Adhering to tightly knit plots was of little importance to the early opera composers. Choruses and instrumental music served as introductions, interludes, or fillers between songs.

Often, when it was time for an aria, all action on stage stopped. The performers stood frozen in tableau while the soloist crossed downstage and, with little regard for the dramatic situation, delivered his or her aria to the audience. Suddenly the fair maiden, about to die in bed, would throw off her covers, stand up, and sing. Following the aria, the death scene continued. The hero, about to plunge his sword into the villain's chest, postponed the kill until after his aria.

Opera Stars

Since its beginning, opera has attracted loyal fans to hear their favorite singers. Just as they enjoy virtuoso concerto soloists, audiences marvel at a singer's range, special tone quality, and *bel canto* abilities.

Great opera stars are capable of far more than just the musical performance. They transform into the characters they are playing: The resounding bass voice becomes a fierce villain; the ringing tenor with his high "C" becomes the handsome prince; the warm, lilting soprano becomes the fair young maiden.

Quality Plots

Romantic composers—Carl Maria von Weber, Richard Wagner, Giuseppe Verdi, Giacomo Puccini, Georges Bizet, Charles Gounod, and others—

HISTORICAL PERSPECTIVE

Opera in North America

Inaugurated in 1883, the Metropolitan Opera Company in New York City became the first major opera company in North America. Though many limited-season opera companies held occasional performances in various cities throughout North America after 1883, the next permanent opera company did not start until fifty years later, in 1923: the San Francisco Opera Company.

Today, there are more than 50 major opera companies in North America with productions rivaling those anywhere in the world.

elevated the significance and quality of the stories and heightened the drama of their operas. Now, audiences began to come to the opera for its drama, not solely for the vocal abilities of the stars or for the grand spectacle of its production values.

⁓ *Italian Romantic Opera*

Italian Language

Italian composers and the Italian language had dominated opera from its inception. Even Mozart used the Italian language. To continue that dominance into the Romantic Period, early-nineteenth-century Italian composers such as Gioacchino Rossini (roh-*see*-nee, 1792–1868), Gaetano Donizetti (don-ih-*tzeh*-tee, 1797–1848), and Vincenzo Bellini (beh-*lee*-nee, 1801–35) created a new round of exciting Italian operas.

Bel Canto Style of Singing

Romantic-period Italian composers perpetuated the *bel canto* style that characterized early Italian opera. Their aria melodies became elaborate vocal gymnastics, designed to astound audiences with the soloist's virtuosity.

Verdi's Opera Innovations

Both Verdi and Wagner are credited with developing opera into a fully integrated art form. Verdi's characters continued to sing appealing arias, but their songs grew out of the plot more convincingly than ever before. Though audiences still applaud at the end of his arias, Verdi tried to manipulate the action on stage and the orchestration to sustain the mood of the drama throughout the scene without applause.

GAETANO DONIZETTI (1797–1848)

One of the most prolific of all opera composers, Donizetti (don-ih-*tzeh*-tee) was born in the northern lake district city of Bergamo, Italy. He studied opera composition with the German composer Johann Simon Mayr (1763–1845). Some of his early operas were produced in northern Italy, but his career took off with the Rome and Naples productions of his works.

Later, the Parisians came to enjoy his operas because Donizetti spent most of his later years in France and used the French language in his works.

Donizetti became famous for his dazzling arias, such as the "Mad Scene" from *Lucia di Lammermoor*, which requires singers with great flexibility who can reach extremely high tones.

PRINCIPAL WORKS

Operas: 70 operas: *Lucrezia Borgia* (1833); *L'elisir d'amore* (The Elixir of Love, 1832); *Lucia di Lammermoor* (1835); *La Favorita* (1840); *La Fille du regiment* (The Daughter of the Regiment, 1840); *Don Pasquale* (1843)

Other Works: About 100 songs, several symphonies, concertos, oratorios, cantatas, chamber music, and church music.

VINCENZO BELLINI (1801–35)

Bellini's (beh-*lee*-nee) ten operas brought him great success and fame before his death at 33. Like Donizetti, Bellini wrote in both Italian and French and was adored by opera audiences in both Italy and France. Most of his works are still produced regularly today by opera companies around the world.

PRINCIPAL WORKS

Operas: La Sonnambula (The Sleepwalker, 1831); *Norma* (1831); *I Puritani e i Cavalieri* (The Puritans and the Cavaliers, 1835).

GIOACCHINO ROSSINI (1792–1868)

Rossini (roh-*see*-nee) was born in the northern Italian town of Pesaro on the Adriatic coast. After studying music in Bologna, he made his debut as an opera composer in Venice at the age of 18 with a comic opera. His reputation as an entertaining composer quickly spread across Europe, and commissions poured in. Soon he was composing for the important opera houses in Italy, including La Scala in Milan.

A highly prolific composer, by the age of 21 Rossini had composed 10 operas; by the age of 30 he had produced 32 operas—the most famous of that era was *The Barber of Seville*. Composing operas that combined appealing, flowing melodies, wit, comedy, and brilliant stage effects, Rossini became one of the most important composers of the early nineteenth century.

Though he achieved tremendous success and wealth with his outpouring of operas and lived to the age of 75, Rossini unexpectedly stopped composing operas at the age of 37. He wrote his last opera, *William Tell*, using the French language while he was living in Paris.

After a series of disappointing love affairs and bouts with ill health, Rossini turned away from opera. He continued composing mostly religious music and songs throughout the remainder of his life.

PRINCIPAL WORKS

Operas: L'Italiana in Algeri (The Italian Girl in Algiers, 1813), *Il barbiere di Siviglia* (The Barber of Seville, 1816), *La Cenerentola* (Cinderella, 1817), *Semiramide* (1823), *Guillaume Tell* (William Tell, 1829)

Sacred Choral Music: Petite messe solennelle (1864), *Stabat mater* (1841), Masses

Secular Vocal Music: Les Soirées musicales (Musical Evenings, 1835), cantatas

GIUSEPPE VERDI (1813–1901)

Busseto, a small town in northern Italy, was Verdi's (*vehr*-dee) birthplace. And it was there he studied music until the age of 18, when he applied for admission to the Milan Conservatory. But Verdi couldn't pass the entrance examinations because the administrators of the conservatory claimed that his pianistic abilities were substandard. Instead, Verdi had to study with various private music teachers in Milan.

In 1839, Verdi's first opera, *Oberto*, was staged at the famous Teatro alla Scala (La Scala) in Milan. But the joy of this success was negated by the death that year of his wife and two young children, all from a mysterious disease. Fifty-four years and twenty-five operas later, Verdi's last opera, *Falstaff*, premiered at Teatro alla Scala when the composer was 80.

For a time, Verdi became involved in Italian politics and Italy's struggle for independence from the Austro-Hungarian Empire. His name was used as a rally acronym—*Vittore Emanuele Ré D'Italia* (Victor Emanuel, King of Italy). When Victor Emanuel became the first king of a united Italy, Verdi was appointed to the new parliament and was later elected to the Senate. Among his accomplishments was the establishment of a home for retired opera singers and musicians. His death in Milan stirred Italy, and his funeral drew some of the largest crowds in that nation's history.

PRINCIPAL WORKS

Operas: Nabucco (1842), *Ernani* (1844), *Macbeth* (1847), *Rigoletto* (1851), *Il trovatore* (The Troubadour, 1853), *La Traviata* (The Courtesan, 1853), *Un ballo in maschera* (A Masked Ball, 1859), *La forza del destino* (The Force of Destiny, 1862), *Don Carlos* (1867), *Aïda* (1871), *Otello* (1887), *Falstaff* (1893)

Sacred Music: Requiem (1874), *Quattro pezzi sacri* (Four Sacred Pieces, 1889–97)

Summary of Verdi's Opera Innovations

- His libretto (book or story) for each opera was of high quality— adapted from stories by Shakespeare, Hugo, Dumas, and Schiller.
- His characters were believable and human.
- His arias blended into the action.
- His orchestral interludes and accompaniment were highly expressive and contributed substantially to the mood of the entire work.

↝ French Romantic Opera

During the first half of the nineteenth century, the aftershocks of the French Revolution, the turbulent Napoleonic Empire, and the rising middle class all contributed to making Paris an important European political and cultural center. Its elaborate opera productions at this time made it the opera capital of the continent.

Composers of all nations flocked to Paris to have their new works performed—Luigi Cherubini (1760-1842), Gasparo Spontini (1774-1851), Gioacchino Rossini, Gaetano Donizetti, Vincenzo Bellini, and Giacomo Meyerbeer (1791-1864).

French Grand Opera

Designed mainly to appeal to the relatively unsophisticated middle class, nineteenth-century French operas emphasized the spectacle known as *grand opera*. As important as the music was, it was the spectacle that drew audiences. Elaborately costumed crowd scenes, large choruses, plenty of ballet, and lavish sets are the hallmark of French grand opera.

French Comic Opera

Also popular was the less pretentious *opéra comique* (comic opera). With fewer singers and extras and less elaborate staging, *opéra comique* emphasized wit and satire both in the libretto and in the music.

Jacques Offenbach (1819–80) was the first to write in the French comic-opera style. His operas *Orpheus in the Underworld* and *Tales of Hoffman* later influenced the operettas of the famous English team of William Gilbert (1836–1911) and Arthur Sullivan (1842–1900)—*The Mikado, H.M.S. Pinafore, Pirates of Penzance*—and those of Johann Strauss, Jr. (1825–99) in Vienna (*Die Fledermaus* "The Bat," *Zigeunerbaron* "Gypsy Baron"), as well as the Broadway musical of the twentieth century.

Scene from Verdi's opera *Falstaff*.

Cherubini
(keh-roo-*bee*-nee)
Spontini
(spohn-*tee*-nee)
Meyerbeer
(*my*-er-beer)

Offenbach

Gilbert and Sullivan

Strauss

French Lyric Opera

Developing a style with characteristics from both *opéra comique* and grand opera, the French *lyric opera* became popular in the mid-nineteenth century. Its main appeal was its emphasis on melody and romantic or fantasy-based stories.

Many extremely popular operas from this category remain in the repertories of the world's major opera companies: *Faust* by Charles Gounod (1818–93), *Mignon* by Ambroise Thomas (1811–96), and *Carmen* by Georges Bizet (1838–75).

CARMEN One of the most popular operas in music, *Carmen* premiered at the Opéra Comique in Paris in 1875. The opera is also important historically. With its focus on two passionate lovers, Carmen and Don Jose, infidelity, and Carmen's realistic death in the Seville square, the opera began a trend of operatic realism (*verismo*) that inspired, among others, Mascagni's *Cavalleria rusticana* and Puccini's *La Bohème*.

Gounod
(goo-*noh*)
Thomas
Bizet
(bee-*zay*)

GIACOMO PUCCINI (1858–1924)

Born in Lucca, Italy, into a family of church composers and musicians, Puccini (poo-*tchee*-nee) early on planned a career as a church composer. But at 17, when he saw a production of Verdi's *Aïda,* he became hooked on opera. Changing his plans, Puccini enrolled at the Milan Conservatory to study opera composition.

After his studies, Puccini began composing opera, finishing his first, *Le villi,* when he was 25. The famous music publisher Giulio Ricordi was in the audience at that first production in Teatro alla Scala in Milan. He commissioned Puccini to write more operas, and their association lasted throughout Puccini's life.

Many of Puccini's operas are tragic love stories set far from Italy: Japan (*Madama Butterfly*), China (*Turandot*), and even California (*The Girl of the Golden West*).

PRINCIPAL WORKS

Operas: Manon Lescaut (1893), *La Bohème* (The Bohemian Life, 1896), *Tosca* (1900), *Madama Butterfly* (1904), *La fanciulla del west* (The Girl of the Golden West, 1910), *Turandot* (posthumous, 1926)

LISTENING ACTIVITY ❧

PUCCINI, TURANDOT
ACT III ARIA, "NESSUN DORMA"
LARGE FORM: OPERA; DETAILED FORM:
STROPHIC-FORM ARIA

Cassette Tape: Side C, Example 6
Compact Disc 2, Track 38

In 1924, while working on his last opera, *Turandot*, Puccini complained of hoarseness in his throat. Unaware until a month before his death that his discomfort was due to throat cancer, Puccini underwent an operation that at first seemed successful. A few days later his heart failed, and he died before completing the last act of the opera. His student Franco Alfano (1876–1954) completed the opera according to Puccini's notes.

One of Puccini's closest friends and admirers, the great conductor Arturo Toscanini, conducted the premiere of *Turandot* at La Scala in Milan on April 25, 1926. At the point where Puccini had stopped working on the opera, Toscanini halted the performance. After a few words of explanation to the audience, Toscanini left the orchestra pit. The orchestra followed. Then, in relative silence, the cast and audience left La Scala. At the second performance, Toscanini conducted the entire opera, including Alfano's reconstruction of the ending.

Using an abundance of Chinese pentatonic scales, Chinese ceremonies, and imaginative orchestration, Puccini invokes portraits of ancient China. Somewhat reminiscent of Verdi's works, the chorus in *Turandot* is an essential element. Puccini's style of melody and orchestration were a strong influence on Andrew Lloyd Webber's *Phantom of the Opera* and on Boublil and Schönfeld's *Le Misérables* and *Miss Saigon*.

Synopsis of Acts I and II

The setting is ancient Peking, China. Act One opens with a Mandarin's reading a decree to an assembled crowd: Princess Turandot will marry only if a prince of royal blood comes forward and solves her three riddles. However, anyone who attempts but fails to solve them will meet death, the fate about to befall the Prince of Persia. The crowd gleefully calls for the prince's execution. When Turandot appears on the balcony, the people fall to the ground and hide their faces. She signals the executioner, and the Persian dies.

Cristina Deutekom as Turandot and Carlo Bini as Calaf in San Diego Opera's production of *Turandot.*

In the crowd is an unknown prince, driven from his native land after its overthrow. Catching a glimpse of Turandot's beauty, he resolves to win her for himself. He approaches the ceremonial gong to signal his readiness to solve the riddles. Ping, Pang, and Pong, Turandot's ministers, try repeatedly to dissuade the young prince. Nonetheless, he resolutely runs to the gong and strikes it three times.

In Act Two, before the assembled crowd, Turandot poses the three riddles to the unknown prince. He quickly answers the first riddle: "Hope." Considering the second more carefully, the prince replies, "Blood." The suspense mounts as Turandot poses the third riddle: "What is the ice that gives you fire?" The prince answers, "Turandot."

Although all three answers are correct, the princess protests. The prince gallantly offers Turandot an opportunity to get out of her agreement on one condition: If she can discover his name by morning, he is prepared to die.

Act III, Scene 1

Act III opens with a scene in the palace garden. In the distance, heralds sing "Nessun Dorma" (No one shall sleep). They proclaim that the prince's name must be discovered.

Recording:

In one of the most popular tenor arias in opera, the prince repeats those words as he sings "Nessun Dorma." (Full text appears in the Listening Guide.)

After the prince's aria, the crowd reassembles. Turandot's guards drag in a blind old man and Liu, the prince's servant girl, both of whom were seen earlier with the prince. Unknown to the princess, the old man is really the prince's father. The guards start to torture the old man, and to save him, Liu insists that only she knows the prince's name. She is not only loyal, but she loves the prince.

Turandot's guards torture Liu while the prince, restrained by the guards, watches helplessly. Asked how she can endure such torture, Liu answers, "Through my love." When she can bear it no longer, Liu asks the guards to bind her mouth so the prince cannot hear her screams. Then she sees an opportunity to take a dagger from one of the guards. She stabs herself and dies. The old man is grief-stricken and tells Liu that she is kindness itself. He vilifies everyone for having allowed her to die. Fearing his condemnation, the crowd exits, asking Liu's spirit to forgive them. The guards release the prince and exit.

Alone on stage with Turandot, the prince reprimands her for her cruelty and repeatedly professes his love. At first she resists him on the grounds that he must not profane her because she is pure—her soul is in a higher place. The unheeding prince embraces Turandot and kisses her passionately. The princess shows the first signs of relenting.

Dawn is breaking, and the chorus sings a hymn to the morning. Turandot cries for the first time. Touched by her tears, the prince again vows his love and reveals his name to Turandot. He is Calaf, son of Timur. Then, he declares his love for her is so great that he is ready to have her kill him if she wishes.

The scene expands to include the emperor's throne room. Turandot announces to her father and the court that she knows the stranger's name. Anxiously, the crowd waits. "His name is *love*," Turandot proclaims. As she and her beloved come together, everyone sings jubilantly, and the curtain falls.

Eva Marton as Turandot in Act III of Houston Grand Opera's production of Puccini's *Turandot*.

LISTENING GUIDE

PUCCINI, TURANDOT
ACT III, "NESSUN DORMA"
LARGE FORM: OPERA;
DETAILED FORM: STROPHIC-FORM ARIA

Cassette Tape, Side C, Example 6
Compact Disc 2, Track 38
Running time: 3:00

38	0:00	**THE PRINCE**		
		Nessun dorma.	No one shall sleep	
		Nessun dorma.	No one shall sleep	
		Tu pure, o Principessa,	Oh Princess, you are awake	
		nella tua fredda stanza	in your lonely room	
		guardi le stelle	watching the stars	
		che tremano d'amore	that tremble with love	
		e di speranza!	and longing!	
		e di speranza!	and longing!	
	0:49	Ma il mio mistero è chiuso in me,	But my secret is locked within me,	
		il nome mio nessun saprà!	No one will know my name!	
		No, no, sulla tua bocca io dirò	No one until I confess upon	
		quando la luce splenderà!	your mouth!	
39	1:32	**THE PRINCE** *repeat of previous melody with new text*		
		Ed il mio bacio scioglierà	When the dawn breaks!	
		il silenzio	And my kiss shall break the silence	
		che ti fa mia!	that makes you mine!	
	1:50	**CHORUS** *offstage, pp*		
		Il nome suo nessun saprà	What is his name, none shall know	
		E noi dovrem ahimè morir, morir!	And all of us, alas, shall die, shall die!	
40	2:06	Dilegua, o notte!	Vanish, oh night!	
		Tramontate, stelle!	Grow dim, stars!	
		Tramontate, stelle!	Grow dim, stars!	
		All'alba vincerò!	At dawn, I will be victorious!	
		Vincerò! Vincerò!	I will be victorious! Victorious!	
	2:37	**ORCHESTRA CONCLUSION**	*ff; emotional—hurried and rubato, tremolo low strings, cadence and final chord.*	

GEORGES BIZET (1838–75)

Bizet was born in Paris, the son of professional musicians. His father was a singing teacher and composer; his mother, an excellent pianist. Georges was very young when he displayed his talents at the piano, and when he was nine, his parents enrolled him at the Paris Conservatory. There, at 14, he won first prize in piano.

As part of his composition and orchestration studies at the Conservatory, Bizet wrote his now highly popular Symphony No. 1 in C. At 19, he won the Offenbach Prize for a one-act opera, *Le Docteur miracle* (1857). That same year he won the coveted Grand Prix de Rome.

The Grand Prix provided Bizet tuition to study in Rome. As part of the obligations for accepting the Grand Prix de Rome, the recipient must compose a Mass for the Church. Bizet fulfilled his obligation by writing his *Te Deum* (1858).

Returning to Paris, Bizet threw himself into opera composition. However, both audiences and critics received his operas coolly. Even his last and best-known opera, *Carmen*, performed 37 times at the comic-opera theater during its first season, had mixed reviews.

Bizet's untimely death at 36 came at the end of that first season, and he never realized the acclaim his works would receive years later.

PRINCIPAL WORKS

Operas: *Le Docteur miracle* (1857); *Les pêcheurs de perles* (The Pearl Fishers, 1863), *La jolie fille de Perth* (1867), *Djamileh* (1872), *Carmen* (1875)

Orchestral Music: Symphony No. 1 in C (1855), *Vasco da Gama* (1859), a symphonic ode with chorus; Souvenirs de Rome (1869), a symphonic suite; *L'Arlésienne* Suites 1 and 2 (1872)

Choral Music: Cantatas: *David* (1856), *Clovis et Clothilde* (1857), *Te Deum* (1858)

Piano Music: More than 150 piano pieces including *Jeux d'enfants* (1872) for four hands

Katherine Prinz, appearing in the role of Carmen, and Salvador Novoa in the role of Don Jose, in Act IV of Bizet's Carmen.

With the appealing arias, brilliant orchestration, colorful dancing, haunting rhythms, and realistic drama of *Carmen*, it is difficult to understand why its first performances were not received as enthusiastically as they are today. Perhaps its realism was too stark for nineteenth-century audiences who had become used to distant settings and otherworldly stories.

By contrast, *Carmen* draws you into the action until you can empathize with its characters. When Carmen is unfaithful and the tension mounts as Don Jose threatens to kill her, you become anxious that he will carry out his threat. And when he does, the drama becomes real.

჻ German Romantic Opera

Nowhere in Europe was the bonding between music and literature as strong as in Germany. With Mozart's singspiel *Die Zauberflöte* (The Magic Flute) and Carl Maria von Weber's mystical opera *Der Freischütz* (The Freeshooter), German opera composers began using their native German instead of the traditional Italian language.

Imbued with the ideals of Romanticism, German composers sought out librettos incorporating magic, mystery, the supernatural, the mystical, distant lands, exotic cultures, love, and heroes (see Chapter 12). Middle-class audiences were ready to embrace the new subjects and reject the typ-

Der Freischütz
(der *fry*-shoots)

Carl Maria von Weber (1786–1826)

Weber (*vay*-ber) was born in the north of Germany into a family of musicians—Costanze, Mozart's wife, was one of Weber's cousins. Weber's early musical studies were with Michael Haydn (1737-1806), Joseph's brother, in Salzburg. He wrote his first opera at 12 and two more before he was 15.

As a pianist and composer, Weber traveled extensively throughout central Europe, finally settling in Prague as music director for the Prague Opera Company. Weber's most influential opera, *Der Freischütz*, premiered in Berlin. It was a huge success. Audiences were stunned by its special stage effects and mysticism, especially in the Wolf's Glen scene. Weber composed other operas, but none achieved the success of *Der Freischütz*.

Weber never reached his 40th birthday. He died in London at the age of 39 during a production of his opera *Oberon*.

Principal Works

Operas: Der Freischütz (The Freeshooter, 1821), *Euryanthe* (1823); *Oberon* (1826)

Orchestral Music: 2 piano concertos; 2 clarinet concertos; 1 bassoon concerto; Konzertstuck for piano and orchestra (1821); opera overtures: *Der Freischütz, Euryanthe, Oberon*

Choral Music: 2 Masses; 6 cantatas

Piano Music: Invitation to the Dance (1819) [modern transcription for orchestra], 4 sonatas; misc. pieces.

ical court intrigues and farces that had been so popular with the mostly aristocratic audiences of the eighteenth century.

Wagner's Music Dramas

Richard Wagner carried Romantic opera to its extreme. His vision was to create a total art work (*Gesamtkunstwerk*) that he called *music drama*. Toward that goal, he exerted total control: He wrote his own librettos; composed, orchestrated, and conducted the music; designed the sets; and directed the staging.

Gesamtkunstwerk
(guh-*zamt-koonst*-vehrk)

RICHARD WAGNER (1813–83)

Richard grew up in Leipzig, Germany, his birthplace. Although Wagner (*vahg*-ner) claimed he was mostly self-taught in music, he did attend St. Thomas' School, where a century earlier Bach had been choirmaster. Later Wagner continued his music studies at Leipzig University.

At 20, while employed as rehearsal director of the choir in a small opera house in Leipzig, he had a love affair with Minna, one of the sopranos in the chorus. Two years later they were married.

During the next ten years, Wagner and Minna lived in poverty while he was writing his first operas. Their restless, stormy marriage was plagued with infidelities from both sides. After *Rienzi* (1842) was produced, several other successes followed. Wagner's work caught the attention of the King of Saxony, who hired Wagner to be the Saxon State conductor.

In 1848, Wagner became a political activist and published articles calling for revolution. To avoid arrest, he fled to Switzerland. His marriage to Minna ended, and he became involved with a succession of married women.

When Ludwig II, also known as "Mad King Ludwig," was crowned king of Bavaria, one of his first acts was to summon Wagner to Munich to produce operas. There, Wagner married Franz Liszt's daughter, Cosima, with whom he had been having an extended affair.

Cosima, a shrewd businesswoman, used her wiles to inveigle financial backing out of the "mad" king. The Wagners used the money to build Festspielhaus at Bayreuth, devoted entirely to staging Wagnerian operas. Although artistically successful, the productions were far too costly, and the Bavarian treasury always had to subsidize Wagner heavily.

Exhausted after composing his last opera, *Parsifal*, Wagner went for a rest in Venice. He died there of heart failure at the age of 70. Carried by gondola in an elaborate procession down the Grand Canal to the railway station, Wagner's body was transported to Bayreuth for burial.

PRINCIPAL WORKS

Operas: Rienzi (1842); *Der fliegende Holländer* (The Flying Dutchman, 1843); *Tannhäuser* (1845); *Lohengrin* (1850), *Tristan und Isolde* (1865),

Die Meistersinger von Nürnberg (The Mastersingers of Nuremberg, 1868); *Der Ring des Nibelungen* (The Ring of the Nibelung); four operas, 1) *Das Rheingold* (The Rhine Gold, 1869), 2) *Die Walküre* (The Valkyrie, 1870), 3) *Siegfried* (1876), 4) *Götterdämmerung* (Twilight of the Gods, 1876); *Parsifal* (1882)

Orchestral Music: Siegfried Idyll (1870)

Songs: Wesendonk-Lieder (1858)

You might think all that involvement would have satisfied Wagner. Hardly. He persevered until he could design and build his own opera house—Bayreuth—a shrine to himself. Dedicated to performing only his music exactly the way he envisioned it, the opera house continues that tradition today.

Wagner delighted in composing long works, some lasting as long as five hours. As a way of unifying the music and drama throughout these long works and sustaining the interest of his audiences, he used specific melodies and harmonies to represent particular characters or ideas. He called this pervasive theme a **leitmotif** (leading motive). You may recall that Berlioz used this idea (called the *idée fixe*) throughout his *Symphonie fantastique* to represent his beloved Harriet.

Wagner and Hitler

Richard Wagner was and still is a highly controversial figure. He was an artistic genius and wrote great music; however, many feel that as a person, Wagner was despicable. To achieve his ends, he lied, cheated, walked out on debts, exploited people, and had affairs with some of his friends' wives.

LISTENING INSIGHTS

Understanding Wagnerian Opera

One of the keys to following and understanding Wagner's operas is to associate the melodies or leitmotif with the characters or ideas they represent. For instance, when the hero Parsifal silently contemplates his quest for the Holy Grail, the orchestra plays the Holy Grail leitmotif. Although Parsifal isn't singing and action onstage is static, we know that he is thinking about the quest because we recognize the theme.

Born six years after the composer's death, Adolph Hitler embraced Wagner's anti-Semitism. He adored Wagner's music and played it constantly, even during war-strategy meetings. How much was Hitler influenced by Wagner? We'll never really know. But there is an ironic similarity between the ending of the Third Reich and the ending of Wagner's opera *Götterdämmerüng* (Twilight of the Gods).

During the finale of that opera, the great warrior, Siegfried, is killed. His body is then burned on a funeral pyre. But the flames get out of control, and Walhalla, the home of the dead battle heroes, goes up in flames and collapses in the conflagration. To end the opera, the Rhine River overflows, flooding the land and drowning the flames.

Hitler, too, staged his own dramatic finale by deliberately ignoring several opportunities to end World War II, particularly in the last few days when Berlin was surrounded by the allies. Instead of surrendering, Hitler locked himself in a Berlin bunker, leaving the city and thousands of its residents to die in the firestorm following the bombing and shelling of the city. He himself was consumed in flames in his bunker after committing suicide.

Walhalla
(vahl-*hah*-luh)

LISTENING ACTIVITY ॐ

WAGNER, OVERTURE TO DIE MEISTERSINGER
VON NÜRNBERG
LARGE FORM: OPERA OVERTURE

▌*Compact Disc 4, Track 1*

DIE MEISTERSINGER   Die Meistersinger von Nürnberg (The Mastersingers of Nuremberg) concerns the relationship between the creative artist and his critics, the conflict between tradition and innovation. The opera is set in sixteenth-century Nuremberg, Germany, when the craft guilds (professional unions) were at their zenith. Older members of these guilds represent the Establishment—reluctant to upset the status quo. Membership as mastersinger had elevated them into the middle class.

Wagner opens the opera with a scene in the local church in Nuremburg where Walther, a young stranger, spies Eva, the goldsmith's beautiful daughter, seated near him. They become mutually attracted to each other.

After the church service, the town begins preparations for its annual singing contest. We soon learn that it is the contest that brings our young stranger to town hoping to enter the competition.

Seemingly insurmountable bureaucratic hurdles are thrown into Walther's way to prevent him from competing. Even Hans Sachs, a respected member of the Mastersinger's Guild, cannot successfully intercede in Walther's behalf.

The goldsmith has offered his daughter, Eva, and her dowry as the prize to the winner of the singing contest. Further adding interest to the plot, Walther does not yet know Eva is one of the prizes.

On the day of the singing festival, all masters and apprentices of Nuremberg's trade guilds parade onstage. Clad in robes, ribbons, and insignias, they carry their guilds' banners.

Just before the contest, Hans Sachs, favoring Walther, deliberately obscures the rules, saying that audience response will be one of the criteria. Beckmesser, a petty local clerk who also serves as judge, starts the contest with a bungled rendition of Walther's song. When the audience laughs at him, he is furious. Beckmesser's philosophies closely paralleled those of a music critic named Hanslick, who consistently denigrated Wagner's music as departing from tradition.

Hans Sachs seizes the opportunity. He tells everyone that the song is really lovely and suggests that the composer should sing it himself. The mastersingers accede to Sachs' suggestion. Up steps Walther, the composer, who wins the contest with his "Prize Song." Walther claims both his membership in the Mastersinger's Guild and the hand of Eva in marriage.

Listen to the Overture to Wagner's opera *Die Meistersinger von Nürnberg*. An overture or prelude to an opera has the same purpose as in a musical show: to acquaint the audience with the main melodies and to set the mood for the story.

In this overture, Wagner introduces four of the main melodies — *leitmotifs:*

[leitmotif 1] represents the Mastersingers and all that was dependable and noble in the medieval German burgher.

[leitmotif 2] played first by the flute and then by the oboe rep-

Leitmotif
(*lyt*-moh-*teef*)

resents Walther and Eva's love for each other.

[leitmotif 3] introduced by the brass represents the banner and

heritage of the Mastersinger's Guild.

[leitmotif 4] is the Prize Song, a love song in which Walther

imagines Eva in paradise.

The overture climaxes when the full orchestra soars with three

of the four leitmotifs—the Prize Song, the Banner, and the Mastersingers—sounding simultaneously.

LISTENING GUIDE

WAGNER, OVERTURE TO *DIE MEISTERSINGER VON NÜRNBERG*
LARGE FORM: OPERA OVERTURE

Compact Disc 4, Track 1
Running time: 8:39

EXPOSITION

1	0:00	LEITMOTIF 1— Mastersingers	full orchestra, *ff*, moderate march tempo; 4 meter, key of C major
2	0:52	LEITMOTIF 2—Love of Walther and Eva	played by flute and clarinet, imitated by oboe, then flute, then clarinet; *f* with expression, *p* in the strings
	1:20	TRANSITION	transition section; *crescendo* to *f*; violins, starting high, descending in sequences
3	1:30	LEITMOTIF 3— Mastersinger's Heritage	played by brass section, marchlike; strings with upward swoops; *f*
	2:08	LEITMOTIF 1— Mastersingers	played by violins, then joined by winds; *ff*; sequences
	3:07	TRANSITION	transition; agitated fragments in violins; dynamic swells, *f crescendo* to *ff* and back to *f*
4	3:28	LEITMOTIF 4—Walther's Prize Song	played by violins, *p* and expressively, change of key to E major

DEVELOPMENT SECTION

5	4:39	LEITMOTIF 1— Mastersingers	fragments played first by the oboe; *p*; melody is twice as fast as opening, though basic tempo is the same as the opening
	5:49	LEITMOTIF 1— Mastersingers	played by trombones, *f*, original style as opening

POLYPHONIC SECTION

(Leitmotifs 1, 3, and 4 together)

6	6:05	LEITMOTIF 4—Walther's Prize Song	played by first clarinet, first horn, first violin, and cello; *p*; together
		LEITMOTIF 1— Mastersingers	played by bassoon, bass trombone, and string basses; *p*

		LEITMOTIF 3— Mastersinger's Heritage	twice as fast; played by flutes, oboes, horns, violins and violas; *p*
		RECAPITULATION SECTION	
7	8:08	LEITMOTIF 1— Mastersingers	full orchestra, *f*

Summary of Terms

Bayreuth	Gesamtkunstwerk	lyric opera
comic opera	leitmotif	music drama
French Grand opera	libretto	singspiel

CHAPTER 15

Late Romantic Music

✥ State of Music in the Late Romantic Period

By the second half of the nineteenth century, Beethoven's vision for musicians became a reality. As professional composers became highly respected and revered, they also attained financial security. No longer did they have to devote the major portion of their energies promoting and staging concerts of their own works. Throughout Europe, public concert societies had assumed that task.

ADVENT OF PHILHARMONIC AND SYMPHONY ORCHESTRA SOCIETIES Throughout the nineteenth century, most major cities in Europe and the United States were beginning to establish philharmonic and symphony orchestra societies.

HISTORICAL PERSPECTIVE

Early Orchestral Societies in Europe and North America

Founded in 1781, The Gewandhaus Orchestra of Leipzig was one of the earliest permanent orchestras. It was not until 1835, when Felix Mendelssohn took over as conductor, that the orchestra became a full-fledged professional orchestra. As with many orchestras before Mendelssohn, players were only part-time performers. Mendelssohn's Gewandhaus Orchestra inspired other orchestras to attain professional status. Listed below is a brief list of some of the most important orchestras and their founding dates.

1781	Gewandhaus Orchestra, Leipzig	1882	Berlin Philharmonic Orchestra
1842	New York Philharmonic Orchestra	1883	Concertgebouw Orchestra, Amsterdam
1842	Vienna Philharmonic Orchestra	1895	Cincinnati Symphony Orchestra
1874	Cologne Orchestra, Germany	1895	Pittsburgh Symphony Orchestra
1880	St. Louis Symphony Orchestra	1900	Philadelphia Orchestra
1881	Boston Symphony Orchestra	1906	Toronto Symphony Orchestra
1891	Chicago Symphony Orchestra	1935	Montreal Symphony Orchestra

DEMAND FOR NEW MUSIC   As concert audiences expanded throughout the nineteenth century, so did the number of performances. Solo recitals, chamber music, ballet, and opera flourished, creating a constant demand for new music.

Radical Versus the Traditional

Mainstream concert music began to branch into two movements in the mid-nineteenth century. Richard Wagner championed the radical movement; Johannes Brahms, the traditionalist movement. Suddenly, European composers, artists, and audiences took sides. The Schumanns and others sided with Brahms. Liszt and later Richard Strauss were in Wagner's camp.

WAGNERIANS   With formal control now subordinate to emotion, music took new directions. Expanding harmonic movement away from its traditional tonic or home key rooting, Wagner and his followers embraced a wandering tonality, conveying the feeling of an extended journey. Using loose and often vague forms, composers began to rely increasingly on extra-musical associations (stories, ideas, poems) for continuity. They built their symphonic poems, overtures, symphonies, and chamber music around programs or descriptive titles.

BRAHMSIANS   To those composers who aligned with Brahms, formal control still mattered. They adhered to the classical traditions of Haydn, Mozart, Schubert, and especially Beethoven. Tonality and form, they believed, should remain recognizable, with minimal extra-musical associations and overcharged emotionalism.

Continuing the classical tradition, both Schumann and Brahms focused their efforts on chamber music, three-movement concertos, and four-movement symphonies. Of the two, only Robert Schumann attempted to write an opera, though his *Genoveva* is rarely performed today.

Brahms's Orchestral Music

Brahms idolized Beethoven. So much in awe was he of Beethoven's nine symphonies that Brahms labored over his own First Symphony for 20 years, reworking it until he felt he had finally attained the Beethoven standard. He was right: Audiences hailed the first performance of Brahms's First Symphony as "Beethoven's Tenth."

Unlike Beethoven, Brahms was not an innovator. Proudly declaring himself a musical conservative, he avoided extreme changes in musical expression as proposed by the followers of Lizst and Wagner.

Brahms and Beethoven had many similarities. Both were born in Germany and composed their major works in Vienna. Both profited from freelance employment and publishing royalties. Both expressed their love of mankind yet led reclusive lives, devoting their main creative energies to their art, never marrying.

Brahms's desire for personal freedom seems to have superseded his ability to develop close personal relationships. Although he had been in love with Clara Schumann for many years, he moved away from her after Robert Schumann's death. Possibly it was a conflict between his love for her and his devotion to his mentor that drove Brahms from Düsseldorf. Yet he remained close to Clara and loved her seven children throughout his life. Perhaps it was due to their age difference—Clara was 14 years older than he. In Brahms's own family, though, his mother was 17 years older than his father.

A mystery in Brahms's life was his deliberate avoidance of obligations that might restrict his freedom. A fine conductor and recognized as the foremost musician of his time, Brahms could have secured any post he wanted. Yet he accepted only minor positions—coaching women's choirs and directing minor orchestras. Throughout his life he remained a freelance musician, earning his living from private teaching, publishing royalties, occasional piano performances, and guest conducting appearances.

JOHANNES BRAHMS (1833–97)

Brahms's first piano teacher was his father, a bass player in a salon orchestra in Hamburg, Germany. To add to the family income, Brahms began playing at 17 in bars and brothels of the seedy Reeperbahn and dock sections of his home town. His enormous talent soon became evident to concert musicians, and at 20 he began a three-year tour with the Hungarian violinist Remenyi, considered the best European violinist of his time.

After this experience, Brahms decided to devote himself to serious music composition, seeking out the highly respected Robert Schumann in Düsseldorf. Not only was the 23-year-old Johannes accepted for study, but the Schumanns warmly welcomed the young man into their home as a boarder.

Soon after their first meeting, in an article in his influential publication *Neue Zeitschrift für Musik* (The New Magazine for Music), Schumann described Brahms as the "new genius of music." After Schumann's death, Brahms moved back to Hamburg and later relocated to Vienna.

Brahms's main employment in Vienna was as director of a women's choir. He was also a frequent guest conductor of various orchestras throughout Europe. Eventually Brahms was celebrated as the leading German composer, though his permanent residence remained Vienna until he died at 64.

PRINCIPAL WORKS

Orchestral Music: 4 symphonies: No. 1 in c minor (1855–76), No. 2 in D Major (1877), No. 3 in F Major (1883), No. 4 in e minor (1885); 2 piano concertos: No. 1 in d minor (1858), No. 2 in B-flat Major (1881); other works: Violin Concerto (1878); *Academic Festival Overture* (1880); *Tragic Overture* (1881)

Chamber Music: 2 string sextets, 2 string quintets, 3 string quartets, Piano Quintet in f minor, 3 piano quartets, 3 piano trios; Clarinet Quintet; violin sonatas

Piano Music: sonatas, rhapsodies, intermezzos, ballades, capriccios, variations, *Liebeslieder Walzer, Hungarian Dances*

Choral Music: A German Requiem (1868), *Alto Rhapsody* (1869), and more than 180 songs

LISTENING ACTIVITY ॐ

BRAHMS, *ACADEMIC FESTIVAL OVERTURE*, OP. 80
LARGE FORM: CONCERT OVERTURE; DETAILED
FORM: MEDLEY OF UNIVERSITY SONGS

Cassette Tape: Side C, Example 7
Compact Disc 2, Track 42

The background of the *Academic Festival Overture* gives us a glimpse of Brahms's great prestige in the late nineteenth century. In 1880, the University of Breslau honored him with a Doctor of Philosophy degree for being "Germany's leading composer."

In appreciation, Brahms composed the *Academic Festival Overture*. Its form is that of a *concert overture*—an overture not associated with either a ballet or an opera. Nineteenth-century concert overtures are usually highly descriptive works.

Brahms described his overture as a "very boisterous *potpourri* of student songs." Most of them were actually drinking songs. The piece ends with the well-known "Gaudeamus igitur," a noble anthem-like tune played by the full orchestra.

LISTENING GUIDE

BRAHMS, ACADEMIC FESTIVAL OVERTURE, OP. 80
LARGE FORM: CONCERT OVERTURE;
DETAILED FORM: MEDLEY OF UNIVERSITY SONGS

Cassette Tape: Side C, Example 7
Compact Disc 2, Track 42
Running time: 10:22

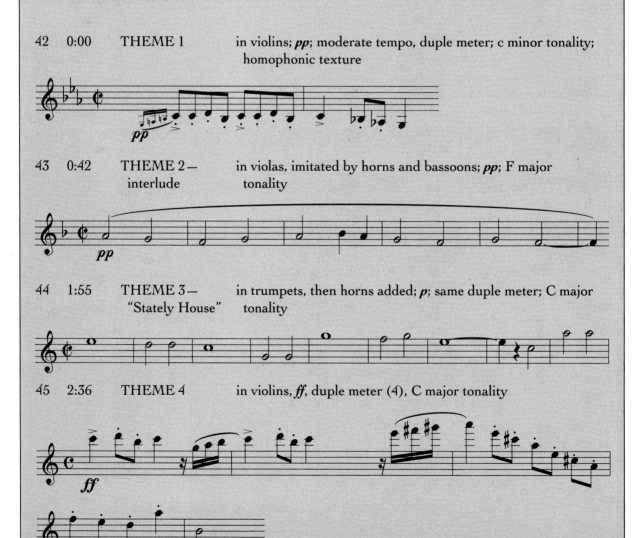

42   0:00   THEME 1   in violins; *pp*; moderate tempo, duple meter; c minor tonality;
                             homophonic texture

43   0:42   THEME 2 —   in violas, imitated by horns and bassoons; *pp*; F major
            interlude   tonality

44   1:55   THEME 3 —   in trumpets, then horns added; *p*; same duple meter; C major
            "Stately House" tonality

45   2:36   THEME 4   in violins, *ff*, duple meter (4), C major tonality

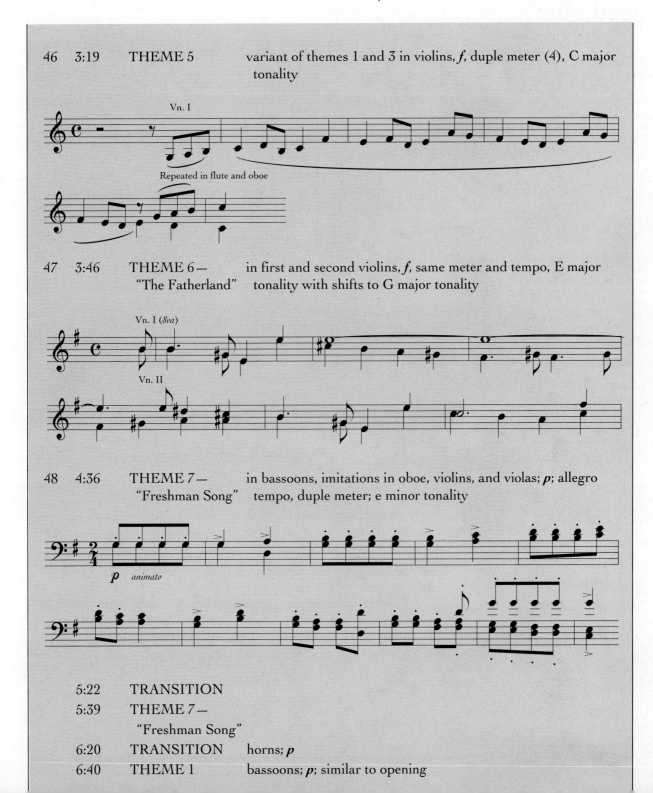

46   3:19   THEME 5   variant of themes 1 and 3 in violins, *f*, duple meter (4), C major
                           tonality

47   3:46   THEME 6 —   in first and second violins, *f*, same meter and tempo, E major
            "The Fatherland"   tonality with shifts to G major tonality

48   4:36   THEME 7 —   in bassoons, imitations in oboe, violins, and violas; *p*; allegro
            "Freshman Song"   tempo, duple meter; e minor tonality

     5:22   TRANSITION
     5:39   THEME 7 —
            "Freshman Song"
     6:20   TRANSITION   horns; *p*
     6:40   THEME 1   bassoons; *p*; similar to opening

7:16	THEME 4 —	
	fragments	
7:58	THEME 6 —	strings, then woodwinds
	"The Fatherland"	
8:49	TRANSITION	woodwinds; *p*
9:15	THEME 7 —	returns briefly
	"Freshman Song"	
9:27	THEME 8 —	finale, in full orchestra, *ff*, triple meter, C major tonality
	"Gaudeamus igitur"	

49

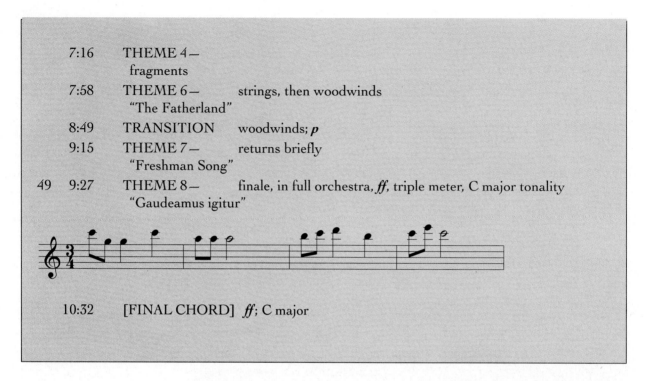

| 10:32 | [FINAL CHORD] | *ff*; C major |

LISTENING INSIGHTS

Enjoying Chamber Music

The key to enjoying chamber music is to become involved in the intimacy of the performance. During a chamber music performance — usually in a small concert hall and close to the audience — chamber musicians communicate closely with one another. You'll notice that they sit close together, often in a semicircle facing the audience. As a member of the audience seated close to the stage, you can see as well as hear each player's performance.

Chamber music is usually woven like a conversation among friends. Players subtly pass musical ideas to one another and add gentle support when a background role is required. Because there is only one player on each part of music, all are equally important.

Romantic-period Chamber Music

Increasingly during the nineteenth century, wealthy art patrons opened their homes for chamber music performances. Artists, writers, and friends gathered to hear the latest compositions of Mendelssohn, Schumann, Brahms, and others.

During the eighteenth century, string trios and quartets were the favorite chamber music groups. By the nineteenth century, string and wind chamber ensembles often added a piano. Works for these groups are *piano trios, piano quartets,* and *piano quintets*.

Though concertgoers know the romantic composers mainly by their large orchestral works, Schubert, Mendelssohn, Schumann, Brahms, and others actually wrote more chamber music than orchestral pieces. Schumann and Brahms, for instance, each wrote four symphonies, yet each composed exactly 23 works for chamber music ensembles.

LISTENING ACTIVITY ♂

BRAHMS, TRIO IN E-FLAT, OP. 40
FOURTH MOVEMENT: ALLEGRO CON BRIO
LARGE FORM: CHAMBER MUSIC TRIO;
DETAILED FORM: SONATA FORM

Instructor's Set: Compact Disc 4, Track 8
Running time: 6:20

This work is found only on the *Listening to Music* Compact Disc recordings and not on the Cassette Tapes.

Brahms scored his Trio in E-flat for horn, violin, and piano. In listening to the work and following with the listening guide, notice that the piano's role is equal to those of the horn and violin.

LISTENING GUIDE

BRAHMS, TRIO IN E-FLAT, OP. 40
FOURTH MOVEMENT: ALLEGRO CON BRIO
LARGE FORM: CHAMBER MUSIC TRIO;
DETAILED FORM: SONATA FORM

▌*Compact Disc 4, Track 8*
▌*Running time: 6:20*

Exposition

8	0:00	THEME 1	played by violin, piano with staccato (short tones); *p* crescendo to
	(1:36)		*f*; fast, duple meter (2); major tonality (E-flat); homophonic texture.

	0:08	THEME 1	horn, one octave lower, joins melody with violin; *mf* crescendo to *f*
	0:15	THEME 1,	in both violin and horn, *f*, sequences

		PART 2	
	0:34	THEME 1	both violin and horn, *f*
	0:42		repeated tones in horn, imitated by violin; *p* crescendo to *f*
9	0:43	THEME 2	in piano, imitated by violin, then back to piano; *f*

	0:51	THEME 2	in violin, *pp*
			entire section played again from the beginning (see alternative timing)

Development

10	3:10	THEME 1— fragments	mostly in violin, changes of dynamics between *p* and *f*, change of key to D major
	3:48	THEME 1, PART 2	in horn, *f*
			transition section, started with piano arpeggios (broken chords); *p*; ritardando, then accelerando
	4:09	THEME 1, PART 2	in horn; *p*; gradual accelerando

Recapitulation

11	4:15	THEME 1	in violin, similar to beginning; *p*; gradual accelerando of tempo until the end
	4:22	THEME 1	horn joins violin playing the melody
	4:29	THEME 1, PART 2	both violin and horn, *f*, still accelerando
	4:57	THEME 2	in piano then violin, *p*
	5:47	THEME 1— fragments	in horn, imitated by violin, *mf* crescendo to *f*
	5:59	THEME 1	in piano, imitated by horn, then violin; *f* then *ff*; still accelerando
	6:16	FINAL CHORD	held; *ff*

GUSTAV MAHLER (1860–1911)

When Bohemia was part of the Austro-Hungarian Empire, Gustav Mahler (*mah*-ler) was born into a family living next to a military barracks. As a boy, Mahler was fascinated by two kinds of music. One was military music, with its strong emphasis on brass. The other was folk music he heard in his village and the surrounding towns. He later incorporated both types into his symphonies.

At 15, Mahler's parents sent him to Vienna to study at the Conservatory. After three years, he was awarded a diploma in composition. Now, Mahler's career as a conductor began. He gradually secured increasingly important conducting positions as he moved from Prague to Leipzig to Budapest to Hamburg and then to the Vienna State Opera. His last two conducting positions were in the United States with the Metropolitan Opera Company (1908) and the New York Philharmonic (1909–11). Ironically, although he spent most of his life conducting operas, Mahler never wrote one.

Mahler's demanding perfectionism earned him a reputation as a tyrant. Other problems plagued him, too. Fighting against the tide of anti-Semitism developing in Austria, in 1897, at the age of 37, Mahler had to resort to trickery to secure his appointment at the Vienna State Opera. Because the management wouldn't give the post to a Jew, Mahler promptly though reluctantly converted to Christianity. Unfortunately, once he was appointed, the anti-Semitic Viennese critics continued to hound him.

In 1902, he married Alma Schindler, a famous Viennese beauty. The death of their young daughter strongly affected Mahler.

Falling ill during his second season as conductor of the New York Philharmonic, Mahler returned to Vienna seeking medical help. He died there at the age of 50.

PRINCIPAL WORKS

Orchestral Music: 10 symphonies: No. 1 (*The Titan*, 1888); No. 2, with soprano (*Resurrection*, 1894); No. 4, with soprano (1900); No. 8, with soloists and choruses (*Symphony of a Thousand*, 1909).

Songs (with orchestra): Song cycles: *Lieder eines fahrenden Gesellen* (Songs of a Wayfarer, 1885); *Kindertotenlieder* (Songs on the Death of Children, 1904); *Des Knaben Wunderhorn* (Youth's Magic Horn, 1893-98); *Das Lied von der Erde* (The Song of the Earth, 1909)

Choral Music: Das klagende Lied (The Song of Sorrow, 1880)

Silhouettes of Mahler conducting by Otto Boehler.

MAHLER, SONGS OF A WAYFARER "GING HEUT
MORGEN ÜBERS FELD." ("I WALKED THIS
MORNING OVER THE FIELDS.")
LARGE FORM: SONG CYCLE

**Cassette Tape: Side C, Example 8
Compact Disc 2, Track 50**

How ironic that Mahler, who spent most of his conducting career in opera, never wrote one. However, he did compose several song cycles with orchestra that are among his most performed works.

Mahler's songs are quite different from the art songs (*leider*) of Schubert and Schumann that you heard earlier. Those composers and others wrote piano accompaniment for a singer performing in an intimate setting—a small hall or a private home. The music more or less "whispered" their innermost romantic feelings. On the other hand, Mahler "proclaimed" his feelings, bearing his soul for large audiences. For his songs, a full symphony orchestra accompanied a singer on a full stage in a large concert hall.

Mahler's emotionalism exemplifies the wonderful excesses of the Romantic period: "You never know what is enough until you know what is too much." Mahler's detractors see his self-indulgent displays of emotionalism as excessive. Others consider them glorious expressions of true feeling.

Keep Mahler's wide range of emotionalism in mind when you listen to the second song in his *Songs of a Wayfarer* cycle, "Ging Heut morgen übers Feld" ("I Walked This Morning Over the Fields"). Mahler's highly personal lyrics are mostly autobiographical, written between 1883 and 1885, after singer-actress Johanna Richter spurned his love. The first of the four songs of the cycle, "Wenn mein Schatz Hochzeit macht" ("When My Love Has Her Wedding Day"), conveys Mahler's sadness over his rejection.

However, by the second song, "Ging Heut' morgen übers Feld," Mahler seems to have recovered as a new day dawns. On this beautiful day, the wanderer (Mahler) walks through sunlit fields, with birds chirping greetings to him as he rediscovers the wonder of nature. His exuberance is short-lived as he plunges into sadness, asking, "When will my luck begin?" ("Wenn sind mein glück voll an?"). He answers himself, "No! No! I don't think it ever will" ("Nein, nein, das ich mein...").

Born a Jew in Bohemia, Mahler worked for most of his career in staunchly anti-Semitic Austria and Germany. Therefore, he considered himself an outsider and often commented that he thought of himself as a "wanderer," at home nowhere. His perfectionism and fiery temperament did not help his cause. Perhaps this inner turmoil contributed to his decision to move to the United States to conduct the Metropolitan Opera Orchestra and the New York Philharmonic.

LISTENING GUIDE

MAHLER, SONGS OF A WAYFARER,
"GING HEUT MORGEN ÜBERS FELD"
LARGE FORM: SONG CYCLE

Cassette Tape: Side C, Example 8
Compact Disc 2, Track 50
Running time: 4:37

50   0:00   *Flutes and piccolo staccato, duple meter,* **p,** *in D major, soloist enters with "walking" theme*

Ging heut' mor-gens ü-bers Feld,   Tau noch   auf den Grä-sern hing;

Ging heut' morgen übers Feld,	I walked this morning over the fields;
Tau noch auf den Gräsern hing;	Dew still hung on the grass;
Sprach zu mir der lust'ge Fink:	The merry finch spoke to me:
Ei du! Gelt?	Hey, you! Is that right?

51   0:19   *mostly strings accompany singer,* **pp**

Gu-ten   Mor - gen! Ei gelt?   Du!
So   good   morn - ing! Good morn - ing!

Wird's nicht— ei - ne   schö - ne Welt?   schö - ne Welt!?
Is— it   not a   love - ly world?   love - ly world?

Walking Theme—second part

Guten Morgan! Ei gelt?	Good morning! Isn't it?
Du! Wird's nicht eine schöne Welt?	You there! Isn't it a lovely world?

0:33   *full orchestra,* **ff,** *then,* **pp**

Zink! Zink! Schön und flink!	Sing! Sing! Pretty and quick!
Wie mir doch die Welt gefällt"	How I love the world!"

0:45   *Short orchestral transition, loud diminishing to soft, "walking theme" returns*

Walking Theme

Auch die Gockenblum' am Feld	Also the bluebell in the meadow
Hat mir lustig, guter Ding'	—cheerful, kind creature—
Mit den Glöckchen, klinge, kling.	With its bells went ring-ring.
Klinge, kling.	Ring, ring.

1:08   ### Walking Theme — second part

Ihren Morgengruss geschellt:	And rang a morning greeting for me:
Wird's nicht eine schöne Welt?	Isn't it a lovely world?
Kling, kling! Kling, kling!	Ring-ring! Ring-ring!
Schönes Ding!	Pretty thing!
Wie mir doch die Welt gefällt!	How I love the world!
Heia!"	Hey-ho!"

1:36   *orchestral interlude with soaring flutes and violins, modulating to key of B major,* **pp**

1:55   ### Walking Theme

Und da fing im Sonnenschein	Then in the sunshine
Gleich die Welt zu funkeln an:	The world suddenly began to glitter;

2:13   ### Walking Theme — second part

Alles, alles Ton und Farbe gewann	All things took on sound and color
Im Sonnenschein!	in the sunshine.
Blum' und Vogel, gross and klein!	Flowers and birds, both large and small!
Guten Tag, guten Tag!	"Good day, good day!
Ist's nicht eine schöne Welt?"	Isn't it a lovely world?
Ei, du, gelt? Ei, du, gelt?	Hey you, Is that right?
Schöne Welt?	Lovely world?

52   2:56   *tempo slows, orchestra very soft, tonality modulates to F-sharp major*

Nun fängt auch mein Glück wohl an?	When will my luck begin?
Nun fängt auch mein Glück wohl an?	When will my luck begin?
Nein, nein, das, ich mein,"	No, no, I don't think
Mir nimmer blühen kann!	it ever will!

4:15   *orchestra ends the song, fading softer and softer toward an F-sharp major chord.*

Mahler's Symphonies

Although Mahler's symphonies abound with extra-musical references, including poetry and philosophy, he considered them to be evolutions of the classical tradition. Awash with intermingled extra-musical ideas, his long symphonies contain some of the most highly charged, emotional music of the Romantic period. The music reflects the composer's own emotional swings, for which he sought therapy from Vienna's leading psychiatrist, Sigmund Freud (1856–1939).

Freud
(froid)
Longest Symphony
Largest Symphony

Mahler established two records in music: one in length and one in number of players. His Third Symphony lasts 1 hour and 35 minutes, longer than any other. His Eighth Symphony, "Symphony of a Thousand," the largest work ever written for a symphony orchestra, used more than 1,000 performers at its premiere: an orchestra of 171, 8 vocal soloists, a children's choir of 350, and two choruses of 250 each.

Early in the twentieth century, his music was somewhat neglected. While Mahler was composing his last works—from 1900 to 1911—modern musical trends had begun. Yet, he was rooted in the past and didn't follow the changing times. Many listeners began to regard Romantic music as outmoded and overly sentimental in contrast to the cerebral, more concise twentieth-century music.

After Mahler's death, his music was still considered old-fashioned. In the 1930s and 1940s, Hitler banned Mahler's music throughout Germany and Austria, along with the music of other Jewish composers.

Then, in the 1950s, as many listeners began moving away from the harsh dissonances of modern music, seeking more consonant and emotional music, they rediscovered Mahler. Since the 1960s, Mahler's music has been enjoying a popularity greater than any he knew in his lifetime.

The Virtuoso Orchestra

Economics had a favorable influence on music just as it did on other professions. After Mendelssohn elevated the performance standards and professional prestige of his Gewandhaus Orchestra, higher-paying positions attracted players. Two outstanding composer/conductors continued the Mendelssohn tradition: Gustav Mahler and Richard Strauss.

Knowing that jobs usually went to the best players, musicians strove to improve their abilities. Beginning in the late nineteenth century, each player in the major symphony orchestras was a virtuoso, capable of performing as soloist.

LISTENING ACTIVITY ⌇

MAHLER, SYMPHONY NO. 1 (THE TITAN) IN D
FIRST MOVEMENT
LARGE FORM: SYMPHONY;
DETAILED FORM: SECTIONAL

▮ *Compact Disc 4, Track 12*

Mahler composed his First Symphony over a period of several years, mostly during summer breaks from his various conducting duties. After hearing Richard Strauss's tone poems, Mahler set about to write a symphonic poem as his first symphony, which he titled *The Titan*. His original plan was to produce a five-movement symphony with a program about nature—patterned after Beethoven's *Pastoral* Symphony. After reworking it a number of times, he finally decided on four-movements without a program.

Because Mahler had built his first movement on ideas of youth, flowers, early dawn, the forest, and endless spring, the Introduction may remind you of Beethoven's *Pastoral* Symphony with its bird calls and sounds of nature. This is no coincidence. Mahler even retraced Beethoven's steps through the Vienna Woods, trying to recapture the feeling and sounds that had inspired the *Pastoral*.

After the slow Introduction, full of forest sounds, the first movement proceeds at a faster tempo into "Days of Youth." For its main theme, Mahler reuses the "Walking Theme" from *The Songs of a Wayfarer*.

LISTENING GUIDE

MAHLER, SYMPHONY NO. 1 (THE TITAN) IN D
FIRST MOVEMENT
LARGE FORM: SYMPHONY; DETAILED FORM: SECTIONAL

▮*Compact Disc 4, Track 12*
▮*Running time: 12:27*

First movement: *langsam, schleppend wie ein Naturlaut*
(Slowly and drawn out like a sound of nature)

Note on the Listening Guide

Melodies and their fragments enter and leave and are commented on by various instruments of the orchestra. Mahler uses a highly flexible and complex form, mainly relying on melodic ideas for continuity. So varied is the form that a listening guide noting every sound event would detract from following the mood and broad sweep of the music. Therefore, only major events are included here.

Introduction

12	0:00	FOREST SOUNDS	the pitch "A" high strings (harmonics); ***ppp***; slow tempo, duple (4) meter
	0:31	FANFARE	in clarinets, ***pp***
	1:07	FANFARE	played by distant (off-stage) trumpets, ***ppp***
13	1:33	FOREST MELODY	played by horns; ***pp***

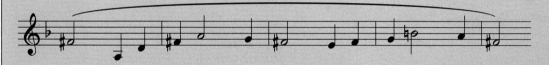

	1:48	FANFARE	played by trumpets, slightly faster tempo
	1:58	FOREST MELODY	in horns, ***pp***
	2:13	FANFARE	in trumpets
	2:20	***Transition Section***	played by cellos and basses; ***p***, faster tempo, horns and woodwinds in background
	2:58	BIRD CALL—cuckoo	played by clarinet, ***p***

Main Section

14	3:02	TRANSITION	played by cellos; ***pp***; imitated by bassoon, then solo trumpet; [BIRD CALL] in clarinets; then violins enter, completing
		WALKING THEME— Days of Youth	the melody; extensions of the melody in violins and woodwinds; rubato tempo; D major tonality

	4:36	WALKING THEME —Days of Youth	started again by horns, *ff*, continued by strings and woodwinds
	5:00	FOREST SOUNDS	slower; introduction music returns—forest sounds; [BIRD CALLS] played by woodwinds
	7:32	HUNTING HORNS	played by horns; *ppp*
	7:49	WALKING THEME—fragments	played by cellos; faster
15	9:09	WALKING THEME—Days of Youth	returns Long developmental section, using new themes and hints of all themes already played; changing tempos and styles cymbals crash, full orchestra, fanfares, *ff*

Finale Section

16	10:41	HORN CALL	containing the interval of a fourth, similar to other melodies and earlier Forest Melody; *ff*
17	11:21	WALKING THEME—Days of Youth	returns in trumpet, *ff*, imitations by other instruments, tempo accelerates; pause; fast, agitated woodwinds; *ff*; pause; full orchestra cadence to final chord, *ff*

LISTENING INSIGHTS

Enjoying Programmatic and Highly Descriptive Music

It is possible to enjoy music without knowing its background. A fine orchestral work can stand on its own without associations to literature or any other art. Most music has no direct reference to a specific, extra-musical source.

When we encounter a work that openly calls attention to its source, we should look into that source—beyond the music alone—for greater understanding and enjoyment. A piece becomes more interesting after you have read the nonmusical ideas that inspired the composer.

If the story of a programmatic or descriptive work does not appear in your printed program or on a record jacket, a little detective work will pay off. Composers' biographies, histories of music, books, and magazine articles on specific composers or works can yield further insights into a composition. Often, the search for meanings and the concomitant pleasure provide some of the joys of music.

RICHARD STRAUSS (1864–1949)

Strauss (*shtrowss*—no relation to the waltz composers) was born in Munich, the son of the principal horn player in the Court Orchestra. (Notice how often Strauss favors the horn in his orchestral works; he also wrote two great concertos for that instrument.) Music was a large part of his family life, and Strauss began composing at the age of six. Soon he was studying composition and orchestration with members of his father's orchestra.

Strauss's earlier compositions were in the conservative tradition of Schumann and Brahms. After taking a series of conducting posts, he veered toward the more radical Wagner and Liszt camp.

In 1898, Strauss was appointed conductor of the Royal Court Opera in Berlin and soon after devoted most of his remaining years to composing operas. In 1919, he was made director of the Vienna State Opera, a post formerly held by his longtime friend Gustav Mahler. During World War II, Strauss chose to remain in Nazi Germany, spending most of the war in retirement in Bavaria. At the age of 85, he died in the Bavarian town of Garmisch.

PRINCIPAL WORKS

Orchestral Music: Symphonic poems: *Aus Italien* (1886), *Don Juan* (1889), *Death and Transfiguration* (1889), *Till Eulenspiegels lustige Streiche* (Till Eulenspiegel's Merry Pranks, 1895), *Also sprach Zarathustra* (Thus Spake Zarathustra, 1896), *Don Quixote* (1897), *Ein Heldenleben* (A Hero's Life, 1898), *Symphonia Domestica* (1903); Horn Concertos: No. 1 in E-flat (1883), No. 2 in E-flat (1942); Oboe Concerto (1945)

Operas: *Salome* (1905), *Elektra* (1909), *Der Rosenkavalier* (The Cavalier of the Rose, 1911), *Ariadne auf Naxos* (1912), *Die Frau ohne Schatten* (The Woman without a Shadow, 1919), *Arabella* (1993)

Songs: *Four Last Songs* (with orchestra, 1948), about 200 with piano

Late Romantic-period Program Music

Searching for new ways of expression, Romantic composers began to depict an entire "program" or story through music. (These stories are not the same as the "program notes" that give background information about a composition.)

Music following stories and nonmusical ideas is not new. Songs, oratorios, cantatas, and operas usually translate textual ideas into musical ideas. Handel's oratorios, such as *Messiah*, abound with such treatments.

Other composers have written highly descriptive instrumental music. Based on a set of sonnets, Vivaldi created a musical description of each of *The Four Seasons:* bird calls in the *Spring*, thunderstorms in the *Summer*, harvesting in the *Fall*, shivering and ice in *Winter*.

In his *Pastoral* Symphony of 1808, Beethoven suggests the idea of program music by specifically titling each of the five movements. However, he cautioned that the titles indicate only "expression of feelings" (see Chapter 11). Later nineteenth-century composers carried these ideas further. Mendelssohn's *Hebrides (Fingal's Cave) Overture* describes his journey to the seascape and caves surrounding the islands off the western coast of Scotland.

Program

The term *program* music or *programmatic* music describes music based on a story or text. Often, that story or *program* appears in the printed concert program.

Berlioz provides the listener with a blow-by-blow account of what is happening in his *Symphonie fantastique*. He specifically intended his story to be included in the printed concert program for the audience to follow. Franz Liszt used programs for several of his works. His *Dante* Symphony and *Faust* Symphony have particularly detailed programs associated with them.

Many pieces suggest that the composer followed a detailed program even though no story was written out to appear on the concert program. Several of Tchaikovsky's concert overtures and symphonic fantasies obviously follow a detailed story: *1812 Overture*, *Francesca da Rimini*, and *Romeo and Juliet*.

Tone Poems (Symphonic Poems)

Of all the programmatic music composers, Richard Strauss was the most successful in wedding a program with music. Calling his programmatic works *tone poems* or *symphonic poems*, Strauss asks the listener to follow his orchestral accounts of detailed poems and stories.

In *Don Juan*, for instance, Strauss describes the infamous rake—the same character who inspired Mozart's *Don Giovanni*. Strauss's symphonic poem depicts Don Juan's searchings, seductions, flights from relationships, and emotional moods, ending in bitterness and despair.

Summary of Terms

chamber music	program music	symphony orchestra
descriptive music	programmatic music	societies
philharmonic	program notes	tone poem
societies	symphonic poem	virtuoso orchestra

CHAPTER 16

Nationalism

ᔥ *Political Influences*

A spark of nationalism ignited Europe, Scandinavia, and Russia throughout the nineteenth century. Wars that followed, including the devastating World Wars I and II of the twentieth century, periodically rekindled the flames until the creation of the Common Market in 1957 (later becoming the European Economic Community).

As countries finally realized the value of pooling their resources, European nationalism subsided. Today, Eastern European countries formerly cut off by political and economic differences are rejoining the family of nations.

Historians are divided on the precise onset of nationalism, but it seems to have coincided with the American and French Revolutions toward the end of the eighteenth century. Weary of oppression, citizens began overthrowing monarchies and taking control of their own countries.

For centuries, without regard for the interests of citizens, rulers had been arranging marriages and royal successions in conquered lands intended to maintain family holdings. In fact, royalty often held the people over whom it ruled in disdain. And since French or German was the language of the courts, most rulers in Russia, Scandinavia, and the Baltic and Slavic nations could not even communicate with their subjects.

NEW INDEPENDENT REPUBLICS FORMED With the people's demanding a greater role in their governments, clusters of independent cities and states consolidated, forming new, independent republics:

- 1830   The Grand Duchy of Luxembourg was divided into the two independent kingdoms of the Netherlands (Holland) and Belgium.
- 1861   The Italian parliament proclaimed that the independent city-states were a unified kingdom.
- 1871   Germany unified as an empire.
- 1872   Spain became a republic.
- 1910   Portugal became a republic.
- 1917   The Russian people overthrew the czarist regime.

INDUSTRIAL AND TECHNOLOGICAL INFLUENCES Further contributing to the growing nationalistic phenomenon was the Industrial Revolution. Leaving their small towns, a newly created middle class of farmers flocked to the cities and factories in search of a better life. Crowded together with citizens from different parts of their homelands, they discovered their shared values and aspirations. Gradually, these countrymen developed a sense of national pride and dared to become more politically active.

TRAVEL INFLUENCES *Wanderlust* also gave impetus to nineteenth-century nationalism. As early tourists boarded France's new passenger trains in 1828, railways replaced stagecoach lines as the primary means of mass transportation. On the seas, the steamship replaced the sailing ship. Now, the difficult, uncertain, three-week Atlantic crossing passed with greater safety in only nine-and-a-half days.

These new, relatively inexpensive means of transportation allowed more people to travel and become acquainted with other cultures. Artists also explored the world, incorporating their discoveries into their poetry, novels, paintings, and music. Some typical examples are the poem "Home Thoughts from Abroad" by Robert Browning, the novel *Lord Jim* by Joseph Conrad, the exotic Tahitian paintings of Paul Gauguin, and *The Hebrides Overture,* and *Scottish* and *Italian* Symphonies by Felix Mendelssohn.

∽ *Nationalism in Music*

Since the time of Vivaldi and Bach, French, German, and Italian music and musicians had dominated almost every court, opera house, and concert hall from Moscow to Madrid. But as nationalism gained momentum, composers in Russia, Scandinavia, Spain, and other countries began examining their own culture. Many realized that they could incorporate it into compositions indigenous to their countries. Thus, nationalistic music became the new fashion.

Russian Nationalism

The scene   St. Petersburg, Russia, on the Baltic Sea.

The time   Latter half of the nineteenth century.

The situation   Five Russian composers band together to create Russian nationalistic music.

Their training   Having had very little formal musical training in Western European music, they were free from most of those influences.

Their goal   To promote purely Russian music.

Their approach   Incorporating situations from history, folklore, legends, and native instruments and music.

The Russian Five

- Nikolai Rimsky-Korsakov (*rim*-skee *kor*-sa-kof, 1844–1908)
- Modest Mussorgsky (moo-*zorg*-skee, 1839–81)
- Alexander Borodin (*bor*-uh-deen, 1833–87)
- César Cui (*say*-zar *kwee*, 1835–1918)
- Mily Balakirev (*mee*-lee bah-*lah*-kih-ref, 1837–1910)

LISTENING INSIGHTS

Listening to Nationalistic Music

Nationalist composers expected their listeners to focus on the native resources in their music. Listen then for the folk and patriotic melodies and indigenous instruments such as Russian balalaika and bells, and Spanish castanets, guitars, and tambourines.

The more rigid, intellectual forms that German composers favored held little interest for most nationalist composers. Their forms were loose, usually relying on forms suggested by descriptions, stories, and titles. You will generally hear many contrasting sections of music with only a smattering of repeated ideas and very little thematic development.

MODEST MUSSORGSKY (1839–81)

A militant nationalist, Mussorgsky was born in Pskof, Russia, into an aristocratic family. He studied at the Preobrazhensky Guard school in St. Petersburg and later spent three years on active duty with the Guard.

Though he was a fine pianist and had dabbled in composition, he hadn't considered music seriously until his later years. He resigned his commission in the Guard to earn his living as a clerk in the civil service—composing on the side.

His great difficulties with money and health were mainly due to his excessive drinking. Although his little formal musical training was primarily from Balakirev, he was one of the most original and influential Russian composers of his day. Searching for a new Russian musical language, Mussorgsky became fascinated with the Russian spoken language, incorporating its unique inflections into his songs and operas.

In spite of his older appearance in the 1881 portrait, Mussorgsky was only 42 when he died.

PRINCIPAL WORKS

Operas: Boris Godunov (1869), *Khovanshchina* (completed by Rimsky-Korsakov, 1886)

Songs: The Nursery (1870), *Sunless* (1874), *Songs and Dances of Death* (1877); more than 50 other songs

Orchestral Music: A Night on Bald Mountain (tone poem) (1867)

Piano Music: Pictures at an Exhibition (later orchestrated by Ravel); numerous songs and piano pieces

Kremlin Square in front of the Church of the Redeemer, setting for the "Coronation Scene" from *Boris Godunov*, and also the location of the first performance of Tchaikovsky's *1812 Overture*.

LISTENING ACTIVITY ॐ

MUSSORGSKY, BORIS GODUNOV, "CORONATION SCENE"
LARGE FORM: OPERA

Cassette Tape: Side D, Example 1
Compact Disc 2, Track 53

Listen to the nationalistic resources that Mussorgsky used in the "Coronation Scene" from his opera *Boris Godunov*.

THE TEXT   Alexander Pushkin (1799–1837), the great Russian Romantic writer exiled to south Russia because of his "liberal" writings, wrote the text for this opera. Although set in Russia under Czar Boris (1598–1605), many of the events in the opera actually had their origins during the reign of Ivan the Terrible (1530–84).

SYNOPSIS OF THE SCENE   The "Coronation Scene" opens in Moscow's Kremlin Square, where a festive crowd of mostly peasants awaits the appearance of Boris on his coronation day. With no particular love for Boris or for any czar, the crowd is celebrating mainly because there is free food and drink and a day off from work.

The music begins very dramatically with the sounding of the great bells of Moscow. In fact, the whole orchestra sounds like a giant, dissonant bell. Prince Schuisky (tenor), an important member of the court, appears in front of the great cathedral to a fanfare of trumpets. He cheers to the crowd (in Russian) "Long life to the Czar Boris, son of Feodor."

The peasants become jubilant and, using the melody of a Russian folk song, sing praises to the new czar.

Boris (bass) enters. Brooding over the recent death of his young nephew—the rightful heir—he is reluctant to take over as czar. Ironically, he had ordered the boy's murder in order to become czar.

Encouraged by the crowds, Boris consents to accept the title of czar. Turning now to the people, in a brighter mood, he invites them all to the traditional coronation feast.

The crowd responds with "Glory! Glory! Glory! Long may you live and reign, O Czar, our father!" Again the great bells of Moscow sound, on and on.

MUSIC   Mussorgsky used an authentic Russian folk song and Russian Orthodox Church hymns. Sung in rich harmony, these hymns demonstrate the pervasive influence of the church.

Many of the melodies in the opera are based on modal scales prevalent in Russian folk and church music, but rare in other countries.

INSTRUMENTS   Mussorgsky's choice of the bells signifies their great importance in Russian life, especially in the "Coronation Scene." In his day, the famous bells of the Moscow churches sounded on Sundays and important occasions. Old and large, the bells hold a particular nostalgia for the Russian people.

The character of Boris is one of the few lead roles written for bass voice, an appropriate vocal type for the heavy vowels of the Russian language. Russian choirs pride themselves on their unusually deep male vocal sections.

OVERALL STYLE   Russian music characteristically resounds with power, drama, and expansiveness—much like our image of Russia today.

LISTENING GUIDE

MUSSORGSKY, BORIS GODUNOV, "CORONATION SCENE"
LARGE FORM: OPERA

Cassette Tape: Side D, Example 1
Compact Disc 2, Track 53
Running time: 9:33

53   0:00   BELL-LIKE CHORDS   dissonant chords, *f*, the orchestra imitates the sounds of bells together with actual bells, chimes, and gongs (Chinese tam-tams); moderately slow tempo in quadruple meter

0:17   BELL-LIKE CHORDS   high woodwinds and strings playing subdivisions of the beat, joining the bell-like chords in the lower instruments; crescendo to a *ff*, held chord

0:55	BELL-LIKE CHORDS	the ideas of the opening section are repeated, this time louder and with the whole orchestra playing. Quicker subdivisions of the beat press the orchestra forward again to a climax chord, with bells ringing on some beats
54	1:48	TRUMPET FANFARE	*ff*
	1:50	TOAST—RECITATIVE	sung by the tenor (Prince Shuisky—*shoo*-skee) all on one pitch

Trumpets

ff

Long life and reign, Czar Bo - ris Fe - o - d - ro - vich!

	2:00	CHORUS	the chorus (crowd) answers, *ff*, slightly faster tempo, chimes cease

Like unto the bright sun in the sky, Glory! Glory!
Is the glory of Russia's Czar Boris! Glory!
Long may you live and reign, O Czar, our father!

55	2:08	CHORUS	the chorus (crowd) sings the main melody of this scene, a Russian folk song in the key of C major; *f*; faster tempo

RUSSIAN FOLK SONG

To the sun in all splen - dor ris - en be glo - ry, glo - ry

2:28	RUSSIAN FOLK SONG	imitated by the orchestra, *f*, the chorus again sings the same folk song
3:02		alternating forte and piano sections, both chorus and orchestra together, a crescendo gradually builds
3:25	RUSSIAN FOLK SONG	fanfares in the brass, bells ring, both orchestra and chorus with [RUSSIAN FOLK SONG], *ff*, in triple meter
4:46		full orchestra *fff*; sections of the chorus imitate each other, while bells chime; change of meter from triple to duple

56	5:00		over a soft timpani roll, horns and woodwinds play quietly in a slow duple meter
	5:12	CZAR BORIS	bass voice (Boris) enters with brooding, emotional melody, shifting tonalities between several major and minor keys

> My soul is sad!
> Strange, dark forebodings and evil feelings
> Oppress my spirit.
> Oh, Holy Saint, oh my Almighty Father!
> Look down from heaven on the tears of thy sinful servant,
> And send down Thy Holy blessing upon my reign!
> May I be as honest and merciful as Thou,
> And reign in glory over my people.

	6:56	CZAR BORIS	a short pause; change of mood, beginning with *p* woodwinds in minor, then major as Boris sings a short prayer in recitative style

> Now let us go to kneel
> Before the tombs of Russia's former monarchs.
> Then all the people are summoned to a feast;
> All, from the boyars to the blind beggars,
> All are invited, all shall be my honored guests.

	7:19	CZAR BORIS	Boris sings louder and higher with the orchestra following and then answering in loud chords.
	7:31	CHORUS	The chorus answers Boris, *ff*, faster tempo with short orchestral interludes

> Glory! Glory! Glory! Long may you live and reign, O Czar, our father!

57	7:41	BELLS	The bells sound repeatedly
	7:55	BELL-LIKE CHORDS	a repeat of opening bell-like chords, *f*, followed by the chorus singing [RUSSIAN FOLK SONG] in imitation
	8:04	RUSSIAN FOLK SONG	sung and played by both chorus and orchestra; *ff*; triple meter
	8:55	CHORUS	Orchestra, *fff*, chorus imitating, meter shifting to duple for ending cadence

9:21	FINAL CHORD	final chords, orchestra and chorus, *ff*
	BELLS	bells continue ringing

PETER ILYICH TCHAIKOVSKY (1840–93)

A favorite composer of audiences around the world, Tchaikovsky was born in Votinsk, Russia. After studying law in St. Petersburg, he grudgingly worked as a clerk in the Ministry of Justice.

Returning at 23 to school at the newly founded St. Petersburg Conservatory of Music, Tchaikovsky studied composition with Anton Rubinstein (1829–94). Three years later he was hired to teach music at the new Moscow Conservatory, where he remained until his retirement at the age of 37. Then, he was able to devote his full time to composing and conducting.

As guest conductor with various orchestras, he toured Russia, London, and Europe extensively. In 1891, the New York Philharmonic invited Tchaikovsky to the United States as guest conductor for the opening of Carnegie Hall.

Hounded by bigots and disgraced in court because of his homosexuality, Tchaikovsky fell into a severe depression. The cause of death was listed as cholera, but there is little doubt that he committed suicide at the age of 53.

PRINCIPAL WORKS

Operas: Eugene Onegin (1865), *Mazeppa* (1884), *The Queen of Spades* (1880)

Orchestral Music: 6 symphonies: No. 2 (*Little Russian*, 1872), No. 3 (*Polish*, 1875), No. 4 (1878), No. 5 (1888), No. 6 (*Pathétique* 1893); Concertos: Violin Concerto (1878); 3 piano concertos, No. 1 (1875); Ballets: *Swan Lake* (1877), *Sleeping Beauty* (1889), *The Nutcracker* (1892); Fantasy Overtures: *Romeo and Juliet* (1869), *Francesca da Rimini* (1876), *Capriccio italien* (1880), *1812 Overture* (1882), *Marche slav*

Chamber Music: String sextet (1890), string quartets, piano trio

A New York Philharmonic performance of Tchaikovsky's *1812 Overture* in Central Park.

TCHAIKOVSKY AS A NATIONALIST   Although he was their contemporary, the so-called "Russian Five" excluded Tchaikovsky from their group. They considered him an outsider—too cosmopolitan, too influenced by the music of other nations through his frequent travels, especially to Germany, France, and Italy.

Despite his exclusion by "The Five," their music influenced Tchaikovsky to compose nationalistic music. However, he did not limit his nationalistic sources to Russia. His ballets *Swan Lake* and *Nutcracker* (see Plate 10) include folk dances of other countries. His six symphonies, *March Slav*, operas, and numerous other works contain Russian songs. His orchestral work *Capriccio italien* is not Russian; it's a musical diary of his travels to Italy. (Rimsky-Korsakov, a member of "The Five," similarly memorialized his travels to Spain in his work *Capriccio espagnol*.)

Perhaps "The Five" were right. Tchaikovsky did not consistently display the nationalistic fervor that they did. But the *1812 Overture* epitomized his passion as a Russian nationalist.

HISTORICAL PERSPECTIVE

The 1812 Overture:
Its First Performance and Modern Performances

The original performance of Tchaikovsky's *1812 Overture* took place outdoors in front of the Cathedral of the Redeemer in Kremlin Square (see photograph on page 254)—the same setting as the "Coronation Scene" from *Boris Godunov*. For the premiere, rifle and cannon fire from the czarist troops augmented the huge cathedral bells. How impressive that performance must have been!

Scored for a large orchestra, the *1812 Overture* has full brass and percussion sections. A military or university band sometimes joins the orchestra for the finale.

Church bells are often replicated by chimes, or occasionally by pre-recorded tapes. When the Moscow Symphony performs this work, it traditionally uses heavy, five-foot-diameter, authentic church bells. For outdoor performances around the world, real cannons and rifles are often used.

Tchaikovsky featured Russian folk songs, "La Marseillaise," and the "Czar's Hymn" in this fanciful work. Until the breakup of the socialist government, the Soviet Union forbade performances of the "Czar's Hymn," even in a classic work such as the *1812 Overture*. (Tchaikovsky used the same theme in *Marche slav*.) Instead of the "Czar's Hymn," the Soviets substituted a new, considerably less exciting melody in both works. Today, even in Russia, the original "Czar's Hymn" has been reinstated for performances.

LISTENING ACTIVITY ❧

Tchaikovsky, *1812 Overture*
Large Form: Programmatic Concert Overture

▌*Compact Disc 3, Track 42*

This work is found only on the *Listening to Music* Compact Disc recordings and not on the Cassette Tapes.

Tchaikovsky's *1812 Overture* is one of the most nationalistic works ever written. The programmatic piece celebrated the 70th anniversary of Napoleon's defeat by the Russian army in Moscow and his subsequent retreat to Paris with only 20,000 of his original 550,000 troops.

THE PROGRAM The work opens with a Russian hymn, "God Preserve Thy People." In an agitated section, Napoleon's troops advance toward Moscow. The horns introduce a slow march as the Russian troops prepare for battle. The armies clash and fall back, as the orchestra sounds fragments of the French national anthem, "La Marseillaise."

Freezing in the bitter winter's evening, the Russian troops think of their warm homes and families, as we hear a Russian lullaby and a playful Russian folk song.

Morning, and the French troops advance with the "La Marseillaise" as a minor battle ensues. Both sides retreat to their camps for another cold night, as we again hear the lullaby and the folk song.

Then a new, more furious battle begins—armies clashing, cannons and rifles blasting over the music. We hear the opening hymn again, this time with church bells and chimes signifying the Russian victory.

Triumphantly, the Russian troops march back to Moscow, greeted by the "Czar's Hymn." Bells chime. Rifle and cannon fire signal victory.

LISTENING GUIDE

TCHAIKOVSKY, *1812 OVERTURE*
LARGE FORM: PROGRAMMATIC CONCERT OVERTURE

Compact Disc 3, Track 42
Running time: 14:34

42	0:00	THEME 1—Russian Orthodox Church hymn	in string section; *p*; very slow (largo) tempo, triple meter; E-flat major tonality; homophonic texture

	1:20	THEME 1—fragments	imitation and sequences between woodwinds and strings, crescendo to *fff*
43	2:00	THEME 2—Russian folk song	played by the oboe, *p*, imitations flutes and cellos; c minor tonality

	2:44	THEME 2—modified	imitation of short, rhythmic motive in minor tonality, *f* to *fff*, tempo gets faster, sixteenth notes
	2:54	THEME 2—fragments	full orchestra, sequences, two loud chords bring the music to a one-beat halt
	3:20	THEME 2—Russian folk song	played in strings, *fff*, slightly slower tempo, same c minor tonality
44	3:39	THEME 3—fanfare-type march	played by woodwinds and horns over snare drum; *mf*; slower tempo (andante), duple meter; E-flat major tonality

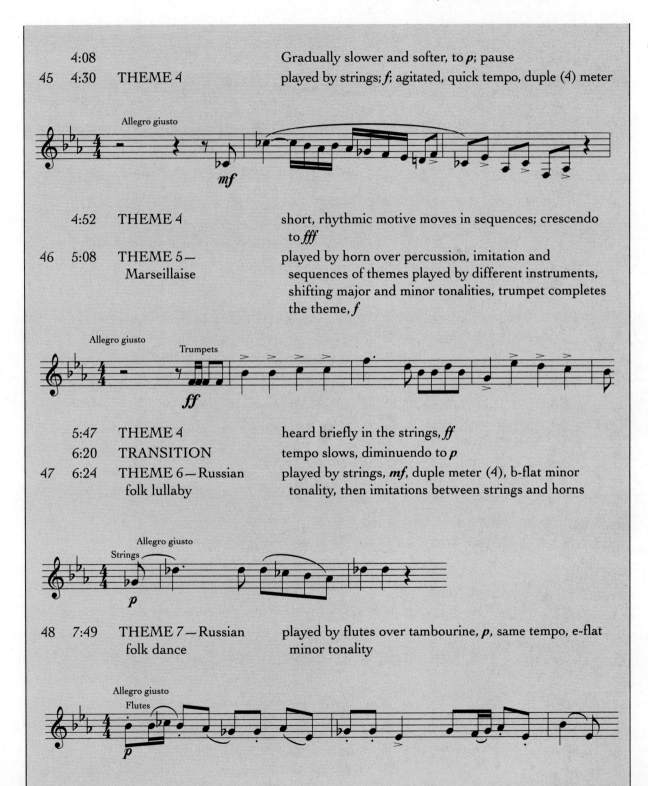

| | 4:08 | | Gradually slower and softer, to *p*; pause |
| 45 | 4:30 | THEME 4 | played by strings; *f*; agitated, quick tempo, duple (4) meter |

Allegro giusto

mf

| | 4:52 | THEME 4 | short, rhythmic motive moves in sequences; crescendo to *fff* |
| 46 | 5:08 | THEME 5 — Marseillaise | played by horn over percussion, imitation and sequences of themes played by different instruments, shifting major and minor tonalities, trumpet completes the theme, *f* |

Allegro giusto

Trumpets

ff

	5:47	THEME 4	heard briefly in the strings, *ff*
	6:20	TRANSITION	tempo slows, diminuendo to *p*
47	6:24	THEME 6 — Russian folk lullaby	played by strings, *mf*, duple meter (4), b-flat minor tonality, then imitations between strings and horns

Allegro giusto

Strings

p

| 48 | 7:49 | THEME 7 — Russian folk dance | played by flutes over tambourine, *p*, same tempo, e-flat minor tonality |

Allegro giusto

Flutes

p

8:31	THEME 5—Marseillaise	held pitch in bass; *p*; change of key; agitated tempo; played by trumpets, fragments imitated by horns; crescendo to *f*
9:18	THEME 4	briefly returns in strings, *ff*, interspersed with fragments of [THEME 5], fanfares in brasses; slowing of tempo
9:56	THEME 6—Russian folk lullaby	returns in high strings, *p*, imitated by low strings
10:37	THEME 7—Russian folk dance	returns played by violins over tambourine, *mf*, minor tonality
10:55	THEME 5—Marseillaise	played by horns, fanfare fragments in a series of sequences; *mf*; shifting major and minor tonalities
11:27	THEME 5—Marseillaise	played by trumpets, *ff*, rifles and cannons fire
11:39	TRANSITION	high strings play descending pattern of sequences, gradually slowing
12:17	THEME 1—Russian Orthodox Church hymn	in full orchestra, *fff*, church bells and chimes added
13:29	THEME 3—fanfare-type march fragments	faster tempo, *ffff*, continues to the end, major tonality
49 13:39	THEME 8—Czar's Hymn	in E-flat major tonality, cannons and rifles fire and bells ring

| 14:10 | THEME 3—fragments | full orchestra and bells on one held E-flat pitch, *ffff*, final chord |

Twentieth-century Russia

Many communist-era composers retained a nationalistic approach in their music. The government not only encouraged them to do so but reprimanded them when their music became too "international." Most of these composers are discussed in Chapter 21: Alexander Scriabin (1872–1915), Sergei Rachmaninov (rahk-*mah*-nih-nof, 1873–1943), Sergei Prokofiev (1891–1953), Dmitri Shostakovitch (shos-tah-*koh*-vich, 1906–75), Aram Khachaturian (kahtch-a-*tur*-ee-an, 1903–78), and Dmitri Kabelevsky (kab-a-*leff*-skee, 1904–87).

NIKOLAI RIMSKY-KORSAKOV (1844–1908)

Born in Tikhvin, Russia, Rimsky-Korsakov (*rim*-skee–*kors*-a-cuff) later served eleven years as a naval officer with the title of Inspector of Naval Bands.

But Rimsky-Korsakov's interests were not in the military, and he joined the faculty of the St. Petersburg Conservatory of Music to teach composition and orchestration. Like his colleagues in the "Russian Five," Rimsky-Korsakov used native folk melodies in his compositions and also arranged and edited collections of Russian folk music.

A highly renowned orchestrator and composer, Rimsky-Korsakov edited many of Mussorgsky's and Borodin's works to facilitate their performance. His most famous students were Igor Stravinsky and Sergei Prokofiev (discussed in Chapters 19 and 20). Although his compositions include symphonies, chamber music, choruses, and songs, his most well-known works are his symphonic poems and operas.

PRINCIPAL WORKS

Orchestra Music: Concerto for Trombone and Brass Band (1877); Symphonic suite *Scheherazade* (1888); *Capriccio espagnol* (1887); and the *Russian Easter Overture* (1888)

Operas: 16 operas, *Sadko* (1898); *Snegurochka* (Snow Maiden, 1882); *Mozart and Salieri* (1897); *Skzka o Tsare Saltane* (Tale of Czar Saltan, which includes "The Flight of the Bumble Bee," 1900); *Le Coq d'or* (The Golden Cockerel, 1909)

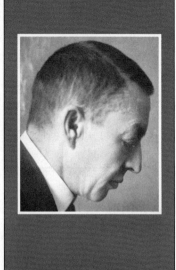

SERGEI RACHMANINOV (1873–1943)

Rachmaninov's (rahk-*mah*-nih-nof) early musical studies were at the St. Petersburg Conservatory. Later, he studied at the Moscow Conservatory, graduating at 19. A brilliant career as a pianist, conductor, and composer followed, affording him enough economic security to travel extensively.

When his First Symphony (1895) was not well received by the Moscow public, Rachmaninov withdrew from composition for a while. But with the completion and successful premiere of his Second Piano Concerto in 1901, Rachmaninov regained his stride and went on to compose some of his most popular works.

In 1917, fleeing the Russian Revolution, Rachmaninov and his family emigrated to the United States, where he was immediately acclaimed for his pianistic abilities. Subsequent concert tours and record contracts kept him extremely busy. Yet he found time to compose, premiering several of his works with the Philadelphia Orchestra.

With his nineteenth-century Romantic style becoming increasingly anachronistic, Rachmaninov decided to abandon composition. He continued as a successful concert pianist until his death at his Beverly Hills home at the age of 69.

PRINCIPAL WORKS

Orchestral Works: Piano Concertos: No. 1 in f-sharp minor (1891); No. 2 in c minor (1901); No. 3 in a minor (1909); No. 4 in g minor (1926); Symphonies: No. 1 in d minor (1895); No. 2 in e minor (1907); No. 3 in a minor (1936); *The Isle of the Dead* (1909); *Rhapsody on a Theme by Paganini* for piano and orchestra (1934); *Symphonic Dances* (1940)

Piano Music: Preludes (23) (1904, 1910), sonatas, études, and variations

Choral Music: Liturgy of St. John Chrysostom (1910); *The Bells* (1913)

Opera: Aleko (1893)

Miscellaneous songs and chamber music

Other Nationalist Composers

THE CZECH REPUBLIC   Until 1919, the country we know today as the Czech Republic was part of the Austro-Hungarian (Hapsburg) Empire. It was home to several outstanding nationalist composers. Antonin Dvořák (1841–1904) and Bedrich Smetana (1824–84) are the most widely known.

BÉLA BARTÓK (1881–1945)

Bartók (*bahr*-tok) was born in Hungary during the last years of the Hapsburgs' reign. After early piano training with his mother, he studied at the Budapest Royal Academy of Music.

Following graduation, Bartók embarked on a successful career as a concert pianist, composing in his spare time. Throughout most of his life, Bartók's main source of income was from piano teaching—30 years at the Budapest Academy.

Bartók's studies had been mainly in the Austro-German tradition until 1904, when he began discovering the vast resource of folk music. Together with the Hungarian composer Zoltán Kodály, Bartók compiled and analyzed the folk music not only of his native Hungary but also of other countries. Both men utilized their findings in composing nationalistic music.

In 1940, when Hungary entered into a collaboration with the Nazis, Bartók fled with his family to the United States. In their haste, they had to leave most of their possessions in Hungary, settling in New York City with meager resources.

Unable to find work immediately, Bartók used what was left of his money to support his family. Their financial difficulties were compounded by his bouts with leukemia.

Columbia University came to the family's rescue by appointing Bartók to a position as a folk music researcher at the university library. Also, a few composing commissions helped ease Bartók's circumstances, especially the Boston Symphony's commission in 1943 for the *Concerto for Orchestra*. Bartók died at 64 in a New York City hospital.

PRINCIPAL WORKS

Orchestral Music: Kossuth (1903); *Dance Suite* (1917); *Music for Strings, Percussion, and Celesta* (1936); *Concerto for Orchestra* (1943); 3 piano concertos; 2 violin concertos, Viola Concerto (1945)

Ballets: The Wooden Prince (1917); *The Miraculous Mandarin* (1926)

Opera: Bluebeard's Castle (1918)

Chamber Music: 6 string quartets; *Contrasts* for Violin, Clarinet and Piano (1938); Sonata for Solo Violin (1944); sonatas for violin and piano

Piano Music: 14 Bagatelles (1908), *Allegro barbaro* (1911), *Suite* (1916), *Sonata* (1926), *Out of Doors* (1926), *Mikrokosmos* volumes 1-6 (1926-39)

Choral Music: Cantata profana (1930)

Miscellaneous choral works, songs, and folk song arrangements

Dvořák
(*dvohr*-zhahk)
Smetana
(*shmeh*-tuh-nuh)

Dvořák is particularly interesting to Americans. After having achieved fame as a composer in his native Bohemia, he moved to New York City to become director of the National Conservatory of Music (no longer in existence) from 1892-1895. During that time, he wrote his famous New World Symphony (Symphony No. 9).

Kodály
(koh-*dye*)

HUNGARY   Franz Liszt (see biography in Chapter 13) and the twentieth-century composers Zoltán Kodály (1882–1967) and Béla Bartók (1881–1945) are the Hungarian composers whose music you are most likely to hear at concerts.

Grieg
(greeg)
Sibelius
(sih-*bayl*-yus)

SCANDINAVIA   Edvard Grieg (1843–1907) of Norway wrote many Norwegian songs and is well known for his nationalistic *Peer Gynt Suites*. Jean (*yan*) Sibelius (1865–1957) of Finland is best known for his *Finlandia* Violin Concerto, tone poems, *Valse triste*, and his symphonies—especially Symphony No. 2.

Elgar

Vaughan Williams

UNITED KINGDOM   Edward Elgar (1857–1934) was a distinctly English composer. His most famous works are the *Pomp and Circumstance* Marches and *Enigma* Variations. Ralph Vaughan Williams (1872–1958), another English nationalist composer, once wrote:

> *Art, like charity, should begin at home. If it is to be of any value, it must grow out of the very life of himself (the composer), the community in which he lives, the nation to which he belongs.*

To accomplish this task, Vaughan Williams incorporated English folk songs into many of his works, notably his *English Folk Song Suite* and *Fantasia on "Greensleeves."*

Grainger

Percy Grainger (1882–1961) is less easy to classify. Born in Australia and educated in London, he lived in the United States during the latter part of his life. For many years, Grainger wandered through the English and Irish countrysides with an Edison cylinder-recorder and music paper, recording and notating folk songs he heard. Then, he abundantly incorporated these songs into his music. He is best known for his many British folk song settings, such as *Irish Tune from County Derry, Country Gardens*, and his wind band work *Lincolnshire Posy*.

ITALY   Several famous opera composers are considered Italian nationalists. The greatest were Giuseppe Verdi (*vehr*-dee, 1813–1901) and Giacomo Puccini (poo-*tchee*-nee, 1858–1924), both discussed in Chapter 14.

Respighi
(res-*pee*-ghee)

Ottorino Respighi (1879–1936) is best known for his orchestral works: *Roman Festivals, The Pines of Rome, The Fountains of Rome*, and *The Birds*.

Jean Siebelius at the age of 23.

SPAIN   Isaac Albéniz (1860–1909), Enrique Granados (1867–1916), and Manuel de Falla (1876–1947) incorporated lively flamenco and Andalusian dance rhythms into their colorful music. Also, because of the use of instruments indigenous to Spain such as castanets, tambourine, and guitars, their music sounds distinctly Spanish.

Albéniz (ahl-*bay*-neeth)
Granados (grah-*nah*-dohs)
de Falla (*fah*-yah)

NORTH AMERICA   Chapters 23 through 25 discuss composers in the United States.

Summary of Terms

Andalusian rhythms	Czar's Hymn	La Marseillaise
balalaika	flamenco dance rhythms	Russian Five
bells	folk song	tambourine
castanets	guitar	wanderlust

CHAPTER 17

Impressionism

ﾐ *Impressionistic Poetry and Painting*

A Claude Monet painting, *Impression — Soleil Levant* (*Impression of the Eastern Sunshine*; see Plate 9), provided the inspiration for the name of a new movement in France. Alienated by German intellectualism and "oversentimentality," French artists of the late nineteenth century felt more spiritually attuned to quieter, more sensual expression. For example, the poet Mallarmé was more interested in beauty and sound of the French language than he was in the content.

French painters reflected their interest in the "impression" of a subject rather than in its detailed, specific content. The works of Monet, Manet, Renoir, and others epitomize the Impressionistic style—uncomplicated subject matter portrayed in the quiet of pastel colors with vague definition.

New Inventions Influence Art

Two practical inventions boosted Impressionistic painting: the camera and the paint tube (similar to the toothpaste tube).

THE CAMERA   Until the invention of the camera, a painter's primary role was that of a "photographer"—to capture the moment for posterity. Notice how Hans Holbein's portrait of Henry VIII looks almost like a snapshot of the king.

In 1827, Joseph Niépce produced the earliest photographs on a metal plate, encouraging painters to look at a subject with a fresh eye. Painters gathered in Parisian cafés, intently discussing new options for capturing the feelings and impressions of the moment. Although the details of their paintings may seem veiled, as though you were looking at them through a slight haze, the mood is always clear (see Monet's *Les Meules* below).

THE PAINT TUBE   Before the invention of the lead tube of oil paint, artists rarely worked outdoors. When the did, they found it very inconvenient. Oil paint thinned with alcohol dries in minutes in the open air. To avoid lugging containers of paints and alcohol everywhere, artists were limited to making pencil sketches of their outdoor subjects. Later, in their studio, they had to recreate the scene, mixing paint to match whatever colors they could recall.

With the freedom of a tube, an artist could dab colors on a palette, cap the tube, and quickly paint a scene. And though artists still had to wait for sunlight and to paint quickly, they could capture the spontaneity and mood of the moment. Impressionistic painting, with its sparse details, invites each perceiver to fill in the gaps with personal impressions.

Painting *Henry VIII* (1540) by Hans Holbein the Younger.

Les Meules (The Haystacks, 1891) by Monet.

Painting *Rouen Cathedral, West Facade, Sunlight* by Monet.

Photograph of Rouen Cathedral, West Facade.

Aided by the new tube, Claude Monet (1840–1926) painted the west facade of the Rouen Cathedral from the same location at various times of the day. Changes in light and shadow make each painting different (see Plate 9). Monet was also fascinated by the effect of changing lights, shadows, and colors on the lily pads in his pond in Giverny, France. He thus created a series of masterpieces—his impressions of these lily pads as the sun progressed through the day.

ᨊ Impressionism in Music

Toward the end of the nineteenth century, French composers rejected the Germanic mainstream in favor of their own music. Championed by Claude Debussy, the new French music reflected some of the new trends in poetry and painting. It came to be known by the same name: Impressionism.

Paris World Exposition

The Paris World Expositions of 1878 and 1889 profoundly influenced Debussy, who was searching for new materials at the time. Hearing the Indonesian *gamelan* ensemble use delicate finger cymbals, Debussy decided to incorporate the instrument into his orchestral works. Groups from Japan and China also attracted his interest, and soon thereafter, Debussy incorporated Asian scales into his music.

Characteristics of Impressionism

Creating a new world of sound was Debussy's challenge. To do this, he developed techniques that contrasted with those of the late Romantic composers.

FORM: AVOIDING HARD OUTLINES   Debussy avoided clear-cut cadences and resting points. Instead, his music has a feeling of wandering or floating. (Some have said that the undulating sounds of *La mer* [The Sea] make them feel "seasick.")

ORCHESTRAL COLORS: USING DELICATE TONE COLORS   Debussy's instrumental effects were delicate, subtle, and full of color, bearing a similarity to Impressionistic painters' choices of delicate colors. He preferred the following instruments (in order of importance):

flutes
oboes
clarinets
strings (often muted)
harp (sweeping arpeggios veil
  tonality)

brass (used sparingly, usually with
  mutes)
percussion (used sparingly, avoiding
  military instruments; employed
  antique cymbals and triangles)

CLAUDE DEBUSSY (1862–1918)

Debussy (de-byoo-*see*) was born in Saint-Germain-en-Laye, a small town near Paris. At 11, he entered the Paris Conservatory, studying piano and composition. After winning the prestigious Prix de Rome, he went to study in that great city.

At 25, returning to Paris to compose and perform as a pianist, Debussy became part of a wide circle of artists, writers, and musicians who met often to discuss new directions for the arts. He became the main developer of Impressionistic music.

Toward the end of his career, Debussy became associated with the Ballets Russes, composing his last work, *Jeux*, for that ensemble. World War I had its effect on Debussy: He produced only a few minor works until his death in 1918 at the age of 55.

PRINCIPAL WORKS

Orchestral Music: Prélude à l'après-midi d'un faune (Prelude to The Afternoon of a Faun, 1894); *Nocturnes* (1899); *Danses sacrée et profane* (1904); *La mer* (The Sea, 1905); *Première Rapsodie for Clarinet and Piano* (1910); *Images* (1912)

Ballet: Jeux (Games, 1913)

Incidental Music: Le Martyre de St. Sébastien (1911)

Chamber Music: String Quartet (1893), *Petite Pièce for clarinet and piano* (1910), *Sonata for Cello and Piano* (1915), *Sonata for Flute, Viola, and Harp* (1915); *Sonata for Violin and Piano* (1917)

Piano Music: Suite, pour le piano (1901); *Suite bergamasque* (1909); *Estampes* (1903); *Images* (1905); *Children's Corner* (1908); Préludes, 2 books (1910, 1913); *Études* (1915)

Opera: Pelléas et Mélisande (1902)

Songs: Fêtes galantes (1881, 1904); *Chansons de Bilitis* (1898); more than 60 others

Choral Music: La Demoiselle élue (The Chosen Maid, 1888)

RHYTHMS: DE-EMPHASIZING SOLID, SYMMETRICAL RHYTHMS To deviate from the predictability of typical rhythms (for example, those found in marches and waltzes), Debussy calls for vague beats and complex subdivisions (7, 11, 13). A run of 7 tones to a beat may follow 13 tones to a beat.

The Eiffel Tower in 1989, celebrating its centennial.

SCALES: INCORPORATING THE NONTRADITIONAL Rather than use diatonic scales (do, re, mi), which give the feeling of a solid base, Debussy incorporated three other scale types: *pentatonic, chromatic,* and *whole-tone.*

Pentatonic Scales. Debussy had heard Asian performers use a variety of five-tone scales at the Paris Fair. The following is only one of the many pentatonic scales:

The pentatonic scales that Debussy incorporated were not completely new to Western music. Many concert pieces and folk songs use them—European folk songs, cowboy songs, and Native American songs.

Good - by, old Paint, I'm a leav- ing Chey - enne.

Chromatic Scales. The chromatic scale, though sparingly used, appears in Western concert music since the music of Bach. In music, "chromatic" refers to all the black and white keys on a keyboard. Moving in half steps, these scales incorporate all the tones used in Western music.

Because each interval in the chromatic scale is of equal size—a half step—the scale seems to avoid a home base or tonal center.

ASCENDING CHROMATIC SCALE

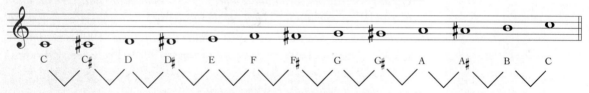

half steps

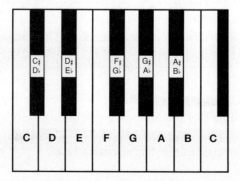

Traditional diatonic scales are constructed with a mixture of whole and half steps, giving the feeling of key-based stability.

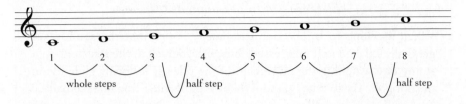

Whole-tone Scale. In his search for music materials to convey the vagueness of Impressionism, Debussy used a *whole-tone scale*. A whole-tone scale consists of equal large steps (whole-step intervals). Similar to the chromatic scale, which consists of equal small steps (half-step intervals), the whole-tone scale seems to avoid a key centered on a specific pitch.

HARMONY   Because it provided a feeling of solidity based in a certain key base, traditional harmony did not fit easily into Debussy's style. So, he ex-   Extended chords
tended the traditional chords of three and four tones built on any degree of
the diatonic scale. (See music notation in Appendix A)

Notice that the 13th chord contains all the pitches of the scale. Because all pitches are equal, the 13th chord has only a remote reference to the root tone or key center.

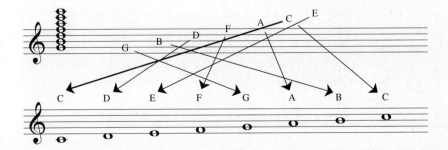

LISTENING INSIGHTS

Listening to Impressionistic Music

When listening to Impressionistic music, notice that the sounds are generally relaxed and unstressed. Imagine yourself at the seashore on a sunny day watching the movement of the tides as sailboats glide by on the horizon. Try to relax without following the music too intellectually.

LISTENING ACTIVITY ❧

DEBUSSY, *PRELUDE TO THE AFTERNOON OF A FAUN*
LARGE FORM: DESCRIPTIVE CONCERT PRELUDE
DETAILED FORM: A B A

❘ *Compact Disc 4, Track 18*

Stéphane Mallarmé's poem provided the inspiration for Debussy's *Prélude à L'après-midi d'un faune* (Prelude to the Afternoon of a Faun). The poem concerns a mythical half-man, half-animal forest creature.

Awakening from a dream of lovely nymphs, the creature is disoriented. Is he awake or still dreaming? Because the afternoon is warm and lazy, he decides to go back to sleep. Not much action, but the scenario is perfect for Impressionism.

The concert prelude here is similar to the concert overture, which is a concert opener, rather than a work preceding an opera or ballet.

A flute opens and closes the piece with a dreamy, chromatic scale. Fast runs in the orchestra make the middle section slightly more active. Notice the use of the Indonesian antique cymbals at the end.

ABOUT THE LISTENING GUIDE: Since Debussy and other Impressionists expected audiences to listen more sensually than intellectually, the listening guide presents a less-than-detailed analysis. Furthermore, late nineteenth-century music contained changing meters, chromatic harmony, extended chords, and highly complex forms, making detailed analysis extremely difficult for most listeners.

LISTENING GUIDE

DEBUSSY, *PRELUDE TO THE AFTERNOON OF A FAUN*
LARGE FORM: DESCRIPTIVE CONCERT PRELUDE; DETAILED FORM: A B A

Compact Disc 4, Track 18
Running time: 10:21

Section A

18	0:00	CHROMATIC MELODY	flute solo, unaccompanied at beginning; *p*; slow tempo, changing meters, rubato; chromatic and pentatonic scales; extended chords; harp glissandos blur tonality

0:56	CHROMATIC MELODY	mainly in solo flute, tremolo strings; *pp*
2:01	CHROMATIC MELODY	flute solo expressively with harp arpeggios
2:42	CHROMATIC MELODY	flute solo with harp arpeggios
3:16	TRANSITION	cadence; clarinet
3:35	WHOLE-TONE MELODY	solos by clarinet, then flute; faster tempo, changing meters; whole-tone scales

4:21	TRANSITION	faster and animated; crescendo to *f*; gradual diminuendo and slowing; modulating and cadencing to A-flat tonal area

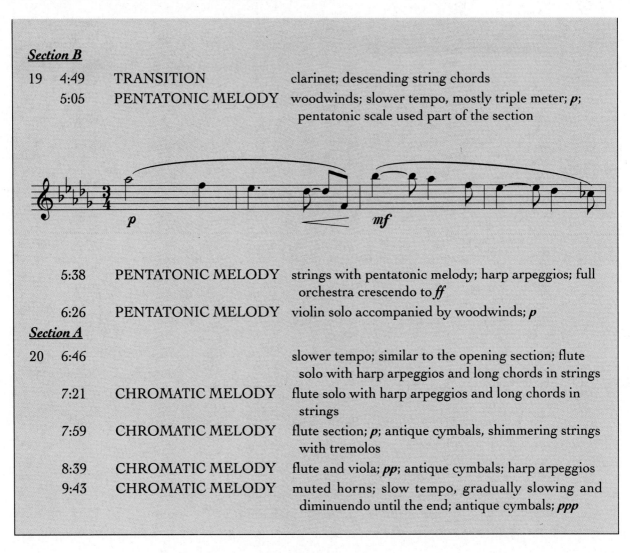

Section B

19 4:49   TRANSITION   clarinet; descending string chords
    5:05   PENTATONIC MELODY   woodwinds; slower tempo, mostly triple meter; *p*;
                                      pentatonic scale used part of the section

    5:38   PENTATONIC MELODY   strings with pentatonic melody; harp arpeggios; full
                                      orchestra crescendo to *ff*
    6:26   PENTATONIC MELODY   violin solo accompanied by woodwinds; *p*

Section A

20 6:46   slower tempo; similar to the opening section; flute
                                      solo with harp arpeggios and long chords in strings
    7:21   CHROMATIC MELODY   flute solo with harp arpeggios and long chords in
                                      strings
    7:59   CHROMATIC MELODY   flute section; *p*; antique cymbals, shimmering strings
                                      with tremolos
    8:39   CHROMATIC MELODY   flute and viola; *pp*; antique cymbals; harp arpeggios
    9:43   CHROMATIC MELODY   muted horns; slow tempo, gradually slowing and
                                      diminuendo until the end; antique cymbals; *ppp*

Debussy was the most prominent of the Impressionist composers, but others used the same techniques. Maurice Ravel (1875–1937) was one of them. Although he composed in many styles, including jazz, several of his pieces were influenced by Impressionism—*Pavane pour une infante défunte* (Pavane for a Dead Princess) and the *Daphnis et Chloé* ballet.

Summary of Terms

antique cymbals	gamelan	Prix de Rome
Ballets Russes	Paris World Exposition	13th chord
chromatic scale	pentatonic scales	whole-tone scale
extended chords		

❧ Plate 8

An early nineteenth-century grand pianoforte. (See Chapter 13)

Source: The Metropolitan Museum of Art, Gift of Mrs. Henry McSweeny, 1959.

❧ Plate 9

Impression: Soleil Levant (Impression of the Sunrise) *by Claude Monet which inspired the name of the Impressionism movement in painting, poetry, and music. (See Chapter 17)*

Source: Giraudon/Art Resource

ひ Plate 10 (below)
Cynthia Giannini and Edward Stierle in "Tea from China" from The Joffrey Ballet's Production of Tchaikovsky's **The Nutcracker.** *(See Chapter 16)*
Source: © Herbert Migdoll

ひ Plate 11 (above)
The Fiddler by Marc Chagall. Painted in Paris in 1911, the painting recreates a surrealistic scene from Chagall's childhood village in his native Russia. (See Chapter 16)
Source: Errch Lessing from Art Resource

ひ Plate 12
The Persistence of Memory (1931) *by the notorious Spanish painter Salvador Dali. Twentieth-century Surrealistic painters such as Dali often depicted distorted images inspired by the mind's dream and unconscious states. (See Chapter 18)*
Source: Collection, The Museum of Modern Art New York, Given anonymously

≈ Plate 13

Painting Number 200, *a painting by Russian artist Vassily Kandinsky,
who became the leading member of a group of nonobjective or abstract painters
working in Munich, Germany, early in the twentieth century.*

Source: Collection, The Museum of Modern Art New York. Mrs. Simon
Guggenheim Fund

≈ Plate 14

Les Demoiselles d'Avignon *(The Ladies of Avignon, 1907) by Pablo
Picasso. This is an early cubist-modern painting.*

Source: August/Zorn Slide collection. Original source: Picasso Museum Barcelona

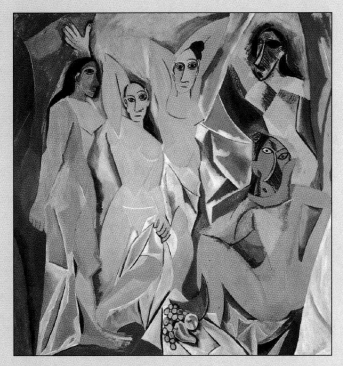

MAURICE RAVEL (1875–1937)

Ravel (rah-*vel*) was born in the Pyrenees in the south of France. Like Debussy, Ravel studied at the Paris Conservatory of Music. Though clearly the most outstanding student composer, Ravel was denied the prestigious Prix de Rome four times. So outraged were Ravel's teachers, friends, and the public about his not receiving the award that they forced the resignation of the director of the Conservatory.

During World War I, Ravel drove an ambulance on the front lines. The war over, Ravel resumed composing and was soon recognized as France's leading composer.

Early in 1928 when George Gershwin visited Paris, the two composers became friends. Gershwin had wanted to study European styles with Ravel. Instead, Ravel advised him to continue his unique style of incorporating jazz into his concert music. As a result of their discussions, Gershwin went home to compose the tone poem *An American in Paris*, and Ravel wrote his Piano Concerto in G in which he used Gershwin-style jazz.

Ravel developed into a master of orchestration as displayed in works like *La Valse, Daphnis et Chloé,* and his orchestration of Mussorgsky's *Pictures at an Exhibition* (1922). At 60, Ravel contracted a brain disease and died two years later.

PRINCIPAL WORKS

Orchestral Music: Alborada del gracioso (1905); *Rapsodie espagnole* (1908); *La valse* (1920); *Bolero* (1928); *Piano Concerto in D Major for Left Hand* (1930); *Piano Concerto in G Major* (1931)

Chamber Music: String Quartet (1903); *Trio for Violin, Cello and Piano* (1914); violin sonatas

Ballets: Ma Mère l'Oye (Mother Goose, 1912); *Daphnis et Chloé* (1912)

Operas: L'enfant et les sortilèges (The Child and the Spells, 1925), *L'Heure espagnole* (1909)

Piano Music: Pavane pour une infante défunte (Pavane for a Dead Princess, 1899, later orchestrated); *Jeux d'eau* (1901); *Sonatine* (1905); *Miroirs* (1905); *Valses nobles et sentimentales* (1911); *Le tombeau de Couperin* (1917)

Songs: Shéhérazade with orchestra (1903); *Histoires naturelles* (1906); *Chants populaires* (1910)

CHAPTER 18

The Twentieth-Century Style Period

✣ Influence of the World Wars

The fever of nationalism in Europe, so charmingly conveyed in the nineteenth century, veered out of control in 1914. As country after country entered the hostilities, Europe was swept into a world war.

When the war ended in 1918, many of Europe's prized libraries, theaters, concert halls, and museums were in ruins. Throughout the continent, economies were in shambles.

The toll of World War I was staggering: 8.5 million killed, 21 million wounded, 7.5 million prisoners and missing.

World War I also had a devastating effect on the European artistic community. Drafted into service to fight the war, many artists were killed. Some fled to the United States. Others sought refuge in neutral countries where they could continue working. The November 1918 armistice finally halted "the war to end all wars."

After only a brief period of recovery in the late 1920s, the Great Depression paralyzed Europe and North America. Playing on the panic of the people, the fascist governments of Adolf Hitler, Benito Mussolini, and Hideki Tojo laid the groundwork for World War II (1939–45).

When peace finally returned in 1945, 57 countries of the world were scarred by the greatest trauma in human history: an estimated 54.8 million people killed—most of them civilians. Millions more were left crippled and homeless. The extent of the war's cruelty brought civilization to its knees. Nazi genocide killed at least 14 million Jews, Poles, Slavs, gypsies, homosexuals, and political dissidents.

Devastated, the artistic community revived slowly. With the cost of war, and post-war rebuilding, each nation's resources allocated toward funding of the arts were strained. For approximately fifty years (1914–64), the arts in Europe struggled. Aided partly by the United States' Marshall Plan, most European nations gradually regained financial and artistic stability by the 1960s.

Art Redefined

Before the twentieth century, most art was defined by the adjective "beautiful." Music was beautiful, harmonious sound; painting, beautiful pictures; dance, beautiful movement, and so on.

Could music, painting, poetry, dance, and the theater seem "ugly," and still be "art"? Picasso's *Guernica* (see painting) depicts a hideous scene:

Closeup of a section of *Guernica* by Pablo Picasso.

Hitler's *Luftwaffe* testing their new weapons by bombing the peaceful Spanish town of Guernica in 1937. Twisted, wrenching victims expose the horror of this despicable act.

Igor Stravinsky and Pablo Picasso were friends and shared views on art. Adhering to an outlook similar to Picasso's, Stravinsky composed his ballet *Rite of Spring* (discussed in the next chapter). Subtitled "Scenes from Pagan Russia," the ballet is characterized by angular dancing, stark scenery, and dissonant music. Its infamous 1913 debut changed the direction of music for the rest of the twentieth century.

ॐ *Overview of the Twentieth-century Period (1900 to the present)*

COMPOSERS

Samuel Barber, Béla Bartók, Alban Berg, Leonard Bernstein, Ernest Bloch, Nadia Boulanger, Pierre Boulez, Benjamin Britten, Carlos Chávez, Aaron Copland, Edward Elgar, Edward Kennedy "Duke" Ellington, Manuel de Falla, Gabriel Fauré, George Gershwin, Edvard Grieg, Paul Hindemith, Gustav Holst, Arthur Honegger, Charles Ives, Leos Janácek, Jerome Kern, Zoltán Kodály, Franz Lehár, Witold Lutoslawski, Oliver Messiaen, Gian Carlo Menotti, Darius Milhaud, Francis Poulenc, Sergei Prokofiev, Sergei Rachmaninoff, Maurice Ravel, Ottorino Respighi, Richard Rodgers, Sigmund Romberg, Arnold Schoenberg, William Schuman, Alexander Scriabin, Dmitri Shostakovich, Jean Sibelius, Karlheinz Stockhausen, Richard Strauss, Igor Stravinsky, Edgard Varèse, William Walton, Kurt Weill, Ralph Vaughan Williams, Anton Webern, Ellen Taaffe Zwilich

VISUAL ARTISTS

Mateo Alonso, Max Beckmann, Georges Braque, Alexander Calder, Marc Chagall, Jean Cocteau, Salvador Dali, Willem De Kooning, Walt Disney, Marcel Duchamp, Max Ernst, Buckminster Fuller, Juan Gris, Wassily Kandinsky, Paul Klee, Le Corbusier, Henri Matisse, Mies van der Rohe, Joan Miró, Amedeo Modigliani, Piet Mondrian, Claude Monet, Henry Moore, Georgia O'Keeffe, Pablo Picasso, Jackson Pollock, Auguste Renoir, Diego Rivera, Auguste Rodin, Georges Rouault, Henri Rousseau, Eero Saarinen, Maurice Utrillo, Andy Warhol, Frank Lloyd Wright, Andrew Wyeth

WRITERS

Edward Albee, Bertold Brecht, Truman Capote, Paddy Chayefsky, Joseph Conrad, e. e. cummings, T. S. Eliot, William Faulkner, F. Scott Fitzgerald, Robert Frost, Gregorio López Fuentes, Lillian Hellman,

Ernest Hemingway, Aldous Huxley, A. E. Housman, Henrik Ibsen, Henry James, James Joyce, Franz Kafka, Federico Garcia Lorca, Norman Mailer, Thomas Mann, Arthur Miller, O'Henry, Eugene O'Neill, Dorothy Parker, Carl Sandburg, George Bernard Shaw, Neil Simon, Gertrude Stein, John Steinbeck, August Strindberg, Leo Tolstoi, Mark Twain, H. G. Wells, Tennessee Williams, Thomas Wolfe

PHILOSOPHERS

Alfred Adler, Martin Buber, Teilhard de Chardin, John Dewey, Sigmund Freud, Eric Fromm, Mohandas K. (Mahatma) Gandhi, Carl Jung, Martin Luther King, Jr., Mao Tse-tung, Bertrand Russell, George Santayana, Jean-Paul Sartre

SOCIAL, POLITICAL, AND CULTURAL EVENTS

Freud's psychoanalytic theories, jazz, Einstein's relativity theories, United Nations, World Wars I and II, Russian Revolution, communism, Great Depression (U.S. and Europe), Korean War, Vietnam War, Common Market, European Economic Community, pop art, Malcolm X, chance music and painting, dadaism, Nonviolence (Gandhi), Civil Rights Movement (Martin Luther King), racial integration

SCIENCE, TECHNOLOGY

Ford's production-line automobile, telephone, airplane, computer, films, television, phonograph, microchip, semiconductor, laser technology, penicillin, smallpox vaccine, polio vaccine, *Sputnik*, man on the moon, organ transplantation, DNA research, gene-splicing

Characteristics of Twentieth-Century Music

GENERAL	Music often sounds dissonant, complex, asymmetrical, non-emotional, objective, satirical; often experimental, eclectic resources
PERFORMING MEDIA	Chamber orchestra and ensembles used more often than symphony orchestra; all previous media still used; electronic synthesizers and keyboards; mixed media: pre-recorded electronic sounds combined with traditional instruments; computer-generated sounds
RHYTHM	Polyrhythms (layers of different rhythms), polymeters, irregular rhythmic patterns, ostinato (recurring patterns)

MELODY	Wide ranges, both for voices and for instruments; fragmented, disjunct, exotic intervals and scales (Asian, chromatic, pentatonic, whole-tone, twelve-tone, quarter-tone)
HARMONY	Extensive use of dissonance; polychords (two or more different chords together), clusters (chords by seconds), quartal harmony (chords by fourths); exotic, experimental sounds
EXPRESSION	All previous techniques still used; extreme effects, including silence
TEXTURE	Polyphonic texture often used; mixes of polyphonic and homophonic; layers of ideas and sounds
FORMS	All forms of the previous periods used, but highly modified; experimental forms; forms incorporate new sound sources and compositional techniques:

Musique Concrète: traditional and environmental sounds pre-recorded and manipulated on the tape recorder

Chance Music: also called aleatory—improvised, unpredictable, vague or nonspecific notation, leaving much to the performer to decide

Electronic Music: electronically produced sounds, also called synthesizer music

Computer Music: electronic music organized and manipulated by the computer.

Igor Stravinsky (right) and Pablo Picasso, in a caricature by Jean Cocteau.

⁓ *The Evolution of Musical Resources*

		Innovations	*Forms/Styles*	*Composers*
1600	↓	tonal music	opera perfection of the violin	Monteverdi Stradivarius
1700	↓	traditional scales	concerto	Vivaldi
		traditional chords	cantata, oratorio	Bach, Handel
1750	↓	traditional forms	symphony, string quartet	Haydn, Mozart
1800	↓	loosening of forms	orchestra expands brass valves, keyed woodwinds, art songs	Beethoven, Berlioz Schubert, Schumann
1850	↓	expanding harmony	large, virtuoso orchestra	Brahms, Wagner, Strauss, Mahler
		folk songs and instruments search for new materials	Nationalism	Tchaikovsky, Mussorgsky

1900	↓	whole-tone, pentatonic,
		  chromatic scales, expanded
		  chords by thirds
			Impressionism	Debussy, Ravel

1910	↓	polychords, polytonality, polyrhythms, polymedia	discussion	Stravinsky, Ives
		atonality, 12-tone	serial music	Schoenberg, Berg, Webern

1920	↓	back to tonality,	neo-Classicism
			  traditional forms
				Stravinsky, Prokofiev,
				  Shostakovich

		jazz, improvisation	performer control	Joplin, Gershwin
1930	↓	eclecticism		Gershwin, Copland
1940	↓	natural sounds manipulated by tape recorder — composer control	*musique concrète*	Varèse, Cage

1950	↓	vague-graphic notation
		  process not product
			chance (aleatory) music	Cage, Stockhausen,
				  Feldman

		electronic synthesizer
		  composer control
		  new sound sources, also
		  recreates music of past
			electronic music	Babbitt, Luening,
				  Subotnick, Carlos

1960	↓	multi-track recording, amplified
		  guitars, synthesizers
			pop, rock, eclectic,
			  folk, blues
				Beatles, Bob Dylan
				  Rolling Stones

1970	↓	mix of resources	eclecticism, fusion	Bernstein, Lloyd Webber
1980	↓	computer assisted electronic sounds	eclectic, growing neo-Romantic	Lesemann
1990	↓	home electronic keyboards computer-synthesizer	neo-Romantic	Del Tredici

CHAPTER 19

Stravinsky: Into the Twentieth Century

Just as audiences had started to grow comfortable with the soothing "new" music of Debussy and the Impressionists, Igor Stravinsky burst on the scene with music to jar the senses.

ᔓ Stravinsky's Pivotal Position

At the beginning of the twentieth century, Stravinsky held a position similar to Beethoven's a century earlier. During Beethoven's time, the pendulum of change had begun to swing from the objectivism of the Classical period toward the subjectivism of the Romantic period. A century later, the pendulum began to swing back to objectivism.

Both Beethoven and Stravinsky guided those changes in music, giving credence to the so-called Great Man Theory of anthropology: When the time is right, a "great man" can move society into a new era.

IGOR STRAVINSKY (1882–1971)

When Stravinsky (stra-*vin*-skee) was born, his father was a leading bass at the Imperial Opera in St. Petersburg (Leningrad), Russia. Music wasn't Igor's earliest interest. Instead, Stravinsky pursued painting and theater.

Despite his own musical success, the elder Stravinsky encouraged his son to study civil law. But soon after enrolling in St. Petersburg University, Stravinsky revealed his real interests. He willingly dropped his law studies to study composition with Rimsky-Korsakov at the St. Petersburg Conservatory.

In the audience at the St. Petersburg debut of Stravinsky's first major work, *Fireworks*, was his distant cousin Diaghilev, a prominent avant-garde thinker. So impressed was Diaghilev by his cousin's music that he commissioned Stravinsky to compose music for his newly formed Ballets Russes, a Paris-based dance company of Russian expatriates. The collaboration resulted in the *Firebird* ballet of 1910, *Petrushka* in 1911, the monumental *The Rite of Spring* in 1913, and other works.

The outbreak of World War I in 1914, along with his wife's illness, convinced Stravinsky to move to Switzerland. In 1917, the Russian Revolution made it impossible for them to return to their homeland. In 1925, with Stravinsky as their conductor, the Ballets Russes toured the United States. The outbreak of World War II in Europe coincided with the deaths of his daughter, wife, and mother in 1939 and 1940.

When Harvard extended an invitation to Stravinsky to lecture there, he decided to move to the United States. After a year at Harvard, Stravinsky, newly remarried to Vera Soudeikine, settled in Los Angeles with his bride. There, he composed most of his remaining works.

In 1969, after several illnesses, he and Vera moved into the Essex House Hotel in New York City, where he died in 1971 at the age of 88. Following his funeral in New York, Stravinsky's body was taken to Venice (Stravinsky's favorite city). After a gondola procession through the Grand Canal, he was buried in a modest grave.

PRINCIPAL WORKS

Operas: Oedipus Rex (1927); *The Rake's Progress* (1951)
Ballets: The Firebird (1910); *Petrushka* (1911); *The Rite of Spring* (1913);

Pulcinella (1920); *Les Noces* (The Wedding, 1923); *Apollo Musagetes* (1928); *The Fairy's Kiss* (1928); *Jeu de Cartes* (The Card Party, 1937); *Orpheus* (1947); *Agon* (1957)

Music-theater: L'histoire du soldat (The Soldier's Tale, 1918)

Orchestral Music: Symphonies of Wind Instruments (1920); Violin Concerto (1931); *Dumbarton Oaks* Concerto (1938); *Symphony in C* (1940); *Symphony in Three Movements* (1945); *Ebony Concerto* for Clarinet (1945); *Concerto for Strings* (1946)

Chamber Music: Duo Concertante for violin and piano

Choral Music: Symphony of Psalms (1930); *Mass* (1948); *Cantata* (1952); *Threni* (1958); *A Sermon, a Narrative and a Prayer* (1961); *Requiem Canticles* (1966)

Vocal Music: Pribaoutki (1914); *Abraham and Isaac* (1963)

Piano Music: Sonata (1924); *Concerto* (1925): *Sonata for Two Pianos* (1944)

Debussy (standing) and Stravinsky (seated).

Today, as we reflect on musical giants and assess their influence, Stravinsky looms as one of the most dominant musical forces of the twentieth century. Stravinsky's early masterpiece *The Rite of Spring* had an effect similar to that of Beethoven's Ninth Symphony. Both the works and their composers influenced music throughout and beyond their lifetimes.

Painting *Three Musicians* (1921) by Pablo Picasso.

Cubism in Painting

Just as music departed from the predictable lines and harmonies of the nineteenth century, so did the visual arts.

Employing similar techniques around 1910, painters such as Picasso, Braque, and other artists created a style called "cubism." To grasp the essence of three musicians in costumes and masks on stage, Picasso breaks images into geometric shapes in his *Three Musicians* (page 280).

HISTORICAL PERSPECTIVE

The Rite of Spring—Its Infamous Debut in 1913

Paris, 1912   Audiences enjoyed two new Impressionist-style ballets premiered by Diaghilev's Ballets Russes—Ravel's *Daphnis et Chloé* and Debussy's *Afternoon of a Faun*, both choreographed by Nijinsky.

Paris, 1913   The Téâtre des Champs-Elysées—the Ballets Russes opened its season with the premiere of Debussy's *Jeux*. But Paris audiences were totally unprepared for the unleashing of the next work, *The Rite of Spring: "Scenes from Pagan Russia."*

Audience Reaction: At first, not knowing what to make of these new sounds, many in the audience began laughing. Soon, others began heckling and protesting, trying to stop the performance. A few slaps across the faces of the protesters—some from women—and a full-fledged riot broke out. Demonstrators tore out seats. Spilling out into the Paris streets, the melée continued until the Paris police brought it under control by arresting more than 40 of the rioters.

What Was New in Stravinsky's Music?

Unprepared for what they heard, the audience was disturbed. What was this music that reached out and assaulted them? Unfamiliar with Stravinsky's new musical language, many listeners felt lost and alienated.

Even today, some people are unable to accept *The Rite*'s dissonance and "modern" techniques. Curiously, audiences seem not to mind similar dissonances and modern techniques that effectively establish a mood in films or television. Hollywood film and television composers owe a great deal to Stravinsky.

MUSICAL DOUBLE EXPOSURE   In *The Rite of Spring* and many of his other works, Stravinsky often superimposes two or more coherent ideas on each other, resulting in an entirely new idea. A double exposure in photography is the closest illustration. For instance, suppose you take a front-view snapshot of your friend. Without your knowing it, the film does not advance.

Then, you snap a side-view picture. In the developed film, you see a novel effect. Although you can still recognize your friend, he or she looks different—because front and side views have been superimposed.

Stravinsky employed musical double exposure through many elements:

Polychords

Polychords. Two or more triads performed simultaneously, producing a novel harmony.

Polytonality

Polytonality. A section of music with parts simultaneously residing in different keys produces polytonality.

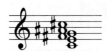

Here is the opening of Mozart's Sonata in C Major in its original form. Both upper and lower parts are in C major:

Here is a twentieth-century treatment of the same section of the Mozart Sonata. This time, the upper part is in C major and the lower is in F-sharp major, producing polytonality:

Polyrhythms

Polyrhythms. Two or more contrasting rhythms sounded simultaneously produce polyrhythms. Even if you don't read music, you can still see that in the duration of each beat, there are several different rhythmic patterns. On the first beat: 2-note pattern, 6-note pattern, 4-note pattern, and a 7-note pattern. On the second beat: 4-note pattern, 6-note pattern, and a 5-note pattern.

The Rite of Spring

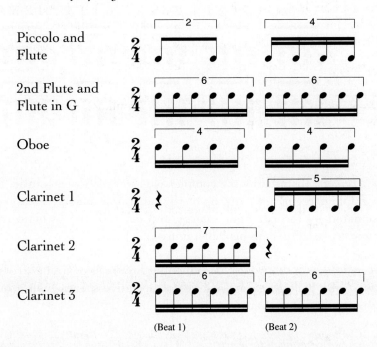

Polymeters. These occur when two or more contrasting meters are sounded simultaneously. In this example, the upper part is in four meter plus a five meter, while the lower part is in a nine meter with three groups of three eighth notes.

Polymeters

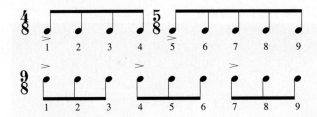

OTHER STRAVINSKY INNOVATIONS For centuries, music had predictable, recurring rhythm patterns—meters: for example, the three pattern of the waltz, minuet, and mazurka; the two and four patterns of the march. But does music need predictable rhythmic patterns? Stravinsky and others began employing irregular metrical patterns in their music. Later, most twentieth-century composers followed.

Changing Metrical Patterns. Here is a section from *The Rite of Spring*, "Dances of Youth and Maidens," which uses constantly changing metrical patterns. Almost randomized, the patterns are difficult to predict. Imagine how difficult they are to dance to.

Changing metrical patterns

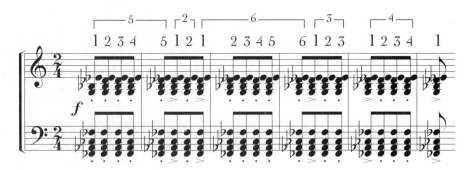

Ostinato

Ostinato. Inspired by the complex rhythms of African music, Stravinsky employs recurring patterns of rhythmic and melodic ideas—*ostinato.* Fascinated by the rhythmic energy and drive of the ostinato rhythms, Stravinsky used them in his ballet music.

MORE ON THE RITE OF SPRING   Subtitled by Stravinsky "Scenes from Pagan Russia," the ballet presents a series of primitive scenes built around the spring fertility rites of ancient Russia.

Part I: The Adoration of the Earth

1.   "Introduction." The birth of spring. A group of girls is seated before the sacred mound, each girl holding a long garland. The tribal Sage appears and leads them toward the mound.

Martha Graham Company dancing *The Rite of Spring,* 1984.

2. "Omens of Spring: Dances of the Youths and Maidens." They dance around the mound in celebration of spring.

3. "Dance of Abduction." In this frenzied ritual, one of the maidens is abducted and carried off.

4. "Spring Rounds." Four couples remain. Each man lifts a girl on his back and, with a solemn procession, begins making the Rounds of Spring.

5. "Games of the Rival Tribes." Young warriors from the rival tribes display their prowess. The Sage pushes his way through the crowd.

6. "Entrance of the Sage." The village Sage enters and assumes direction of the proceedings.

7. "Adoration of the Earth." The dancers prostrate themselves in adoration of the mystical powers of the earth.

8. "Dance of the Earth." An exuberant dance in praise of the earth's fertility.

Part II: The Sacrifice

1. "Introduction: Pagan Night." The Sage and the girls sit motionless around the fire in front of the sacred mound. Their task is to choose the girl who is to be sacrificed to ensure the earth's fertility.

2. "Mystic Circles of the Adolescents." The girls dance the mystic circles until one stands suddenly transfixed as she realizes that she is the Chosen One.

3. "Dance to the Glorified One." In honor of the sacrificial victim, all dance vigorously, building into a frenzied climax.

4. "Evocation of the Ancestors." Strong rhythmic dances invoke the blessings of the ancestors.

5. "Ritual Performance of the Ancestors." Undulating, pulsating rhythmic patterns to which the village elders perform a shuffling, swaying dance.

6. "Sacrificial Dance." The Chosen One begins a frenzied dance and continues until she collapses and dies. The men carry her body to the foot of the sacred mound as an offering to the gods of fertility.

LISTENING ACTIVITY ❧

STRAVINSKY, *THE RITE OF SPRING*,
"SACRIFICIAL DANCE"
LARGE FORM: BALLET; DETAILED FORM: RONDO

Cassette Tape: Side D, Example 2
Compact Disc 3, Track 1

Listen to the "Sacrificial Dance." While many of Stravinsky's innovative techniques will be obvious on first hearing, others may require several hearings.

- polychords
- polytonality
- polyrhythms
- polymeters
- changing metrical patterns
- ostinato

LISTENING GUIDE

STRAVINSKY, *THE RITE OF SPRING*
"SACRIFICIAL DANCE"
LARGE FORM: BALLET; DETAILED FORM: RONDO

Cassette Tape: Side D, Example 1
Compact Disc 3, Track 1
Running time: 4:33

| 1 | 0:00 | MOTIVE 1 | After a string section dissonant chord, the rhythmic-melodic motive is played by the large orchestra, *f*; polychords; fast tempo, unpredictable, changing meters and rhythmic patterns; ostinatos |

Violins

| 2 | 0:29 | RHYTHM PATTERN 1 | introduction to motive 2, played mainly by strings and horns, suddenly *p*; less dissonant polychords; ostinato with changing meters |
| 3 | 0:41 | MOTIVE 2 | introduced by muted trombones, *f*, imitated by muted trumpets several times, and then by horns, while strings and horns continue ostinato, |

Trombones

	0:52	RHYTHM PATTERN 1	in lower strings and horns, *p*, then *f*, ostinato with changing meters
	1:04	MOTIVE 2	played by muted trumpet and piccolos, *f*, imitated by horns
4	1:19	RHYTHM PATTERN 2	full orchestra, *ff*, ostinato with changing meters, polychords
5	1:31	OSTINATO PATTERN	played by lower strings and horns, *p*
	1:38	MOTIVE 2 OSTINATO PATTERN	played by muted trombones, alternating imitations with trumpets, *f*, while [Ostinato pattern 1] is played by strings and horns softly
	1:47	TRANSITION SECTION	played by full orchestra, *f*, strings and flutes have fast running patterns of 5 notes to a beat, section ends with a loud chord, then short pause.
	1:56	MOTIVE 1	returns, similar to opening section, *f*, repeats several times, polychords, changing meters
6	2:24	RHYTHM PATTERN 3	polyrhythms, triplet patterns played by timpani, duple patterns played by lower strings, changing meters, loud trombone glissandos
	2:33	MOTIVE 3	played by horns, then horns and strings, changing meters

Horns

2:46	MOTIVE 3	played by trumpets and strings, ostinato rhythm in duple meter, polychords, crescendo to *ff*, then short pause
3:01	MOTIVE 1	returns, similar to beginning section, *f*, changing meters, short pause
3:12	MOTIVE 3	played by brass, then overlapping imitations throughout the orchestra, mostly duple meter, ostinato
3:32	MOTIVE 1	played by low strings, *f* then *ff*, changing meters, polychords, changing ostinato patterns, then gradual crescendo to loud chord
4:29	FINAL CHORD	flute upward run to piccolo and high strings to a loud final chord emphasized by low strings and drums

LISTENING INSIGHTS

Listening to Twentieth-century Music

Twentieth-century music often uses new musical language. Be patient at first hearing. Once you get used to the sound, you'll discover the composer's intentions. Then you can begin to form a more educated opinion about this "different" music and to find a place for it among your personal values.

Summary of Terms

Ballets Russes

cubism

changing metrical patterns

double-exposure

irregular metrical
  patterns

objectivism

ostinato

polychords

polymeters

polyrhythm

polytonality

CHAPTER 20

Expressionism: Atonal Music

The term *Expressionism* is used to describe music, painting, and poetry developed in Vienna during the early decades of the twentieth century. The movement began as a rejection of *Impressionism* that focused on the "outer" world, inspiring artists such as Monet and Debussy.

Expressionism, in contrast, centered on the "inner" world described in the writings of Sigmund Freud (1856–1939).

In music, Arnold Schoenberg led the Expressionistic movement. His colleagues, Anton Webern and Alban Berg, followed. Some of the painters associated with expressionism include Pablo Picasso (1881–1973), Wassily Kandinsky (1866–1944), and Paul Klee (1879–1944).

End of Tonality?

In use since the 1600s, the major-minor tonal system of Western music had been bent and stretched by many composers, especially Wagner and Debussy. In 1908, it snapped. A young Viennese composer, Arnold Schoenberg, pushed tonality beyond its former limits. Disciples gathered, establishing a major movement still alive today: *atonality*.

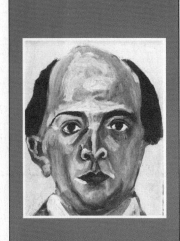

ARNOLD SCHOENBERG (1874–1951)

Schoenberg (*shurn*-behrg) grew up in his native Vienna at the same time Brahms, Mahler, and Richard Strauss were working there. By eight he was studying violin and soon began composing his own string chamber music—an interest that continued throughout his life.

Just after Schoenberg completed his schooling, his father died, leaving the family poor. Needing to support himself, young Arnold had to forsake his musical interests in order to earn a living in a Viennese bank.

Mostly self-taught as a composer, Schoenberg continued composing and performing in chamber music groups in his spare time. Not until he took a position as music director for a Berlin cabaret was he able to make his entire income as a professional musician. Finally, he returned to Vienna to teach and compose, interrupted by World War I when he had to serve in the Austrian army.

Between 1918 and 1923 he had formulated his twelve-tone method, which he used throughout most of his remaining compositions. In 1925, he was appointed professor of composition at the Berlin Academy of Arts.

Because he was Jewish, Schoenberg had to flee to the United States from Germany when Adolf Hitler seized power. Settling in southern California, Schoenberg attained citizenship and taught at both the University of Southern California and the University of California at Los Angeles. (The Arnold Schoenberg Institute is located on the University of Southern California campus, and Schoenberg Hall is a major performing arts auditorium at UCLA). He died in Los Angeles at the age of 76.

PRINCIPAL WORKS

Orchestral Music: Verklärte Nacht (Transfigured Night, 1917); *Pelleas und Melisande* (1903); Five Pieces for Orchestra (1909); Variations (1928); Violin Concerto (1936); Piano Concerto (1942); 2 chamber symphonies

Chamber Music: 4 string quartets, 1 string trio, 1 wind quintet, Octet (1922)

Operas: Erwartung (Expectation, 1909); *Die glückliche Hand* (The Fortunate Hand, 1913), *Von Heute auf Morgen* (From Today to Tomorrow, 1930), *Moses und Aron* (1932)

Choral Music: Gurrelieder (1911); *A Survivor from Warsaw* (1947)

Vocal Music: The Book of the Hanging Gardens (1909); *Pierrot lunaire* (1912); cabaret songs

Piano Music: Three Piano Pieces, Op. 11 (1909); Six Little Pieces, Op. 19 (1911); Five Piano Pieces, Op. 23 (1920); Suite (1923)

✺*Atonality*

Atonal, or nontonal, music contains pitches, but melodies and harmonies are carefully constructed to avoid creating tonal centers, or home keys.

Early Atonal Experiments

Strongly influenced in his youth by Brahms, Wagner, Strauss, and Mahler, Schoenberg composed his earlier works with roots in late-nineteenth-century Viennese romanticism. New directions and experiments in music always interested him, and he often discussed his ideas with his friend Gustav Mahler.

Schoenberg concluded that because music had been gradually moving away from tonality throughout the nineteenth century, we would take that idea to its logical destination: atonality. Experimenters such as Wagner, Strauss, Debussy, and Stravinsky had approached the threshold; Schoenberg made a quantum leap, and from 1908 on, many of his works are atonal.

Once he had crossed over, his Viennese colleagues—Anton Webern (1883–1945) and Alban Berg (1885–1935)—followed. Throughout the twentieth century, other composers saw atonality as a progressive avenue of self-expression.

In Street, Berlin (1913). Painted by Ernst Ludwig Kirchner.

Schoenberg's Twelve-tone System

Atonal music was an inevitable development, and Schoenberg, Webern, and Berg became absorbed by it. Even Stravinsky admired the orderly procedures and intellectual nature of Schoenberg's atonal music and spent some time later in life composing twelve-tone music.

By 1923, Schoenberg formulated a theoretical system for composing atonal music that would ensure both its unique status and its departure from traditional tonal music. His system is known variously as the *serial, twelve-tone,* or *dodecaphonic* method.

The twelve-tone method is highly disciplined. At its core is an ordered set, or *tone-row*, of the twelve different tones of the chromatic scale. Because Western music has only twelve different tones within an octave, each tone-row uses all of them. Only their order is different.

Looking at the model of the keyboard, you'll notice that there are only twelve tones within an octave. Using tones or pitches from a higher or lower octave doesn't change the *names* of the pitches or the *order* of the row—only the *register* of the pitches.

Dodecaphonic music

Tone-row

ALBAN BERG (1885–1935)

Berg (*behrg*) was born into a financially comfortable Viennese family. Although he had no training in composition as a teenager, Berg wrote many songs. After graduating from school, he took a position in Vienna as government accountant.

A newspaper advertisement caught Berg's attention when he was 19: Arnold Schoenberg was inviting composers to study with him. Berg, financially secure, responded to the ad and studied with Schoenberg for the next seven years.

During World War I, Berg spent more than three years in the Austrian army. After the war, he composed one of the twentieth century's most interesting operas, *Wozzeck* (*vo*-tseck). Mostly atonal, the work captured the torment and anxiety of the common man caught in the societal and psychological upheavals between the two World Wars.

A year after *Wozzeck*, Berg wrote his *Lyric Suite* for string quartet, using a musical language that was gentler, though still atonal. He began his next opera, *Lulu*, in 1928. The main character, Lulu, is another victim of a decaying society. After shooting her wealthy husband, she is sentenced to years of degrading experiences in prison. Once released, she becomes a prostitute, murdered at the end of the opera by Jack the Ripper.

Berg's chronic ill health restricted his composing output. At 50, when he died in Vienna, he left *Lulu* not quite finished.

PRINCIPAL WORKS

Orchestral Music: Chamber Concerto (1925), Violin Concerto (1935)
Chamber Music: String Quartet (1910), *Lyric Suite* (1926)
Operas: *Wozzeck* (1925), *Lulu* (1934)
Songs: more than 75 songs, *Altenberg Songs* (with orchestra, 1912)
Piano Music: Sonata (1908)

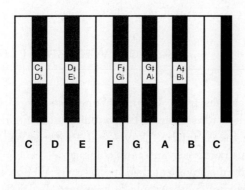

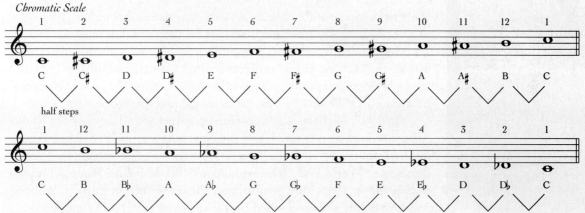

Schoenberg claimed the tone row could be manipulated in a similar fashion, and proposed four basic treatments of the row. Here's an example from Schoenberg's Suite for Piano, first movement:

ANTON WEBERN (1883–1945)

Like his colleagues from Vienna—Schoenberg and Berg—Webern (*vay*-bern) studied music there: cello, piano, and music theory. At 18, after attending the Wagner Festival in Bayreuth, Webern decided to become a serious composer and musicologist.

He studied musicology at the University of Vienna and composition for two years privately with Arnold Schoenberg. In 1908, to earn a living, Webern began a conducting career with orchestras throughout Austria.

Following his obligatory service in the Austrian army in World War I, Webern lived near Schoenberg in Vienna, turning his efforts mainly to teaching music and composing. Using Schoenberg's twelve-tone system and experimenting with works of extreme brevity, Webern's postwar compositions became more atonal and dissonant.

In 1927, Webern was appointed conductor and adviser for Radio Austria, where he remained until the Nazi takeover in 1938. Although he differed politically with the Nazis, Webern chose to remain in Vienna throughout World War II, losing his son in battle and his home to bombs. In September 1945, only months after the war ended in Europe, Webern was mistakenly shot and killed by an American occupation soldier.

PRINCIPAL WORKS

Orchestral Music: Six Pieces for Orchestra, Op. 6 (1909); Five Pieces for Orchestra, Op. 10 (1913); Symphony, Op. 21 (1928); Variations, Op. 30 (1940)

Chamber Music: Five Movements for String Quartet (1909); Six Bagatelles for String Quartet (1913); Four Pieces for Violin and Piano, Op. 7 (1910); Quartet for Violin, Clarinet, Tenor Saxophone, and Piano, Op. 22 (1928); three string quartets

Piano Music: Variations, Op. 27 (1936)

Vocal Music: Das Augenlicht (Eyesight, 1935), three cantatas, several songs

TRANSPOSED ROWS Keeping the series intact, entire rows and their treatments can also be transposed to higher and lower pitches, and the row will retain its integrity. This is also true for traditional melodies and harmonies. Moving a melody to a different key (higher or lower) doesn't change our recognition of that melody or harmony.

ENSURING ATONALITY   In Schoenberg's method, tones of the row are rarely repeated until all have been sounded. This helps to ensure atonality: With all pitches having equal importance, there can be no suggestion of a tonal center around any one pitch. Repeating pitches often tends to force a tonal center.

ATONAL HARMONY   Rows can provide a source of harmony as well. Taking three or four tones from any portion of the sample tone row, we can sound them simultaneously to produce chords.

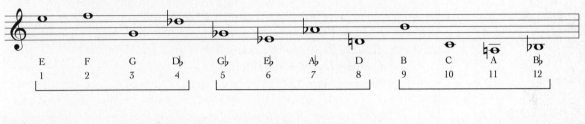

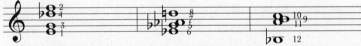

How to Listen to Twelve-tone Music

Twelve-tone row, atonal music sounds different from most other music. For the listener, melodies often seem fragmented and difficult to follow. Unfamiliar harmonies are usually dissonant, and it is easy for a listener to feel lost.

Schoenberg and his colleagues didn't expect listeners to follow the row completely through all its transformations. Most musicians have difficulty doing this. Instead, they felt that the tone row provides an integral infrastructure for the work that may not be always apparent in the listening.

To get the most out of the music, you have to remain totally attentive, focusing especially on the opening section. Here is where the tone row is revealed, usually in its basic form before it undergoes transformation. This is similar to traditional forms, such as the theme and variations or rondo, which state the theme at the beginning. Though a challenge, memorizing the tone row, or as many of the intervals as possible, will help you recognize it through its transformations.

Although the resulting chords are dissonant, usually they are compatible with the atonal nature of the row. Since it adheres to strict principles, twelve-tone music tends to be short and concise. Webern's *Symphony*, Op. 21 (1928), lasts only ten minutes in contrast to Gustav Mahler's Third Symphony (1896), which lasts about one hour and twenty minutes.

LISTENING ACTIVITY ✺

SCHOENBERG, *SUITE FOR PIANO*, OP. 25,
FIRST MOVEMENT; RASCH (QUICK)

Cassette Tape: Side D, Example 3
Compact Disc 3, Track 7
Running time: 0:51

Listen to the "Praeludium" from Schoenberg's *Suite for Piano*, Op. 25. The piece starts with the entire tone row in its original form in the upper register of the piano. After only two of the row's tones are sounded, the bass register begins an imitation using a different rhythm. Following that, the row is manipulated and transformed using retrograde, inversions, retrograde-inversions, transpositions, and harmony.

Original Form of Tone Row

| 1 | 2 | 3 | | 4 | 5 | 6 | 7 | 8 | 9 | | 10 | 11 | 12 |
| E | F | G | | Db | Gb | Eb | Ab | D | B | | C | A | Bb |

Here is the tone row:
Listen to the opening of the *Suite* several times until you feel that you know the row. Then listen to the entire movement.

Summary of Terms

atonal	expressionism	tone row
atonal harmony	major-minor tonality	transposed rows
atonality	nontonal	twelve-tone method
atonal music	serial music	twelve-tone music
dodecaphonic music	tonal center	twelve-tone row

CHAPTER 21

Neo-Classicism: Mainstream Music

✎ Beginnings of Neo-Classicism

Was it the public's uproar over his musical language in *The Rite of Spring* (1913) that influenced Stravinsky to question his choices? Perhaps it was the pagan subject matter. As a composer, he expected to communicate with his audiences. Composers in the past had met with audience resistance, but a riot? And if his audiences were apparently not ready for his innovations, should he try a more familiar style?

Contemplating his next direction, Stravinsky turned to a leaner style. Taking his inspiration from the music of the Baroque and Classical periods, he adapted the forms, idioms, and instrumental sounds of those times to his own personal compositional techniques.

Stravinsky was shaken by the outbreak of World War I. Both Russia and his new homeland, France, were under siege in 1914. Ever the pragmatist, Stravinsky retreated to neutral Switzerland. The disorder of war was anathema to his exacting, orderly nature, and he made his 1940 move to the United States for similar reasons.

During and after World War I, composing for large European orchestras was impossible. Orchestras were in shambles: Players were in the armed services, and funding was non-existent.

So when in 1917 Diaghilev commissioned Stravinsky to write *The Story of a Soldier (L'histoire du soldat)*, a play with musical interludes, he wisely scored it for a chamber ensemble of seven musicians. The scarcity of orchestral performers was an important factor in Stravinsky's decision to use techniques from the eighteenth century, with its sparer instrumental resources. The result was *Neo-Classicism*.

An Approach, Not a Style Period

Neither a style nor a style period, Neo-Classicism is a creative approach. During the postwar years, many composers began to adopt resources from former musical style periods to produce new and fresh music.

Generalizing about Neo-Classical music is difficult. Although it is mostly tonal with prominent melodies, composers merged these qualities with their twentieth-century compositional techniques.

Broadening the concept of Neo-Classicism, Stravinsky began using techniques from earlier style periods such as the Medieval and Baroque. Neo-Classicism now meant incorporating techniques from any previous musical style periods—even including several styles within one piece.

For the Ballets Russes, Stravinsky went on to compose the ballet *Pulcinella* (1920), based on the music of the Baroque composer Pergolesi. With his Octet (1922), his shift to Neo-Classicism was complete. Except for a period of exploration in atonal music when he was in his 70s, Stravinsky continued composing Neo-Classical music for the rest of his life.

Neo-Classicism in Russia

The same year Stravinsky was composing *The Story of a Soldier* (1917), Prokofiev had already reached the same conclusion about Neo-Classicism: Audiences would be more willing to accept modern techniques as long as the musical language was familiar.

LISTENING INSIGHTS

Neo-Classical Approaches

In discussing and listening to these works, it isn't necessary to label them Neo-Baroque when using Baroque-period techniques, or Neo-Renaissance when using Renaissance styles. *Neo-Classical* will do.

SERGEI PROKOFIEV (1891–1953)

Born in the Ukraine in southern Russia, Prokofiev (proh-*kohf*-yef) studied piano with his mother, who also encouraged him to compose at an early age. By the age of nine he had written a three-act opera. After the family moved to Moscow, his parents sent him to the Conservatory in St. Petersburg, where he studied composition with Rimsky-Korsakov.

When the turmoil of the Russian Revolution became intolerable, Prokofiev followed Diaghilev and Stravinsky to Paris. He was taken into the Russian expatriate community that included members of the Ballets Russes. Prokofiev used Paris as his home base while traveling through post-World War I Europe and the United States.

When he decided to return to Russia in 1933, Prokofiev was greeted warmly by both the public and the government. But he soon found himself in trouble with the Stalin Regime: they accused him of writing music that was too "formalistic, too technically complicated and alien to the Soviet people." The Party Central Committee constantly pressured Prokofiev to publicly apologize for his "transgressions." Though he tried to shrug off these attacks, the stress finally affected his health. Ironically, both Joseph Stalin, his tormentor, and Prokofiev died of brain hemorrhages on the same day.

PRINCIPAL WORKS

Orchestral Music: Symphonies: No. 1 (*Classical*, 1917); No. 2 (1925); No. 3 (1928); No. 4 (1940); No. 5 (1944); No. 6 (1947); No. 7 (1952); *Peter and the Wolf* (1936); *Lieutenant Kijé Suite* (1934) from the film score; 5 piano concertos, 2 violin concertos, and a cello concerto

Chamber Music: string quartets; Flute Sonata; Violin Sonata; Cello Sonata

Piano Music: Mostly sonatas

Operas: The Love for Three Oranges (1921); *The Fiery Angel* (1928); *The Gambler* (1929); *War and Peace* (1944)

Ballets: The Prodigal Son (1929); *Romeo and Juliet* (1938); *Cinderella* (1945)

Choral Music: Alexander Nevsky (1939) for chorus and orchestra—from the film score

Prokofiev wrote his *Symphony No. 1 (Classical Symphony*, 1916–17) as a modern work using Classical-period compositional techniques. Scored for an orchestra similar to Haydn's, Prokofiev's four-movement symphony followed the typical late-eighteenth-century plan:

First Movement:	Allegro (fast, sonata form)
Second Movement:	Larghetto (moderately, slow rondo form)
Third Movement:	Gavotte (moderate dance in duple meter, song form and trio—similar to minuet and trio)
Fourth Movement:	Allegro (fast, sonata form)

OTHER RUSSIAN NEO-CLASSICAL COMPOSERS   A group outlook on modern composition emerged from Russia. Working independently, other composers concurred with the idea of expanded Neo-Classicism and incorporated techniques from previous style periods, including the recent Romantic.

In addition to Prokofiev, the composers working in this genre include Sergei Rachmaninov (1872–1943; see biography in Chapter 16), Dimitri Shostakovich (see biography in this chapter), Dmitri Kabalevsky (1904–87), and Aram Khachaturian (1903–78).

LISTENING ACTIVITY ❧

PROKOFIEV, *SYMPHONY NO. 1* (CLASSICAL),
FIRST MOVEMENT: ALLEGRO
LARGE FORM: FOUR-MOVEMENT SYMPHONY;
DETAILED FORM: SONATA FORM

Cassette Tape: Side D, Example 4
Compact Disc 3, Track 8

Prokofiev's *Classical Symphony* is quite similar in style to Haydn's. In comparing the two composers' use of orchestral instruments, however, notice that Prokofiev utilizes the capabilities of modern, technically improved instruments. For example, violinists are required to play extremely high on their fingerboards, and woodwinds and brass have parts that are considerably more demanding than in Haydn's day. Also, many of the melodies contain large leaps, requiring highly skillful performers.

LISTENING GUIDE

PROKOFIEV, *SYMPHONY NO. 1* (CLASSICAL),
FIRST MOVEMENT: ALLEGRO
LARGE FORM: FOUR-MOVEMENT SYMPHONY;
DETAILED FORM: SONATA FORM

Cassette Tape: Side D, Example 4
Compact Disc 3, Track 8
Running time: 3:37

Exposition

8   0:00   THEME 1   played by the strings and woodwinds, quickly changing
dynamics, *ff*, *p*, crescendo, *ff*, *p*, key of D major, duple meter

	0:11	THEME 1	repeats played only by the strings and in the key of C major
9	0:19	TRANSITION THEME	played by flute, *p*, imitated by oboe and clarinet, *p*, then by bassoon, *p*

10   0:46   THEME 2   played by first violins in dominant key, *pp*, light arpeggio
accompaniment played by bassoon, theme repeated several
times, then *ff* cadence to pause (exposition is not repeated)

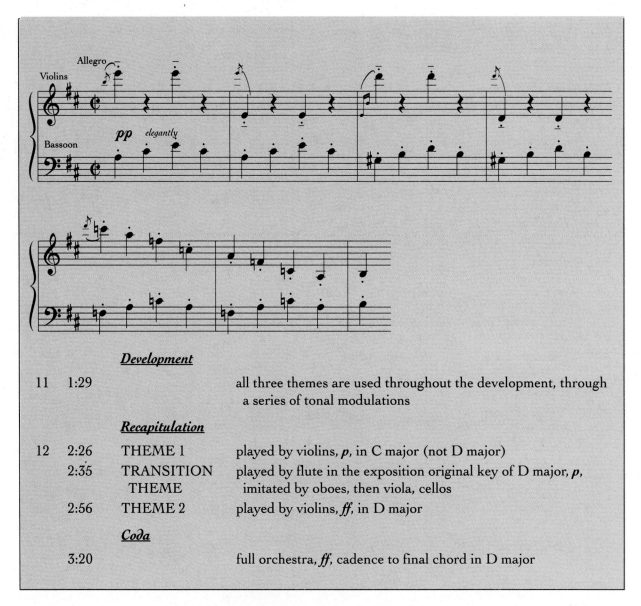

Development

11	1:29		all three themes are used throughout the development, through a series of tonal modulations

Recapitulation

12	2:26	THEME 1	played by violins, *p*, in C major (not D major)
	2:35	TRANSITION THEME	played by flute in the exposition original key of D major, *p*, imitated by oboes, then viola, cellos
	2:56	THEME 2	played by violins, *ff*, in D major

Coda

	3:20		full orchestra, *ff*, cadence to final chord in D major

✣Moving Back to the Mainstream

Viewed broadly, Neo-Classicism can be seen as an attempt to move back to the mainstream of music. According to mainstream composers, lack of communication with audiences runs contrary to the role of music—the tradition of Bach, Haydn, Beethoven, Schumann, and Brahms. However interesting atonal experimental music may be to the knowledgeable musician, most audiences seemed to prefer tonal music. Composers need audiences, for without them there is only an empty hall.

To pigeonhole the diverse lot of twentieth-century mainstream composers into rigid categories would be misleading. Despite their differences, however, they shared a goal: to express their musical individuality in a way audiences can understand.

United Kingdom

For a country that produced many of the greatest performers, presented some of the finest concerts, and nurtured many outstanding composers from other countries, England boasted few prominent composers until the twentieth century. Since then, a notably prolific group of English composers has surfaced.

EDWARD ELGAR (1858–1935) Active as a performer and composer in the latter part of the nineteenth century, Elgar wrote his most popular works beginning in the 1890s and into the twentieth century: the "Serenade for Strings" (1892), "Enigma" Variations (1899), and the "Cello Concerto" (1919). Perhaps Elgar is best known for his *Pomp and Circumstance* Marches (1901-30), widely identified with school commencement exercises.

Vaughan Williams.

RALPH VAUGHAN WILLIAMS (1872–1958) Following his interest in English folk music, Vaughan Williams composed *Fantasia on "Greensleeves"* (1934) and *English Folk Song Suite* (1923). His nine symphonies, especially *A Sea Symphony* (No. 1, 1910) and the popular *London Symphony* (No. 2, 1914), demonstrate his considerable talent for orchestration and the influence of his studies in Paris with Maurice Ravel. Vaughan Williams also wrote a sizable collection of choral music for the Church of England.

GUSTAV HOLST (1874–1934) A contemporary and close friend of Vaughan Williams, Holst also incorporated English folk songs (Suites 1 and 2 for band) in his music. The influence of Hindu mysticism is evident in his *Choral Hymns from the Rig-Veda* (1912). Brilliantly scored for orchestra, his best-known work is *The Planets* (1914–16).

Benjamin Britten (center).

WILLIAM WALTON (1902–83) Walton composed a wide variety of works: symphonies, concertos, chamber music, ballet, and even ceremonial music for coronations (*Crown Imperial*, 1937, and *Orb and Sceptre*, 1953).

BENJAMIN BRITTEN (1913–76) Britten was the most prolific and most famous English composer of the mid-twentieth century. His outstanding works include *A Ceremony of Carols* (1942, for choir), *Spring Symphony* (1947, for vocal soloists and chorus), and *War Requiem* (1962). Britten is one of the most important contributors to twentieth-century opera, most notably with *Peter Grimes* and *Billy Budd*. His composition *The Young Person's Guide to the Orchestra* is often used to introduce newcomers to orchestral instruments (Compact Disc 4, Tracks 21–40)).

DIMITRI SHOSTAKOVICH (1906–75)

Like many composers in the past, Shostakovich (shos-tah-*koh*-vich) received his earliest piano training from his mother, an accomplished pianist. At 13, Shostakovich entered the Conservatory in his native St. Petersburg, focusing his studies on composition. By 19, he had completed his first symphony. Over his lifetime, he composed 15 symphonies and a considerable legacy of various types of music.

Communist bureaucrats in control of the arts continuously assailed Shostakovich's music as "too formalistic," "too self-serving," "chaotic," "coarse and primitive," and "not subservient to the Soviet State."

To continue composing, Shostakovich, like Prokofiev, often had to sign humiliating, phony apologies addressed to his public, promising to do better in the future. After withstanding many years of these types of harassment by the Stalinist bureaucrats, Shostakovich died at the age of 69.

PRINCIPAL WORKS

Orchestral Music: 15 symphonies (1925-66); piano concertos, violin concertos, cello concertos; *Festival Overture* (1954); Suite from *The Age of Gold* (1929)

Chamber Music: 15 string quartets; Piano Quintet (1940); 2 piano trios

Piano Music: 2 sonatas; 24 Preludes (1933); 24 Preludes and Fugues (1951)

Operas: The Nose (1930); *Katerina Izmaylova* (1963)

Ballets: The Age of Gold (1929)

PERCY GRAINGER (1882-1961)   Best known for his tune "In an English Country Garden," the brilliant, eccentric Grainger was born in Australia, educated in England, and lived in the United States most of his life. His early influences were little-known British folk songs that he discovered while roaming the countryside with music pad and portable recorder.

During World War II, he was an arranger in the United States Coast Guard Band, using many of his folk song discoveries in compositions for band—for example, *Irish Tune, Shepherd's Hey from County Derry,* and *Lincolnshire Posy.*

France

ERIK SATIE (sah-*tee*, 1866–1925)   A unique composer, Satie is famous for giving intriguing, surrealistic titles to his works: *Three Pieces in the Form of a Pear, Three Flabby Preludes for a Dog,* and *Jack in the Box.*

Satie was strongly opposed to Impressionism, which had become the popular music style in his country. His clever, anti-sentimental music influenced many younger French composers: Honegger, Milhaud, Poulenc.

ARTHUR HONEGGER (ohn-ne-*geh*r, 1892–1955)   Perhaps Honegger's best-known work is the oratorio *King David,* written for amateur choruses. He wrote *Joan of Arc at the Stake* for children's chorus and large orchestra. One of his most intriguing works is *Pacific 231* (1923), a musical translation of the sounds of a speeding locomotive. The "231" in the title refers to the number and placement of wheels on the locomotive as seen from the side: *2* wheels, followed by *3* wheels, followed by *1* wheel. This configuration is well known in railroad circles.

Les Six, a group of six French composers. From left to right, Darius Milhaud, Georges Auric, Arthur Honegger, Germaine Tailleferre, Francis Poulenc, and Louis Durey (not shown). Seated at the piano, the poet, artist, and novelist Jean Cocteau.

SPOTLIGHT: OUTSTANDING ARTIST-TEACHER NADIA BOULANGER (1887–1979)

The influence of some musicians extends far beyond their personal triumphs as composers, performers, and conductors. Such distinction belongs to Nadia Boulanger (boo-lahn-*zhay*).

Few artist-teachers have earned such high esteem not only for their knowledge of music but also for their ability to transmit their knowledge. Despite her reputation for being austere and authoritarian, Boulanger had a sincerity and warmth of spirit that opened up the universe of music to the countless young people who sought her tutelage.

Many details of her life will remain secret until the year 2009, when documents entrusted to the Bibliothèque Nationale (National Library) become accessible. However, here are some of the highlights currently public.

Nadia's father, the pianist and composer Ernest Boulanger, supervised her first musical studies before she was eight. The following year he enrolled her in a sight-reading/singing (solfège) class at the Paris Conservatoire (Conservatory) and hired a teacher to instruct her in organ and composition. Nine-year-old Nadia revealed a dedication and diligence unusual for a child her age. In 1897, Nadia received a First Prize in solfège.

After her husband's death in 1900, Madame Boulanger accelerated the pace of Nadia's studies. In 1901, she was in Gabriel Fauré's class in composition, that year winning a Second Prize in harmony. Two years later, Nadia won First Prize in harmony, and the following year, 1904, she received First Prizes in organ, piano accompaniment, fugue, and composition. Also in 1904, Nadia earned her first money as a musician.

By 1905, Nadia had established her career as a performer, composer, and teacher, gaining an excellent reputation for her group lessons. Then-prominent pianist Raoul Pugno and her former teachers at the Conservatory sent pupils to her. Through Pugno's recommendation Nadia acquired her first American students, who helped her learn English.

Having Pugno as her champion significantly boosted Boulanger's career, but even his prestige was not enough to help her prevail over the sensitive politics of the French music world. Some attributed her losing the First Grand Prize of the 1908 Prix de Rome to her youth and her sex—the only woman among the finalists. Others suggest it was due to her offending one of the judges, **Camille Saint-Saëns**. Having ruffled his plumage, she settled for second place.

Her youth and sex also deprived her of an appointment to the Paris Conservatory in 1910. It took thirty-five years until she became a duly appointed faculty member. However, in 1913, Boulanger did become the first woman to win the Prix de Rome's First Grand Prize.

Nadia's friendship with **Walter Damrosch**, head of the New York Philharmonic, began in 1918. Damrosch, who had founded American Friends of Musicians in France, had come to Paris to conduct a benefit concert. Nadia performed as organist for the Third Symphony by Saint-Saëns, with whom she had finally reconciled.

After World War I, Damrosch continued his philanthropic activities in France, donating and raising substantial funds to establish several music schools. One such school, for American musicians who wanted to spend summers studying in France, opened in June 1921 in Fontainebleau Castle. With her enthusiasm and innovative techniques, Nadia revolutionized instruction in harmony.

Nadia had begun trying out her teaching concepts two years earlier in her classes in organ, harmony, and counterpoint at *École Normale de musique*. In January 1920, Nadia wrote: "My goal is to awaken my students' curiosity and then to show them how to satisfy that curiosity." So popular were her classes that enrollment was soon limited.

Aaron Copland was among the first students at Fontainebleau. The twenty-year-old Copland had enrolled in another teacher's composition class but out of curiosity sat in on one of Boulanger's classes. He never missed another one, hesitantly asking her for private lessons. "No composer has ever had a woman teacher. It was not Nadia Boulanger I was worried about—it was my reputation!" said Copland. Yet he stayed on with her for three years. In return she introduced him to important contacts, such as the newly appointed conductor of the Boston Symphony, Russian-born **Serge Koussevitzky,** with whom Nadia had been working closely at the time.

Nadia's personal magnetism played a great part in the success of the school at Fontainebleau, which attracted several generations of young Americans. In ever greater numbers they came to France to work with her at the school, followed by extended stays in Paris. For nearly fifty years, interrupted only by World War II, Boulanger's Paris apartment at 36 rue Ballu became a gathering place for these young musicians.

In January 1938, Nadia sailed for America. She was scheduled for forty concerts and sixty lectures and classes. From the moment she landed in New York, she was treated like a star. A high point of that tour was on February 19. Thanks to her friend Koussevitzky, Nadia became the first woman to conduct the Boston Symphony.

The following year—February 1939—Nadia was the first woman to conduct the New York Philharmonic in a sold-out performance at Carnegie Hall. The New York Herald Tribune music critic wrote: "One can already say of her, in the full maturity of her career, that she has enriched her time."

That same year Boulanger also conducted the Philadelphia Orchestra, after which the press noted: "The prejudice against women conductors, which lurks in the bosom of every orchestra player, breaks down instantly when one comes in contact with Mlle. Boulanger's masterful touch." Boulanger's response: "Let's forget that I'm a woman. Let's talk about music."

Fontainebleau was hastily closed at the end of August 1939. When the Nazis invaded France, she requested and received a contract from the Longy School of Music in Boston in order to obtain an exit visa from France. In addition to her classes at Longy, Nadia resumed her activities as a lecturer, conductor, and soloist, mostly in New England. In 1942, she accepted in addition an offer from the Peabody Conservatory in Baltimore, commuting there once a week from Boston to give classes.

After the war, she obtained an exit visa and in January 1946 came home to her beloved France. Although much of the country was rubble, her rue Ballu apartment was intact. By the summer, her life had resumed just about where it had left off, including her classes at the reopened Fontainebleau School. She also accepted an appointment to the Paris Conservatory.

In 1953, Nadia Boulanger became undisputed head of the Fontainebleau School, where she remained for twenty-six summers. Although compulsory retirement ended her classes at the Conservatory upon her seventieth birthday in 1957, she remained engaged in diverse activities, traveling widely until her ninetieth year. However, with her health and eyesight failing in 1976, she was no longer able to give lessons.

In 1977, the president of France made her a Grand Officer of the Legion of Honor, a distinction that was extremely rare for women. It was just one of the many honors bestowed upon her, including the Order of the British Empire, the Gold Medal of the Beaux-Arts Academy, and Medal of the City of Paris.

On Nadia's 92nd birthday, **Leonard Bernstein** visited her in Paris. In a flash of lucidity, she recognized him, heard what he said, spoke a few words, and clung to him. He was one of the last to see her. A few weeks later, in the early hours of October 22, 1979, Nadia Boulanger died in her rue Ballu apartment.

DARIUS MILHAUD (mee-*yoh*, 1892–1974)   Extremely prolific, Milhaud composed in almost every form—even film music. His *Suite provençale* (1937) and *Suite française* (1944) for orchestra are impressions of his native France. North and South America held a fascination for Milhaud, and he incorporated music from both continents into his music.

His ballet *La Création du Monde* (The Creation of the World, 1923) was influenced by his visit to Harlem jazz clubs in the 1920s. To avoid Nazi persecution, Milhaud left Paris in 1940 for Oakland, California, where he was a professor at Mills College until his retirement in 1971.

FRANCIS POULENC (poo-*lahnk*, 1899–1963)   Poulenc's songs (chansons) are among the most charming in the literature. His larger works include the *Mass in G* (1937, for chorus *a cappella*) and his opera *Dialogues des Carmelites* (Dialogues of the Carmelites, 1956).

Germany

Nationalistic aggression during the twentieth century largely displaced creative expression in both Germany and Austria. Most composers had to leave these countries; many emigrated to the United States. These were the lands that produced Bach, Handel, Mozart, Haydn, Beethoven, Schubert, Mendelssohn, Schumann, Brahms, Wagner, and Strauss. So much for war's contribution to civilization!

PAUL HINDEMITH (*hin*-duh-mit, *1895-1963*)   Hindemith stands out as Germany's most important composer and teacher in the twentieth century. Beginning his teaching career at the Berlin School of Music, from 1927 to 1937 he became the model of the artist/teacher. To escape from the Nazi regime, he came to the United States and taught at Yale University from 1940 to 1953. Then he accepted a professorship at the University of Zurich.

Disturbed by the widening gap between composer and audience, Hindemith created a collection of works with a broad appeal, in contrast to pure art works. He called these compositions *Gebrauchsmusik*, or "useful music." Numerous chamber pieces fall into this category, as does his musical playlet for children titled *Wir Bauen eine Stadt* (Let's Build a Town, 1930).

Hindemith used excerpts from his opera *Mathis der Maler* (Mathis the Painter, 1934) to compose a symphony of the same title. His outstanding ballets are *Nobilissima visione* (1938) and *The Four Temperaments* (1940). Works for more unusual instruments such as a saxophone, bassoon, tuba, string bass, and harp are among his notable contributions to sonata literature.

Paul Hindemith.

The musician Sting starring as MacHeath in a 1990 Broadway production of Weill's *Three Penny Opera*.

KURT WEILL (vile, 1900–1950)   Close friends, Weill and Hindemith collaborated (a rare occurrence for composers) on the music for several interesting stage works. Inspired by Lindbergh's daring flight across the Atlantic is a choral piece called *Der Lindberghflug* (The Lindbergh Flight), with a text by Berthold Brecht (1898–1956).

Weill collaborated again with Brecht on the opera *The Rise and Fall of the City of Mahagonny* (1929). Written in pre-Nazi Berlin, it is a scathing commentary on twentieth-century materialism, power struggles, and sex.

The Three Penny Opera (1928) characterizes city life of the early twentieth century. One of the hit songs, "Mack the Knife," depicts modern, low-life, street and cabaret people. Written in a popular chamber-opera style, *The Three Penny Opera* (1928) is based on the 1728 William Gay work *Beggar's Opera*.

When the rise of the Nazis in Germany became intolerable in 1933, Weill and his wife Lotte Lenya fled to Paris, and then, in 1935, emigrated to the United States where Weill composed mainly for films and Broadway shows. His last work, *Lost in the Stars* (with Maxwell Anderson, 1949), is a brilliant Broadway-style musical that comments on the Apartheid problem in South Africa from the black worker's point of view.

CARL ORFF (1895–1982)   Orff based his well-known dramatic cantata *Carmina Burana* on a collection of thirteenth-century student songs and poems discovered in an old Bavarian monastery. With its driving rhythms and ostinati, Orff's music has been frequently used as background music in films and television.

Italy

OTTORINO RESPIGHI (reh-*spee*-ghee, 1879–1936)   Writing in both Neo-Classical and Impressionistic styles, Respighi distinguished himself by composing nationalistic symphonic poems: *Fountains of Rome, Pines of Rome*, and *Roman Festivals*. To create a feeling of reality in portraying the countryside on the outskirts of Rome, Respighi calls for a recording of birds to be played over the loudspeaker at performances of *Pines of Rome*.

Central Europe

BÉLA BARTÓK (1881–1945)   One of the leading twentieth-century composers, Bartók was born in Hungary and studied and taught at the Conservatory in Budapest. Collaborating and traveling with his friend Zoltán Kodály (koh-*dye*, 1882–1967), he collected and edited Hungarian folk music, which they both used extensively in their music.

When he emigrated to the United States in 1940, Bartók joined the hordes of artists escaping from Europe. Although suffering from leukemia and oppressed by financial problems, Bartók wrote his last and most popular works in the United States between intermittent hospitalizations. Finally, his problems were somewhat eased when he was invited to join a folk music research group at Columbia University.

Reflective of Hungarian peasant music, much of Bartók's music contains interesting dissonances. Bartók's most famous work, the Concerto for Orchestra (1943), resulted from a commission from the Boston Symphony Orchestra.

One of his last works before his death in New York in 1945 was the *Third Piano Concerto*. Gravely ill and aware of his imminent death, Bartók worked feverishly to finish the concerto so he could leave his family less impoverished.

Hebrew Music

ERNEST BLOCH (blohk, 1880–1959)   An international musician, Bloch was influenced by his Jewish heritage. A popular work of his, *Schelomo* (Solomon, 1915), is a plaintive rhapsody for cello and orchestra. *Baal Shem* (1923) is for violin and piano. Another popular work, *Sacred Service* (*Avodath Hakodesh*, 1930–33), is for cantor (baritone), chorus, and orchestra.

Latin America

HEITOR VILLA-LOBOS (vee-lah-*loh*-bohsh, *1887–1959*)   Villa-Lobos and Darius Milhaud met in 1915 in Brazil. Milhaud, then the French ambassador's secretary, encouraged Villa-Lobos to incorporate Brazilian folk material into his music.

Of his more than 2,000 works, his *Bachianas brasileiras* are the most widely known. In this group of nine works, Villa-Lobos blended his Brazilian heritage with the style of Johann Sebastian Bach.

CARLOS CHÁVEZ (chah-vez, 1899–1978)   Incorporating Native American folk tunes into his music, Chavez was Mexico's most outstanding composer. *Sinfonia india, Toccata for Percussion*, and the ballet *Horsepower* are among his most important works.

Summary of Terms

Broadway-style   musical folk songs   Neo-Classicism

Béla Bartók (right) with violinist Rudolph Kolisch during a rehearsal of *Music for Strings, Percussion, and Celesta* (1940).

CHAPTER 22

Experimental and Technological Music

During the first half of the twentieth century, the momentum of accelerating progress swept artists toward the future. Radical changes were inevitable. Traditionalism was the past; experimentalism, the future.

Following this trend, composers have been writing works that fall into disparate categories:

- *musique concrète*
- electronic music
- computer music and mixed media music
- aleatoric music
- chance music

∿ *Musique Concrète*

French composers use the term *musique concrète* to refer to everyday sounds they capture and manipulate with tape recorders. The techniques were startling: overdubbing, cutting and splicing, playing backward and forward, changing the speed.

Varèse

It was in 1942, during World War II, that the magnetic tape recorder was invented. Edgard Varèse (vah-*rehz*, 1883-1965), a French-born musician who later emigrated to the United States, saw possibilities for using the new invention to create musical sounds. Soon other musicians followed his lead. Lugging the clumsy portable machines, musicians headed outdoors, microphones in hand, to record the "real" (concrete) world.

For centuries composers had tried to replicate the sounds of the world around them: Vivaldi (*The Four Seasons*), Beethoven (*Pastoral* Symphony), Mahler (Symphony No. 1), Honegger (*Pacific 231*). In *Pines of Rome*, Respighi came closest with recordings of nightingales played during live performances. Now, with the amplification ability of the tape recorder, composers could capture sounds from everywhere, no matter how puny the original source.

Music with Composer Control

By the 1950s, the composer with a tape recorder had final control over his or her music. Performers were not necessary: The composer was the performer. Pointing the microphone, the composer could choose the sound sources. Then, back in the studio, the composer made all the decisions about manipulating the various sound events he had recorded and how the final tape recording should sound.

Important *musique concrète* composers:

John Cage (1912–1992)
Karlheinz Stockhausen (b. 1928)
Edgard Varèse (1883–1965)

ᢒᢛ *Electronic Music*

Electronic music refers to sounds produced on electronic oscillators and then usually recorded and stored. At first, the term *electronic music* was used to distinguish electronically produced sounds from the manipulated sounds of *musique concrète*.

As the 1960s approached, the analog electronic music synthesizer changed recording techniques. Storing individual sounds on tape was now obsolete. Instead, both natural sounds—birds, thunder, rain—and "musical" sounds could now be produced synthetically—"synthesized"—in the electronic music laboratory.

Early synthesizers had some faults. Because they produced music that was *too* precise, it sounded synthetic. Singers and instrumentalists do not perform like machines. Depending on their interpretations, live artists deliberately vary beats, tempo, pitches, and other elements of music. Realizing this, later electronic music composers used *digital* synthesizers to incorporate these variations into their music to "humanize" its sound.

Important electronic music composers:

Milton Babbitt (b. 1916)
Wendy (née Walter) Carlos (b. 1939)
Mario Davidovsky (b. 1934)
Charles Dodge (b. 1942)
Philip Glass (b. 1937)
Frederick Lesemann (b. 1936)

Otto Luening (b. 1900)
Karlheinz Stockhausen (b. 1928)
Morton Subotnick (b. 1933)
Vladimir Ussachevsky (b. 1911)
Edgard Varèse (1883–1965)
Charles Wuorinen (b. 1938)
Iannis Xenakis (b. 1922)

❧ Computer and Mixed Media

Invented in 1942, the same year as the magnetic tape recorder, the computer may prove to be the most important invention since the wheel. Musicians are just taking the first steps in exploring its possibilities.

Electronic music studio.

LISTENING ACTIVITY ≈

LESEMANN, *METAKINETIC INVENTION, VERSION 2* EXCERPT
LARGE FORM: ELECTRONIC MUSIC RECORDING

Cassette Tape: Side D, Example 5
Compact Disc 3, Track 13

Listen to Frederick Lesemann's *Metakinetic Invention, Version 2*
(1984), which displays the wide versatility of electronic music.

About the Guide: Because electronic, computer, and highly
complex contemporary music uses radically different music resources, describing the musical events in traditional terms is rarely
successful. Therefore, the guide here uses descriptions different from
the others in the text.

Three main sound events permeate the excerpt of *Version 2*:

STACCATO TONES	staccato (short) tones
SLIDING TONES	sliding tones, similar to the wail of a siren, are heard at different pitch levels
RHYTHMIC MOTIVE	reminiscent of Beethoven's opening motive in his *Symphony No. 5* (Cassette Tape, Side C, Example 1)

LISTENING GUIDE

LESEMANN, *METAKINETIC INVENTION, VERSION 2* EXCERPT
LARGE FORM: ELECTRONIC MUSIC RECORDING

Cassette Tape: Side D, Example 5
Compact Disc 3, Track 13
Running time: 2:00

13	0:00	STACCATO TONES	bursts of staccato tones, followed by silence, then
		SLIDING TONES	descending sliding tone

0:10	STACCATO TONES SLIDING TONES	staccato tones followed by moderately high ascending sliding tones, then repetition of both staccato and sliding tones with different pitches
0:21	RHYTHMIC MOTIVE	used as a motive
0:29	STACCATO TONES SLIDING TONES	similar to beginning
0:32		repetitions and development of all previous material including rhythmic motive
0:46	STACCATO TONES	longer staccato section, followed by silence
0:54	RHYTHMIC MOTIVE	sounded twice, then imitated at a lower pitch, repetitions of rhythmic motive together with staccato bursts and sliding pitches—ascending and descending crossing
1:28	STACCATO TONES SLIDING TONES	repetition, similar to beginning
1:38	RHYTHMIC MOTIVE	repeats
1:46	STACCATO TONES	staccato tones trailing off

Common Terms Used in Computer Music:

MIDI

MIDI   An acronym for Musical Instrument Digital Interface, MIDI is a set of agreed-upon standards for use by keyboards, computers, and other devices. Standards make the sharing of information possible through a common "language."

Sampling

SAMPLING   Using a series of numbers to represent sounds of an instrument, the sound is digitally recorded and stored on disc. A composer can recall samples of a particular sound from that disc and use it in new music. Thus, the composer can access computerized information to put together an entire ensemble of mixed instruments.

Music with Performer Control

Aleatoric music

ALEATORIC MUSIC   This music leaves many important decisions to the performer but is otherwise specific in its notation. "Alea" is the Latin word for one die in a pair of dice. "Aleator," Latin for gambler, suggests the risk and chance involved in playing this twentieth-century music.

Jackson Pollock's painting
Number One (1948), using
elements of chance.

CHANCE MUSIC   Chance music is less precise in its notation than aleatoric music. Instructions to performers are mainly general: details (pitches, duration) happen as they will, allowing the players to create a performance that is a matter of "chance." Therefore, no two performances of the same work are identical.

Chance Music

SILENCE   John Cage's *4'33"* is typical of the playfulness of chance music. To perform this work, the player comes out on stage, sits at the piano, starts a stopwatch, and remains there in silence, allowing the audience to fill that time with their own musical imaginations and to become aware of the sounds already present in the concert hall. Four minutes and thirty-three seconds later, the player rises and walks off the stage.

Silence

In another Cage composition, *Imaginary Landscape*, his directions call for 12 radios and "random noise assemblages." Each of the 12 radios is tuned to a different station. The performance consists of constantly changing stations. Microphones placed outside the concert hall provide random noise. A pair of loudspeakers picks up the sounds onstage. *Che será, será!*

Notation and directions in chance music are rarely conventional. With specific notes and duration left to the performer, only sound events and suggestions appear. In essence, chance music is similar to improvisational theater, where actors use only a situation or character and create dialogue at their discretion. "Action" painters, such as Jackson Pollock and Salvador Dali, who drip and throw paint on the canvas and allow things to "happen," operate in a similar way.

DECK OF CARDS   Another interesting way to make music by chance is to use a deck of cards to select materials randomly. The technique is to translate card numbers and suits into music. For instance:

Number on card determines pitches on the 12-tone scale:

card:	ace (1)	2	3	4	5	6
pitch:	C	C-sharp	D	D-sharp	E	F

card:	7	8	9	10	Jack	Queen
pitch:	F-sharp	G	G-sharp	A	A-sharp	B

king and joker = wild cards (your choice of any pitch)
Suits on card determine duration:

clubs = eighth note or eighth rest	**spades** = quarter note or quarter rest
diamonds = half note or half rest	**hearts** = whole note or whole rest

To create a chance piece, shuffle the deck, deal out the cards, and assign the results to one player. Repeat the process for the other players. Then perform the piece. This may seem simplistic, but this kind of chance music can become very complicated in its execution. Because of the random nature of each shuffle of the deck, each player will have an entirely different part.

Important composers of chance music:

Earle Brown (b. 1926)	Karlheinz Stockhausen (b. 1928)
John Cage (b. 1912)	Christian Wolff (b. 1934)
Morton Feldman (1926–89)	Iannis Xenakis (b. 1922)
Lukas Foss (b. 1922)	LaMonte Young (b. 1935)

❧ *Other Experimentalists*

Here are some other important composers, each with a unique vision.

LISTENING INSIGHTS

Listening to Chance Music

Though serious in its philosophical position, most chance music has a "tongue in cheek" element, leaving room for playfulness. *Process*-oriented rather than *product*-oriented, chance music may at times sound chaotic. Most of the focus for the listener is on the unusual happenings on stage and the novel sound combinations that spontaneously develop.

Pierre Boulez in 1971.

athematic

PIERRE BOULEZ (boo-lez, B. 1925) Boulez favors an athematic (themeless) approach to atonal music. Using a variety of compositional techniques, his music is highly organized yet sounds very different from traditional music. In his words:

> *After the war we felt that music, like the world around us, was in a state of chaos. Our problem was to create a new musical language.*

Karlheinz Stockhausen.

KARLHEINZ STOCKHAUSEN (shtohk-how-zen, B. 1928) An important post-World War II German composer, Stockhausen composes in a variety of styles. Extremely complex rhythms abound in his music, along with un-usually detailed instructions to the performer. Already mentioned for his work in *musique concrète*, electronic music, and chance music, Stockhausen also incorporates ideas from older styles. His popular work *Gruppen* (Groups, 1955-57), for example, is played by three orchestras located in different areas of the concert hall—influenced by Giovanni Gabrieli's six-teenth-century polychoral style (see Chapter 8).

KRYSZTOF PENDERECKI (kris-tof pen-der-ets-kee, B. 1933) An eclectic com-poser, Penderecki combines musical elements from his native Poland with various "mainstream" and experimental techniques. Having witnessed Nazi persecution of the Jews in Poland, he composed music full of com-passion for human suffering. You can hear this in his powerful *Threnody for the Victims of Hiroshima.*

PHILIP GLASS (B. 1937) A New York-based composer, Glass has achieved popularity through his mesmerizing film music: *Koyaanisqatsi* and *Powaqqatsi.* His operas, including *Einstein on the Beach* (1975) and *1,000 Air-planes on the Roof* (1987), have won critical acclaim.

Philip Glass.

Minimalism

Often referred to as a *minimalist*, Glass takes bits of rhythm and pitches and repeats them over and over, while subtly changing their character.

From his extensive travels, Glass has incorporated Asian, North African, and South American percussion music into his minimalistic techniques.

STEVE REICH (ryʃh, B. 1936)   Also a minimalist, Reich uses ostinato to help his music evolve hypnotically, gradually—similar to a slowly changing sunset. *Musique concrète* recording techniques provide the basis for Reich's ostinati. He then moves the ostinati out of phase on other recording tracks, creating interesting polyphonic effects. His "Come Out" is an example of this technique.

✌ What Lies Ahead?

The future is difficult to predict: Today's experiment may be tomorrow's mainstream. Many new approaches may evolve as technology advances. With world migration and new media of communication, the world as a "global community" is rapidly approaching. As cultures interact, each leaves residuals on the others. Undoubtedly, a greater mix of ethnic and diverse cultural resources will spawn new art works.

Summary of Terms

aleatoric music	electronic music	minimalism
athematic	electronic music synthesizer	mixed media music
chance music	MIDI (Musical Instrument	*musique concrète*
computer music	Digital Interface)	sampling

CHAPTER 23

Music in North America

℘ *Immigration*

Around the turn of the twentieth century, into the port cities of New York, Boston, and Philadelphia poured the most diverse immigrant population in the history of the world. Never before had so many people come to so relatively small an area.

Russian and Polish Jews fled czarist pogroms; earlier, the Irish, Scandinavians, and Germans, and later, the Italians were forced off their farms by crop failures. Others left their homelands to avoid persecution. To all of them, North America represented "the promised land" of freedom and limitless opportunities.

The Arts in North America

The same freedom and opportunities attracted artists. America became a refuge and a home for some of the world's greatest musicians: Stravinsky, Schoenberg, Bartók, Hindemith, Milhaud, Arturo Toscanini, Jascha

Heifetz, Gregor Piatigorsky, Artur Rubinstein, Vladimir Horowitz, and scores of others. As they resettled, the arts flourished in North America.

ORCHESTRAS IN NORTH AMERICA   The influx of great artists from Europe helped elevate the standards of American orchestras to a world-class level. Of the great symphony orchestras in the world today, many are in the major cities of North America:

Atlanta Symphony	Minnesota Orchestra
Baltimore Symphony	Montreal Symphony
Boston Symphony	National Symphony (Washington, D.C.)
Buffalo Philharmonic	New Orleans Symphony
Chicago Symphony	New York Philharmonic
Cleveland Orchestra	Philadelphia Orchestra
Dallas Symphony	Pittsburgh Symphony
Detroit Symphony	St. Louis Symphony
Houston Symphony	San Francisco Symphony
Indianapolis Symphony	Seattle Symphony
Los Angeles Philharmonic	Toronto Symphony

SCHOOLS OF MUSIC   Artist-teachers found employment in America's colleges and schools of music. Today, many of the world's finest schools of music are in the United States and Canada:

Curtis Institute of Music
Indiana University School of Music
Juilliard School of Music
McGill University
New England Conservatory of Music
Northwestern University School of Music
Oberlin College Conservatory of Music
Peabody Conservatory of Music
University of British Columbia School of Music
University of Illinois School of Music
University of Miami School of Music
University of Michigan School of Music
University of Rochester Eastman School of Music
University of Southern California School of Music
University of Toronto School of Music

North American-born graduates of these schools now perform in the major orchestras and opera companies around the world.

ARTS SUPPORT   Despite popular appeal, the arts in the United States have always faced a predicament: lack of significant financial support from the

U.S. government. Most European governments allocate five to ten times as much for arts organizations.

WPA Arts Projects

Except for brief periods of federal funding, such as the WPA arts projects in the 1930s during the Great Depression, the arts in America have had to rely on ticket sales, private patrons, and corporate underwriters for funding. Fund raising is a continuous concern.

Some have said that in the United States there seems to be a suspicion about supporting the arts—probably due to the country's Puritan heritage of equating pleasure with sin.

Only recently have Americans begun to understand what the Greeks knew 2,500 years ago: The arts contribute to the quality of life—a benefit that cannot be quantified as television ratings are.

Because musical organizations receive the bulk of their support from their ticket sales, their programs must have broad appeal. Artistic directors program music that communicates easily. Ensembles whose concerts deviate from popular taste have dwindling audiences.

CHARLES IVES (1874–1954)

Born in Danbury, Connecticut, Ives was influenced by his father, who had been a bandmaster in the Civil War. The elder Ives gave Charles his first lessons in music.

Music inventiveness was part of their household as Ives's father experimented with new scales and quarter tones—the tones that fall between the traditional notes of the chromatic scale. In the 1880s, Charles experimented with *polytonality* (some years before Stravinsky), singing in one key and accompanying himself in another.

Once accepted at Yale, Charles majored in music. But upon graduation, he realized that he would have a difficult time earning a living as a musician. So this practical Connecticut Yankee went to New York City to find a job in the business world. Charles did extremely well in business and founded one of the largest agencies for the New York Life Insurance Company.

His wealth as a businessman made it possible for him to compose as a hobby without concern for compensation. On weekends and during vacations in his country home in Connecticut, Ives composed hundreds of works without having most of them performed.

By the time of his death in New York in 1954, only a few of his works had had public performances. His wife, Harmony, later uncovered dozens of works that had been gathering dust in their barn and arranged for their performance and publication.

PRINCIPAL WORKS

Orchestral Music: 4 symphonies; First Orchestral Set (*Three Places in New England*, 1914); Second Orchestral Set (1915); *The Unanswered Question* (1906); *Central Park in the Dark* (1906); *Emerson Overture* (1907); *Washington's Birthday* (1909); *Robert Browning Overture* (1912); *Decoration Day* (1912); *The Fourth of July* (1913)

Chamber Music: String quartets and sonatas

Piano Music: Sonatas and studies

Choral Music: Psalm 67 (1894); *The Celestial Country* (1899)

Organ Music: Variations on "America" (1891)

Songs: More than 150

LISTENING ACTIVITY ✎

IVES, "MEMORIES"
LARGE FORM: SONG; DETAILED FORM: TWO-PART SONG

❙ *Cassette Tape: Side D, Example 6*
❙ *Compact Disc 3, Track 14*

Listen to "Memories," a surrealistic journey back in time that Ives composed in 1897, early in his career. Ives labels the first section **(A) "Very Pleasant."** Section A portrays a young person's excitement waiting for the curtain to open at a theatrical production or concert in the local opera house. Ives requests that the singer whistle and hum in different sections.

The second section **(B) "Very Sad"** is a melancholy remembrance of an uncle who used to constantly hum a simple tune.

LISTENING GUIDE

IVES, "MEMORIES"
LARGE FORM: SONG; DETAILED FORM: TWO-PART SONG

Cassette Tape: Side D, Example 6
Compact Disc 3, Track 14
Running time: 2:42

Section (A) "Very Pleasant"

19   0:00   *Presto (very fast); 2 meter; C major tonality*
We're sitting in the opera house,
the opera house, the opera house;
We're waiting for the curtain to arise
with wonders for our eyes;
We're feeling pretty gay,
and well we may,
"O, Jimmy, look!" I say,
"The band is tuning up
and soon will start to play."
We whistle and we hum,
beat time with the drum.

0:15   *Singer whistles, then sings:*
We whistle and we hum,
beat time with the drum,

0:19   *Singer whistles, then sings*
We're sitting in the opera house,
the opera, house, the opera house;
We're waiting for the curtain to arise
with wonders for our eyes,
a feeling of expectancy,
a certain kind of ecstasy,
expectancy and ecstasy,
expectancy and ecstasy, Sh......Curtain!

Section (B) "Very Sad"

20   0:42   *Adagio (very slow) E-flat major; **p**; arpeggios, rubato*
From the street a strain on my ear doth fall,

A tune as threadbare as that "old red shawl,"
It is tattered, it is torn, it shows signs of being worn,
It's the tune my Uncle hummed from early morn,
'Twas a common little thing and kind 'a sweet,
But 'twas sad and seemed to slow up both his feet;
I can see him shuffling down to the barn or to the town,
a humming.

2:10   *Singer hums until the end, **pp**; E-flat arpeggios to cadence*

♫ American Composers

Charles Ives was the first outstanding, distinctly American composer. Although well-versed in European music, Ives used American songs and rhythms, capturing the American spirit in his music—making him an American nationalist composer.

Ives's Songs

You'll come to know Ives best through his songs. American eclecticism abounds. Mixing European art song tradition with American speech and temperament, Ives called for a unique sound. He expected full-voiced concert singers to use twangy American pronunciation.

Subjects for his songs range from a child singing about his father ("The Greatest Man"), to a man's impressions of a circus parade ("The Side Show"), to the reflections on the death of a cowhand ("Charlie Rutlage").

Ives's piano accompaniments are novel, too. Behind the calm, tonal melodies of his songs, Ives relishes accompaniments in contrasting keys (bitonal or polytonal) and even employs atonality—although not the Schoenberg variety.

Ives was an experimenter. Predating Stravinsky in using polychords, polytonality, polymeters, and polyrhythms, Ives felt free to follow his creative ideas without regard for what people thought. To him, creating music was a joyful process. Just for fun, Ives worked into his music some of the popular tunes of his day, church hymns, and patriotic songs. Combined with dissonant, occasionally atonal passages, the familiar tunes seem to anchor the listener to reality, while Ives moves off into uncharted regions.

Ives's favorite holiday was the Fourth of July. He wrote several works to capture the exuberance of the occasion, including "Putnam's Camp, Redding, Connecticut" from his *Three Places in New England*, and "The Fourth of July" in the third movement of his *Holidays Symphony*.

LISTENING INSIGHTS

Listening to Ives

Listen particularly for some of the dissonant, surrealistic sound journeys on which Ives takes you. Look for the fun in the music. Try to find the buried treasure—the hymns and popular and patriotic tunes that he has hidden everywhere. If you listen expecting traditional musical sounds, you might often feel lost. If you open your mind to the possibilities, you'll be surprised.

In all these works, Ives tried to project the American spirit he acquired during his New England childhood. His music expresses it: a wonderful American holiday, full of warmth and celebration and joyful din.

POLYMEDIA Ives enjoyed mixing media. Many of his works are surrealistic in that they juxtapose seemingly unconnected tunes and situations, much the way events occur in a dream. Favorite experiments of his are combining a symphony orchestra playing in one key with a marching band playing a patriotic march, or mixing two orchestras with two conductors playing two seemingly different works on the same stage.

LISTENING ACTIVITY ॐ

IVES, FIRST ORCHESTRAL SET
(*THREE PLACES IN NEW ENGLAND*)
"*PUTNAM'S CAMP, REDDING, CONNECTICUT*"
LARGE FORM: DESCRIPTIVE ORCHESTRA PIECE

Cassette Tape: Side D, Example 7
Compact Disc 3, Track 16

As you listen to the "Putnam's Camp" from *Three Places in New England*, imagine a turn-of-the-century band playing popular patriotic music on the town square. In the nearby park, children rush about in play, shouting and laughing. The Stars and Stripes unfurl everywhere, making the townspeople feel festive and patriotic.

In his preface to the music, Ives supplies a written program, which is paraphrased on page 328.

In a Revolutionary War Memorial Park near Redding, Connecticut, a child attends a Fourth of July picnic. General Israel Putnam's soldiers spent the winter of 1778–1779 in that park. The child wanders into the woods beyond Putnam's camp ground and rests on a hillside. As the tunes of the band and the songs of the children grow fainter, the child falls asleep and dreams of the discouraged American soldiers breaking camp, marching out with fife and drum to a popular tune of their day. Suddenly, the soldiers turn back and cheer—Putnam is coming over the hills.

Waking from his dream, the child hears the songs of the children at the picnic. He runs down to join them and listen to the band.

Three sections (A B A), reflect the events in the program:

Section one (A) sets the raucous, happy mood with a quick-step march that Ives reused from an earlier piece he wrote for band. Also featured are melody fragments, including the British army's quick-step march, "The British Grenadiers," contrasted with the American army's "Yankee Doodle" and "Battle Cry of Freedom" composed by George Frederick Root (1820–95) during the War Between the States.

Section two (B) depicts the child's dream state. First, the music gradually fades to a pause. Then a surrealistic collage of tunes begins: overlapping melodic fragments of "Yankee Doodle," "The British Grenadiers," bugle calls, church hymns, and popular tunes from Ives's day.

Section three (A) depicts the exciting celebration when the boy awakens and rejoins his friends. Polyrhythms, polytonality, and polyphonic treatment of fragmented tunes characterize the music. A short quote from "The Star Spangled Banner" brings the piece to a resounding end.

LISTENING GUIDE

IVES, FIRST ORCHESTRAL SET (*THREE PLACES IN NEW ENGLAND*)
"*PUTNAM'S CAMP, REDDING, CONNECTICUT*"
LARGE FORM: DESCRIPTIVE ORCHESTRAL PIECE

Cassette Tape: Side D, Example 7
Compact Disc 3, Track 16
Running time: 6:14

Section one (A) Fourth of July Celebration

16	0:00	MARCH INTRODUCTION	full orchestra; allegro; *ff*; changing meters, syncopation
	0:10	BRITISH QUICK STEP	mainly strings, musical show style; *f*; dissonant chords

17	0:26	BRITISH GRENADIERS	fife and drum tune; quadruple meter with syncopation and polyrhythms; imitations of tune fragments; polytonal

"The British Grenadiers"

	0:52	BRITISH QUICK STEP BUGLE CALLS	bugle calls played by trombones and tubas; polyrhythms, syncopation
18	1:03	BATTLE CRY OF FREEDOM	fragments of several tunes; polytonal

"The Battle Cry of Freedom"

YANKEE DOODLE

"Yankee Doodle"

	1:12	POPULAR TUNE	played by strings, smoothly; *p*; consonant harmony
	1:37	TRANSITION	syncopation, polyrhythms; gradually slower and softer
	Section two (B) Dream Scene		
19	2:20	BUGLE CALL	polychords and clusters; slow tempo; very soft
	2:37	OBOE TUNE	slightly faster; polyrhythms; melancholy oboe tune; *p*
	3:38	BRITISH GRENADIERS	faster; march tempo; louder
	4:13	PATRIOTIC TUNES	faster and louder; still 4 meter; polytonal
	Section three (A) Awakening and Fourth of July Celebration		
20	4:28	POPULAR TUNE	suddenly softer and calmer; 4 meter, then changing meters
	4:50	BRITISH QUICK STEP	polymedia — brass band and orchestra; overlapping tunes
	5:07	BRITISH GRENADIERS	march tempo; *f*; polyrhythms
	5:23	TRANSITION	brass; *ff*; syncopation
	5:28	BRITISH QUICK STEP	polymedia — brass band and orchestra; overlapping tunes
	5:55		fast and very loud; polyrhythms; dissonant harmony
	6:07	STAR SPANGLED BANNER	fragment in brass; then very loud, dissonant polychord

✼ Jazz: The American Art Form

Fortuitously, turn-of-the-century New Orleans was a musical breeding ground. Several ingredients came together to produce a distinctive style of American music enjoyed throughout the world today: jazz.

Origins of Jazz

Slave trade

Prize captives for the slave trade in the 1600s and 1700s were the tribal musicians of west Africa. Understanding that music could help keep their steerage slave cargo calmer during the arduous journey across the Atlantic, the traders insisted that their agents select representative musicians from the tribes they raided. Once they had arrived in the Americas, music helped to prevent further deterioration of the slaves' spirits. This music was passed down through generations of African-Americans, and elements of it were absorbed into the mainstream of American music.

African Singing

CALL AND RESPONSE In call and response, characteristic of most African vocal music, a leader would sing a phrase (question), and the group would promptly repeat or answer it—comparable to a responsive reading in a religious service. Today, call and response permeates jazz, gospel, rhythm and blues, and rock music and is an integral part of African-American church services, both spoken or sung. The minister constantly throws out a question or stirring statement, and the congregation responds, often by saying, "Amen!"

Call and response

RIFF Heard throughout African singing and instrumental groups, and later in jazz, a *riff* is a short phrase repeated over and over. It fits our defini-

Riff

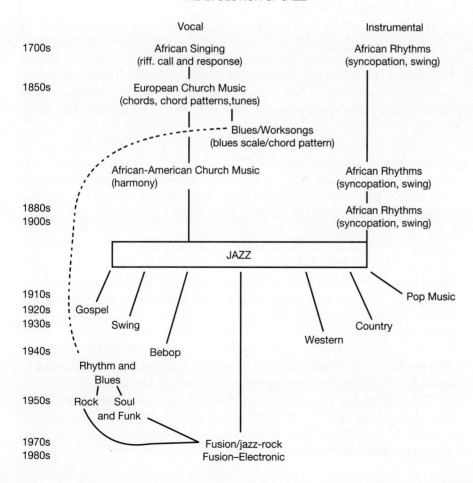

THE EVOLUTION OF JAZZ

tion of an *ostinato*, a repeated pattern that unifies the music. Originally, riffs or ostinatos were improvised by various members of the African percussion ensemble and then imitated by the entire ensemble. Today, *riff* may refer to any repetitive passage.

African Rhythms

Rhythm has often been called the "soul of Africa." Almost every African social gathering had its rhythmic accompaniment. Every tribal occasion also brought out the percussion instruments played by male members of the tribe.

Especially throughout western Africa, each percussionist had a discrete role in the ensemble. Choosing a particular instrument while still a young boy, each tribesman continued playing that instrument throughout his lifetime. Exceptional percussionists often developed into soloists, responsible for improvising new rhythmic patterns that the rest of the ensemble answered or imitated.

Syncopation

SYNCOPATION   Complexities of rhythm have always been the essence of African percussion ensembles. Playing the same rhythm hour after hour at ceremonies can be boring. To maintain interest, players created variations. *Syncopation* is a variation that accents parts of the beat not usually accented. Constant use of syncopation results in a *swing* or forward motion to the music.

When musicologists first analyzed African percussion music in the nineteenth century, they couldn't understand it. Comparing it with European music, the musicologists heard beats accented in unusual places (syncopation). They finally concluded that "Africans don't know how to keep time."

Off-beat

OFF-BEAT   The fact that African percussionists didn't all play continuously on the beat also disturbed early musicologists. Later, they came to learn that African percussionists have fun trying *not* to play on the beat. Great jazz players and singers have been influenced by this relaxed, *offbeat* performing. (It's not "cool" to play on the beat—that's for Lawrence Welk.)

Polyrhythms

POLYRHYTHMS   African percussion ensembles utilize *polyrythms*—several overlays of conflicting rhythms that add interest to the music. Through the several World Expositions in Paris in the early 1900s, Debussy, Stravinsky, and others were so impressed with African Percussion ensembles' use of polyrhythms that they incorporated them into their compositions.

Influence of European Church Music

HARMONY   Early jazz performers used the harmonies they found in the European Christian hymns. For instance, you can find the popular "When the Saints Go Marchin' In" in many turn-of-the-century Christian hymn books. This hymn and many others were used as a harmonic basis for many jazz arrangements.

When the Saints Go Marchin' In

Bessie Smith (1928).

Blues

Predating jazz, mainly through the worksongs of African-American workers, the *blues* songs convey sadness.

BLUES SCALE AND BLUE NOTES   Contributing to jazz and other jazz-related music, the blues use a scale containing *blue notes*, which were part of the African singing tradition. Blue notes "bend" some degrees of the traditional Western scale, usually the 3rd, 5th, and 7th degrees.

Blues Scale
and Blue Notes

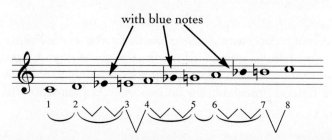

Creole Jazz Band (1923). Louis "Satchmo" Armstrong (cornet in the middle), Joe "King" Oliver (trombone on Armstrong's right), and Lil Hardin Armstrong (Armstrong's wife) at the piano).

CHORD PATTERN   Characteristic of blues is its use of predictable chord patterns. Called *blues progressions*, these patterns were derived from church hymns.

12-Bar Blues Progression

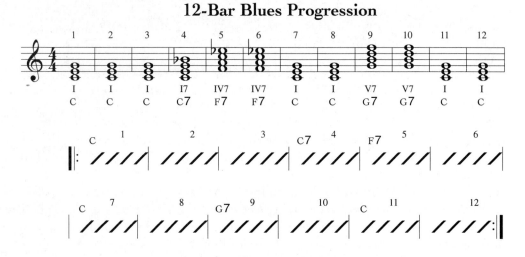

Military Bands

At the turn of the century, American military bands, as well as the French military bands in New Orleans, influenced the beginnings of jazz. A band played at every important occasion, especially if a parade was part of the celebration. Even a funeral procession for an important person would be headed by a band.

United States Marine Band (1880) with its leader, John Philip Sousa (1854–1932), playing cornet (with black cape, front right).

THE FUNERAL In New Orleans, the African-American funeral procession became a tradition. Mainly centered around the African-American church, the New Orleans African-American community was a proud, distinctive society. Ultimately, their use of funeral procession bands spread into other cities—particularly Memphis, St. Louis, and New York.

At the death of one of the community leaders, a band would assemble, usually playing secondhand instruments that had been traded in by the military bands. Performing mainly church hymns, these African-American-society marching bands headed the long, solemn parade of mourners through the streets.

Cakewalk

Originating as a demeaning entertainment on Southern plantations, the *cakewalk* was a high-kicking dance. Slave couples competed for a prize, generally a cake. Those with the highest, proudest steps would "take the cake." On some plantations, the dancers moved with pails of water on their heads. The winners were the couples who could maintain the most erect posture while spilling the least amount of water.

The cakewalk's rhythms are full of syncopation. As the dance craze became widespread, concert bands and military bands obliged their audiences with band arrangements of the music.

New Orleans funeral
procession.

Introduced to Europe by the New Orleans pianist and composer Louis Gottschalk (1829–69), the cakewalk caught on in Europe as well. Even Debussy composed one: "Gollywog's Cakewalk," 1908.

Ragtime

Ragged time
Rag

Around the turn of the century, the syncopated cakewalk, originally described as *ragged time*, was renamed *ragtime*, or just *rag*. Military bands continued to play the cakewalk music, now called ragtime, but in the parlors of society, pianists such as Scott Joplin entertained their audiences with their original ragtime compositions and arrangements. Shortly after the turn of the century, ragtime had become the favorite music played in saloons and bordellos throughout North America.

George Gershwin

Closing the gap between the jazz idiom and classical music, Gershwin was one of America's greatest composers. He was also among the most financially successful.

Gershwin was one of those tremendous talents—like Mozart, Mendelssohn, and Chopin—whose art seemed to pour effortlessly out of him. All of them, like supernovas, lit up the world, then suddenly died— Gershwin at 39, Mozart at 35, Mendelssohn at 38, Chopin at 39.

Gershwin had an easier life than Mozart. Almost everything he touched was successful. Writing music for radio, recordings (even piano rolls), Broadway shows, films, popular songs, and classical concert music, Gershwin achieved fame and fortune while still in his twenties.

SCOTT JOPLIN (1868–1917)

Called the "King of Ragtime," Joplin grew up in a musical family in Texarkana, Arkansas. Everyone in the house sang or played an instrument. His father, despite meager earnings as a railroad laborer, scraped together enough money to buy Scott a used grand piano. Mostly self-taught, Joplin caught the attention of a German-trained local piano teacher who gave him free lessons and introduced him to European music.

At first, Joplin played his music in saloons and bordellos around the country. In 1895, he teamed up with a vocal group as their accompanist and composer. His rags quickly became popular with the public. By 1898, the ragtime craze had swept the country, and Joplin had his first set of rags published the next year. In 1899, playing at the Maple Leaf Club, Joplin composed his "Maple Leaf Rag." The royalties from this work and other rags made him a wealthy man.

Settling in New York in 1909, Joplin began writing operas. His second one, *Treemonisha*, was rejected by all opera companies. Finally, personally producing a scaled-down version in a Harlem hall in 1915, he was devastated by the public's negative reception to the opera. Two years later he died at the age of 48.

PRINCIPAL WORKS

Rags: "Maple Leaf Rag" (1899); "The Entertainer" (1902)—used in the film *The Sting*; "The Sycamore" (1904); "Gladiolus Rag" (1907); "Sugarcane Rag" (1908); "Wall Street Rag" (1909)

Ragtime Opera: Treemonisha (1911)

Gershwin loved jazz. He played it. He expanded it. During his early years as a song plugger and improviser in the theater, he incorporated jazz elements into his music. Syncopation, ragtime, blues scales, blue notes, and bent tones abound in Gershwin's music.

Porgy and Bess Written in 1935, two years before Gershwin's death, *Porgy and Bess* was his last important composition and perhaps his greatest work. After years of hit musicals, Gershwin's emphasis shifted to composing serious concert music. However, he did not move too far away from his roots. Perhaps Gershwin heeded Maurice Ravel's advice to stick with jazz and jazz-influenced concert music rather than try to imitate European composers.

GEORGE GERSHWIN (1898–1937)

George's Russian-Jewish immigrant parents didn't know he had musical talent. Born in Brooklyn, New York, George showed little interest in music until the age of 12. Up to that time he was a typical New York street kid.

Then, at a school assembly, he heard classmate Max Dreyfus play the violin. Tracking down Dreyfus after school, Gershwin asked all about music and where he could learn. Studying piano without his parents' knowledge, Gershwin became highly proficient after only four years of lessons.

Life was hard in the economically unstable years before World War I. George quit school at 16 and was hired as a Tin Pan Alley song plugger for the Remick Music Publishing Company. Soon he began writing his own songs. In 1919, hearing Gershwin playing his new song "Swanee" at a party, Al Jolson asked to use it in his Broadway show. The song was a hit and sold two-and-a-half million copies of the sheet music. The royalties netted Gershwin a small fortune.

From 1920-1924, he wrote the music for the *George White Sandals* on Broadway. With his brother Ira, a brilliant lyricist, George wrote a string of successful Broadway musicals (see Chapter 25).

George made it possible, in 1924, for jazz to break into the classical-music concert hall for the first time. A controversy arose among concertgoers, concert hall managers, and board members when Paul Whiteman, a noted conductor, commissioned Gershwin to compose *Rhapsody in Blue* for performance in Aeolian Hall in New York City. Because the work is scored for piano soloist and jazz band, they considered it unfit for the classical concert hall. After negotiation, the management allowed this new jazz music to have its premiere, with George Gershwin at the piano and Paul Whiteman conducting.

In 1937, after playing his Concerto in F with the Los Angeles Philharmonic at the Hollywood Bowl, Gershwin was hospitalized. He died a few days later from a brain tumor at the age of 39.

PRINCIPAL WORKS

Orchestral Music: Rhapsody in Blue (piano concerto, 1924), Concerto in F (piano concerto, 1925), *An American in Paris* (tone poem, 1928), *Second Rhapsody* (piano and orchestra, 1931), *Cuban Overture* (1932)

Chamber Music: Lullaby for string quartet (1919)

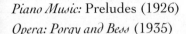

Piano Music: Preludes (1926)

Opera: Porgy and Bess (1935)

Stage Works: Lady Be Good (1924); *Tip Toes* (1925); *Oh, Kay* (1926); *Strike Up the Band* (1927); *Funny Face* (1927); *Treasure Girl* (1928); *Show Girl* (1929); *Girl Crazy* (Hollywood film, 1930); *Of Thee I Sing* (1931); *Pardon My English* (1933)

The 1925 novel and later serious play *Porgy* by South Carolinians Du-Bose Heyward and his sister Dorothy interested Gershwin. He envisioned it as the basis for a distinctly American folk opera. George was excited about the project when he approached DuBose Heyward with his idea. His excitement was contagious. Heyward invited him to come to South Carolina with him, where the two began writing the opera.

Although a wealthy white man, Heyward had carefully and lovingly captured the rhythms and spirit of the Southern African-American community in his play. In an effort to preserve that, DuBose wanted to be the lyricist. He later agreed that Ira Gershwin could also write some of the lyrics. George sent for his brother, and they both soaked up the culture on the remote islands off the coast of South Carolina where *Porgy and Bess* is set. Both Gershwins attended church services and musical gatherings, and they became familiar with the distinctive dialect, speech patterns, and musical style and performance of the islanders.

∞*Mainstream American Music*

Aaron Copland

If Gershwin's music leans to jazz, Copland's music epitomizes eclecticism—music with a wide variety of influences.

Scene from *Porgy and Bess*.
Krister St. Hill as Sportin' Life.

LISTENING ACTIVITY ∞

GERSHWIN, *PORGY AND BESS*,
"BESS, YOU IS MY WOMAN NOW"
LARGE FORM: OPERA (MUSICAL THEATER);
DETAILED FORM: THREE-PART SONG FORM (DUET)

Cassette Tape: Side D, Example 8
Compact Disc 3, Track 21

"Bess, You Is My Woman Now" comes from Act II of the opera *Porgy and Bess*, which is set in Catfish Row, Charleston, South Carolina.

After the overture, the curtain rises and the music starts for the haunting song "Summertime." The love story begins between the crippled beggar Porgy and the street woman Bess. In their duet, "Bess, You Is My Woman Now," Porgy and Bess declare their need for, devotion to, and love for each other.

As you listen to this appealing duet, notice the use of blues scales and harmonies.

LISTENING GUIDE

GERSHWIN, *PORGY AND BESS*,
"BESS, YOU IS MY WOMAN NOW"
LARGE FORM: OPERA (MUSICAL THEATER);
DETAILED FORM: THREE-PART SONG FORM (DUET)

Cassette Tape: Side D, Example 8
Compact Disc 3, Track 21
Running time: 4:42

21   0:00   (A) *Moderate tempo, orchestra introduction with cello solo leads into Porgy's entrance; B-flat major blues scale; complex chromatic harmonic accompaniment, syncopated rhythms*

Porgy
Bess, you is my woman now,
  you is, you is,
An' you mus' laugh an' sing an' dance
  for two instead of one.
Want no wrinkle on yo' brow, nohow,
because de sorrow of de past
  is all done done.
Bess, my Bess!
De real happiness is jes' begun.

1:19   *(A) section, main melody returns, higher key of D major; Bess Sings*

                        Bess
                        Porgy, I's yo' woman now,
                          I is, I is!
                        An' I ain' never goin' 'less you shares de fun
                        Dere's no wrinkle on my brow, no how, but

22   1:53   *(B) bridge section, faster, then slowing for return of main melody*

                        Bess
                        I ain' goin'
                        You hear me sayin'
                        if you ain' goin'
                        wid you I'm stayin'

2:04   *(A) main melody and tempo returns; higher key F-sharp major*

                        Bess
                        Porgy, I's yo' woman now!
                        I's yours for ever,

2:19   *transition section; imitations; softer, recitative-style*

                        Bess
                        Mornin' time and ev'nin' time an'
                        summer time an' winter time.

23   2:45   *song repeats as a duet; (A) section; D major; original tempo*

Porgy

Bess, you is my woman now an' forever,
Dis life is jes' begun

Bess, we two is one now an' forever
Oh, Bess, don' min' dose women.
You got yo' Porgy,
You loves yo' Porgy,

Bess

Porgy, I's yo' woman now,
I is, I is!
An' I ain' never goin' nowhere
'less you shares de fun.
Dere's no wrinkle on my brow, nohow,

3:13   *(B) section; faster, then slowing back to main melody*

Porgy

I knows you means it.
I seen it in yo' eyes, Bess.

Bess

I ain' goin! You hear me sayin'
if you ain' goin' wid you I'm stayin'.

3:24   *(A) section; original tempo; F-sharp major*

Porgy

We'll go swingin' through de years
a singin'

Bess

Porgy, I's yo' woman now!
I's yours forever.

3:38   *transition section; imitations; softer, recitative-style*

Porgy

Hmm—
Hmm—
Mornin' time and ev'nin' time an'
summer time an' winter time.

Bess

Mornin' time and ev'nin' time an'
summer time an' winter time.
Hmm—
Hmm—

3:52   *coda; orchestra with jazzy clarinet, then duet,*

Porgy

My Bess,
My Bess,

Bess

Oh, my Porgy,
my man Porgy,

4:07   *faster, rubato till the end cadence*

Porgy

From dis minute I'm tellin' you
I take dis vow:
Oh, my Bessie,
We's happy now,
We is one now.

Bess

From dis minute I'm tellin' you
I take dis vow:
Porgy,
I's yo' woman now.

LISTENING   INSIGHTS

Eclecticism in Music

Eclecticism incorporates into a musical work materials, styles, and ideas from a variety of sources. The search for new materials was underway during the late nineteenth century when nationalist composers gathered resources from within their own borders—folk songs and dances, indigenous instruments, and so on. Around the turn of the twentieth century, Debussy incorporated scales and instruments from Asia that he had heard at the Paris World Exposition. Stravinsky, Prokofiev, and others incorporated into their Neo-Classical compositions materials and compositional methods from other style periods.

For American and Canadian composers exposed to the tremendous waves of immigration from all over the globe, incorporating the cultural influences from their new citizens was inevitable. Thus, the United States and Canada became the first *world* communities. The rise of jazz and popular music developed in North America offered additional materials into the great mix of concert music.

Listening to the eclectic music of Ives, Gershwin, Copland, Bernstein, and others, you'll find a grand mixture of ideas: folk songs, folk-influenced songs, folk instruments, jazz and popular music melodies, harmonies, rhythms, patriotic songs, and tunes from a variety of churches—for example, the Shaker Church tune "Simple Gifts" woven into Copland's *Appalachian Spring*.

Much of the enjoyment in listening to eclectic music is in identifying the sources of the various musical resources.

ॐ *Other American Composers*

WILLIAM SCHUMAN (B. 1910)   Raised in his native New York City, Schuman began a lively music career as a Tin Pan Alley songwriter and song plugger—à la Gershwin.

Coming late to classical music, Schuman did not hear his first symphony concert until he was 20. The next day he changed his major at Columbia University to music. He continued composing and later taught at the Juilliard School of Music, serving as its president from 1945 to 1961.

An eclectic composer, Schuman purposely incorporated composition techniques similar to Copland's. With syncopation and other interesting rhythms, Schuman's music has a distinctly American flavor. Among his most popular music are his symphonies, ballet music (*Undertow*, 1940), and his works for band (*Chester* Overture).

AARON COPLAND (1900–90)

Like Gershwin, Aaron Copland (*cope*-land) was born in Brooklyn, New York, of recently immigrated Russian-Jewish parents. But he showed early musical talent and began to study music as a child. At 20, he went to Paris and was one of the first of many American composers to study with the famous teacher Nadia Boulanger.

Ironically, Copland had his first real exposure to jazz in Paris. Returning to the United States in 1924, Copland was determined to compose music that would be identified as "Americana" and would appeal to a wide variety of audiences.

A series of commissions from Agnes de Mille (*Rodeo*) and Martha Graham (*Appalachian Spring*) launched Copland into the ballet world, for which he produced some of the finest works of the twentieth century. Incorporating jazz and American-folk syncopations, Stravinsky's techniques, and Neo-Classical influences, Copland developed a highly appealing style many call American Nationalistic music.

By 1945, Copland had written the majority of his most popular compositions. He began devoting himself to conducting (mostly his own music) and teaching, spending many of his summers at the Tanglewood Music Center in Massachusetts. His most famous pupil was Leonard Bernstein.

PRINCIPAL WORKS

Orchestral Music: Symphonies: No. 1 (1928), No. 2 (1933), No. 3 (1946), *Music for the Theater* (1925), *El salón México* (1936), *An Outdoor Overture* (1938), *Quiet City* (1940), *Lincoln Portrait* (with narrator, 1942), *Fanfare for the Common Man* (1942), Orchestral Variations (1957), *Music for a Great City* (1964), *Inscape* (1967), *Three Latin American Sketches* (1972), Piano Concerto (1926), Clarinet Concerto (1948)

Ballets: Billy the Kid (1938), *Rodeo* (1942), *Appalachian Spring* (1944)

Film Music: Of Mice and Men (1939), *Our Town* (1940), *Red Pony* (1948), *The Heiress* (1949)

Operas: The Tender Land (1955)

Chamber Music: Study on a Jewish Theme (1928), Violin Sonata (1943); Piano Quartet (1950), Nonet for Strings (1960), *Threnody I: Igor Stravinsky, in memoriam* (1971)

Piano Music: Variations (1930), Sonata (1941), Fantasy (1957), *Night Thoughts* (1972)

Songs: Old American Songs, Twelve Poems of Emily Dickinson (1950)

LISTENING ACTIVITY ✒

COPLAND, *RODEO* "HOE DOWN"
LARGE FORM: BALLET

| *Cassette Tape: Side D, Example 9*
| *Compact Disc 3, Track 24*

Copland composed his Old West ballet *Rodeo* in 1942. Agnes de Mille choreographed it and danced the leading role in its premiere.

Rodeo is about a cowgirl infatuated with the head wrangler and championship roper. To attract his attention, she shows off her skills as a rider. But none of the cowboys pays attention to her until she appears in a feminine dress near the end of the ballet. Then, she has to fight off the competing cowboys. Finally, the head wrangler asks her to dance, and they join the other cowboys in a wild hoe down.

Notice how the syncopation and exciting dance rhythms of Copland's "Hoe Down" capture the sound and spirit of country fiddlers.

LISTENING GUIDE

COPLAND, *RODEO* "HOE DOWN"
LARGE FORM: BALLET

| *Cassette Tape: Side D, Example 9*
| *Compact Disc 3, Track 24*
| *Running time: 3:18*

24   0:00   FIDDLE TUNE 1   played by strings and winds; *ff*; fast tempo, duple meter;
                                  D major tonality

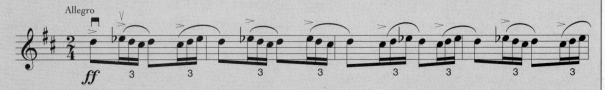

	0:03	FIDDLE TUNE 1— variation 1	played by trumpets, imitated by oboes and strings; *f* variation of tune 1
	0:12	FIDDLE TUNE 1	like the beginning, *ff*
	0:17	RHYTHM INTERLUDE	rhythm interlude played by strings and piano, *mf*
	0:36	FIDDLE TUNE 1	similar to beginning, played by strings and clarinet, *f*
	0:43	FIDDLE TUNE 1— variation 2	played by strings and woodwinds, *f* variation 2
	0:57	FIDDLE TUNE 1	played by strings and woodwinds, *f*
	0:59	FIDDLE TUNE 1—	played by strings, imitated by woodwinds, *mf* played by full orchestra, *fff*
	1:14	FIDDLE TUNE 1	similar to beginning, *f*
25	1:32	FIDDLE TUNE 2	played by trumpet, imitated by violins, then woodwinds, *f*, then *mf* sudden pause
	2:15	RHYTHM INTERLUDE	played by strings and piano; *mf—p*; rubato tempo, then slowing to held E-flat chord
	2:42	FIDDLE TUNE 1	like beginning, *f*; fast tempo again
	2:49	FIDDLE TUNE 1— variation 2	played by woodwinds, *mp*, then imitated by full orchestra, *fff*
	3:11	FIDDLE TUNE 1	played by strings and winds; *f*, crescendo to *ff* to *fff*. Three quick final chords; played by full orchestra, *fff*

Neo-Classical American Composers

Following Copland's goal to create music that could be accessible to the general American population, several important American composers incorporated Neo-Classical influences in their music.

WALTER PISTON (1894–1976)   A contemporary of Copland, Piston studied in France with Nadia Boulanger, as well as with Paul Dukas. He is known for his books on music theory and his teaching at Harvard (Bernstein was one of his students). Piston wrote eight symphonies, numerous concertos, and chamber music works. His ballet *The Incredible Flutist* (1938) is his most popular work.

LEONARD BERNSTEIN (1918–90)

Lawrence, Massachusetts, Bernstein's (*burn*-styne) birthplace, was a mill town when he was born. Luckily for Bernstein, Lawrence was close to Boston. Displaying an early talent for piano performance, composition, and literature, he studied music at Harvard.

The 1943-44 musical season thrust Bernstein into the public spotlight when he substituted for an ailing Bruno Walter as conductor on a nationally broadcast New York Philharmonic concert. Later that season, his *Jeremiah* Symphony won the New York Music Critics Circle award, his ballet *Fancy Free* was performed to critical acclaim, and his first Broadway show, *On the Town*, was an instant hit.

Composition in many styles continued, including film and theater music. In 1957, his most successful Broadway musical, *West Side Story*, opened and became a classic.

Concentrating on conducting, Bernstein became permanent conductor of the New York Philharmonic from 1958-1968. Since 1971, after composing his theater piece *Mass*, he divided his efforts between composing and conducting, becoming a revered guest conductor for the world's most prestigious symphony orchestras.

PRINCIPAL WORKS

Orchestral Music: Symphony No. 1 (*Jeremiah*, soprano and orchestra; 1943), Symphony No. 2 (*Age of Anxiety* for piano and orchestra, 1949); Symphony No. 3 (*Kaddish*, mixed chorus, boys' choir, soprano, speaker, and orchestra, 1963); *Chichester Psalms* (mixed chorus, boy soloist, and orchestra, 1965), *Songfest* (A Cycle of American Songs for Six Singers and Orchestra, 1977); Slava! (1977); *Halil* (Nocturne for Solo Flute, String Orchestra, and Percussion, 1981)

Ballets: Fancy Free (1944), *Facsimile* (1946), *Dybbuk* (1974)

Chamber Music: Clarinet Sonata (1942), Fanfares (1961)

Piano Music: Seven Anniversaries (1943), *Touches* (1980)

Stage Music: On the Town (1944), *Trouble in Tahiti* (1951), *Wonderful Town* (1953), *Candide* (comic operetta, 1956), *West Side Story* (1957), *Mass* (Theater Piece, 1971)

LISTENING ACTIVITY ∿

BERNSTEIN, *OVERTURE TO CANDIDE*
LARGE FORM: MUSICAL THEATER OVERTURE

Cassette Tape: Side D, Example 10
Compact Disc 3, Track 26

Though the original 1956 run on Broadway of *Candide* was short-lived—only 73 performances—the overture has remained a concert favorite. Lillian Hellman's book and Richard Wilbur's lyrics for the original production were adapted from Voltaire's classic about mindless optimism. When it was revised in 1974, with added lyrics by Stephen Sondheim and staging by Harold Prince, the new Broadway run was highly successful.

In the musical, we accompany Candide, his frivolous fiancée Cunegonde, and his teacher Dr. Pangloss as they leave Westphalia, Germany, their home and "The Best of All Possible Worlds," and travel to Lisbon, Paris, Buenos Aires, and Venice. During their voyage they endure such devastations as the treachery of the Spanish Inquisition, an insurrection, a war, the rape of Cunegonde, an earthquake, the plague, and the humiliation of slavery. By the time they finally return home to Westphalia, they realize that perfection can never be attained: One must accept life's realities and try to do one's best.

Listen to Bernstein's *Overture to Candide*. The function of the overture is to set the tone, style, character, and spirit of the musical before the curtain rises. Bernstein's *Overture to Candide* is one of the most effective overtures to any musical theater work, achieving all those requirements. Although several tunes from the musical are previewed in the overture, the music focuses on the optimistic and witty tune "Glitter and Be Gay" ("If I'm not pure, at least my jewels are").

LISTENING GUIDE

BERNSTEIN, *OVERTURE TO CANDIDE*
LARGE FORM: MUSICAL THEATER OVERTURE

Cassette Tape: Side D, Example 10
Compact Disc 3, Track 26
Running time: 4:22

26	0:00	INTRODUCTION MUSIC	very fast, mostly duple meter; *ff*; full orchestra; tonal with some dissonant chords
	0:38	BATTLE SCENE MUSIC	duple meter; march; *f*; mainly band instruments
27	1:19	OH, HAPPY WE	low woodwinds and strings; meters changing between 2 and 3; *mf*
	1:32	OH, HAPPY WE	violins and oboes added higher
	1:44	OH, HAPPY WE	full orchestra; *f*
	2:01	OH, HAPPY WE	full orchestra; *ff*
	2:12	INTRODUCTION MUSIC	duple meter; *ff*
	2:34	BATTLE SCENE MUSIC	mostly band instruments; *ff*
	2:49	OH, HAPPY WE	melody in oboes and horns; *p*
	3:00	OH, HAPPY WE	full orchestra; *ff*; section ends with silent pause
28	3:18	GLITTER AND BE GAY	woodwind melody; *pp*; then gradually getting louder and adding more instruments
	3:31	GLITTER AND BE GAY	full orchestra, horns and woodwinds imitate one beat after flutes and violins

Coda Section

	3:37	GLITTER AND BE GAY	suddenly faster and softer
	3:55	GLITTER AND BE GAY	full orchestra; *ff*
	4:07	BATTLE SCENE MUSIC	full orchestra, *fff*
	4:13	OH, HAPPY WE	horns in counterplay; two final chords, first soft, last loud

GIAN CARLO MENOTTI (B. 1911)

An Italian by birth, Menotti later became a naturalized citizen of the United States. He grew up, however, in a country town on Lake Lugano on the Swiss-Italian border. Menotti's father was a prosperous businessman, and his mother, an amateur musician.

By the time he entered the Milan Conservatory of Music at the age of 13, Menotti had written two operas. In 1928 at the age of 17, he continued his musical studies at the Curtis Institute of Music in Philadelphia, where he met his lifelong friend, the composer Samuel Barber.

After graduating with honors from the Curtis Institute, Menotti began receiving commissions for opera works. In 1936, his *Amelia Goes to the Ball*, a comic opera in Italian, premiered in Italy, and then played at the Metropolitan Opera in New York. It was then that Menotti decided to remain in the United States to become a citizen.

From 1958 until recently, Menotti spent most of his efforts directing the Spoleto Festival of Two Worlds located in Spoleto, Italy.

Menotti's operas have been some of the most successful of the twentieth century. He has the distinction of having composed the first opera for television, *Amahl and the Night Visitors*, commissioned by NBC. His concerns have been to make his operas realistic and accessible to North American audiences. Caring for the voice and vocal melody, Menotti has often been compared to Puccini. Though he has composed entirely in the twentieth century, Menotti's compositional techniques have been mostly traditional, conservative, and somewhat reminiscent of nineteenth-century Romanticism.

PRINCIPAL WORKS

Orchestral Music: Piano Concerto in F (1945); *Sebastian*, ballet suite (1947); Concerto for Violin (1952)

Operas: Amelia al ballo (Amelia to the Ball, 1936); *The Old Maid and the Thief* (1939); *The Medium* (1945); *The Telephone* (1946); *The Consul* (1949); *Amahl and the Night Visitors* (1951); *The Saint of Bleecker Street* (1954); *Help, Help, the Globolinks* (1968); *The Hero* (1976); *Tamu-Tamu* (1973)

Cantatas, Madrigal Ballets: The Unicorn, the Gorgon and the Manticore (1956); *The Death of Bishop Brindisi* (1963); *Landscapes and Remembrances* (1976)

Chamber Music: Four Pieces for string quartet (1936); Suite for Two Cellos and Piano (1973)

Piano Music: Poemeti per Maria Rosa, 12 pieces for children (1937); *Ricecare and Toccata on a Theme from The Old Maid and the Thief* (1953)

ROGER SESSIONS (1896–1985)   Born in Brooklyn, New York, Sessions wrote complicated, abstract music (without extra-musical ideas attached) and twelve-tone music. He taught at Smith College in Massachusetts, Cleveland Institute of Music, Princeton University, University of California/Berkeley, and the Juilliard School of Music.

Session's most successful students include Miriam Gideon, Hugo Weisgall, Vivien Fine, Donald Martino, and Ellen Taaffe Zwilich.

ELLEN TAAFFE ZWILICH (B. 1939)

Born in Miami, Florida, Zwilich began to study violin at an early age. After receiving both her bachelor's and master's degrees in music from Florida State University, she studied composition with Roger Sessions and Elliot Carter at the Juilliard School of Music in New York City. Zwilich was the first woman to be awarded a doctorate in composition from Juilliard.

Commissions from the San Francisco and Indianapolis orchestras and several chamber music groups gave Zwilich opportunities to compose for a variety of performing media. Her Symphony No. 1 earned her a Pulitzer Prize in 1983.

As with other North American composers, eclecticism characterizes Zwilich's music, which draws on a wide range of diverse styles. Twentieth-century compositional techniques blended with Romantic tonality and thematic treatment have given her works an appeal to a wide range of audiences—untypical of much of contemporary music. In fact, some of her admirers call her the champion of a "new Romanticism."

PRINCIPAL WORKS

Orchestral Music: Symposium (1973); Chamber Symphony (1979); Symphony No. 1 (1982); Symphony No. 2 (1985); *Celebration* (tone poem, 1984); Prologue and Variations (1984); Concerto Grosso (after Handel, 1985); *Symbolon* (1988)

Chamber Music: Sonata for Violin and Piano (1974); String Quartet (1974); String Trio (1981); Divertimento (1983); Double Quartet for Strings (1984); Concerto for Trumpet and Five Players (1984)

Vocal Music: Einsame Nacht (Lonesome Night, song cycle, 1971); *Passages* for Soprano and Instrumental Ensemble; several other songs

Neo-classical American
composers

SAMUEL BARBER (1910–81)   An eclectic, Neo-Romantic composer, Barber
was born in Philadelphia and studied at the Curtis Institute there. Some of
his most popular works are his overture for *School of Scandal* (1933), String
Quartet (1936), *Vanessa* (opera, 1958), "Adagio for Strings" (1936, used in
the film *Platoon*), *Medea* (ballet, 1946), and many interesting songs.

HOWARD HANSON (1896–1981)   From 1924 to 1964, Hanson was director of
the Eastman School of Music, where he also founded and conducted the
Eastman Philharmonic Orchestra. Symphony No. 1 (*Nordic*, 1923) and
Symphony No. 2 (*Romantic*, 1930) are two of his popular works, along with
his opera *Merry Mount* (1934).

LISTENING ACTIVITY ✏

ZWILICH, *CONCERTO GROSSO 1985*
FIRST MOVEMENT: MAESTOSO

Cassette Tape: Side D, Example 11
Compact Disc 3, Track 29

Listen to the *Concerto Grosso 1985* by Ellen Taaffe Zwilich. It is
scored for a chamber orchestra consisting of a small group of winds,
harpsichord, and strings reminiscent of Baroque style Period. The
work was commissioned by the Washington Friends of Handel for
the commemoration of George Frideric Handel's birth.

Zwilich patterned the *Concerto Grosso* on a violin sonata by Handel. The first movement contains several musical quotes from the
original Handel work. The Handel sections are juxtaposed with contemporary polytonal arpeggios. To contrast Handel's style with
Zwilich's unique contemporary style, she instructs the performers to
perform the Handel sections in obvious Baroque style.

The composer states that the concerto is "both inspired by Handel's sonata and, I hope, inbued with his spirit." More specifically, in
Neo-Classical style (neo-Baroque here), she uses terraced dynamics—contrasting imitations of loud and soft sections—repeated
melodic phrases, and sequences.

Interestingly, at the world premiere in 1986, the Handel violin
sonata was performed preceding the Zwilich *Concerto Grosso 1985*.

LISTENING GUIDE

ZWILICH, *CONCERTO GROSSO 1985*
FIRST MOVEMENT: MAESTOSO

Cassette Tape: Side D, Example 11
Compact Disc 3, Track 29
Running time: 2:41

29	0:00	HELD TONES	3 long tones on the pitch "D," *f*, maestoso
30	0:24	ARPEGGIO THEME	intervals based on Handel's theme, 16th note, polytonal arpeggios in flutes, oboes, violins over held "D," *f*, repeated *p*
31	0:41	HANDEL THEME	played by violin, harpsichord continuo in Baroque style, ornamented stately melody, *mp*, duple meter
	1:02	ARPEGGIO THEME	*f*, 16th note polytonal arpeggios played by flute and violin, imitated by various instruments
	1:22	HANDEL THEME— fragments	*p*, oboe, ornamented melody over harpsichord and basso continuo
	1:38	HANDEL THEME— fragments	violins, *f*, alternating imitations with flute and oboe, oboe fragments from the Handel theme
	1:57	HANDEL THEME— fragments	*f*, woodwinds and strings, ornamented melody in Baroque style with continuo, section ends with cadence
	2:10	ARPEGGIO THEME	woodwinds and strings together play polytonal arpeggios
	2:20	POLYCHORDS	*f*, three held polychords with harpsichord arpeggios

Summary of Terms

African-American church music
bebop
bitonal
blue notes
blues
blues progressions
blues scale
cakewalk
call and response
country
eclecticism
fusion

fusion/electronic
fusion/jazz-rock
gospel
jazz-rock
off-beat
ostinato
polychords
polymedia
polymeters
polyrhythms
polytonality
pop music

quarter tones
rag
ragtime
rhythm and blues
riff
rock
song plugger
soul and funk
swing
syncopation
Tin Pan Alley
worksongs

CHAPTER 24

Part IV: Adjunct Music
North American Popular Music

How does popular music fit into a study of concert music? Drawing a dividing line between classical and popular music can be difficult—especially since many popular artists have classical-music backgrounds, such as Wynton Marsalis, Herb Alpert, and Cleo Laine.

Some musicians claim that classical music is for serious listening and will be a legacy for future generations, and that popular music is for sheer entertainment, satisfying the changing tastes of today's audiences. In that case, much of Mozart's music would have been considered popular in his day. In the 1780s, Viennese from all walks of life sang tunes from Mozart's *The Magic Flute*.

Also, many popular music hits cross over into symphony orchestra "pops" concerts and summer festivals. You may find popular music on the same program as opera, ballet, and traditional orchestral music. For example, the Boston Pops Orchestra has regularly programmed music by the Beatles.

People have always used popular music to enhance their lives. Songs have helped to uplift the spirit and ease the rigors of daily existence. African-American slaves in America's South sang their popular spirituals to mitigate the pain of their toil. Lonely cowboys out on the vast prairies sang to relieve their boredom. Work songs accompanied the hammering of spikes into railroad ties across America. Caught in a traffic jam today, what do we do? Turn on the radio or put in a tape and listen to music.

❧ *Early American Popular Music*

"Yankee Doodle," originally a British tune, became a popular song throughout the colonies during the Revolutionary War. Later during the War Between the States, "Yankee Doodle" and "John Brown's Body" ("The Battle Hymn of the Republic") were identified with the North, and Dan Emmett's (1815–1904) "Dixie" with the South. Popular in their day, they are still with us.

Foster

Stephen Foster (1826–64) wrote hundreds of popular songs in the nineteenth century. "Jeanie with the Light Brown Hair," "Oh, Susanna," and "Camptown Races"—hit songs of his day—are still sung. Foster's "My Old Kentucky Home" sold 90,000 copies of sheet music. His "Old Folks at Home" reached an all-time record, with sales topping $10,000, a considerable sum in the nineteenth century.

Twentieth-century technology and a host of inventions have created an unprecedented mass market for popular music. Radio, television, music videos, phonograph records, compact discs, and audio tape recordings (reel to reel, cassette, digital audio tape) deliver popular music to millions of people around the world.

Irving Berlin's "Alexander's Ragtime Band"

When Irving Berlin (1888-1989) wrote the popular song "Alexander's Ragtime Band" in 1911, jazz crossed over into popular music, and for the first time jazz style became commercially successful. Berlin intended to capture the flavor of a New Orleans street-parade jazz band and bring it to Tin Pan Alley in New York City. Within a few years after its introduction, a whole nation was singing and dancing to that tune.

Until that time, the highly syncopated ragtime music, blues, and jazz was the sole province of African-American musicians. They played to small audiences in their churches, social clubs, and society street parades in Memphis and New Orleans. By 1916, the new jazz style had influenced popular music, sweeping across the nation.

✲ Tin Pan Alley

Until the late 1930s, Tin Pan Alley was the commercial hub of American popular music. Rows and rows of four-story brownstone buildings on New York's West 28th Street housed music publishing companies and related businesses. From there they distributed their products throughout the Western world.

Where did that peculiar name come from? During the hot, stifling New York City summers, music businesses would open all their windows for fresh air. The sounds they produced spilled out into the streets, mixing the pounding of pianos of song pluggers, squealing saxophones and blaring trumpets, and musical show singers trying out the latest tune. The din must have reminded someone of the banging of tin pans.

✲ The Commercialization of Popular Music

With the wind-up phonograph of Thomas Edison and the crystal radio of Guglielmo Marconi still luxury items, no mass market had emerged for the expensive wax recordings. Nor were there commercial radio stations to play "Alexander's Ragtime Band." To hear the latest Irving Berlin or George M. Cohan songs, music lovers had to go either to the theater or to a department store where song pluggers would play music to entice customers to buy the sheet music. Royalties from sheet music sales and from vaudeville and musical theater performances were the only mass market for songwriters.

Record Companies

The first African-American owned recording company, The Black Swan Phonograph Company, started in 1921. The blues singer Ethel Waters gave the company its first big hit, "Down Home Blues."

By the late 1920s, major record companies were electronically recording and mass producing brittle shellac phonograph records that were now flat discs, 8 to 12 inches in diameter. Turntables for the discs spun at 78 revolutions per minute.

Popular and affordable, phonograph records introduced musical artists and their songs to people around the world. In 1928, for instance, Al Jolson's recording of "Sonny Boy" sold four million copies in just four weeks! Jolson, a Russian-Jewish immigrant, made a fortune imitating African-American minstrels.

Sheet Music cover of Berlin's "Alexander's Ragtime Band."

Edison phonograph
Marconi Radio

Radio Broadcasts

With the opening in 1920 of America's first public broadcast station, KDKA in Pittsburgh, mass-produced home radio sets became a hot-selling item. Disc jockeys created a new market for popular music.

Popular Music in Films

The 1927 film *The Jazz Singer*, starring Al Jolson, became the first commercially produced "talkie." With the advent of sound film, musicals became another important outlet for popular music.

America in the '20s became the world's commercial center for popular music. Through the media of radio, sound films, and sound recordings, people everywhere could hear the music of George Gershwin, Irving Berlin, W. C. Handy, Eubie Blake, Jerome Kern, Cole Porter, Richard Rodgers, Harold Arlen, and many others.

♫ *The Swing Era*

The big bands of the 1930s and 1940s brought popular swing music into dance halls and ballrooms. Band buses rolled around the country bringing live music to millions from Bridgeport to Boise. Through the media and live performances, Americans heard the seventeen-piece bands of trum-

Benny Goodman with his big band.

peter Bunny Berrigan, pianist Fletcher Henderson, trombonist Tommy Dorsey, saxophonist Jimmy Dorsey, trombonist Glenn Miller, trumpeter Harry James, clarinetist Artie Shaw, and the American royalty: "Duke" Ellington (piano), "Count" Basie (piano), and the "King of Swing," Benny Goodman (clarinet).

Highly skilled performers staffed their bands. Audiences crowded around the bandstand to hear these popular music virtuosos. Because big bands provided music for listening as well as dancing, they gave their audiences unforgettable performances.

Each big band featured a male and a female vocalist. "Crooners" such as Russ Columbo, Frank Sinatra, Bing Crosby, Dick Haymes, Perry Como, and Vaughan Monroe launched their careers singing with the big bands. So did female vocalists: Sarah Vaughan, Helen Forest, Ruth Etting, Peggy Lee, Rosemary Clooney, Doris Day, Billie Holiday, and Ella Fitzgerald.

Billie Holiday.

Popular Music and World War II

To boost the morale of English-speaking troops during World War II, Armed Forces Radio broadcast music throughout the war zones. Glenn Miller and many members of his band eventually joined the Army Air Corps. Based in London, they broadcast to all the fighting forces—on both sides of the conflict. After the Allies liberated Paris, Glenn Miller obtained a small aircraft and pilot to fly him there to relocate the Air Force band. His plane crashed in the Normandy fog, killing him and the crew.

Popular Music in Industry

To increase production during World War II, factories introduced music. Researchers studied different music throughout the day and noted its effect on production. As a result of these studies, a new branch of music emerged—*environmental* music.

Environmental music

Today, music is everywhere—in elevators, offices, medical and dental waiting rooms, airport lounges, restaurants, bowling alleys, shopping malls, supermarkets, lawyers' offices—even when you're on "hold" during a phone call. Environmental-music companies provide sound tracks designed to increase employees' efficiency by creating a cheerful environment. Theoretically, you don't even have to listen to the music intently: It surrounds you and helps shape your mood.

Decline of the Big Bands

After World War II, with America focusing its economy on housing and consumer goods for the returning G.I.s and their expanding families, music retrenched. Spending priorities changed from expensive entertainment

Juke box.

_____

Ray Charles.

_____

to buying automobiles, housing, furniture, and kitchen appliances. Gone was the costly big band era. Now, small groups became fashionable.

THE JUKE BOX   The juke box, an offshoot of the record industry, was an economical replacement for live music. The "box" also made popular music available in ice cream parlors, bowling alleys, bars, and restaurants. By 1959, over a half million juke boxes across the nation were swallowing dimes and quarters.

During and immediately after World War II, with money scarce for most young families, they often had stay-at-home parties. They danced to radio programs such as "Juke Box Saturday Night" and "Your Hit Parade." In the 1950s "Your Hit Parade" moved to television, where it was seen along with new dance programs such as Dick Clark's "American Bandstand" and in the '60s, "Soul Train."

❧ Country Music

Replacing the big bands throughout America were the four- to seven-piece bands with the all-important lead singer. Guitars—acoustic, electric, and the Hawaiian steel guitars—replaced trumpets, trombones, and saxophones.

A "down-home" eclectic music became popular. Combining elements from Southern folk music (simple tunes and predictable harmony) with elements of jazz, blues, and gospel, a new sound echoed throughout the music industry. Called "country," "country-western," "country-folk," "rock-a-billy," or at times "honky-tonk," the music became popular everywhere, notably in the South and Southwest.

The Grand Ole Opry and other country music broadcasts made Nashville, Tennessee, a significant commercial center for country-popular music.

Country music is not only thriving but has also earned respect. Among the artists associated with country music are Merle Haggard, Waylon Jennings, Brenda Lee, Loretta Lynn, Hank Williams, Johnny Cash, Charlie Rich, Buck Owens, Dolly Parton, Kris Kristofferson, Kenny Rogers, K. T. Oslin, Reba McIntyre, The Judds, Willie Nelson, and Bonnie Raitt.

❧ Rhythm and Blues

R & B, a transitional style between swing and rock, first became popular in the African-American communities in big cities such as Chicago and Detroit. Chuck Berry, "Fats" Domino, Little Richard, Muddy Waters, Otis

Redding, James Brown, Ray Charles, and Aretha Franklin were the leading exponents of rhythm and blues. Using electronic amplifiers, a four-piece band now could not only match but exceed the volume of the 17-piece band of the swing era. And did they ever turn up the volume!

R & B influence became even stronger in the 1960s. Berry Gordy organized Motown Records (from "*mo*tor *town*," i.e., Detroit) to handle the careers of R & B artists. Specializing in black artists, Motown had its first big hit in 1964 with a recording by The Supremes with Diana Ross.

❧ *Rock 'n' Roll/Rock*

In the mid-1950s, a relatively obscure group, Bill Haley and the Comets, recorded "Rock Around the Clock." The music became background music for a 1955 film, *Blackboard Jungle*, which portrayed the inner-city, teenage subculture of the time.

The music caught on, especially with teenagers, and has remained popular through four decades. Rock 'n' roll (later "rock") was originally a music mixture of jazz, blues, rhythm-and-blues, folk, and country. From its early days, rock was characterized by its hard-driving beat—a departure from the subtle syncopated rhythms and prominent melodies of the swing era. In rock, melody and text are subordinate to rhythms.

The Rolling Stones, featuring Mick Jagger (center).

Elvis Presley

"You Ain't Nothin' But a Hound Dog," "Blue Suede Shoes," and other Elvis Presley hits added a new dimension to early rock music. A young "country boy" gyrating in leather and glittering studs, Elvis was dubbed "The King." He exuded a sensuality that teenagers couldn't resist. Crowding to hear him, screaming their adulation, teenagers had found not only a music but an idol all their own. Hoards of imitators followed.

The Beatles

Something was different about those long-haired young men—the four-piece group from Liverpool, England, who made their North American television debut February 8, 1964 on "The Ed Sullivan Show."

For their first number, the Beatles sang a rather simple love song, "I Wanna Hold Your Hand," and crowds of teenagers screamed and yelled and tore their hair in virtual hysteria. The Beatles achieved immediate popularity, and from that moment on, they arguably had a profound, lasting influence on popular music throughout the world for the rest of the decade.

Something was different about 1964: The American consciousness had begun to change. As the Beatles' popularity spread, they verbalized the feelings many people shared toward the government, the military, and industry. They sang about the absurdity of war, and we listened. Youth protested the Establishment in a twentieth-century version of Romanticism.

Many of the Beatles' songs, especially those of John Lennon and Paul McCartney, have become standards. For example:

"Yesterday"   "Penny Lane"
"Michelle"   "Eleanor Rigby"
"Sgt. Pepper's Lonely Hearts Club Band"

The Beatles.

Woodstock rock festival in
upstate New York, August
1969.

Inevitably, other rock groups followed, notably the Byrds and the
Rolling Stones.

Woodstock Rock Festival

The 1969 Woodstock Festival and the 1994 twenty-fifth anniversary concerts became an explosive manifestation of rock music. More than
300,000 people listened to Joan Baez, Janis Joplin, Jimi Hendrix, and
the Jefferson Airplane, among others, at the largest music gathering in
history. An attitude of "sex, drugs, and rock 'n' roll" prevailed, but considering the size of the crowd, the festival was relatively peaceful. Rock
music proved it was no passing fad; it would remain on the world scene
for generations.

Folk-Rock

Folk-rock music was a prominent part of Woodstock and many subsequent festivals. Promoting contemporary causes such as civil rights and the
end of the Vietnam War, these modern-day troubadours echoed the troubled, changing times.

Many artists blended folk and rock music styles. Performing for large
crowds, artists took advantage of amplification systems, though folk-rock
artists favored the traditional acoustic guitar over rock music's electronic
instruments.

Some of the most influential folk-rock artists include:

Bob Dylan	Joni Mitchell	John Denver
Joan Baez	Simon and Garfunkel	Cat Stevens
Judy Collins	Peter, Paul and Mary	Donovan

Jazz-Rock

During the late 1960s, seven- and eight-piece rock groups began featuring trumpets, trombones, and saxophones as well as electronic and orchestral instruments. These groups include:

Chicago	Yes
Blood, Sweat & Tears	Ten Wheel Drive
Earth, Wind, and Fire	The Mothers of Invention

With performers more highly trained than those of some previous rock groups (many were college music school graduates), they were able to incorporate more complex four- and five-part harmony. Moving toward the fusion of rock and jazz styles (jazz-rock), these groups created music that appealed to more sophisticated audiences than earlier rock groups had.

Characteristics of Live Rock Music Performances

- Heavy, driving bass (usually played by amplified bass guitar and/or electronic keyboards).
- Persistent ostinato in rhythms.
- Catchy, repetitive refrain (the "hook").
- Extensive modal harmonies and tonalities, generally avoiding traditional major and minor tonalities.
- Live sounds augmented with electronic synthesizers and pre-recorded tapes.
- Performers wear theatrical costumes, unusual hairdos and makeup.
- Pyrotechnics in lighting, stage sets, and visual displays (smoke, lasers, strobes, etc.).

Summary of Terms

country	folk-rock	Marconi radio
country-folk	Grand Ole Opry	rhythm and blues
country-western	honky-tonk	rock 'n' roll
Edison phonograph	jazz-rock	rock-a-billy
environmental music	juke box	

CHAPTER 25

Broadway Musical Theater

Ever since the Middle Ages, when the troubadours of Provence sang their poetic notions of love, song has been the vehicle for communicating romantic ideas and ideals. As all music does, song enriches the spirit with its fundamental messages: Life is worth living, love conquers all, good ultimately prevails over evil, and a rainbow may indeed lead us to a pot of gold.

As North America's contribution to world theater, the Broadway musical offers us not only optimistic messages but also an exciting, carefully constructed entertainment package. We can sit back, relax, and enjoy its art, color, universal theme, drama, believable characters, distinctive form, and demanding production.

Above all, there's an engaging story—the "book"—that can sweep us away for a couple of hours. Afterward, we leave the theater humming an enchanting new melody.

⁓ *The Broadway Musical: Its Roots*

European Predecessors of the Broadway Musical

Ballad opera

BALLAD OPERA   Starting in the first half of the eighteenth century, ballad opera differed from other opera mainly by having spoken dialogue between songs instead of the recitative. Also, much of the music was from popular tunes and folk songs of the day to which composers set new lyrics. Most ballad operas contained simple melodies with uncomplicated harmonies, designed to appeal to middle-class audiences. Similar to Greek tragedy, plots were based on familiar material.

In England, the most popular work of the eighteenth century was John Gay's *The Beggar's Opera* (1728). Included in the repertory of every touring company at that time, the work satirized Italian opera—especially those by Handel—the aristocracy, the British government and its then-prime minister, Robert Walpole. Using English for its language, *The Beggar's Opera* presented an alternative to Italian, which had been the dominant opera language. With its strong book, *The Beggar's Opera* set the standard for the form and style of musical productions that followed: The book comes first.

Exactly two hundred years after the introduction of Gay's *Beggar's Opera*, the German-born composer Kurt Weill (1900-50) wrote his popular *Dreigroschen Opera* (*The Three Penny Opera*, 1928), a modern-setting imitation of *The Beggar's Opera*.

The year 1735 marked the production of *Flora*, the first ballad opera farce staged in North America. Without scenery, costumes, or footlights, the show played in the Charleston, South Carolina, courthouse to only the handful of people who could fit into the room.

Mozart took inspiration from the English ballad operas and wrote his delightful *Abduction from the Harem* in 1782 for the German *singspiel* employing the German language.

Comic opera

COMIC OPERA   From the French, Italian, and English repertory, comic opera resembled the French *opéra bouffe* and the German operetta. In the United States, the comic opera incorporated the English emphasis on comedy over romance.

Mozart had a special flair for comic opera. His witty and charming *Le nozze di Figaro* (*The Marriage of Figaro*, 1786) and *Don Giovanni* (1787) are two of his most often performed comic operas.

Operetta

OPERETTA   Originating in Germany and the Austro-Hungarian Empire, the operetta incorporated every aspect of the late-nineteenth-century romanticism: love, idealism, adventure, and bravery. Wrapped in a trivial plot combined with appealing music and graceful dance, life in operettas was a delightful fantasy.

Roots in North America

MINSTRELSY   Minstrel shows of the nineteenth century were the first truly all-American musical theater. Until then, American musical theater imitated European musical theater in both form and style.

Minstrelsy

North American composers realized that minstrel shows offered an opportunity to introduce original songs to the public. Some of those who took advantage of this outlet for their work became famous. For example, Stephen Foster (1826–64) wrote more than 200 minstrel songs.

Using burnt cork for their blackface, white men imitating African-Americans dressed in gaudy costumes sat on stage facing the audience in a semicircle. The typical format was in three parts:

Part 1 featured jokes and solo songs backed by the humming of the other performers.

Part 2 was similar to vaudeville theater and featured whatever diverse talents the minstrel performers possessed—juggling, dancing, magic, and the like.

Part 3 was usually a parody of a play or opera. Most often it took the form of a sentimental operetta based on plantation life.

Although his titles seem to identify Foster with the Deep South— "Old Folks at Home," "De Camptown Races," "Oh, Susanna," and "My Old Kentucky Home"—he lived, worked, and died in the North in the area around Pittsburgh, Pennsylvania. In fact, "Oh, Susanna" premiered in Pittsburgh at the Eagle Ice Cream Saloon.

Perhaps the most important of the African-American writers and entertainers who joined minstrel troupes after the War Between the States was James A. Bland (1854–1911). A well-educated man born in the North, Bland was the son of one of the first African-Americans in the United States to receive a college education. Bland started as an entertainer, but he is best remembered for the songs he wrote: "Carry Me Back to Old Virginny," "In the Evening by the Moonlight," and "Oh, Dem Golden Slippers." Unfortunately, all but 38 of his songs have been lost.

"Dixie" was the best-known minstrel song. Written originally for banjo by Dan Emmett, the song later acquired new lyrics and became the battle hymn of the Confederacy during the War Between the States.

Early Broadway Musicals

VAUDEVILLE   Vaudeville's roots go back to a fifteenth-century French village, Val-de-Vire, in Normandy. The villagers were famous for entertaining one another by composing and performing ballads and satirical songs.

Vaudeville

The North American stage form of vaudeville, which flourished from 1878 to 1925, was a succession of unrelated specialty acts: singers, dancers,

Sheet music cover for collection of songs by James Bland.

actors, acrobats, comics, magicians, jugglers, midgets, monkeys, dogs, dancing elephants, skating bears, fire-eaters, Swiss bell ringers, xylophonists, female impersonators, and anything that was sensational and startling.

When Tony Pastor, a former minstrel showman, opened the doors of his Paterson, New Jersey, variety theater in 1865, he opened the doors to vaudeville in North America. In both his New Jersey and New York theaters, Tony Pastor promoted family entertainment only—no smoking, no drinking, no vulgarity. E. F. Albee continued the crusade for purity, setting the moral tone for the Albee Theater in Brooklyn, the great Palace Theater in Manhattan, and the Keith circuit—a nationwide chain of vaudeville houses.

Some of America's most popular songs emerged from vaudeville. "Sidewalks of New York" (1894) by vaudevillian Charles Lawlor became the unofficial anthem of New York City. Other surviving vaudeville hits include:

"In the Good Old Summertime"
"Waltz Me Around Again, Willie"
"The Band Played On"

"My Wild Irish Rose"
"Sweet Adeline"
"When You Were Sweet Sixteen"
"After the Ball Is Over"
"Shine on Harvest Moon"

During the early heyday of vaudeville, the popular song developed in both form and content. It matured with the influence of ragtime, blues, Tin Pan Alley, and such greats as Jerome Kern, Irving Berlin, George Gershwin, and Richard Rodgers.

BURLESQUE   In direct contrast to the Keith "Sunday School Circuit," as vaudeville artists called the chain, burlesque was raucous, bawdy, musical sex-and-comedy-travesty entertainment. Starting about 1868, touring companies played to audiences of men eager for naughty, grown-up amusement, though performances were fairly modest in the early years. Not until the 1920s, when striptease replaced "hootchie-cootchie" dancing, did burlesque degenerate into sexual exhibitions.

Burlesque

Innovative "travesty" comedy—broad parody—was burlesque's real contribution to musical theater. In fact, around 1900 it was the great vaudeville team of Joe Weber and Lew Fields who decided to try out a travesty-comedy routine in burlesque. After their successful burlesque debut, Weber and Fields left the show to open their own music hall. Critics praised their show, saying that the combination of lavish musical numbers and outrageous travesty offered the best "musical comedy" available.

Burlesque had begun with a tradition of satire and comedy. After World War I, when the shows replaced their hallmark comedy with vulgar sexuality, burlesque had a decline from which it could never recover. Fortunately, musical theater learned its lesson from that: Never abandon comedy.

EXTRAVAGANZA AND SPECTACLE   The embodiment of extravaganza/spectacle was New York's Hippodrome Theater (1905–35), which occupied the entire block on Sixth Avenue between Forty-third and Forty-fourth streets. Inside, as many as 5,200 paying customers could thrill to unobstructed views of floods and fires, sensational water ballets, cavalry charges of 480 soldiers on horseback, entire baseball games, and a brilliantly costumed female chorus of 280 dancers. Six hundred performers could fit comfortably on the half-acre stage.

Extravaganza and spectacle

The Great Depression affected the economics of all theatrical forms, especially the costly extravaganza. Paying customers decreased and public taste changed at the same time, signaling the demise of the Hippodrome.

Renowned showman Billy Rose tried to revive the theater in 1935 with a spectacular production of *Jumbo* by Richard Rodgers and Lorenz Hart. The show was only a moderate success, and the era of the extravaganza was over.

Revue

THE REVUE   America borrowed the name *revue* from the French musical variety show that satirized Parisian high life. The new, more cohesive North American version was an energetic, nonbook show—usually built around star performers—featuring musical numbers, comedy acts, dramatic sketches, and specialty routines.

After its Broadway debut with *The Passing Show* in 1894, the revue grew in popularity. It reached its height equally in England and in North America between the two World Wars.

On Broadway, the longest-running annual revues included:

The Ziegfield Follies	(1907–31)	25 editions
The Passing Show	(second series, 1912–24)	12 editions
George White's Scandals	(1919–31)	11 editions
Earl Carroll Vanities	(1923–32)	11 editions
The Greenwich Village Follies	(1919–28)	8 editions

Ziegfield

Florenz Ziegfield (1867–1932), whose shows epitomized glamor and extravagance, was the greatest exponent of the American revue. He dedicated each of his editions to the glorification of the American woman, packaging the show with a pace that built to climaxes and a spectacular finale.

The Ziegfield Follies of 1918, featuring (left to right) W. C. Fields, Will Rogers, Lillian Lorraine, Eddie Cantor, and Harry Kelly.

Ziegfield was a starmaker. Through his casts paraded the celebrities of the era: Fanny Brice, Nora Bayes, Eva Tanguay, Marion Davies, Barbara Stanwyck, Ed Wynn, Marilyn Miller, Irene Dunne, and comedians W. C. Fields, Eddie Cantor, and Will Rogers.

Over the years, Ziegfield commissioned more than 500 songs from such composers as Jerome Kern, Victor Herbert, and Irving Berlin. Berlin is the composer most identified with the Follies and its theme song, "A Pretty Girl Is Like a Melody," which he wrote for the 1919 edition.

The 1992 musical *Will Rogers' Follies* is a modern revue based on Will Rogers' career with *The Ziegfield Follies*.

Other long-running revues spawned great American composers such as Cole Porter and Harold Rome. Between 1920 and 1924 George Gershwin wrote his first scores for *George White's Scandals*. Richard Rodgers and Lorenz Hart wrote their first complete Broadway score for *The Garrick Gaieties of 1925*. One of the songs in the score, "Manhattan," became a hit and launched their successful career collaboration.

Categories of Modern Broadway Musicals

The majority of Broadway musicals fall into several broad classifications:

- modern operetta
- musical comedy
- musical play
- play with music
- popular opera

MODERN OPERETTA   Viennese composers Johann Strauss in *Die Fledermaus* and Franz Lehar (*lay*-har, 1870–1948) in *The Merry Widow* perfected the form. Both operettas remain in the modern repertory. Victor Herbert, Sigmund Romberg, and Rudolf Friml refined operetta and introduced it to North American audiences.

Modern operetta

The Great Depression affected operetta as it had the extravaganza spectacular. Ragtime and jazz had taken the place of quaint old tunes. With the emergence of Jerome Kern, George Gershwin, Cole Porter, Irving Berlin, and Richard Rodgers, the popular song that had begun to develop in vaudeville had come of age. Composers were leading American musical theater into a new era.

Some of the roots of modern Broadway musical comedy are traceable to the early works of George M. Cohan (1878–1942). His "plays with music" were punctuated with songs created for singing actors rather than for full-voiced operetta singers. And Cohan's thin plots had a "hometown" flavor that Americans easily related to. (continued on page 374)

SIGMUND ROMBERG (1887–1951)

The most prolific composer of popular musicals, Romberg was born in Hungary and raised in Vienna, coming to America in 1909. Among his 60 operettas are *Maytime* and *Over the Top* (1917), *Blossom Time* (1921), *The Student Prince* (1924), *The Desert Song* (1926), *The New Moon* (1928) and *Up in Central Park* (1945).

His most enduring songs include "Deep in My Heart," "Serenade," and "Drinking Song" from *The Student Prince*; "One Alone" from *The Desert Song*; and "Lover Come Back to Me" and "Stout-Hearted Men" from *The New Moon*. From 1929 on, he wrote songs for motion pictures, including "When I Grow Too Old to Dream."

VICTOR HERBERT(1859–1924)

Herbert was born in Dublin, Ireland, and emigrated to the United States in 1886. He became the first important composer of the American musical stage.

From 1893 to 1898, Herbert conducted the 22nd New York Regiment band. For the next six years he conducted the Pittsburgh Symphony, until organizing and conducting his own orchestra in 1904.

Herbert's first success, *The Wizard of the Nile* (1895), was set in Egypt. This was followed in 1898 by *The Fortune Teller*, which premiered at the Grand Opera House in Toronto preceding its Broadway run. Set in Hungary, the operetta gave us "Gypsy Love Song," which has endured for many generations.

Legend has it that in 1899 and 1900, while simultaneously composing four operetta scores, Herbert, a great lover of food and drink, kept four bottles of wine chilled in a washtub of ice, sipping a different one with each score.

Among his greatest hits were *Babes in Toyland* (1903), *The Red Mill* (1906)—which had the first moving electric sign on a Broadway marquee—and *Naughty Marietta* (1910). Herbert also wrote musical scores for *The Ziegfeld Follies* of 1917 and 1921–24 and composed two grand operas.

RUDOLF FRIML (1879–1972)

Considered an infant prodigy at the piano, Friml studied in Prague with his Czech countryman Antonin Dvořak. In 1901 and 1906, Friml was accompanist for the U.S. tours of the famous Czech violinist Jan Kubelik (1880–1940). After the second tour, Friml decided to remain in the United States, becoming a naturalized citizen in 1925.

In his more than 30 operettas, Friml's formula for success was a combination of rich melody, rousing choruses, and passionate romance.

His works include: *The Firefly* (1912), *You're in Love* (1917), *Rose Marie* (1924, which featured the song "Indian Love Call"), *The Vagabond King* (1925, which included "Only a Rose" and "Someday"), *The Three Musketeers* (1928), and *Bird of Paradise* (1930).

From 1930, Friml composed for movies. He wrote the famous "Donkey Serenade" for the 1937 film version of *Firefly*.

IRVING BERLIN (1888–1989)

Berlin came to New York's Lower East Side from his native Russia in 1892. Although he had no musical training, he taught himself to compose by picking out melodies on the black keys of the piano. He even worked as a singing waiter in Chinatown, performing his own songs.

Berlin's 1914 show *Watch Your Step* introduced ragtime into the theater. *As Thousands Cheer* (1933), which ranks among his finest works for the theater, includes "Heat Wave," the show-stopper he wrote for Ethel Waters, and the timeless "Easter Parade." For that song, Berlin did something that was common among musical composers at that time. He unearthed a tune he had written earlier titled "Smile and Show Your Dimple" and simply changed the lyrics.

Later, Irving Berlin wrote two long-running Broadway hits—*Annie Get Your Gun* (1946) and *Call Me Madam* (1950)—both starring the great Ethel Merman.

George M. Cohan

Little Johnny Jones (1904) was Cohan's first Broadway hit, giving us such songs as "Yankee Doodle Boy" and "Give My Regards to Broadway." His other popular shows included *Forty-Five Minutes from Broadway* (1906), *The Little Millionaire* (1916), and *Little Nelly Kelly* (1922). During World War I, his song "Over There" from *The Cohan Revue of 1918* became a symbol of patriotic fervor.

Early African-American Musicals

A number of African-Americans have enriched the legacy of musical theater. As early as 1898, there were full-length musical productions composed and performed by African-Americans. In 1903, the first black musical to open at a major, previously whites-only Broadway theater was *In Dahomey* by Will Marion Cook and Paul Lawrence Dunbar.

Eubie Blake

One of the most important descendants of the early pioneering works was the 1922 production of *Shuffle Along*, with music by Eubie Blake (1883–1984), who also conducted the orchestra. Best remembered from his score is the lively song "I'm Just Wild About Harry."

Over There, 1918, with a Norman Rockwell illustration on the cover.

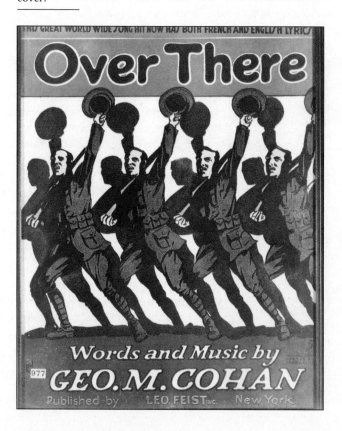

Jerome Kern (1885–1945) brought a new attitude into musical the-   Jerome Kern
ater: He insisted on a partnership between the story, or "book," and the
music. Kern had been leading a revolution in musical theater even in his
co-authored series of shows known as the Princess Theater musicals.
Staged in a 299-seat house, Kern's shows could be more intimate, a departure from the European operetta. And each show had a simple, modern,
farce-oriented plot:

Nobody Home and *Very Good Eddie* (1915)
Oh, Boy! and *Leave It to Jane* (1917)
Oh, Lady! Lady! (1918)

During the 1930s, Kern spent much of his time in Hollywood writing
film musicals, returning to Broadway intermittently with *Cat and the Fiddle*
(1931), *Roberta* (1933, "Smoke Gets in Your Eyes"), and *Very Warm for May*
(1939).

The music of George Gershwin (1898–1937) and lyrics of his broth-   George Gershwin
er Ira (1896–1983) were a remarkable collaboration. On December 1,
1924, at the Liberty Theater, the show *Lady Be Good* opened—with the first
complete score by the Gershwin brothers produced on Broadway. Giving
us both the title song, "Lady Be Good," and "Fascinating Rhythm," the
show was the jazz-age equivalent of Kern's Princess Theater musicals of
the preceding decade.

HISTORICAL PERSPECTIVE

Kern's Show Boat: The New Broadway Musical

Show Boat (1927), Jerome Kern's milestone musical produced by Florenz Ziegfield, demonstrated
that dramatic literature could merge successfully with romantic song to create good theater. The
New York Times singled out for exceptional praise the collaborative achievement of Kern's music
and Oscar Hammerstein II's book and lyrics.

Daring for its time, *Show Boat* deals with delicate and controversial subjects such as love
gone sour, miscegenation (racially mixed marriages), racial prejudice, alcohol and gambling ad-
diction, and economic troubles—a major departure from the "happy-go-lucky," "all is well with
the world" musical. Yet audience took to the integration of music and challenging story with
great enthusiasm, pioneering the way for later musicals such as *South Pacific*, *Les Misérables*, and
Miss Saigon.

Paul Robeson singing "Ol' Man River" in the 1936 film version of Kern's *Show Boat.*

LISTENING ACTIVITY ❧

JEROME KERN, *SHOW BOAT,*
"OL' MAN RIVER"
LARGE FORM: MUSICAL THEATER;
DETAILED FORM: VERSE, THREE-PART SONG-FORM

Cassette Tape: Side D, Example 12
Compact Disc 3, Track 32

Listen to "Ol' Man River," one of the opening songs from *Show Boat.* Joe, an African-American dockhand on the Mississippi waterfront, sings about his continuing hardships even after the end of slavery.

In this rare recording by Paul Robeson (1898–1976), the great African-American bass who was a son of a slave, we hear the role of Joe as Kern and Hammerstein conceived it when they created it for Robeson. He sang the role in the 1928 London production, in the 1932 revival, and also in the 1936 film version.

Robeson himself felt oppressed by racial discrimination in the United States and sought refuge in the Soviet Union for a number of years. This 1958 recording marks Robeson's historic return to his native United States for a concert in Carnegie Hall.

As a fighter for racial equality, Robeson slightly alters Hammerstein's lyrics in the recording. For example, to avoid the stereotypical dialect associated with the African-American, he replaces *"dat's de ol' man"* with *"that's the ol' man."* And in the last few lines:

"I git weary
An' sick of tryin',
I'm tired of livin',
An' skeered o' dyin'"

Robeson replaces lyrics about his personal crusade for civil rights:

"But I keep laughin'
Instead of cryin'.
I must keep fightin',
Until I'm dyin'…"

LISTENING GUIDE

JEROME KERN, *SHOW BOAT*
LARGE FORM: MUSICAL THEATER;
DETAILED FORM: VERSE, THREE-PART SONG-FORM

Cassette Tape: Side D, Example 12
Compact Disc 3, Track 32
Running time: 2:17

| 32 | 0:00 | INTRODUCTION | piano, moderately fast, 4 meter throughout, major, mostly pentatonic scale, slowing down to cadence slower tempo; emphasis on text; slowing to cadence |

0:17 VERSE

Dere's an ol' man
called the Mississippi.
That's the ol' man
I don't like to be.
What does he care
If the world's got troubles?
What does he care
if the land ain't free?

| 33 | 0:37 | CHORUS [A] | slower, steady tempo, mostly pentatonic |

That ol' man river,
That ol' man river,
He mus' know sumpin'
But don't say nuthin',
He jes' keeps rollin',
He keeps on rollin' along.

1:00 CHORUS [A] same music, different text

He don't plant 'taters,
He don't plant cotton,
an' dem that plants 'em
Is soon forgotten,
But ol' man river,
He jes' keeps rollin' along.

| 34 | 1:23 | BRIDGE [B] | faster tempo; agitated; rubato; slowing to cadence |

You an' me,
We sweat an' strain,

> Body all achin'
> an' racked wid' pain.
> Tote dat barge!
> Lift dat bale!
> Yo' show a little click,
> An' yo' lands in jail.

1:46   CHORUS [A]   same music as [A] with new text, cadence at end

> But I keep laughin'
> Instead of cryin'.
> I mus' keep fightin'
> Until I'm dyin'.
> An' ol' man river,
> He jes' keeps rollin' along!

Cowboy Curly (Gordon MacRae) singing "Oh, What a Beautiful Morning" in the opening scene from the film production of *Oklahoma*.

LISTENING INSIGHTS

Form in Early Broadway Musical Theater Songs

Most songs in early musicals contained three main elements:

verse   Similar to the recitative in opera. The verse's task was to introduce the song (*aria* in opera) and present story or background. The verse was even more important in early musicals such as the **revue** or **vaudeville** because these shows contained little or no story—magicians, dancers, acrobats, and comics were interspersed between songs. When the singer took center stage, the verse provided a vehicle to engage the audience in the song. Occasionally, when the songs are performed outside the context of the show, the verse is omitted.

chorus [A]   The chorus is the main tune or song.

bridge [B]   A middle, usually contrasting section of music. The tempo, mood, and style of the bridge usually contrasts the chorus. Typical plans for Broadway musical songs are:

VERSE optional)	CHORUS (A)	CHORUS (A)	BRIDGE (B)	CHORUS (A)

or

VERSE optional)	CHORUS (A)	BRIDGE (B)	CHORUS (A)	BRIDGE (B)

Because their first show with book writers Guy Bolton and P. G. Wodehouse had been a hit, the Gershwins again teamed up with them on *Oh, Kay!* (1926). That score contains several Gershwin classics: "Do, Do, Do," "Clap Yo' Hands," and "Someone to Watch Over Me." *Girl Crazy* (1930) gave us "Embraceable You," "I Got Rhythm," and "But Not for Me."

Just as *Show Boat* had brought a new maturity to the American musical stage, *Of Thee I Sing* (1931) introduced an offbeat, adult approach to musical comedy. The show was the first musical to receive the Pulitzer Prize for Drama.

The book by George S. Kaufman and Morrie Ryskind was a sendup of American political institutions and the Establishment. To complement the story, the Gershwins explored a new style of composition, producing a score that interweaves a succession of songs, recitatives, and extended musical scenes. A distinctively native form had emerged.

Cole Porter (1891–1964) brought his own elements to the musical stage: extraordinary style and sophistication. The fact that he was born into great wealth did not help him at first. However, his money did provide the wherewithal for a quick escape following his Broadway debut in 1916. The show was an immediate flop, and Porter retreated to France where he studied composition at the Paris Conservatory with Vincent D'Indy (dan-*dee*).

Porter's first Broadway hit was *The Gay Divorcee* in 1932, which featured the song "Night and Day." He followed this with *Anything Goes* (1934—"I Get a Kick Out of You") and a string of commercial successes over the next ten years. His last three major triumphs were *Kiss Me Kate* (1948), *Can Can* (1953), and *Silk Stockings* (1955).

Leonard Bernstein (1918–90), discussed in Chapter 23, wrote several important works for the American musical stage:

> *On the Town* (1944) with Betty Comden and Adolph Green
> *Wonderful Town* (1953) Tony Award[*]
> *Candide* (1956) with Lillian Hellman, (1974) with Stephen Sondheim
> *West Side Story* (1957) with Stephen Sondheim—The Standard Award[**]

Written in collaboration with lyricist Stephen Sondheim, Bernstein's *West Side Story* became one of Broadway's biggest successes and was later made into a film. Set in the 1950s in one of New York City's ethnically mixed neighborhood, the story was inspired by Shakespeare's *Romeo and Juliet*. The two lovers are from completely different ethnic backgrounds, and the pressures of their clashing cultures bring on a series of tragic events.

Cole Porter

---

[*]"Tony" is the shortened version of the Antoinette Perry Award, presented annually to the best musical on Broadway.
[**]The Standard Award is presented annually by the *London Evening Standard* to the best musical in London, England.

RICHARD RODGERS (1902–79)

One of the most prolific and successful Broadway musical composers, Richard Charles Rodgers was born in Hammels Station on Long Island near New York City. Studying piano from the age of six, he quickly learned to improvise and to play by ear. As a teenager, he attended one Broadway show after another and was particularly impressed by the operettas of Victor Herbert and the musicals of Jerome Kern.

While studying at Columbia University in 1918, he met Lorenz Hart, and they began writing musicals together. Their first collaboration, *Fly with Me*, was written for Columbia's amateur varsity production.

Rodgers and Hart's first Broadway success was *The Garrick Gaieties* (1925), a revue-type show. Between 1926 and 1930 the team produced 14 musicals and revues.

Called to Hollywood, Rodgers and Hart continued working on films together. After a fruitful partnership for nearly 30 musicals, their collaboration ended with the death of Lorenz Hart in 1943.

A new era began in Rodgers' life when he then teamed up with the great lyricist Oscar Hammerstein II. Beginning with *Oklahoma* (1943), their eighteen-year collaboration until Hammerstein's death created a legacy of nine of Broadway's greatest and timeless musicals—including *Carousel* (1945), *South Pacific* (1949), *The King and I* (1951), and *The Sound of Music* (1959).

Even though there were earlier examples of a "book show" such as *Show Boat* (1927), *Pal Joey* (Rodgers and Hart, 1940), and the Gershwins' *Of Thee I Sing* (1931), *Oklahoma!* became the benchmark for musicals in which the songs were fully integrated dramatically and served the play. Rodgers and Hammerstein believed in the importance of music in theater—that it could reinforce emotion beyond words alone. Their songs helped to move the story along, establishing mood and contributing to character development and dynamic.

After Hammerstein's death, Rodgers tried writing both the lyrics and the music. But he was never as successful as he was when he worked with his two great collaborators, Lorenz Hart and Oscar Hammerstein II. Richard Rodgers died in New York City at the age of 77.

PRINCIPAL WORKS

Hit Musicals, Revues, and Films from Musicals: The Garrick Gaieties (with Hart, 1925); *On Your Toes* (with Hart, 1936, film 1939); *Babes in Arms* (with Hart, 1937, film 1939); *Pal Joey* (with Hart and O'Hara, 1940, film 1957); *Oklahoma* (with Hammerstein, 1943, film 1955); *Carousel* (with Hammerstein, 1945, film 1956); *South Pacific* (with Hammerstein, 1949, film 1958); *The King and I* (with Hammerstein, 1951, film 1956); *Flower Drum Song* (with Hammerstein, 1958, film 1961); *The Sound of Music* (with Hammerstein, 1959, film 1964); *Do I Hear a Waltz?* (with Laurents and Sondheim, 1965)

Original Film Scores: Love Me Tonight (with Hart, 1932); *State Fair* (with Hammerstein, 1945); *Words and Music* (with Hart, 1948)

Television Musicals: Cinderella (with Hammerstein, 1957); *Androcles and the Lion* (Rodgers after Shaw, 1967)

Television Documentary Series: Victory at Sea (1952); *Churchill, the Valiant Years* (1960)

STEPHEN SONDHEIM (B. 1930)

Born in New York City, Stephen Joshua Sondheim showed an early interest in Broadway musical theater. He was encouraged to pursue that interest by family friend, mentor, and neighbor Oscar Hammerstein II.

At the small, prestigious liberal arts Williams College in Massachusetts, Sondheim wrote several full-length musicals that earned him a scholarship to study for two years with the avant-garde composer Milton Babbitt.

Working with Babbitt gave Sondheim insight into contemporary sound. He mastered the inventive meters, unusual melodic intervals, and unpredictable harmonies that characterize his music.

Hammerstein passed on to Sondheim what Jerome Kern had passed on to him and Richard Rodgers: an understanding of dramatic construction. The songs in Sondheim's scores grow not only from the dramatic ideas in the story but also from the objective of giving the actor something to act—a theatrical moment. With his success, Sondheim brought another level of maturity into Broadway's musical theater.

Sondheim made his Broadway debut with incidental music to *The Girls of Summer* (1956) and as a lyricist for *West Side Story* (1957, with Leonard Bernstein). The 1962 production of *A Funny Thing Happened on the Way to the Forum*, the first for which he wrote both music and lyrics, won a Tony Award for best musical of the year. Over the years Sondheim collaborated as lyricist with Richard Rodgers (*Do I Hear a Waltz*, 1965), and again with Bernstein in his 1974 revival of *Candide*.

PRINCIPAL WORKS:

Musicals: The Girls of Summer (1956, incidental music); *West Side Story* (1957, lyrics, with music by Leonard Bernstein); *Gypsy* (1959, lyrics, music by Jule Styne); *A Funny Thing Happened on the Way to the Forum* (1962, lyrics and music); *Company* (1970, lyrics and music—Tony Award); *Follies* (1971, lyrics and music—Tony Award), *A Little Night Music* (1973, lyrics and music—Tony and The Standard Awards); *Pacific Overtures* (1976, lyrics and music); *Sweeney Todd* (1979, lyrics and music—Tony and The Standard Awards); *Merrily We Roll Along* (1981, lyrics and music); *Sunday in the Park with George* (1984, lyrics and music—Pulitzer Prize); *Into the Woods* (1987, lyrics and music)

Film Music: Stavisky (1974); *The Seven Percent Solution* (1977)

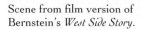

Scene from film version of Bernstein's *West Side Story*.

LISTENING ACTIVITY ↶

SONDHEIM, *A LITTLE NIGHT MUSIC*,
"SEND IN THE CLOWNS"
LARGE FORM: BROADWAY AND MUSICAL THEATER

Compact Disc 4, Track 41
Running time: 3:14
"Send in the Clowns" is on the compact disc only.

Sondheim's show was one of the big hits of Broadway's 1973 season. Mozart's serenade "Eine Kleine Nachtmusik" (A Little Night Music) provided the title for this charming work. Because of its turn-of-the-century (nineteenth to twentieth) setting, period costumes, sentimental plot, and waltz-filled score, *A Little Night Music* is usually called a modern operetta, similar to those of Franz Lehar and Johann Strauss, Jr.

The story, closely based on Igmar Bergman's film "Smiles of a Summer Night," is set in Sweden and about Fredrik Egerman, a middle-aged attorney, newly remarried to a teenage girl the same age as his son. After 11 months of an unsatisfying marriage in which his wife is still a virgin, Egerman resumes an affair with his former mistress, Desirée Armfeldt—an actress whose current lover is Count Malcolm, a Swedish military officer. "Send in the Clowns" is sung in the musical by Desirée when she and Egerman meet again after years of separation.

Egerman, Desirée, Count Malcolm, and his wife meet at Desirée's mother's country estate for a brief holiday. Madame Armfeldt herself was a beautiful and notorious courtesan in her day.

By the final curtain Egerman is relieved to learn that his wife and his 18-year-old son have fallen in love and run off together. Egerman and Desirée are reunited, and the count is reconciled to being reunited with his wife.

LISTENING ACTIVITY ∿

BERNSTEIN, *OVERTURE TO CANDIDE*
LARGE FORM: MUSICAL THEATER OVERTURE

| *Cassette Tape: Side D, Example 10*
| *Compact Disc 3, Track 26*
| *Running time: 4:22*

See Chapter 23 for background on the musical *Candide* and a Listening Guide for the overture.

LISTENING ACTIVITY ∿

BOCK, *FIDDLER ON THE ROOF*, "SUNRISE, SUNSET"
LARGE FORM: BROADWAY MUSICAL THEATER

| *Compact Disc 4, Track 42*
| *Running time: 3:05*

Fiddler, based on "Tevye and His Daughters" by Sholom Ale-ichem, is set in Anatevka, a *stetl* (small ghetto-town) in turn-of-the-century Russia. Plagued by czarist pogroms, the townspeople live precariously—like a "fiddler on the roof."

"Sunrise, Sunset" is sung at the oldest daughter's wedding. Tevye and Golde reflect on how their family has grown up and how quickly the years have gone by.

Scene from the film production of *Fiddler on the Roof* (1971).

∿ *Other Important Broadway Musicals*

Alan Jay Lerner *(1918–86) and* **Frederick Loewe** *(1901–88):*

> *Brigadoon* (1947)
> *Paint Your Wagon* (1951)
> *My Fair Lady* (1956) Tony Award
> *Camelot* (1960)
> *Gigi* (1958 film)

Frank Loesser *(1910–69):*

>*Where's Charley?* (1948)
>*Guys and Dolls* (1950) Tony Award
>*Most Happy Fella* (1956)
>*How to Succeed in Business without Really Trying* (1961) Pulitzer Prize
>   and Tony Award

Jule Styne *(1905–1994):*

>*Gentlemen Prefer Blondes* (1949) with Leo Robin
>*Gypsy* (1959) with S. Sondheim
>*Two on the Aisle* (1951) with Betty Comden and Adolph Green
>*Peter Pan* (1954) with Comden and Green
>*Bells Are Ringing* (1956) with Comden and Green
>*Say, Darling* (1958) with Comden and Green
>*Do Re Mi* (1960) with Comden and Green
>*Subways Are for Sleeping* (1961) with Comden and Green
>*Fade Out—Fade In* (1964) with Comden and Green
>*Funny Girl* (1964) with Bob Merrill

Jerry Herman *(b. 1933):*

>*Milk and Honey* (1961)
>*Hello, Dolly!* (1964)
>*Mame* (1966)
>*La Cage Aux Folles* (1983)

Richard Adler *(b. 1921) and* **Jerry Ross** *(1926–55):*

>*Pajama Game* (1954) Tony and The Standard Award
>*Damn Yankees* (1955) Tony and The Standard Award

Kurt Weill *(1900–50); see biography in Chapter 21:*

>*Threepenny Opera* (1928) with Berthold Brecht
>*Happy End* (1929) with Brecht
>*Mahoganny* (1930) with Brecht
>*Knickerbocker Holiday* (1938, "September Song") with Maxwell Anderson
>*Lady in the Dark* (1940) with Ira Gershwin
>*One Touch of Venus* (1943) with Ogden Nash
>*Street Scene* (1947) with Langston Hughes
>*Lost in the Stars* (1949) with Maxwell Anderson

Meredith Willson *(1902–84):*

>*The Music Man* (1957) Tony Award
>*The Unsinkable Molly Brown* (1960)
>*Here's Love* (1963)

Vincent Youmans *(1898–1946):*

> *No! No! Nanette!* (1925) with Otto Harbach and Irving Caesar

Mitch Leigh *(b. 1928):*

> *Man of La Mancha* (1965) Tony Award

Charles Strouse *(b. 1928):*

> *Bye, Bye, Birdie* (1963) with Lee Adams, Tony Award
> *Applause* (1969), Tony Award
> *Annie* (1978) with Martin Charmin

John Kander *(b. 1932) and* **Fred Ebb** *(b. 1932):*

> *Cabaret* (1972), Tony Award

Jerry Bock *(b. 1928) and* **Sheldon Harnick** *(b. 1924):*

> *Fiorello!* (1959) Tony Award
> *Tenderloin* (1960)
> *She Loves Me* (1963)
> *Fiddler on the Roof* (1964) Tony Award
> *The Apple Tree* (1966)

Burton Lane *(b. 1912):*

> *Finian's Rainbow* (1947) with E. Y. Harburg
> *On a Clear Day You Can See Forever* (1965) with Alan Jay Lerner

Tom Jones *(b. 1928) and* **Harvey Schmidt** *(b. 1929):*

> *The Fantasticks* (1960)
> *110 in the Shade* (1963)
> *I Do! I Do!* (1966)

Andrew Lloyd Webber *(b. 1948):*

> *Joseph and the Amazing Technicolor Dreamcoat* (1968, 1972) with Tim Rice
> *Jesus Christ Superstar* (1971) with Tim Rice
> *Evita* (1976) with Tim Rice, Tony Award
> *Cats* (1981)
> *Starlight Express* (1984)
> *Phantom of the Opera* (1986)
> *Aspects of Love* (1989)
> *Sunset Boulevard* (1993)

Marvin Hamlisch *(b. 1944):*

> *A Chorus Line* (1975) with Edward Kleban, Tony Award

Henry Krieger *and* ***Tom Eyen:***

Dreamgirls (1982)

Alain Boublil *and* ***Claude–Michel Schönberg:***

Les Misérables (1985) with Herbert Kretzmer
Miss Saigon (1990)

Summary of Terms

African-American musicals

ballad opera

bridge

burlesque

chorus

comic opera

extravaganza/spectacle

minstrel shows

modern operetta

musical comedy

musical play

opéra bouffe

operetta

popular opera

Pulitzer Prize

revue

Standard Award

Tony Award

troubadours

vaudeville

verse

Final scene from the film
production of *The Music Man.*

CHAPTER 26

Music for Films

Lights dim, curtains open, and the screen comes alive. The title and credits roll, with music in the background. Even before we see the first scene, we know a great deal about the film. Music—or the absence of it—provides an important clue to what we are about to see: an adventure, a mystery, a horror movie, a romance, a shoot-'em-up Western, or an action thriller.

Since silent-film days, music and the movies have had a unique relationship. As an ingredient of the total entertainment, music heightens action, deepens emotion, reinforces comedy, and augments mystery. In other words, music adds life to the film medium.

✲ *How It Began: The Silent Era*

In 1908, a film company in Paris, Le Film d'Art, created its first musically scored production: *L'Assassinat du Duc de Guise (The Assassination of the Duke of Guise)*. Composer Camille Saint-Saëns had readily accepted the opportunity to create the film's musical score, later developing it into a concert piece—*Opus 128 for Strings, Piano, and Harmonium.*

A year after the Saint-Saëns score, specific music suggestions accompanied movies from the Edison Film Company. Within five years, publishers had catalogued their music for theater orchestras, pianists, or organists according to specific moods or dramatic situations. Giuseppe Becce's 1919 Berlin publication *Kinobibliothek* (or *Kinothek*, as it was called) is the most famous early example of these catalogues.

Cataloguing of Existing Concert Music

Max Winkler, a clerk in the Carl Fischer Music Store in New York City, is customarily given credit for being the first cataloguer in the United States. It was 1912, and filmmakers were demanding more and more music for their productions. Winkler realized that the vast Carl Fischer library was a potential gold mine. Fischer's had enough music stored and catalogued to fit any situation a filmmaker could devise.

So the enterprising Max wrote to the Universal Film Company. He offered to make up music cue sheets for all their films on one condition—that they would let him see each film before they released it. Understanding the value of this idea, Universal's publicity director gave Winkler a chance to show what he could do. Max was successful. Eventually he left Fischer's to work full time in film music.

Buster Keaton in a scene from the silent movie *The General*.

MASTERS TRANSCRIBED FOR FILM To keep pace with the increasing market for his services, Winkler and his partner, S. M. Berg, began to catalog excerpts from the great masters. Any work not under copyright was fair game. Beethoven, Brahms, Bizet, Bach, Verdi, Mozart, Grieg, Tchaikovsky, and others were making their film debuts. The composers might not have recognized their works, however. To create the desired effect, the excerpts would often undergo transformation. They would be jazzed up, slowed down, or played out of tune as needed. For example, Mendelssohn's or Wagner's wedding marches, played intact, might underscore the happiness of a bride and groom. If the marriage grew rocky, the same music would be played out of tune or with dissonant harmonies.

Occasionally, a score might be all-Debussy or all-Tchaikovsky, but usually the production schedule and the scenario did not allow for this. Problems persisted in making smooth transitions between excerpts and synchronizing the music with the picture. In fact, the music director would sometimes have to compose music to accommodate particular scenes.

The score for D. W. Griffith's *The Birth of a Nation* established the standards for orchestration and cueing that remained throughout the silent era. A joint work by Griffith and Joseph Carl Breil, a composer/orchestra leader, the score is a mélange of original music combined with "Dixie," "The Star-Spangled Banner," and quotes from Liszt, Verdi, Beethoven, Wagner, and Tchaikovsky.

Scene from *The Birth of a Nation*.

German composer Edmund Meisel set another milestone in scoring silent films. For his scores, including his legendary work for the 1925 Sergei Eisenstein film *The Battleship Potemkin*, Meisel devised a distinctive system for analyzing film montages to determine the timing of music needed. His contributions earned him recognition as the master of the silent-film score.

In *Potemkin*, discovered in the Eisenstein Archives in Leningrad, the music was much more than background accessory to the picture. Each note strikes to the heart of the drama, making it a component of the film itself.

Another Eisenstein film—*Alexander Nevky* (1938)—was screened at the Hollywood Bowl during the summer of 1989. A live performance by the Los Angeles Philharmonic Orchestra of Serge Prokofiev's original score accompanied the film.

In 1981, after producer/director Francis Ford Coppola (of *Godfather* fame) restored Abel Gance's four-hour silent masterwork *Napoleon*, Coppola arranged for special screenings in theaters that could accommodate a full orchestra. He had commissioned his father, the composer Carmine Coppola, to write a new score for the movie. (Arthur Honegger had composed the original score.) Following the theatrical presentations with live music, Coppola used the new score as a synchronized sound track for the film.

The Role of Music in Sound Films

As a beneficial side effect of silent-film music, employment opportunities burgeoned for instrumental players in hundreds of theaters. With the advent of sound films in 1927, however, the music track displaced live performances, and orchestra pits became empty.

From the earliest days of sound films through the summer of 1930, the most common use of music was in the musical films of the era, such as *Rio Rita, The Street Singer*, and *The Vagabond Lover*. By 1931, a few directors had incorporated music to support love scenes or to bridge silent sequences. For the most part, though, directors felt that music had to be justified by the plot; for example, it had to emanate from a visible source on screen—a theater, a nightclub, a ballroom, or an organ grinder.

Hermione Gingold and Maurice Chevalier in a scene from *Gigi*.

⟋ *Film Music Comes of Age*

During the next several years, composers skilled at writing symphonic music began to get commissions to compose film music, and film music came of age. Each score was unique, like a work of art in any other medium, with the best of them carrying the imprint of the composer. Music had assumed a more important function: to serve the story. A 1935 *New York Times* article characterized film music as "a vital element—an accentuated background for mood and action."

Here are some of the composers, usually associated with concert music, who wrote original scores for films:

Malcolm Arnold	Aram Khachaturian
Leonard Bernstein	Ernesto Lecuona
Benjamin Britten	Gyorgy Ligeti
Mario Castelnuovo-Tedesco	Pietro Mascagni
Aaron Copland	Sergei Prokofiev
Rheinhold Glière	Erik Satie
Ferde Grofé	Dmitri Shostakovich
Hans Werner Henze	Jan Sibelius
Paul Hindemith	Ernst Toch
Gustav Holst	Virgil Thomson
Arthur Honegger	Edgard Varèse
Jacques Ibert	Ralph Vaughan Williams
Dmitri Kabalevsky	William Walton

It was Walt Disney, in his 1940 classic *Fantasia*, who added a new element to the partnership of music and film. In a series of scenes, this timeless motion picture presents animated interpretations of existing concert music, including:

The Rite of Spring by Igor Stravinsky
La Gioconda, "The Dance of the Hours" by Amilcare Ponchielli (1834–86)
The Sorcerer's Apprentice by Paul Dukas (1865–1935)
Symphony No. 6 (*Pastoral*) by Ludwig van Beethoven
A Night on Bald Mountain by Modest Mussorgsky

To synchronize the sound with the animation of the film, Walt Disney built one of the first stereophonic sound-dubbing theaters on his lot in Burbank, California.

The Contribution of Music to Film

In a 1949 *New York Times* article, Aaron Copland said: "Music can create a more convincing atmosphere of time and place. This atmosphere, musically speaking, is 'color.'" As a filmgoer, think of the settings one might associate with a minuet played on a harpsichord, a calypso tune played on steel drums, a hillbilly song played on the banjo, and an energetic dance played on Flamenco guitar.

Copland also said: "Music creates a psychological element better than dialogue can." Finally, Copland cited two other uses for music—as neutral background that fills empty spots without our being aware of it and as an intensifier that builds the drama and helps to deliver the climax.

Composer Bruce Broughton (*Silverado, Sweet Liberty, Young Sherlock Holmes, Moonwalker*, and others) in a 1987 published interview with June August, said: "Music in films should be an emotional adjunct, increasing the amount of tension, feeling."

USE OF LEITMOTIF IN FILMS   The Wagnerian *leitmotif* (discussed in Chapter 14)—a theme associated with a particular character or situation—was a natural device for film music. On hearing the ominous motive by John Williams in *Jaws*, for instance, the audience knows that there is a shark in the vicinity, though it is not always visible.

In his famous musical scoring of *Superman*, Williams uses leitmotifs throughout. We associate the "Love Theme" with the relationship of Superman and Lois Lane. The heroic music over the opening credits, played again when Superman soars to the rescue, lets the audience know that some larger-than-life character is coming to affirm the concept of good triumphing over evil.

There is a striking similarity between Williams's "Love Theme" and a theme from Richard Strauss' *Death and Transfiguration*. Even the lush, romantic orchestral treatment of *Superman* is reminiscent of late-nineteenth-century composers such as Richard Strauss and Richard Wagner.

The Rite of Spring scene from *Fantasia*.

Williams could have chosen futuristic-sounding music, perhaps using electronic media and contemporary harmony. However, the concept of *Superman* is basically a romantic subject. The nineteenth-century German philosopher and poet Friederich Nietzche (1844–1900) promoted a doctrine of glorification of the superman, or *Übermensch* as he called him. Therefore, Williams's choice to emulate Strauss and Wagner was in keeping with the nineteenth-century Germanic concept of Superman.

Summary of Terms

leitmotif	sound dubbing	synchronized sound track
film score	sound film	*Übermensch*
silent film	sound track	

CHAPTER 27

Contributions of World Cultures

As new modes of transportation and electronic communication shrink the world into a "global village," as Marshall McLuhan called it, we learn about and interact with cultures different from ours.

To learn more about the music of these cultures, ethnomusicologists equipped with tape recorders and video cameras travel to some of the world's most remote areas to study the native music. This chapter covers only a sampling of that vast variety of folk and ethnic music.

Thus far, our focus has mainly been on music encountered in the North American and European concert halls. In the past century, an existing and distinctive wealth of folk and ethnic music from world cultures has influenced that main body of traditional Western concert music. Ethnomusicologists predict that ethnic influence will ultimately bring about even more profound changes in Western music.

Early Interactions

THE UNITED STATES' CENTENNIAL   The place is Philadelphia. The year, 1876. The event, a small-scale World Exposition to celebrate the 100th anniversary of the American Declaration of Independence. In response to invitations, music groups from distant lands perform at the event, exposing large groups of Westerners for the first time to music of diverse cultures.

Evidently the interaction was dynamic, because other major European and American cities hosted World Expositions before the turn of the century:

1878 — Paris
1882 — Moscow
1883 — Amsterdam
1889 — Paris
1893 — Chicago
1897 — Brussels

The late nineteenth century was a time when nationalism was taking hold, nurturing an interest in travel and world cultures. Nationalistic music became the vogue — in 1880, Tchaikovsky premiered his musical travel adventures throughout Italy with *Capriccio italien*; in 1888, Rimsky-Korsakov introduced his *Capriccio espagnole* and his Arabian-influenced *Scheherazade*.

In 1889, for the 100th anniversary of the Revolution, the French government financed the construction of the Eiffel Tower and invited a large array of ethnic music groups to perform at the World Exposition in Paris. Musicians flocked to see and hear these groups first-hand. They were impressed, and the direction of traditional Western music began to change.

❧ *Non-Western Influences in Western Art Music*

You have read earlier about some of the influences of non-Western music, some inspired by the international expositions, others through less direct influence:

- Asian scales and percussion instruments used by Puccini in his operas *Madama Butterfly* (about Japan) and *Turandot* (about China); more recently, in the hit musical *Miss Saigon* (about Vietnam and Thailand), Boublil and Schönberg abundantly use Asian scales, flutes, and percussion instruments
- African percussion ensembles inspiring Stravinsky's greater use of percussion instruments and polyrhythms
- African music contributing significantly to American jazz

Other Changes in Western Art Music

SCALES AND TONAL MATERIAL   Some composers considered traditional scales overworked. After hearing non-Western music, they began experimenting not only with Asian and African scales but also with newly devised scales and tonal systems.

INSTRUMENTS   Composers have been incorporating non-Western instruments into their works for some time. Here is a brief list of instruments that you may encounter at contemporary Western music concerts:

From *Africa*	
drums (various shapes, sizes, and construction material) xylophone	wood blocks gourds

From *Islamic North Africa and Turkey*	
cymbals (various sizes, starting in the late eighteenth century) triangle (nineteenth century)	bass drum (starting in the late eighteenth century) timpani or kettledrums (eighteenth century)

From *South and Central America*	
maracas timbales bongos	conga drum claves cowbell

From *Asia*	
Korean temple blocks Indonesian antique cymbals	Chinese gongs (tam tam, starting in the nineteenth century)

☞ *Music South of the Sahara*

Encompassing more than 50 countries, Africa is home to more than 500 million people who have developed hundreds of languages and religions and a wide diversity of music. In spite of the diversity, there are some similar characteristics among African musical traditions about which we can generalize.

Role of Music in African Life

Hardly a tribal or religious activity in African daily life takes place without music. Preparations for, during, and following the hunt, for instance, are all accompanied by prescribed musical activities, enhanced by dances, masks, and costumes. Puberty rites, weddings, and funerals all have their customary music.

In South Africa workers at the mines perform tribal dances in the arenas provided by the mine owners. These are Zulu dancers at the gold mine on the outskirts of Johannesburg.

Like much non-Western music, African music has mainly been passed orally from generation to generation. In rural areas, many African children grow up dancing and contributing their musical talents to the tribal rituals. Everyone participates, and as they grow older, a few become soloists and chant leaders. So integral is music in the life of each person that this interest continues even after a man or woman leaves tribal life to live in the city or among other cultures.

Other Instruments

African musicians use a variety of flutelike instruments, animal horns, whistles, thumb harps, and stringed instruments in addition to instruments that have already crossed over into Western ensembles. This array of different instruments contributes to the richness of the overall sound.

Rhythm

At the core of African music is rhythm. Melody and harmony are usually subordinate to the rhythmic drive of the music.

POLYRHYTHMS   African music often employs multilayers of rhythms. Each percussionist may add a different rhythm, resulting in a highly complex polyrhythmic texture. Dancing adds more complexity to the performance. Each tribal dancer chooses from the various rhythms as the source of inspiration for movement.

A South African six-stringed instrument.

CHANGING METERS AND RHYTHMS   In the nineteenth century, after returning from Africa, one musicologist reported that "African percussionists don't seem to know how to keep time." Because he was unfamiliar with African rhythms, he failed to understand their sophistication. In fact, an important characteristic of African music is its changing rhythms and metrical groups.

OSTINATO   This repetitive rhythmic pattern is at the core of African percussion ensemble music. The ostinato player helps keep a regular pattern moving forward, enabling other percussionists to improvise freely, often skirting around the steady beat.

IMPROVISATION   African musicians strive to avoid the obvious. While some members of a percussion ensemble provide an underlying rhythmic element with a steady beat or ostinato, others are free to play "around the beat" rather than exactly "on the steady beat." After all, the beat is already there; they can feel it. Adding their own rhythmic layers is a valued form of individual expression. Focusing on one player in the group, you will hear changing, imaginative, and complex improvisations.

VOCAL MUSIC   Though usually subordinate to rhythm, African singing is still quite important. Some vocal music uses words; however, most African singing employs varieties of ostinato chants.

Microtones

The pentatonic scale predominates in African music, but some pitches—microtones—differ from Western pitches. *Microtones* fall between the tones in the traditional Western chromatic scale.

Call and response

One characteristic of much of the vocal music of Africa is the use of *call and response*, discussed previously in the chapter on jazz. One member of the tribe, designated as leader, calls out (sings) a melodic-rhythmic phrase. The rest of the singers respond, either with an exact imitation or with a short, ostinato-style answer.

Heterophony

African melodies are often performed using *heterophony*—singers and melodic instrumentalists all perform the same melody at the same time, each with a slightly different interpretation. Some add extra tones or ornaments to the melody, others slightly different rhythms; some players lag behind the others, while others perform their melody slightly ahead of the group. We find this African-style heterophony also in North American jazz.

Transplanted African Music

The eighteenth- and nineteenth-century slave traders transported Africans and their music to many lands, especially to the Americas. We discussed the African influence on jazz in the United States, but the music of Central and South America and the Caribbean Islands also reflects the African influence.

The exciting rhythms of *calypso* music from Trinidad developed through the singing of African slaves living on that island. Other music

African musicians in city dress. Two performers play a wooden slit drum (center) while the others play drums topped with stretched skin.

LISTENING ACTIVITY ~

IF IT COMES TO FIGHTING WITH GUNS
SOUTH AFRICA: GHANA

❙ *Cmpact Disc 4, Track 43*
❙ *Running time: 4:00*

From the South African nation of Ghana, this traditional Ewe dance piece form is known as a *atsiagbekor*. On the recording you will hear the following instruments: 5 drums, 1 double bell (*gankogui*), and several gourds, some with seeds, others with beads or rattles.

emerged: the *mambo* and *rhumba* in Cuba, and the *bossa nova* and *conga* in Brazil. More recently in Jamaica, *reggae* music developed from African, calypso, and rock 'n' roll rhythms.

❧ Music of India

On a land area half the size of the United States reside almost one billion people—one-fifth of the world's population. They speak 15 major languages, with dozens of dialects, most using different alphabets.

British, Islamic, and Asian conquerors of India have helped shape Indian music. *Ragas*, the melodic material of Indian music, have similar counterparts in Iranian and other Islamic Middle Eastern music. European instruments, such as violins, clarinets, and harmoniums, are found in Indian music. These come directly from the English occupation. Other Indian instruments, such as the *sitar*, hand cymbals, and drums, and some Indian scales can be traced to Asia.

Today, in any of the typically overcrowded cities, you will encounter many forms of music: Indian classical, folk, and popular. Recently the predominant popular music has been *film music*. Its popularity reflects the

Raga
(*rah*-gah)

Sitar
(sih-*tar*)

Film music

Indian dancers and musicians.

people's fascination with films and the songs that are part of those films, the majority of which are musicals.

Film music is a curious blend of East and West: energetic melodies, often based on Asian scales over Latin American rhythms. Piercing, nasal-sounding singers are accompanied by instruments that may include a set of American dance-band drums, electric keyboards, guitars, violins, xylophone, celeste, bongos, and Indian sitar, *tabla* drums, or bamboo flute.

Most of India's folk music still being performed has been handed down orally. Street folk musicians earn their livings accompanying acrobats, dancers, or street theater. Others may charm snakes by playing the *punji* (a form of gourd and reed bagpipe). Indian minstrels wander the countryside, singing traditional folk songs and accompanying themselves on a drum or crude stringed instrument.

Indian Classical Music

Classical music in India is distinctively Indian. For more than 2,000 years, trained musicians working in the royal courts or in the religious temples developed the sound and traditions that survive today.

HINDUSTANI AND KARNATIC MUSIC   Since the thirteenth century, when Muslims invaded India and settled in the north, classical Indian music separated into two closely related traditions: north Indian or Hindustani music, and south Indian or Karnatic music. Each style uses slightly different instruments. For instance, the *bin* of the north is called the *vina* in the south. Their sizes and tones differ slightly, but at first glance the two instruments seem identical.

Using for its melodic material *ragas*, or groupings of pitches somewhat similar to Western scales, Indian music is mainly heterophonic with the addition of a drone:

The overall sound of Indian classical music is complex and, at first, seems very different from Western music. With listening, however, it may eventually become more understandable.

ॐ *Typical Classical Indian Musical Texture*

Melody	〰〰〰〰	singers (one or two)
Accompaniment and soloists	⋮⋮⋮⋮⋮⋮⋮⋮⋮⋮⋮⋮⋮	stringed instruments violin, *sitar, sarod, bin* or *vina*
Drone	————————	*tambura* (string instrument, one or two)
Rhythm	– – – – – – – –	*tabla* and other drums

Tabla

Snake charmers
Punji
Minstrels

Bin
Vina

LISTENING ACTIVITY ≻

GHAZAL, BAT KARANE MUJHE MUSHKIL
INDIA

Compact Disc 4, Track 44
Running time: 2:42

From India, the piece *Ghazal, Bat Karane Mujhe Mushkil* features a female vocalist, sitar, tambura (string drone), harmonium (small organ-like keyboard), and tabla (drums).

Several contemporary musicians have incorporated Indian music elements into their Western style. After spending time in India, the Beatles included the sitar among their instruments and worked Indian-type melodies into their music.

More recently, jazz flutist Paul Horn recorded an album of improvisations he performed in the Taj Mahal, the famous mausoleum in Agra, India. To blend Indian music with Western jazz, Horn modified his material closer to the *ragas* he heard in India.

≻ Music of Japan

Throughout history, Japan has incorporated foreign elements into its culture. Today, a wide assortment of music performances in Tokyo include:

American-style Japanese marching bands (on parade)
Japanese kabuki theater
Japanese koto ensemble concert
European chorus concerts of Renaissance music
American popular and rock music
Japanese popular music (American style)
European classical-music orchestra concerts

GAGAKU Japanese music is traceable to the third century B.C. The *gagaku* court orchestra originated in the fifth century A.D. when eighty Korean musicians came to Japan to participate in an imperial funeral. Japanese royalty were impressed by the Korean musicians and set about developing their own court orchestras. Later, gagaku orchestras performed in the Shinto temples. They still can be heard today in the temples.

Japanese koto.

LISTENING ACTIVITY ℛ

NETORI (PRELUDE) ℰ ETENRAKU IN HYOJO
JAPAN

Compact Disc 4, Track 45
Running time: 5:00

The traditional (Gagaku): *Netori* (prelude) & *Etenraku in Hyojo* is performed by singers and an orchestra of assorted instruments, most of which are heard on the recording.

Winds:
- *hichiriki*   double-reed bamboo oboe
- *kakura-bue*   six-holed bamboo flute
- *ryuteki*   seven-holed bamboo flute
- *sho*   mouth organ with seventeen reed pipes

Strings:
- *wagon*   six-stringed zither
- *gaku-so*   thirteen-stringed zither
- *biwa*   pear-shaped lute with four strings

Percussion:
- *da-daiko*   large drum, played with thick sticks
- *tsuri daiko*   medium-size suspended two-headed drum, played with two sticks
- *shoko*   small suspended gong, played with two sticks
- *kakko*   small two-headed drum, played with thin

Musical traditions from other parts of Asia, especially China, entered Japanese music beginning in the seventh century A.D. Many Japanese instruments originated in China, India, Korea, and Manchuria.

From ancient times to the present, an abundance of solo and chamber music has been available for Japan's most popular instruments.

koto—a stringed lutelike instrument
kokyu—a spiked fiddle
shakuhachi—an end-blown bamboo flute
various percussion instruments

Japanese Scales

At the heart of Japanese pitch material are varieties of five-tone, *pentatonic scales*, most of which originated in China. For instance, the following scales used mainly in Japanese sacred music are identical to Chinese scales dating back to 2000 B.C.:

Another extensively used pentatonic scale in modern Japanese music consists of two major third gaps:

The popular *Sakura* or "Cherry Blossom" song uses this scale.

Sakura

Kabuki performance with actors and musicians.

Theater Music

Throughout Japan's history, music usually has accompanied theatrical performances.

NOGAKU   Music is an important part of the traditional *Nogaku* or *No* musical plays. Derived from Buddhism, *No* plays feature singers accompanied by Japanese flutes and drums.

KABUKI   Designed for the masses of common people, kabuki theater began developing its traditions in the sixteenth century. A colorful spectacle, kabuki incorporates acting, dancing, and music. Musical accompaniment also is an integral part of the Japanese puppet theater.

Music in Japanese Schools

Since the Meiji Restoration of 1868, when Emperor Mutsuhito modernized education, Western classical music replaced Japanese classical music in the schools. As a further encouragement, talented Japanese musicians were sent to the music centers of Europe and America to study. They brought back to Japanese schools not only the music but also Western teaching methods.

In the twentieth century, well-known music teachers such as Shinichi Suzuki continued teaching Western music to Japanese children. Through the Suzuki Method, thousands of Japanese youngsters learned in groups to play Vivaldi, Mozart, and other Western composers' violin and cello concertos. As a result, symphony orchestras around the world today employ many Japanese string players.

The Suzuki Method is now used in a number of countries, including the United States. Using the latest methods and instruments, the Yamaha Music Education Foundation teaches Western-style music to hundreds of thousands of youngsters in Japan and the United States.

With this history and emphasis on Western classical music, excellent symphony orchestras and opera companies thrive throughout modern Japan. Composers such as Mozart and Beethoven are as much the favorites of Japanese audiences as they are of European and American audiences. Contemporary Japanese composers are creating new music based on European principles but reflecting the venerable and diverse Japanese cultural history.

LISTENING ACTIVITY ♂

Kabuki Nagauta Music Ayame-Yukata
Japan

Compact Disc 4, Track 46
Running time: 3:30

From Japan and the populat kabuki theater, listen to the *nagauta* music "Ayama-Yukata." Since 1652, kabuki has been performed entirely by male actors. The musicians usually are seated on stage facing the audience and behind the actors (see the photo of a kabuki performance). In this recording we hear an assortment of instruments accompanying the male singer: *shakuhachi* (bamboo flutes), *koto* (stringed instruments), *shamisen* (plucked fiddles).

Summary of Terms

Asian scales
bamboo flute
bin
bongos
bossa nova
call and response
calypso
changing meters
Chinese gongs (tam tam)
claves
conga
conga drum
cowbell
ethnic music
ethnomusicology
film music

gagaku
harmoniums
heterophony
Hindustani music
improvisation
Indonesian finger cymbals
kabuki
Karnatic music
kokyu
Korean temple blocks
koto
mambo
maracas
microtones
minstrels

Nogaku
ostinato
pentatonic scale
punji
raga
Sakura
shakuhachi
shamisen
sitar
Suzuki violin method
tabla
timbales
vina
World Exposition
Yamaha Music Education

Music Notation

To preserve composers' creative ideas, music notation developed gradually over a span of hundreds of years. Notation makes it possible for players to re-create music accurately. Here are some of the basic concepts of modern music notation.

Pitch Notation

STAFF   This structure of five lines and four spaces holds printed notes, graphically indicating the relative highness and lowness of pitches.

CLEFS   A clef is a symbol placed on a staff line to fix the pitch notated on that line. With that reference, performers know the pitches of the other notes on the staff. There are two main clef signs:

The *G clef* or *treble* (high) *clef* is an ornate symbol that circles around the pitch *G*.

pitch *G* ⟶

The *F clef* or *bass* (low) *clef* contains two dots placed on either side of the "F" line to indicate the pitch *F*:

pitch *F* ⟶

GRAND STAFF Because their ranges are limited, most instruments and voices perform music using one *clef*. Keyboards, on the other hand, use a much wider range. Therefore, their parts include both *G* and *F* clefs and are displayed on a *grand staff*. Oval-shaped printed notes represent pitches.

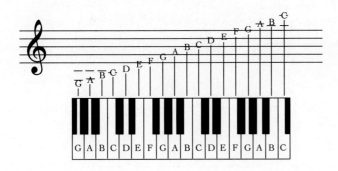

Duration or Time Notation

Shading of notes, together with stems and flags attached to them, indicates duration. Special symbols indicate the specific duration of silence or rest:

NOTES   RESTS

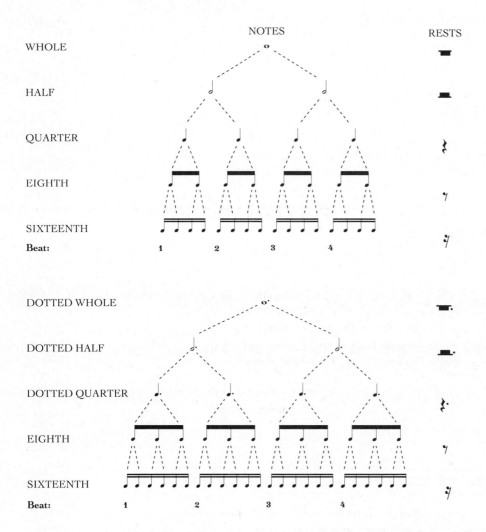

WHOLE

HALF

QUARTER

EIGHTH

SIXTEENTH

Beat: 1   2   3   4

DOTTED WHOLE

DOTTED HALF

DOTTED QUARTER

EIGHTH

SIXTEENTH

Beat: 1   2   3   4

Writing Reports

♪ *The Short Concert Report*

1. Attach the program and ticket stub of the performance to your report.
2. Write a one-paragraph description of each work. Give your personal reaction to each piece. Describe the music as well as you can both in your own words and the terms presented in this course.
3. Try to include:
   - performing medium (also special instruments and soloists)
   - general form (symphony, concerto, dance forms, etc.)
   - outstanding features of melody, rhythms, textures, style, etc.

Other Directions:

Do not copy from printed concert programs, music reviews, or record jackets. That is a breach of copyright. Take a pad and pen so you can jot down a few comments after movements or works. This will help you remember the music. If permitted, record the performance with a small, battery-operated tape recorder. That way you can write your notes later and just enjoy the performance.

Note: Some professional concerts prohibit taping.

♪ *The Long Concert Report*

I. General Directions
   A. Ask your instructor to recommend concerts.
   B. Select one that interests you.

    C. Type your report double-spaced. Make sure your computer printout is legible.

    D. Include a bibliography and possibly footnotes.

    E. Attach your program and ticket stub.

II. Pre-concert Report

Select one major work or a group of short works scheduled on the concert.

    A. Present your research on the historical background of:

      1. the composer

      2. the composition

    B. Listen to a recording and give your general reaction to the performance and specific reaction to the music regarding the composer's use of:

      1. performing media

      2. rhythm, tempo, meter

      3. melodic materials

      4. harmony and tonality

      5. textures

      6. form

III. Post-concert review

    A. Include background information: date, time, place, performer(s), and musical selections.

    B. Discuss your reactions to each work performed. Include both your intellectual and emotional reactions.

    C. Discuss your reactions to the quality of the performance and performer(s). Also comment on the concert ritual the performers follow.

    D. Compare the live concert performance of the major work with the recorded performance you researched.

Other Directions:

Refrain from giving merely a play-by-play account of the concert; your printed program already gives that information.

    Do not copy directly from sources. You may paraphrase researched sources as long as you cite these sources with footnotes and in a bibliography.

    Jot notes after movements or works to help you remember the performance. Try not to write during the live performance so that you will not distract yourself. If permitted, take a tape recorder to help you write your post-concert review.

ᴐ *The Research Report*

Directions

1. Choose one topic.
    *   From the following list of suggested topics, choose one for a research report. Or, choose an alternate topic similar to those suggested. Compare and contrast the musical selections using terminology you learned, research sources, and your experiences attending concerts.
2. Include biographical data on composers.
    *   Explain how events in the composer's life relate to the works you have chosen to compare.
3. What was happening at the time in society, politics, and economics that influenced the general musical style?
    *   Cite specific examples from the music you selected.
4. Include information about the performer and recording.
    *   Identify the ensemble, conductor, soloists, and any other performers mentioned on the recording.
    *   Identify, if possible, the date of the recording and its production label.
5. Include a bibliography.
    *   Cite all sources used to research your topic—books, articles, records, etc.
6. Be original!
    *   Do not copy directly from sources: printed concert programs, music reviews, or record jackets. That is a breach of copyright. You may paraphrase resource material as long as you properly cite sources with footnotes and in the bibliography.

Other Directions:

Take a pad and pen so you can jot down a few comments after movements or works. This will help you remember the music. If permitted, record the performance with a small, battery-operated tape recorder. That way you can write your notes later and just enjoy the performance.

Note: Some professional concerts prohibit taping.

ᴐ *Suggested Research Topics*

1. Compare and contrast an early and a late work by the same composer:
    *   Haydn's Symphony No. 45 (*Farewell*,1772) and Symphony No. 94 (*Surprise*, 1791)

- Beethoven's Symphony No. 1 (1800) and Symphony No. 9 (*Choral*, 1824)
- Beethoven's String Quartets Opus 18 and String Quartets Opus 135.
- Verdi's operas *Rigoletto* (1851) and *Otello* (1887)
- Puccini's operas *La Bohème* (1896) and *Turandot* (posthumous, 1926)
- Mahler's Symphony No. 1 (*The Titan*, 1888) and Symphony No. 8 (*Symphony of a Thousand*, 1909)
- Stravinsky's ballet *The Rite of Spring (1913) and* Ebony Concerto *(1945)*

2. Compare and contrast two similar works by two different composers of the same style period:
   - Bach's *Christmas* Oratorio and Handel's *Messiah* Oratorio
   - Brahms's *Academic Festival Overture* and Wagner's *Die Meistersinger von Nürnberg Overture*
   - Tchaikovsky's *Nutcracker* Ballet and Falla's Suite from *The Three Cornered Hat* Ballet
   - Gershwin's *An American in Paris* and Copland's *Appalachian Spring*
   - Rimsky-Korsakov's *Capriccio espagnole* and Tchaikovsky's *Capriccio italien*

3. Compare and contrast two similar works by two different composers from two different style periods:
   - Haydn's Symphony No. 94 (*Surprise*) and Prokofiev's Symphony No. 1 (*Classical*)
   - Vivaldi's Concerto (*Spring*) from *The Four Seasons* and Schumann's Symphony No. (*Spring*)
   - Bach's *Mass in b minor* and Bernstein's *Mass*
   - Beethoven's Symphony No. 9 (*Choral*) and Stravinsky's *The Rite of Spring*

4. Other topics:
   - Discuss the differences in orchestral music in the Classical, Romantic, and 20th-century style periods.
   - Compare the musical contributions of Felix Mendelssohn and Leonard Bernstein.
   - Trace and discuss the development of the concert tradition from the Baroque period to the present.
   - Describe and discuss the various ways that composers and musicians supported themselves from the Baroque period to the present.
   - Describe, compare, and contrast the different ways of listening to music of the Baroque, Classical, and Romantic style periods.

Glossary of Musical Terms

A cappella Choral music without accompaniment.

Accelerando Gradual quickening of tempo.

Accent Emphasis on a particular tone.

Adagio Slow tempo.

Aleatoric music A twentieth-century method of creating music; uses vague notation to leave many musical decisions to the performer.

Allegretto Less quick than allegro; moderately fast tempo.

Allegro Lively, fast tempo.

Allemande A Baroque dance in moderate tempo and two-beat meter.

Alto A low female voice, also called contralto.

Andante Moderate, walking tempo.

Andantino Slightly faster tempo than andante.

Antiphony, antiphonal Music in which two or more groups are separated to create an echo effect and contrast.

Arco A string instrument bowing direction where the bow is used as opposed to plucking the string.

Aria An elaborate solo song with instrumental accompaniment, generally in an opera, oratorio, or cantata.

Arpeggio Chord tones sounded in succession rather than simultaneously.

Art song An elaborate solo song, usually composed to an existing poem, sung with accompaniment.

Athematic Music without discernible themes or melodies.

Atonality Music without tonality or key.

Avant-garde A French term used to describe radical or advanced composers or other artists.

Ballad A narrative-style folk song.

Ballad opera A type of opera, originating in the eighteenth century, that introduced spoken dialogue between songs.

Ballade (1) French trouvère poetry and songs (2) Song-like, nineteenth-century piano pieces.

Bar *See measure*

Baritone A male voice with a range between tenor and bass.

Bass The lowest, heaviest male voice.

Basso continuo A bass line that provides a basis for a harmonic accompaniment; most often used in Baroque music.

Beat The underlying basic rhythmic pulse.

Bebop Originating in the 1940s, a highly innovative jazz style features small groups of instruments.

Bel canto A style of singing, particularly in Italian opera, that displays the singer's vocal agility and beautiful tone.

Bin A string instrument used in the music of northern India.

Blue notes Flatted or "bent" third, fifth, and seventh tones of a traditional major scale used in jazz and blues music.

Blues A melancholy song originating with African-American singers.

413

Blues progression Predictable progressions of chords in jazz and blues music, using patterns derived from church hymns.

Bolero A Spanish dance in moderate tempo with three beats per measure.

Bourrée A fast Baroque dance with two beats per measure.

Bridge (1) A musical passage between two major sections. (2) The part of a stringed instrument that supports the strings.

Buffo A singer of comic roles in Italian opera.

Burlesque A raucous, bawdy, musical sex-and-comedy-travesty entertainment of the late nineteenth and early twentieth centuries.

Cadence A melodic or harmonic progression that gives the effect of closing a section.

Cadenza A virtuoso passage (sometimes improvised) played by the soloist in a concerto, usually without orchestral accompaniment.

Cakewalk Originating on Southern plantations, the *cakewalk* was a high-kicking dance.

Call and response An African and African-American song style in which a leader sings phrases to which a chorus or group responds with phrases.

Canon Music in which one or more lines continue to imitate one another throughout the work.

Cantata Vocal music developed in the Baroque period for solo voice(s), instruments, and often a chorus; based either on a religious or secular text.

Canzona A short instrumental piece popular in the sixteenth and seventeenth centuries.

Castrato Castrated male soprano or alto singers popular mainly in Italian Baroque operas.

Chaconne A work featuring variations on a progression of chords repeated throughout the work.

Chamber music Musical composition suitable for performances by 2 to 8 players in a room or small hall.

Chance music A twentieth-century technique using general instructions to the performer, allowing them to create a performance that is a matter of chance.

Chorale A hymn tune used in the German Lutheran Church.

Chord The simultaneous sounding of three or more pitches.

Choreographer The person who plans the dancer's movements.

Chorus (1) A group that sings choral music. (2) A section of an opera or oratorio sung by the chorus. (3) The refrain or main section of a song.

Chromatic A scale or harmonic movement of half steps.

Cine music Blend of Eastern and Western music used in popular musical films in India.

Clavier A general term indicating any keyboard instrument.

Coda The Italian word for "tail"; the section that brings the movement to a conclusion.

Col legno A special effect in string performance where the player strikes the strings with the wooden side of the bow.

Coloratura A virtuoso style of singing, usually including fast scales, arpeggios, and ornaments; often associated with a light, high soprano voice, particularly in opera.

Common Time A meter that consists of four beats per measure.

Concertato Contrasting performing groups playing together.

Concertmaster (*Konzertmeister* in German) The first chair player in the first violin section of an orchestra.

Concerto A work for solo instrument(s), usually with three movements, accompanied by an orchestra.

Concerto grosso A concerto for a small instrumental group accompanied by a small orchestra.

Concert overture An overture not associated with an opera or drama.

Consonance A group of sounds that seems pleasing or restful.

Continuo *See basso continuo.*

Contrabassoon A large bassoon pitched an octave below the usual bassoon.

Contralto *See alto.*

Counterpoint Two or more independent melodic lines occurring at the same time.

Counter subject The second theme in a fugue.

Country Popular music originating in the Appalachian region of the United States.

Courante A lively dance in triple meter and fast tempo.

Crescendo Gradual increase in volume.

Decrescendo Gradual decrease in volume. Also called diminuendo.

Development (1) The process of developing themes. (2) The section in sonata form featuring the development of themes.

Dissonance A group of sounds that seems disagreeable or unpleasant.

Dodecaphonic music *See serialism.*

Double stop The sounding of two different pitches simultaneously on a stringed instrument.

Downbeat The accented first beat of a measure.

Duet A musical work for two performers.

Dynamics The various levels of intensity or loudness in music.

Eclectic An incorporation of many different styles.

Electronic music Sounds produced on electronic oscillators and then usually recorded and stored.

English horn An alto oboe.

Etude A short, instrumental composition concentrating on a particular technical aspect of performance.

Exposition The opening section of fugue and sonata forms.

Fantasia A short composition in free form.

Finale The concluding movement of some multimovement works and operas.

Flat A sign indicating that a pitch is to be lowered by a half step.

Form The structure or plan of a composition.

Fortepiano *See pianoforte*

Fugue A composition in which the main subject (theme) is presented in imitation in several parts.

Fusion A blend of jazz and rock music.

Gagaku Ancient Korean and Japanese court orchestras.

Gamelan A Javanese orchestra.

Gavotte A dance with a moderate tempo in two-beat meter.

Gesamtkunstwerk Meaning "total art work" in German; Wagner used this term for his music-dramas over which he exerted total control of the librettos, music, orchestrations, sets, and staging.

Gigue A baroque dance in compound meter with a fast tempo.

Glissando A performance effect provided by rapid sliding up or down scales.

Grand opera Usually serious, nineteenth-century French opera which utilized elaborately costumed crowd scenes, large choruses, ballet, and lavish sets.

Grave Very slowly and solemnly.

Gregorian chant Monophonic church music of the Middle Ages named after Pope Gregory I; also called *plainchant.*

Harmonics (1) Secondary tones that form a part of most tones. (2) High-pitched tones that are produced on a string instrument by placing the finger lightly on a string.

Harmony The simultaneous sounding of pitches.

Harpsichord A popular keyboard instrument of the sixteenth through eighteenth centuries on which the strings are plucked when the keys are depressed.

Heldentenor In German operas, a tenor who sings heroic roles.

Hindustani music Music of northern India.

Homophony, homophonic A texture consisting of a line of melody and accompaniment.

Idée fixe Berlioz' name for the melody or theme used throughout all movements of his *Symphony fantastique.*

Imitation The repetition of a melody or portion of a melody in another part.

Impromptu A short piano composition that sounds improvised.

Improvisation Spontaneous performance without notated music.

Incidental music Music composed for performance in connection with a drama.

Instrumentation The parts assigned to particular instruments in an ensemble.

Interval The distance between two notes.

Jazz A twentieth-century American musical style incorporating complex rhythms and improvisation.

Kabuki Traditional Japanese theater incorporating acting, dancing, and music.

Kapellmeister German term for music director

Karnatic music Music of southern India.

Key *See Tonality.*

Kokyu A Japanese spiked fiddle.

Koto A stringed lute-like instrument of Japan.

Largo Very slow and broad tempo.

Legato Smooth, connected style of performance.

Leitmotif A motive or theme associated with a particular character or idea, used extensively by Richard Wagner.

Lento Very slow.

Libretto The text of an opera or oratorio.

Lied (pl., Lieder) The German term for art song.

Lutheran cantata A choral work, often with instruments, for the musical portion of a Lutheran church service.

Lyric opera Nineteenth-century French opera emphasizing melody and romantic or fantasy-based stories.

Madrigal A secular work for small choir popular in the Renaissance style period.

Maestro de cappella Italian term for music director.

Major One of the two basic scales used in Western music, see also *minor.*

Ma non troppo A performance indicating meaning "but not too much," used to qualify another term, as in *allegro ma non troppo — "fast, but not too much."*

Mass The Roman Catholic Church's main service, frequently set to music (*Missa* in Latin).

Mazurka A polish dance in triple meter.

Measure A group of beats set off in written music by vertical lines called bar lines.

Meistersinger A member of a guild of German master musicians which flourished from the fourteenth to the seventeenth centuries.

Melody A series of consecutive pitches with a recognizable shape or tune.

Meno Means "less" in Italian.

Meter The pattern created by stressed and unstressed beats.

Metronome A device (mechanical or electrical) used to indicate the exact tempo of a composition.

Mezzo-soprano A female voice with a range between a soprano and an alto.

Microtones Pitches falling between the semi-tones of the Western chromatic scale.

MIDI An acronym for Musical Instrument Digital Interface. Standards for use by electronic keyboards, computers, and other devices.

Minimalism Twentieth-century compositional technique using the simplest musical elements, generally repeated over and over, with subtle changes in their character.

Minor One of the two basic scales in Western music, see also *major.*

Minstrel French poet-musicians who performed throughout France during the Middle Ages.

Minuet A popular dance of the seventeenth and eighteenth centuries; uses triple meter.

Minuet and trio form A common Classical period form consisting of three parts: minuet, trio, minuet.

Moderato Moderate tempo.

Modes Scale patterns (including major and minor) derived from early church music.

Monophony, monophonic A texture consisting of a single melodic line without accompaniment.

Motet Sacred polyphonic music for voices popular during the thirteenth through seventeenth centuries.

Motive A short melodic or rhythmic idea.

Movement A large, independent section of an instrumental composition.

Music-drama Wagner's term for his German operas.

Musique concrète Everyday sounds recorded and manipulated on the tape recorder.

Mute A device for dampening and changing the tone of an instrument.

Neo-Classical A twentieth-century style that borrows compositoinal techniques from previous style periods.

Nocturne A short, lyrical piano piece of the Romantic period that evokes feelings associated with the night.

Nogaku Traditional Japanese musical plays..

Notes Symbols written in musical notation to indicate pitches and rhythm.

Octave An interval of eight pitches in which the first and last pitches have the same pitch name.

Octet A work for eight performers.

Opera A dramatic work, comedy or tragedy, set to music.

Opera comique Mid-nineteenth century French opera featuring wit and satire both in the libretto and in the music.

Operetta A light opera with spoken dialogue.

Opus Literally "work"; the number indicates the order in which the composer's works were written.

Oratorio A large work for chorus, soloist, and orchestra usually on a religious topic; performed without scenery, costumes, or action.

Orchestration The art and technique of a scoring music for an orchestra or group of instruments.

Organum Polyphonic choral church music beginning in the ninth century.

Ornament One or more tones that embellish a melody.

Ostinato A short, persistently repeated melodic or rhythmic figure.

Overture An instrumental introduction to a larger work.

Pasticcio A cross between ballad opera and comic opera, combining a dramatic work with music by famous composers.

Pentatonic scale A scale consisting of five tones.

Phrase A relatively short melodic statement similar to a clause or phrase in language.

Piano (1) Keyboard instrument. (2) Quiet.

Pianoforte The complete name for the keyboard instrument usually called a *Piano*. Meaning "soft-loud" in Italian, it was named *pianoforte* when it was invented in the early eighteenth century because it could play both soft and loud.

Pitch The perceived highness or lowness of a musical sound, determined by the number of vibrations per second.

Più Means "more" in Italian.

Pizzicato A direction to string performers to pluck rather than bow the strings.

Plainchant See *Gregorian chant*.

Poco A performance direction meaning "little." For example, *poco accelerando* indicates "gradually play faster."

Polonaise A Polish national dance, also used in piano pieces by Chopin.

Polychord Two or more triads performed simultaneously.

Polymeter Two or more contrasting meters sounded simultaneously.

Polyphony, polyphonic A texture in which two or more melodies of approximately equal importance are present at the same time.

Polytonality Several tonalities present at the same time.

Prelude (1) A short instrumental work usually played as an introduction to a larger work. (2) A short, independent instrumental work.

Presto Very fast tempo.

Programmatic music Instrumental work descriptive of some nonmusical idea or object.

Program notes Short descriptions or background information in the printed concert program about the music, the composer, and the performers.

Quartet A work for four performers.

Quintet A work for five performers.

Raga Ancient melodic material used in Indian music.

Ragtime Syncopated music composed in the 1890s, usually for piano.

Rallentando Gradual slowing of tempo.

Recapitulation The section of sonata form in which the themes from the exposition are heard again.

Recitative A speechlike section found in operas, oratorios, cantatas, and other vocal works.

Requiem The funeral Mass of the Roman Catholic Church.

Revue An energetic popular entertainment show with no story; usually built around star performers, featuring musical numbers, comedy acts, dramatic sketches, and specialty routines.

Rhythm The sensation of motion in music regulated by the duration and grouping of sounds.

Rhythm and blues (R & B) A transitional music style between swing and rock; first became popular in the African-American communities of large, mid-western cities.

Riff Used in African and African-American music, a riff is a short phrase repeated over and over.

Ritardando Gradual slowing of the tempo.

Rock'n'roll/Rock Popular music characterized by its hard-driving beat and use of electronically amplified instruments.

Rococo The highly ornamented style in music and the other arts prevalent in eighteenth-century European courts.

Rondo A form in which the main theme appears several times with contrasting sections between its appearances.

Rubato A performer's slight deviation from strict rhythm for expressive effect.

Sampling A series of numbers which represents sounds that have been digitally recorded and stored on computer disc.

Scale A series of pitches that proceeds upward or downward according to a prescribed pattern.

Scherzo (1) A lively movement usually in triple meter. (2) A self-contained piano piece.

Score The complete notation of a work that includes a number of parts.

Secular music Nonreligious music.

Sequence The immediate repetition of a melodic idea using different pitches.

Serialism A twentieth-century method of composing using tone rows and all twelve tones of the chromatic scale.

Sforzando A loud, accented tone or chord.

Shakuhachi A Japanese end-blown bamboo flute.

Singspiel German eighteenth-century opera with spoken dialogue.

Solo A work in which one player or singer performs alone or is featured.

Sonata (1) A multimovement work for piano or piano and other solo instrument. (2) A Baroque piece for small instrumental ensemble.

Sonata form A large form consisting of an exposition section, followed by a development section and a recapitulation.

Song cycle A group of songs with a unifying theme.

Song plugger A pianist-singer who performed new songs to find customers for them.

Songs without words Mendelssohn's term for melodic piano pieces, written in the style of a Lied or song.

Soprano The highest female voice or boy's voice.

Sprechstimme A vocal style combining speaking and singing.

Staccato A detached style of performing in abrupt bursts.

Stretto A short section mainly found in the fugue where the main subject is imitated in close succession or overlapping voices.

Subscription concerts A series of concerts for advance-purchase subscribers.

Suite (1) An instrumental work in several movements. (2) Portions of a larger work, such as a ballet or opera, performed as a group.

Swing Popular music of the 1930s and 1940s which often featured big bands.

Symphonic poem Programmatic symphony in one movement; also called a tone poem.

Symphony An extended, multimovment orchestral work.

Syncopation Accented beats not normally expected within a particular meter.

Synthesizer An electric instrument used to generate sounds.

Tempo The speed of the beats in a piece of music.

Tenor A male voice higher than baritone or bass.

Texture The way in which the individual parts of music are layered and woven.

Theme The main melody or melodies in a piece of music.

Theme and variations Form consisting of a theme followed by a group of variations on that theme.

Timbre Tone quality or color.

Toccata A display piece for a keyboard instrument.

Tonality A key or tonal center.

Tone poem See *symphonic poem*.

Tone-row music (twelve tone) See *Serialism*.

Tonic (key center) The specific pitch around which a piece of music is centered.

Tonic chord A chord built on the first pitch of a major or minor scale.

Transcription An adaptation of a musical work for a different instrument, voice, or ensemble.

Transposition A piece or section of music written or performed at a pitch other than the original one.

Tremolo Rapid repetition of one pitch, or rapid alternation between two tones.

Triad A chord consisting of three pitches usually separated by intervals of thirds.

Trill A musical ornament consisting of rapid alternations of two tones.

Trio (1) A musical work for three parts or three performers. (2) The second section of a minuet and trio form.

Troubadours During the age of chivalry, singing knights of the twelfth-century court in southern France.

Trouvères Noblemen in the courts of northern France who composed and sang songs during the twelfth and thirteenth centuries.

Tutti An Italian performance term indicating that the entire ensemble plays.

Twelve-tone music See *serialism*.

Unison Performing the same pitches or melody at the same time.

Variation A section of music in which the melody, harmony, or rhythm of a theme is repeated with some changes.

Verismo Late-nineteenth-century opera which uses a realistic story, setting and acting.

Vibrato A rapid fluctuation of pitch or pulsation of tone for expressiveness.

Vina A string instrument used in the music of southern India.

Virtuoso A highly skilled performer.

Virtuoso orchestra An orchestra consisting entirely of highly skilled (*virtuoso*) performers.

Vivace Very fast, lively tempo.

Whole-tone scale A scale in which the octave is divided into six whole steps.

Wind ensemble A wind instrument band smaller than the traditional band.

Photo Credits

Prelude: Page 1, Steve Sherman. **Page 2 (top),** American Society of Composers and Publishers. **Page 2 (middle),** Courtesy ICM Artists, Ltd., photo by J. Henry Fair. **Page 2 (bottom),** Norman McGrath. **Plate 1,** *Le Concert Champetre: La Musique (The Musicians of a Country Concert).* Anon. Italian School, 16th Century, Mus. de l'Hotel l'Allemant, Bourges, Giraudon/Art Resource, NY. **Plate 2,** Codice Squarcilupi: Pagina Miniata, Art Resource. **Plate 3,** *La Primavera (Spring),* Sandro Botticelli, Uffizi Galleria, Florence, Scala/Art Resource, NY. **Plate 4,** Rose Window, Chartres, Photo Resources, Inc. **Plate 5,** Frederick the Great, King of Prussia, performing by candlelight, Archiv Fur Kunst Und Geschichte, Berlin. **Plate 6,** Young Mozart, his father and his sister, Giraudon/Art Resource, NY. **Plate 7,** *The Circle of the Lustful,* Birmingham Museum/Art Gallery. **Plate 8,** Grand pianoforte made for the wife of Lord Foley, baron of Kidderminster, The Metropolitan Museum of Art, Gift of Mrs. Henry McSweeny, 1959. Photograph by Sheldan Collins. **Plate 9,** *Impression, soleil levant (Impression of the Sunrise),* Claude Monet, Giraudon/Art Resource, NY. **Plate 10,** Robert Joffrey's Production of "The Nutcracker", H. Migdoll, The Joffrey Ballet. **Plate 11,** *The Fiddler* by Marc Chagall, Erich Lessing from Art Resource. **Plate 12,** Salvador Dali, "The Persistence of Memory" (Persistence de la memoire). 1931. Oil on canvas, 9½ x 13". The Museum of Modern Art, NY. **Plate 13,** Vassily Kandinsky, "Painting Number 200" 1914. Oil on canvas, 64 x 31½". The Museum of Modern Art, NY. Mrs. Simon Guggenheim Fund. Photograph © 1994 The Museum of Modern Art, NY. **Plate 14,** Picasso, Pablo. "Les Demoiselles d'Avignon". Paris (June-July 1907). Oil on canvas, 8' x 7'8". The Museum of Modern Art, NY. Acquired through the Lillie P. Bliss Bequest. **Plate 15,** The fusion-jazz group "Weather Report" by Andy Freeberg. **Plate 16,** Spanish dancers by Mira.

Chapter 1: Page 3, Steve J. Sherman. **Page 4,** Robert Cahen.

Chapter 2: Page 6, Symphony Hall, Boston, Lincoln Russell. **Page 7 (top),** Courtesy ICM Artists, Ltd. **Page 7 (middle),** Christian Steiner, Cami **Page 7 (bottom),** Courtesy ICM Artists, Ltd. **Page 8 (top),** Courtesy Royal Winnipeg Ballet, David Cooper. **Page 8 (bottom),** Courtesy Boston Pops Orchestra, Photo by Lincoln Russel. **Page 9,** Philadelphia Orchestra, Laird Bindrim. **Page 10,** Boston Symphony Orchestra. **Page 11,** Coutesy of the Boston Symphony Orchestra, Inc., Richard Feldman. **Page 12,** Peter Schaaf.

Chapter 3: Page 16, Peter Cunningham, Courtesy Mendola, Ltd., **Page 20,** Steve J. Sherman. **Page 24,** Nick Sangiamo, Courtesy IMG Artists. **Page 26,** Itzhak Perlman, Courtesy ICM Artists, Ltd., photo by Christian Steiner.

Chapter 4: Page 27, Steve Sherman. **Page 30 (bottom),** Courtesy IMC Artists, Ltd., photo by Peter Schaaf. **Page 30 (top),** Peter Schaaf. **Page 30 (middle),** Courtesy IMG Artists, Martin Reichenthal. **Page 33,** (top) The Toronto Symphony. **Page 33,** (bottom) Courtesy of The Chamber Music Society of Lincoln Center, Harry Heleotis. **Page 34,** Steve Sherman. **Page 35,** Courtesy of Robert Millard. **Page 36,** Courtesy of the New York Philharmonic, photo by David Rentas. **Page 42,** Bettmann. **Page 44,** Bettmann. **Page 53,** Bildarchiv Preussischer Kulturbesitz. **Page 52,** J. Dane. **Page 53,** Bettmann. **Page 55,** Performing Arts Library, Clive Barday.

Chapter 5: Page 57, Art Resource. **Page 58,** Courtesy Houston Grand Opera.

Chapter 6: Page 60, New York Library Picture Collection. **Page 61,** J. Mariani, Leo De Wys, Inc., **Page 64,** New York Public Library Picture Collection. **Page 65,** The Granger Collection. **Page 66,** Joseph Modlens, Black Star. **Page 67,** Alinari, Art Resource. **Page 68,** Alinari, Art Resource. **Page 69,** Images, Inc. **Page 69,** Art Resource. **Page 71,** Bildarchiv Preussischer Kulturbesitz.

Chapter 7: Page 76, Marburg, Art Resource. **Page 77,** Galleria Uffizi. **Page 77,** Alinari, Art Resource. **Page 78,** Courtesy, August/Zorn Collection.

Chapter 8: Page 81, New York Public Library Picture Collection. **Page 82 (top),** Courtesy August/Zorn Collection. **Page 82 (bottom),** Alinari , Art Resource. **Page 86,** Art Resource. **Page 87,** The Granger Collection. **Page 90,** Bettmann. **Page 91,** German Information Center. **Page**

93, Clive Barda. **Page 99,** German Information Center. **Page 104,** New York Public Library Picture Collection. **Page 106,** Bildarchiv Preussischer Kulturbesitz. **Page 110,** Stock Montage, Inc.

Chapter 9: Page 115, Bettmann. **Page 116 (top, left),** Bettmann. **Page 116 (bottom),** Dr. Paul Richer, Images Inc. **Page 117,** J. Messerschmidt, Leo De Wys, Inc.

Chapter 10: Page 119, Bildarchiv Preussischer Kulturbesitz. **Page 120 (top),** Photo Researchers, Inc. **Page 120 (bottom),** Bild-Archiv Der Oesterreichischen Nationalbibliothek, Wien. **Page 129,** Courtesy August/Zorn Collection. **Page 131,** Courtesy August/Zorn Collection. **Page 123,** Bild-Archiv Der Oesterreichischen Nationalbibliothek, Wien. **Page 125,** Bild-Archiv Der Oesterreichischen Nationalbibliothek, Wein. **Page 122,** Bild-Archiv Der Oesterreichischen Nationalbibliothek, Wien. **Page 124,** Bettmann. **Page 136,** J. Messerschmidt, Leo De Wys, Inc. **Page 143,** Clive Barda.

Chapter 11: Page 148, The Granger Collection. **Page 149,** German Information Center. **Page 153 (top),** Bild-Archiv Der Oesterreichischen Nationalbibliothek, Wien. **Page 153 (bottom),** Bild-Archiv Der Oesterreichischen Nationalbibliothek, Wien.

Chapter 12: Page 161, Art Resource. **Page 162,** Louvre/Art Resource, NY.

Chapter 13: Page 165, Bild-Archiv Der Oesterreichischen Nationalbibliothek, Wien. **Page 167,** Bettmann. **Page 168 (left),** Culver Pictures, Inc. **Page 168 (right),** Giraudon, Private Collection., Art Resource. **Page 176,** Bild-Archiv Der Oesterreichischen Nationalbibliothek, Wien. **Page 175,** Culver Pictures, Inc. **Page 180,** Bettmann. **Page 181,** Bildarchiv Preussischer Kulturbesitz. **Page 183,** Hulton Deutsch Collection Limited. **Page 186,** Giraudon, Art Resource, NY. **Page 190,** Lauros-Giraudon/Art Resource, NY. **Page 191,** The Metropolitan Museum of Art, The Crosby Brown Collection of Musical Instruments, 1901. **Page 192,** Culver Pictures, Inc.

Chapter 14: Page 197, Canadian Opera Company, Toronto. **Page 200,** The Granger Collection. **Page 200,** Scala, Art Resource. **Page 201,** The Granger Collection. **Page 202,** Culver Pictures, Inc. **Page 203,** Clive Barda. **Page 204,** Alinari, Art Resource. **Page 207,** Courtesy Houston Grand Opera, photo by Jim Caldwell. **Page 206,** San Diego Opera. **Page 210,** Ken Howard, Courtesy of San Diego Opera. **Page 209,** Bettmann. **Page 211,** Culver Pictures, Inc. **Page 212,** Culver Pictures, Inc.

Chapter 15: Page 219, Sammlungen Der Gessellschaft Der Musikfreunde in Vienna. **Page 222,** Historisches Museum Der Stadt, Vienna. **Page 231,** Bild-Archiv Der Oesterreichischen Nationalbibliothek, Vienna. **Page 230,** Bild-Archiv Der Oesterreichischen Nationalbibliothek, Vienna. **Page 239,** Bild-Archiv Der Oesterreichischen Nationalbibliothek, Vienna.

Chapter 16: Page 242, Martha Swope Associates. **Page 245,** Tass, Sovfoto/Eastfoto. **Page 246,** Galen Rowell, Peter Arnold, Inc. **Page 251,** New York Public Library Picture Collection. **Page 252,** Photo by Chris Lee, Courtesy of The New York Philharmonic. **Page 257,** Bettmann. **Page 258,** Culver Pictures, Inc. **Page 259,** Bartok Archive, Hungarian Academy of Sciences, Budapest. **Page 261 (left),** Bettmann.

Chapter 17: Page 262, Giraudon, Art Resource. **Page 263 (top),** Alinari, Art Resource. **Page 263 (bottom),** Lauros-Girarudon/Art Resource, NY. **Page 264 (top),** Giraudon, Marburg/Art Resource, NY. **Page 264 (bottom),** Bildarchiv Foto Marburg/Art Resource. **Page 265,** Bettmann. **Page 266,** Karen McCunnall/Leo de Wys, Inc. **Page 271,** Bettmann.

Chapter 18: Page 272, Centro De Arte Reina Sofia, Madrid. **Page 273,** Centro De Arte Reina Sofia, Madrid. **Page 276,** Cocteau, New York Public Library Picture Collection.

Chapter 19: Page 278, New York Public Library Picture Collection. **Page 279,** Culver Pictures, Inc. **Page 280 (right),** The Museum of Modern Art, New York, Mrs. Simon Guggenheim Fund. **Page 280 (left),** Archiv Fur Kunst Und Geschichte, Berlin. **Page 284,** Martha Swope Associates.

Chapter 20: Page 289, The Museum of Modern Art. **Page 290,** Arnold Schoenberg Institute University of Southern CA. **Page 291,** The Museum of Modern Art, New York Collection, Purchase. **Page 292,** Arnold Schoenberg Institute University of Southern CA, Los Angeles. **Page 294,** Arnold Schoenberg Institute University of Southern CA, Los Angeles.

Chapter 21: Page 297, Nancy Ellison/Onyx. **Page 299,** Archiv Fur Kunst Und Geschichte, Berlin. **Page 304,** Sovfoto/Eastfoto. **Page 303 (top),** Royal College of Music. **Page 303 (bottom),** Hulton Deutsch Collection Limited. **Page 306,** Bettmann. **Page 305,** Bettmann. **Page 309,** Culver Pictures, Inc. **Page 310,** Nancy Ellison/Onyx. **Page 311,** Bettmann.

Chapter 22: Page 312, Electronic Music Studio University of Illinois EMS. **Page 314,** Electronic Music Studio, University of Illinois EMS. **Page 317,** Soichi Sumani/The Museum of Modern Art. **Page 319 (top),** Bettmann. **Page 320,** Steve Sherman. **Page 319 (bottom),** General Information Center.

Chapter 23: Page 321, Jim Caldwell/Houston Grand Opera. **Page 323,** Sony Music. **Page 333,** Bettmann. **Page 334,** Culver Pictures, Inc. **Page 335,** Hoblitzelle Theatre Arts Harry Ransom Humanities Research Center. **Page 336,** Syndey Byrd. **Page 337,** New York Public Library at Lincoln Center. **Page 338,** Bettmann. **Page 339,** Jim Caldwell, Houston Grand Opera. **Page 344,** Photo Researchers, Inc. **Page 347,** Steve Sherman. **Page 350,** Culver Pictures Inc. **Page 351,** Steve Sherman.

Chapter 24: Page 355, Andy Freeberg. **Page 357,** New York Public Library Picture Collection. **Page 358,** Culver Pictures, Inc. **Page 359,** Culver Pictures Inc. **Page 360 (top),** Max Tharpe, Monkmeyer Press. **Page 360 (bottom),** Ray Charles Michael Cochs Archives. **Page 361,** Andy Freeberg. **Page 362,** Hulton Deutsch Collection Limited. **Page 363,** Elliot Landy, The Image Works.

Chapter 25: Page 365, Springer, Bettmann. **Page 368,** New York Public Library Picture Collection. **Page 370,** Culver Pictures, Inc. **Page 372 (top),** Culver Pictures, Inc. **Page 372 (bottom),** Culver Pictures, Inc. **Page 373 (top),** The Granger Collection. **Page 374,** New York Public Library Picture Collection. **Page 373 (bottom),** Culver Pictures, Inc. **Page 376,** Culver Pictures, Inc. **Page 378,** Culver Pictures, Inc. **Page 380,** Culver Pictures, Inc. **Page 381,** Courtesy American Society of Composers and Publishers. **Page**

Index